NORTHERN LAZIO
AN UNKNOWN ITALY

Other books by Wayland Kennet (Wayland Young)

THE ITALIAN LEFT
THE DEADWEIGHT
NOW OR NEVER
THE MONTESI SCANDAL
STILL ALIVE TOMORROW
STRATEGY FOR SURVIVAL
THE PROFUMO AFFAIR
EROS DENIED
THIRTY-FOUR ARTICLES
EXISTING MECHANISMS OF ARMS CONTROL (ed.)
PRESERVATION
THE FUTURES OF EUROPE (ed.)
THE REBIRTH OF BRITAIN (ed.)

Other books by Elizabeth Young

TIME IS AS TIME DOES
QUIET ENJOYMENT; ARMS CONTROL AND POLICE FORCES
FOR THE OCEAN (ed.)
A FAREWELL TO ARMS CONTROL?
SEA USE PLANNING (ed.)

Other books by Wayland Kennet and Elizabeth Young

OLD LONDON CHURCHES
LONDON'S CHURCHES

NORTHERN LAZIO

An Unknown Italy

Wayland Kennet and Elizabeth Young

JOHN MURRAY

First published in 1990
by John Murray (Publishers) Ltd,
50 Albemarle Street, London W1X 4BD

British Library Cataloguing in Publication Data
Kennet, Wayland, *1923–*
Northern Lazio: an unknown Italy.
1. Italy. Lazio—Visitors' guides
I. Title II. Young, Elizabeth, *1923–*
914.5′6204929

ISBN 0–7195–4643–5

Printed and bound by
Butler & Tanner Ltd, Frome and London

Contents

Illustrations

Acknowledgements

Everyone who helped us with this book, we thank: they are too many to list.

Of those we can list, we thank first of all Dr Vincenzo Ceniti, Director of the Ente Provinciale di Turismo of Viterbo, who not only gained us access to many places but allowed us to tap his own immense knowledge of the Province and its art and architecture.

We thank Richard and Mopsa English for lending us their camera. And for help and advice of all kinds we thank Dr Maria Antonelli, Dr Giovanni Contrucci, Dr Francesco d'Orazi, Prince Giovanni del Drago, Dr Massimo Faggiani, Ing. Dr Alessandro Fioravanti, Dr Mauro Galeotti, the Duke of Gallese, Marchese Carlo Lepri, Princes Francesco and Ascanio Massimo Lancelotti, Arch. Paolo Mezzetti, Dr Bruno Pannunzi, Marchese Enzo Patrizi, Drs Marcella and Marisa Rinaldi, Prince Francesco Ruspoli, and Dr Alessandro Vaciago; Dr Sam Barnish, Dr Milton Gendel, Sir John Hale, Douglas Matthews, Dr Peter Partner, Stephanie Worsley, and Dr George Zamecki.

We also thank the Banca Commerciale Italiana for a valued contribution towards the expenses of writing this book.

All these have contributed to whatever merit it has. Its defects are ours alone; suggestions for improvement will be gratefully received.

Foreword: How to use this book

The book has two main parts: an Introduction, addressing the area as a whole, and separate alphabetical entries for the places in it. Throughout the book place-names with an entry of their own are given in SMALL CAPITALS.

The Introduction starts with two general sections: on the land and on the history. Next come some shorter sections: notes on the landscape, vegetation, animals, food, fish, and wine, and on the waters and baths.

The two Appendices elaborate on topics that some readers may find more interesting than others. There is also a Glossary of Italian words used in the text.

As well as two maps, one for the whole area and one for the City of VITERBO, there are two matrices which analyse things by date, quality, and kind. These will allow readers to compose their journeys *à la carte*: to choose only the best places (middle column 'category'), or everything of one date (from the left-hand columns), or all there is of one kind of thing (the columns on the right), or everything in one part of the area (by using the maps and the map references at the furthest right). Thus on the General Matrix, Column 1 will direct you to what the Etruscans and Romans have left here; Columns 2 (High Middle Ages) and A (churches) to the Romanesque churches (see also pp. 54–8); and Columns 4 (16th and 17th centuries) and C (villas, palazzi, and gardens) will direct you to the explosion described on pp. 59–68. Column H is about nature, more or less: land-, lake- and sea-scapes, the waters, vulcanism, nature reserves. Column I shows the major *festa* and procession places.

VITERBO, the most important town in the area, comes at the end of the entries and has a mini-matrix of its own which works in the same way.

Translations into English are the authors', except for those from the Everyman edition of Vasari, and from Pius II's Commentaries (trans. Florence Gragg).

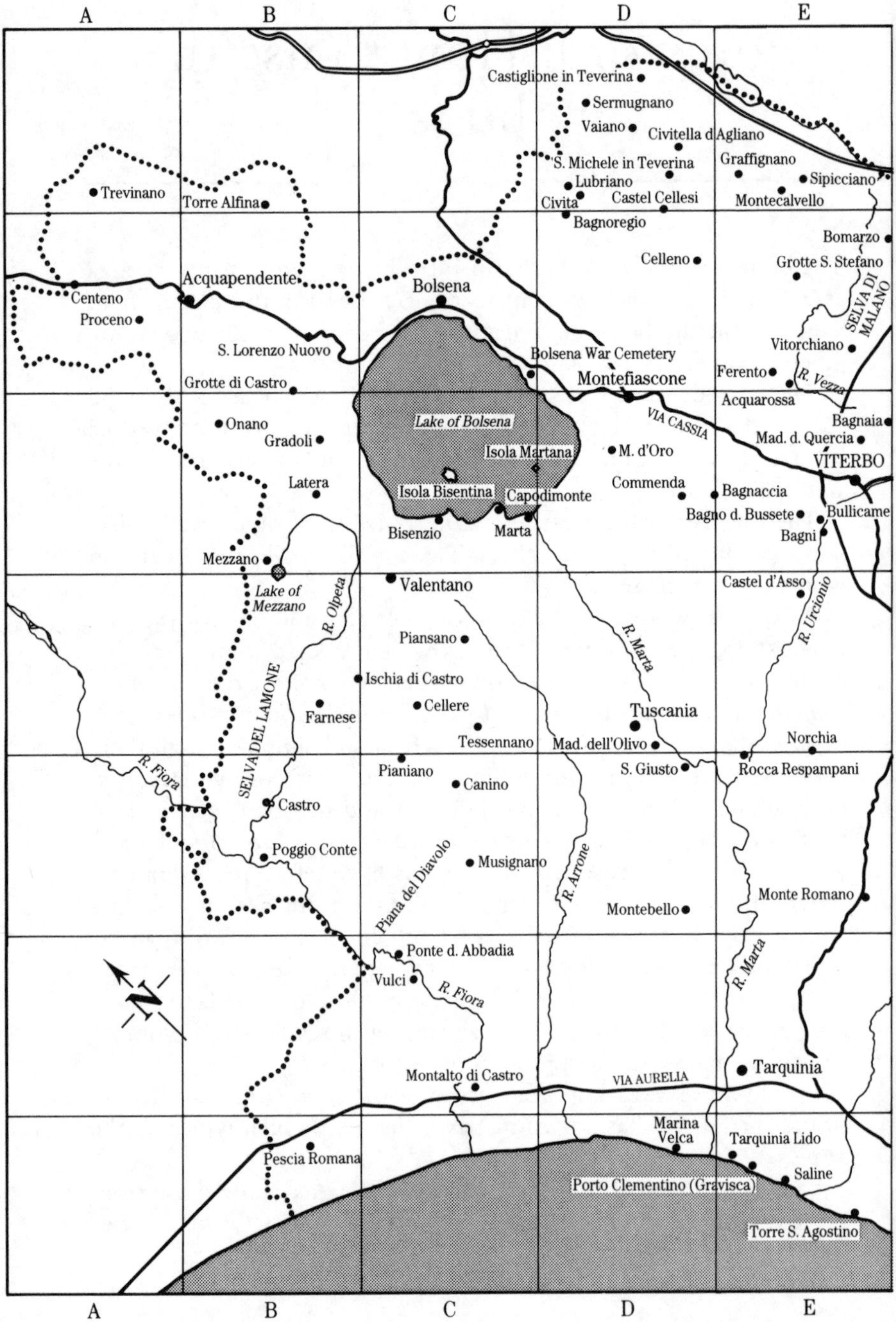

A
B
C
D
E
1
2
3
4
5
6
7
Castiglione in Teverina
Sermugnano
Vaiano
Civitella d'Agliano
S. Michele in Teverina
Graffignano
Lubriano
Sipicciano
Civita
Castel Cellesi
Montecalvello
Trevinano
Torre Alfina
Bagnoregio
Bomarzo
Celleno
Grotte S. Stefano
Acquapendente
Bolsena
Centeno
Proceno
SELVA DI MALANO
S. Lorenzo Nuovo
Bolsena War Cemetery
Vitorchiano
Montefiascone
Ferento
R. Vezza
Grotte di Castro
Acquarossa
VIA CASSIA
Onano
Lake of Bolsena
Bagnaia
Gradoli
Mad. d. Quercia
Isola Martana
M. d'Oro
VITERBO
Latera
Commenda
Bagnaccia
Isola Bisentina
Capodimonte
Bagno d. Bussete
Bullicame
Bisenzio
Marta
Bagni
Mezzano
Lake of Mezzano
Valentano
Castel d'Asso
R. Olpeta
R. Urcionio
Piansano
R. Marta
SELVA DEL LAMONE
Ischia di Castro
Farnese
Cellere
Tuscania
Norchia
Tessennano
Mad. dell'Olivo
R. Fiora
Pianiano
S. Giusto
Rocca Respampani
Canino
Castro
Poggio Conte
Musignano
R. Arrone
Piana del Diavolo
Monte Romano
Montebello
Ponte d. Abbadia
Vulci
R. Fiora
R. Marta
N
Montalto di Castro
Tarquinia
VIA AURELIA
Marina Velca
Tarquinia Lido
Pescia Romana
Saline
Porto Clementino (Gravisca)
Torre S. Agostino

Northern Lazio
F
G
H
I
J
1
2
3
4
5
6
7
Orte
R. Tiber
Mugnano
Vadimone
Bassano in Teverina
Filacciano
Torrita Tiberina
Chia
Gallese
Ponzano Romano
Nazzano
Vasanello
R. Treia
Civitella S. Paolo
M. Soracte
S. Oreste
Corchiano
Fiano Romano
Civita Castellana
VIA FLAMINIA
VIA TIBERINA
Soriano nel Cimino
Vignanello
Vallerano
Il Crocifisso
Falerii Novi
Rignano
Faleria
Lucus Feroniae
M. CIMINO
Canepina
Fabrica di Roma
Calcata
Capena
Cappuccini
Carbognano
Castel S. Elia
Morlupo
Caprarola
Mad. del Barco
R. Vicano
Mazzano
Castelnuovo di Porto
Nepi
Riano
S. Martino al Cimino
Magliano Romano
Ronciglione
S. Eusebio
VIA CIMINA
Sacrofano
M. Fogliano
Lake of Vico
Monterosi
Campagnano di Roma
Sutri
Lake of Monterosi
Mad. del Sorbo
Malborghetto
VIA CASSIA
Capranica
Stracciacappa
Baccano
Vetralla
Lake of Martignano
Formello
To Rome
Bassano Romano
Trevignano
Cesano
Pt. Sodo
Vicarello
Veio
S. Giuliano
Lake of Bracciano
Anguillara
Olgiata
Isola Farnese
Blera
Barbarano Romano
Grotta Porcina
Veiano
Vigna Grande
Fonte Claudia
S. M. di Galeria
Oriolo Romano
San Liberato
Vigna di Valle
Civitella Cesi
Montevirginio
VIA CLODIA
Galeria
Bracciano
Manziana
Pisciarelli
S. Giovenale
Canale Monterano
R. Mignone
Monterano
Luni
Caldara
Tragliata
Rota
Stigliano
Castelgiuliano
La Farnesiana
Tolfa
Ceri
Cibona
Torrimpietra
Cencelle
Allumiere
Sasso
TOLFA
Cerveteri
MONTI DELLA
Palidoro
Ficoncella
Terme Taurine
Palo
Ladispoli
S. Severa
S. Marinella
Civitavecchia

INTRODUCTION

The Land

Between the Tiber and the Tyrrhenian Sea lies Upper Lazio, otherwise known as Southern Etruria, or the Tuscia – a land of lakes and horrids.

There have been many names applied to it and within it and straddling its border: Lazio, from Latium, Rome's original territory on the Tiber's left bank, where Latin was spoken; the Ager Romanus, later Agro Romano, the Roman Field, being the land immediately round Rome; and stretching beyond that, the Roman Campagna (as opposed to Campania, the area round Naples). In ancient days, Etruria, the land of the Etruscans, of the Tusci, began at the Tiber's right bank with the Ager Veientanus, the Field of Veii – VEIO. The Etruscans also threw colonies north into Etruria Circumpadana – round the Po – and south into Etruria Campaniana. When the Romans conquered them, their territory was at first called Tuscia Suburbicaria – 'Suburban' Tuscia – and then Tuscia Romana. In the Dark Ages, it was divided into Tuscia Romanorum – the Romans' – and Tuscia Langobardorum – the Lombards'. Then first a small part, and eventually all of it, became 'the Patrimony of St Peter', the first of the Papal States. Today, the heart of ancient Etruria is again called the Tuscia, a word with the same root as Tuscany, though the Tuscia is not in Tuscany, but in Lazio. Modern Lazio, which covers a different and much larger area than ancient Latium, that is roughly everything between the 18th-century Kingdom of Naples and Grand Duchy of Tuscany, is one of the twelve Regions of mainland Italy, and now has within it five Provinces; Rome is the regional, as well as the national, capital. Northern Lazio, or Alto (Upper) Lazio, as commonly so called, includes the Province of VITERBO and the northern half of the Province of Rome, excluding the Commune, and this is our area.

Geology and Geography

The lakes are the water-filled craters and subsidences of several volcanic systems and periods; BOLSENA's islands are volcanic necks.

The horrids – Italian *orridi* – are the steep and often deep ravines carved by even the smallest water courses in the tufo.

To the east of the Tiber is the Appennine System, which gives Italy its high, rocky spine. To the west, the so-called Tosco-Maremmana System accounts for the Tuscia's very specific geological character, and vulcanism explains most of it: the lakes, the mountains, the texture of the rocks and soils, the behaviour of the rivers and streams. Underlying the volcanic structures are marine clays from the Pliocene, and along the coast are alluvial plains.

The three major lakes – BOLSENA, BRACCIANO, and VICO – have each been lifted high above sea-level by the eruptive processes which began at the end of the Pliocene, went on until about 60,000 years ago, and still rattle and shake and bubble today. One of the lakes, BRACCIANO, is sea-level deep. Each is encircled with hills, and there are other, smaller lakes, some now emptied. The volcanoes appear as craters rather than cones, and it is these that are now filled with water, much of it from submerged springs. The lakes appeared at various times: VICO only about 60,000 years ago. LATERA is a fourth crater system but its only lake, MEZZANO, is tiny. In the Volsinian (BOLSENA) system, 94 cones or craters have been identified.

The TOLFA HILLS were produced by an earlier period of underwater volcanic activity, pushed up and through pre-existing sedimentary layers which left them endowed with copper, iron, tin, and alum. They formed a small, more or less circular mountainous archipelago, which the later great shakes raised up and attached to the mainland, joining them to the Sabatine (BRACCIANO) and Ceretan (CERVETERI) Hills.

The other real mountain, SORACTE, is a solitary, a great streaked limestone outlier from the Appennine System, 5 kilometres long and 600 metres high, stranded on the wrong side of the Tiber. Like the Appennine, it is oriented north-west/south-east, and from either end it is more purely – and confusingly – volcano-like in shape than any of the volcanically produced hills. It too stood as an island in the former Sabine Gulf.

The volcanic rock that once spouted or oozed molten, gassy, and polychrome out of the volcanoes, or shot up and fell as cinders and dust, or collapsed and was re-ejected crystallised and agglomerated, covers most of the pre-existing limestone, clay, sands, and gravels. The sea-level sank, making mountains of what had earlier been islands. The Tiber adopted a course well to the east of its earlier one. Where the waters carved new ways down, previous layers and surfaces emerged or were eroded – the sea-rounded pebbles of CENTENO, the cliffs of the TREIA valley.

Over most of the land, explosive eruptions had caused its surface to be blanketed again and again, tens and even hundreds of metres thick; and because so much matter was thrown out, the new surfaces subsided again and again into the newly evacuated subterranean voids. Even in historical times there have been mini-blanketings: Roman remains have been found in the Alban Hills covered in a layer of crisp dust, and something of the same happened to keep the Etruscan tombs of VULCI safe from the traditional plough. Sometimes the dust and ash were turned into flowing mud by simultaneously ejected steam becoming rain, and over time, the rinsed and bubble-laden mud hardened into, say, travertine, of which much of Rome is built. There are lavas too, liquified rock, which became basalts. And ignimbrites – incandescent gassy clouds – that cooled solid, speckled sometimes with pumice (which is petrified gassy scum), or black cinders, or splinters of crystals. And solid far-flung debris: purple rolls of lava, mixed fragments of earlier rock formations compacted into plum-pudding-like breccias; round, sometimes hollow, balls known as 'bombs'; tiny flutes of obsidian; piled and layered masses of compacted multicoloured sand, washed into 'organ pipes'. The tufo itself comes in different textures and colours – yellow, orange, grey, dark brown, reddish, purple, and white-, yellow-, black- or brown-speckled. And laterites, rock decomposed into rough grains. The native tufo can be quite hard enough to build with, and most towns and villages are built of the rock they stand on. That it is also soft enough to tunnel and to cut through is what allowed the Etruscans to perform their remarkable feats of water and road engineering and to achieve their consequent economic lift-off. Indeed it may have been their penetrable tufo which put them ahead of neighbouring peoples for a while, until that advantage was marginalised by the amazing intellectual grasp of the phenomenon that was Rome.

The harder but less frequent 'peperino', still 'volcanic', but from deeper beneath the surface, the Etruscans did not use. It was later preferred for fine work – it is *pietra* rather than *sasso* – stone rather than rock. It is mostly darkish grey, 'peppered' with darker specks (much of VITERBO is built of it) or a yet harder, darkish pink (as at Santa Maria della QUERCIA).

Signs of active vulcanism abound: waters mineral and thermal, caldaras (see CALDARA), perhaps the mysterious *sessa* of the LAKE OF BOLSENA. And the occasional appalling earthquakes, like that which struck TUSCANIA in 1971. There are a few lava-fields still visible – on the direct road from BOMARZO to SORIANO, just after it has crossed the new motorway, for instance; and by the side of the Cassia near MONTEROSI.

Towards the coast and in the ravines and the Tiber valley, underlying soils appear, sands and conglomerates over clay, and the glowingly pretty limestone called *macco,* of which TARQUINIA is built. The coast has sandy beaches, often glistening black or grey, their great sweeps interrupted by rocky protrusions, the bigger of which sport wet-foot medieval castles (SANTA SEVERA, PALO). Although the level of the sea has risen, a string of one-time ports have silted up with the movement of currents and only CIVITAVECCHIA remains in use.

The Rivers

To the east and south, the Tiber has been both a boundary, cutting the volcanic area off from the Appennines, and a means of communication. It was navigable as far as ORTE until the 19th century, dotted with little ports and ferries and bridged as far down as Rome.

One of its tributaries, the Paglia, together with the seaward-flowing Fiora, both of which rise in Monte Amiata, and the latter's tributary the Nova, more or less bound the Tuscia to the north.

The Marta, also seaward-flowing, emerges from the LAKE OF BOLSENA. With its tributaries – Biedano, Leia, Urcionio – it cuts through and waters the Great Etruscan Plain. It too was long navigable.

The Mignone curls round the east and north of the TOLFA HILLS. In prehistoric and later times there were settlements along its banks: no longer: the sites are hidden in quite ferocious temperate jungle.

There are two rivers called Arrone, one the outlet to the sea from the LAKE OF BRACCIANO, the other flowing seawards between the Marta and the Fiora.

The TREIA is the Tiber's principal tributary from the west and the Rio Vicano, artificially fed from the LAKE OF VICO, joins it. The ravines of its fiercely water-scoured basin on the south abutted the Ager Veientanus (see VEIO): here was the ancient boundary of the Ager Faliscus (see CIVITA CASTELLANA).

The capillary streams dry in summer to mere trickles. Much of the often violent rainfall is absorbed straight into and through the tufo, to reappear where it meets less permeable layers in springs. These feed the hillsides' rich woods, and carve much-used caves in the cliffs. They also provide the human animal with the health-giving mineral and thermal waters it has long recognised and enjoyed.

Flooding was frequent and unreliable, which no doubt in part prompted the Etruscans to develop their various water-management techniques. But during the first centuries AD, there seems to have been a climatic change, and valley bottoms flooded or became water-logged. In some places silt filled them up, burying occupied sites under several metres of alluvium; much of this has since been washed or carved away. At VEIO some Roman baths have come back into view.

Malaria

Malaria appeared in the 2nd century BC; it probably accounted for Roman neglect of the coastal marshlands, and for the millennial delay in their reclamation. In the Middle Ages, French and German popes kept dying in Rome – Romans and Italians less so, presumably – and so moved out of Rome in the summer.

Human Settlements

Most of the human settlements have since the Bronze Age perched on isolated volcanic spurs or necks or shoulders, protected by water courses, and not too conspicuous. This was first for defence, and later to escape the encroaching malaria. There are a few fishermen's hideaways deep in lakeside reeds, a few open townlets (due to Papal States planning in the 17th or 18th century), and in places the single scattershot structures of medieval field-castles and post-war land reform dwellings. Within the woods and the *macchia,* and under the crops and roads and new developments, there are the now invisible remains of innumerable pre-Etruscan and Etruscan settlements, of the Roman villa-farm system (particularly in the south, and along the great roads) and of small fortified farms set up after the Roman system collapsed and before the feudal system took over.

A human presence in the area can be assumed for over a million years. The evidence begins more than half that time ago, along the coast, of hunting for mammoth, rhinoceros, and other animals (see TORRIMPIETRA). Then, after the last Ice Age, as the temperature rose, the deciduous forests appeared – hazel, fir, and finally oak; the settlements were now in clearings. Cereal-growing and the domestication of animals appeared about 5000 BC. There are indications already of 'transhumance' (see below) and a precursor of the Via Cassia.

The slopes of the TOLFA HILLS and the banks of the Fiora show Neolithic settlements. About the 3rd millennium BC appear copper-users, at Rinaldone near MONTEFIASCONE, and in the Fiora valley and the SELVA DI LAMONE. The 2nd millennium Bronze Age provides signs of a widespread trade in increasingly decorated pots, though most settlements were still, apart from sheep-droving, living off their immediate territory. The lakes, too, of BOLSENA, BRACCIANO, and MEZZANO all have remains of the wooden piles and broken crocks of lake-villages.

The Ciminian Forest was an object of horrified awe to the Romans (see VADIMONE) and the whole area was much more densely forested than it is now. The Roman Empire's energy came from the chestnut, beech, and ilex forests, remnants of which still survive high on the CIMINO and on the ISOLA BISENTINA. The TOLFA HILLS provided their own Bronze Age inhabitants, and then CERVETERI, with useful minerals but it was the Metalliferous Hills of Northern Etruria (now Tuscany) that provided more sizeable quantities of iron, copper, lead, and tin. Southern Etruria exported salt (see GRAVISCA) and provided expanding Rome with wine and grain until it became cheaper to import them from Africa, and only the Campagna, the part of Etruria nearest to Rome, was fully cultivated.

Agriculture

The land we see today has thus been cultivated for the last three millennia, depending on where the soil was good and the water plentiful. In Lazio, perhaps 'husbandry' or 'land-use' are better terms than agriculture, because the idea has certainly to include water management at which the Etruscans excelled, and the managed pastoralism of transhumance.

Settlements naturally avoided both the high Appennines and the coastal marsh called the Maremma.* Most cultivation took place as close to them as possible: orchards and gardens closest in; olive groves and vineyards further out; and managed or improved woods between the 'infield' and the 'outfield' beyond it, the *incultum* where nature was used but not cultivated. In the *cultum* only donkeys and working oxen were allowed; pigs had to be in enclosures, though they were let loose among the acorns (and cross-bred with the wild boar). In the valley bottoms where irrigation was sometimes easy, cereals could be grown and crops rotated.

* This name was used until twenty years ago to mean what it says: the Marsh. Now it has expanded in common use among incomers to cover an inland belt many times wider.

To make use of distant pastures, since earliest times transhumance has involved the seasonal transfer of vast flocks of sheep along the valley bottoms, up into the Appennine pastures in summer, and down to the Maremma in winter. Technically, this is 'double transhumance'; the beasts spend no time at habitation level, where there is little or no grazing, and the shepherds very little. Eventually big landowners, the Church and the nobility, came to have properties at either end, and that continued till after the Second World War, since when the lower grazing has been turned over to fertilised crops. The upper continues: flocks with their shepherds and their *Maremmano* dogs can still be seen in summer in the Campo Imperatore, the giant hanging valley under the Gran Sasso d'Italia.

History

Despite all its natural and civil beauties, Northern Lazio figures little in the diaries and books of the innumerable travellers who passed through in the scribbling centuries; and that little tends to disparage. Today, the average British and American traveller and tourist is so stunned by Florence and Siena that they sleep them off all the way to Rome; even to people who know Tuscany well and have heard of Umbria and Calabria, the very name Lazio is unknown. Why?

Many reasons, as we shall see. But above all, the proximity of Rome – Roman Rome, Holy Rome, Papal Rome, Rome the capital of United Italy. At each expansion and contraction of Rome's power, the native wealth and character of this nearest territory to the north was usually obliterated: warfare and the passage of innumerable armies; servitude under Roman, and then a variety of 'barbarian' and then feudal, masters, most of them foreigners; imperial, royal, and papal family rivalries, bringing murderous disputes and penury; economic neglect and decay; earthquakes; disease – endless and repeated: malaria, the plague, cholera, more malaria; the razing of towns and banishment of their inhabitants. And still armies passing through: right until 1944, when in addition the Allied air forces bombed VITERBO, RONCIGLIONE, CIVITA CASTELLANA, MONTEFIASCONE. (For an account of that campaign, see VITERBO; and also BOLSENA WAR CEMETERY.)

The Etruscans

Yet before Rome, seven hundred years before Christ, the ravine-scoured plain of Northern Lazio was the centre of the wealth and power of the Etruscan Confederation, then itself a centre of European civilisation. This wealth and power were founded not only on the Etruscans' wide-ranging trade, but on their understanding and practice of several advanced technologies – their irrigated agriculture and other forms of water management and a network of roads carved in the tufo. Their civilisation was first defeated by Republican and Imperial Romans; then repressed in memory by the Christian Romans and almost deleted from history; and then for centuries it became a subject of universal fantastication.

By the 10th–8th centuries BC, the Faliscan people (see CIVITA CASTELLANA) had a fairly clear identity within their own area, roughly the TREIA basin. And various other, Italic, tribes also dwelt in central Italy. But from that time there are signs of a people, or at least a fashion, moving down from the north, with the new 'urnfield' burial practices, called Villanovan from the first such cemetery to be studied, near Bologna. These tombs were usually shafts dug into the rock with funerary pots and grave goods inserted in them. The Faliscan people were soon swept along with the great Etruscan culture, and the word Villanovan is now increasingly taken to be synonymous with proto-Etruscan.

For the English-speaking traveller, Mrs Hamilton Gray's *Tour to the Sepulchres of Etruria*, published in 1840, was the first proper pointer to the wonders of this culture:

> A journey through Etruria, and a comparison between the frequent and rich records of the dead, and the scarcity and miserable poverty of the living, is enough to confirm our antipathy against those overbearing republican tyrants [the Romans].

This book, intelligent and entertaining though it was, was soon outclassed. In 1848, George Dennis published 'the fruit of several tours made . . . between the years 1842 and 1847' (prompted perhaps by Mrs Gray?): his monumental *Cities and Cemeteries of Etruria*. The scale of the Etruscan presence became clear.

Dennis went everywhere; he had a remarkable eye for an Etruscan site; his mind was fully stored with the classical references; and he turned a good phrase. Behind the sad and oppressed land that was Etruria in the 1840s he saw and conjured for his readers the pride an Etruscan might have felt, two and a half thousand years before, as he regarded the scene northwards from the top of the CIMINIAN HILLS:

> The numerous cities in the plain were so many trophies of the power and civilisation of his nation. There stood Volsinii, renowned for her wealth and arts, on the shores of her crater-lake – there Tuscania reared her towers in the West – there Vulci shone out from the plain, and Cosa from the mountain – and there Tarquinii, chief of all, asserted her metropolitan supremacy from her cliff-bound heights. Nearer still, his eye must have rested on city after city, some in the plain, and others at the foot of the slope

> beneath him ... How changed is now the scene! Save Tuscania, which still retains her site, all within view are now desolate. Tarquinii has left scarce a vestige on the grass-grown heights she once occupied; the very site of Volsinii is forgotten; silence has long reigned in the crumbling theatre of Ferentum; the plough yearly furrows the bosom of Vulci; the fox, the owl, and the bat are the sole tenants of the vaults within the ruined walls of Cosa: and of the rest, the greater part have neither building, habitant, nor name – nothing but the sepulchres around them to prove they ever had an existence.

Dennis had already listed the cities towards Rome in the south – Veii, Fidenae, Falerii, Fescennium, Capena, Nepete, Sutrium, 'all then powerful, wealthy and independent' – and ends his chapter:

> Little did he [the proud Etruscan] foresee that yon small town on the banks of the Tiber would prove the destruction of them all, and even of his nation, name, and language.

(The places in question are now: BOLSENA, TUSCANIA, VULCI, Cosa, TARQUINIA, FERENTO, VEIO, Fidenae, CIVITA CASTELLANA, Fescennium, CAPENA, NEPI and SUTRI.)

The Etruscans called themselves *Rasna*, which might mean just 'people', or 'the people', like the Welsh *Cymru*. The names Etruria and Etruscan came from the Latin, and form a cluster with Tirreno, Tyrrhenian, Toscana, Tuscany, and Tuscia: all probably come from an Indo-European root *tir* or *tur*, a tower. The Greeks seem to have perceived the Etruscans as a tower-people. Aristotle believed they went to Italy from Greece before the Trojan War, that is, in the 13th century BC. A later Greek, Dionysius of Halicarnassus, writing when the Etruscans were subject to the Romans, thought they were indigenous to Italy. From the archaeological evidence, it seems likely that he was right, and that they grew out of the local Iron Age culture. Perhaps it is best to agree with the 19th-century German historian Mommsen that it does not matter where they came from: they were there; they made and did splendid things; let us study them.

They were farmers, fishermen, miners, and ironworkers like other peoples around the Mediterranean, until in the 8th century BC they encountered the first Greek settlers in Italy, who were exploring northwards for minerals from their trading base on the island of Ischia (off Naples). These Greeks traded with them and taught them to write.

Etruscan therefore is written in Greek letters, usually backwards, which sometimes Greek was too. It can be pronounced, but only two or three hundred words are understood, from the 13,000 formal inscriptions that have been found. No literature survives.

Their religion was polytheistic like that of the Greeks; and the Romans later used as many Etruscan names for the Gods as they did Greek. The Etruscans devoted great ingenuity to finding ways to divine the will of the Gods: they divided the sky into sixteen parts and observed what happened in them; the flight of birds, shooting stars, livers, and lightning, for which last they are said to have had more than a dozen distinguishing names, were the raw material of their divination. The will of the Gods could be swayed by the promise of *ex voto* gifts, and these survive in great abundance and variety, often in forms which are still going strong today in the Catholic Church; a limb which had been cured, or an organ.

The main difference between Etruscan society, and Greek and Roman, was that women and men ate together, and on ceremonial occasions women reclined on the couch with their husbands; they also went to public places with men, including the theatre. For this, some Greek writers of their time judged the Etruscans lustful, promiscuous, and shameless, but it is common for a people to project their own hidden desires on to another. Conversely, the modern Etruscologist Larissa Bonfante has written that you might think from its art that Etruscan society consisted entirely of married couples.

In the 8th century the wheel and the made road arrived, and towns began to grow up supported by drainage, irrigation, and widening areas of more intensive agriculture. Trading wealth produced an oligarchy of powerful families, and they built the well-placed cities of Southern Etruria of which we write in this book. Then a more democratically minded middle class grew up in turn, expanding into the countryside, but never quite achieving power. While Rome turned from kingdom to republic and Greece from kingdom and tyranny to democracy, Etruria hung on to an aristocratic or oligarchic form of dynastic government, earning itself a name for theocracy as well as libertinism.

The Etruscan cities came loosely together into the confederation now known as the Etruscan League. They traded greatly with Greece, Sardinia, Spain, Carthage, Egypt. At first they had mainly exported raw materials, particularly metal ores to the Greek colonies in southern Italy, and imported finished goods; ceramics are what survive, and more Greek pots have been found in Etruscan tombs than in Greece. By about the 6th century Etruscan exports of finished goods may have come to predominate over imports; among them great numbers of vases for Greece, with the stories of common Gods and heroes; and scarabs, sometimes with the hieroglyphics wrong, for Egypt. Most of this trade they carried in their own ships, which were like Greek ones.

More than two million tons of ironstone waste have been identified as theirs round the mines of Populonia in Tuscany. Copper, iron, and lead they won from the TOLFA HILLS, and the gold they worked was imported from Spain and Eastern Europe. In metal-working they produced portraits of individuals, temple decorations, chariots, tools and pots, hooks and eyes, and drink trolleys. These, and the brilliant – indeed unsurpassed – delicacy of their gold jewellery, strike in the modern mind prolonged amazement and delight. Their false teeth were pretty good too.

Their temples were just as Vitruvius described them. The columns were painted wood, with stone bases and capitals, and the roofs, friezes, and pediments of ornate tiles, sometimes of great weight and magnificence: the Veii Apollo (see VEIO) was set on a roof with three other figures. Their houses were wood and daub, the still widespread *intonaco*. Their art we know from their tombs, of which tens of thousands, often in great necropoles or cities of the dead, have been opened, legally and illegally, scientifically and carelessly. Every portable thing of any value, as soon as found, has been moved to a museum or a private collection; the 'valueless' was broken up on the spot (see VULCI). Only the traveller's memory, which needs to be well-stocked, and imagination, which needs to be hard-working, can refurnish the tombs and replace things in their proper position or context.

The tombs themselves come broadly in three types: the built-up house-tombs of CERVETERI, the straight-down-in-the-ground tombs of TARQUINIA, and the architectural cliff tombs. These last are 'architectural' in the sense that what there is – or was – to see of them is permanent and designed. Many tens of thousands of façaded cliff tombs, most of them invisibly, honeycomb the *burroni* – the stream-eroded, bushlined, ravines – of the eastern part of the Etruscan Plain. Although cliff tombs abound in Asia Minor and the Near East, in Italy they are found only in Etruria, and mostly in the greater and lesser necropolises of NORCHIA (under which we describe the form), BLERA, GROTTA PORCINA, CASTEL D'ASSO, SAN GIULIANO, SAN GIOVENALE, etc. – to give them their modern names. All were in the hinterland of the coastal centres – Caere (CERVETERI), Tarquinii

(TARQUINIA), and Volcii (VULCI) – and the rise and fall of the hinterland places reflect expansion from (or withdrawal back into) those three centres. The towns are, or were, linked by a network of roads, some of which were driven astonishingly deep through the tufo. Some were inhabited in the Middle Ages, and then disappeared, as did NORCHIA. A few are still inhabited and even flourishing, as are BLERA and TUSCANIA.

The great period was from the 6th century BC, when the Etruscan artistic spirit emerged from a rather stiff and complicated 'Oriental' style, until the 4th, when it effectively merged with the Greek. At their best, Etruscan artists were as graceful as the Greeks, as grand as the Romans, as human as their descendants the Tuscans of the Renaissance, and often they added a cunning and cheerful absurdity of their own.

They produced grain, wine, olives, sheep, cattle, like today. Almost as soon as the wheel was invented, they engineered level roads to allow wheeled traffic between towns, and from farms to towns. Their water management has not even yet been matched in that soil. They drained marshes and small lakes, built aqueducts; above all, they cut miles and miles of tunnels, about five feet high and varyingly broad, in and through the workable tufo, called in Latin *cuniculi*, rabbit-holes, which are still a marvel to us today. Besides obvious uses like urban supply and drainage – possibly Rome's main drain, the Cloaca Maxima, was originally Etruscan – they were used to replenish reservoirs or natural aquifers and to divert streams from one valley into another (see CORCHIANO). Vertical holes were dug for their construction, which sometimes later served for land drainage.

Following the usual rule of international – and indeed interspecies – conflict, the Etruscan League tended to ally itself with its neighbours' neighbours, specifically with the Carthaginians, who were for ever at war first with the Greeks of Sicily and southern Italy and later with the Romans. But in 474 BC the Greeks of Syracuse decisively defeated the Etruscan and Carthaginian fleets off Cumae near Naples, and stepped into their shoes as rulers of the waves round Italy both in war and in trade. By the first half of the 4th century, they were sore beset: Gauls were invading from the north, and Samnites (a people of the Abruzzi, whose language was not far from Latin) from the east.

The little town of Rome came to pre-eminence, if not actually in the very midst of the Etruscan civilisation, then undoubtedly within it. Roman historians believed Rome was originally an Etruscan settlement; Ruma is an Etruscan name. Certainly Servius Tullius, the King of Rome who gave it a famous constitution and was murdered in 534 BC, was an Etruscan, born at VULCI with the name of Macstarna. Roman religion, law, institutions, customs, sewers, and military organisation were all adopted from the Etruscans. What they had that the Etruscans did not was salt under their own control at the Tiber mouth; an instinct for making money work for them – their *tabernae argentariae* in the Forum were more than mere *bureaux de change*; and lastly that great mystery, Organising Ability.

In 396 BC the Romans took VEIO, and in 382 NEPI and SUTRI as well. VEIO was then richer and larger than Rome (though without a port), and barely 20 kilometres away from it. According to some modern writers the Romans, in this almost parricidal attack, felt a guilt they never felt again. The first victorious blow, against this more-than-neighbour, removed all obstacles to the rain of blows to be dealt out thereafter from Scotland to Egypt, from the Black Sea to Morocco. The simple remains of the temple centre of VEIO remind us poignantly today of how small the first step can be that leads to the gigantic, for good or ill.

The Romans imposed direct rule, but did not at first treat their first subjects badly, and the old landlord families of Southern Etruria left their land and went to live in Rome. A sort of slave latifundia ensued, irrigation was abandoned, the land decayed, and depopulation followed. In the 4th to 2nd centuries BC Northern Etruria, now Southern Tuscany, fared better than Southern (now Northern Lazio): there the Romans imposed only what we should now call unequal treaties, and the native landowners stayed.

Etruscan culture was at first cherished by its new masters; the Emperor Claudius in the early 1st century AD wrote a book about it in twenty parts (since lost), and made laws to protect it. Apuleius, in the 2nd century AD, translated the 'Tagetic books', looking for old exotic doctrine to combat the new one of Christianity. (Tages was a divine boy born in a furrow in a field near TARQUINIA.) The Etruscan people mingled with the Roman; the language had already died out by the time of Claudius and, though Romans could still read it even later, they never thought to make a dictionary of it for posterity, any more than they did of Egyptian. Perhaps the Romans were poor linguists and, like later imperial peoples, just shouted louder.

Etruscan art flowed with the great river of Greek art into its Roman successor. What remained intact longest was the Etruscan practice of divination and it was not until the fourth century that

Constantine, the first Christian Emperor, banned it. His brother, the Emperor Julian the Apostate, permitted it again two years after Constantine's death, when he tried to re-establish polytheism in the Roman Empire. Then another Christian Emperor, Honorius, ordered the destruction of all Etruscan books and finally, in the early 5th century, all practice of the Etruscan Discipline, as their divination was called, was banned. So it was not the Romans as such who destroyed the Etruscan writings and forbade their rites, but Christianity in Rome.

This total destruction of Etruscan literature has allowed later Europeans to see in the Etruscans what we have wanted to see, or what it has been in our interest to see, much as we have done with the Druids, about whom even less is known. Villani, in his early 14th-century chronicle of Florence, read a living justification of the Florentine Republic into the Etruscans and their remains: Lars Porsena of Clusium became a Medicean republican hero. He was such also to Alberti in the 15th century; and a contemporary praised Donatello for being 'a real Etruscan'. A little later, down in the Papal State, Annius of Viterbo concluded that Etruscan society had been conservative and monarchical and that Hercules was their hero (see VITERBO). In 1504, soon after Savonarola had given Florence an experience of extremism under a republic, Piero dei Ricci Baldi argued that you still did not need monarchy to hold a society together: the Etruscans provided the example of *honesta disciplina* without it. In 1513 Pope Leo X Medici made it up with his kinsmen Cosimo and Giuliano in front of a picture of Romans making it up with 'Hetruscans'. Macchiavelli drew morals from them, and by the time the Medici Dukes of Florence had finally broken with their republican past, the Etruscans had become good absolutists.

In 1619 Thomas Dempster, a Scottish professor of law at Bologna, completed the first general survey of everything that was known about them; it was only published in 1723–4, edited by one Filippo Buonarroti who thought Etruscan was ancient Egyptian. Contemporaries said that Dempster just about credited them with the invention of breathing.

In 1727 an Etruscan Academy was founded at Cortona which published nine great volumes in the next sixty years: Montesquieu and Voltaire were members. The word *Etruscheria* passed into the Italian language, meaning things made in the Etruscan style, like *Chinoiserie* in French. By this time of course the Etruscans were republican democrats again, and the Spinozist Lampredi lamented the fact that the Romans had ever conquered them.

It had till then been assumed that Herodotus was right, and that the Etruscans had come from Greece. But in the increasingly nationalistic 18th century they were sometimes deemed to have originated in Italy, migrated to Greece, where they founded arts and letters, and then migrated back again to Italy. Or they were Celts. Or a sort of Jew. (Those who thought this cannot have looked at their votive penises.) Their language was Hebrew, or Latin, or of course Greek, or by the early 19th century Punic, Gothic, or Ibero-Celtic. Wolanski claimed it for the Slavonic languages, most likely Russian. The controversy began to be put in proportion in the 1820s by the work of Schlegel and Bopp on the unity of all the Indo-European languages. Modern scholars incline to think Etruscan was not Indo-European at all.

When today you hear a Tuscan aspirate a C or a Ch at the beginning of a word (*Huanto hosta huesto?*), you are hearing an Etruscan trick of speech at which the Romans laughed when they heard it in Latin, just as later colonialists have laughed at colonial pronunciations. And when you go into small old houses in Lazio (see BARBARANO ROMANO), you are in a house built to an Etruscan design: when you see a bishop with his crook anywhere in the world, you are seeing an Etruscan judge shepherding his human flock, and leading it from in front as Etruscan shepherds did and shepherds in Lazio still do to this day.

And we suppose you might, just might, as an American scholar did in the late 19th century, or said he did, find a peasant praying to the Etruscan gods. To Fufluns, the Etruscan Bacchus:

> Faflon! Faflon! Faflon! Hear my prayer. The grapes are scarce on my vine. Hear my prayer, and grant me a good vintage.

Or to Turan, the Etruscan Venus:

> Turanna! Turanna! In this thick wood I kneel down, for I am so unhappy and so unfortunate. I love a lady and she does not love me.

The Romans

Having defeated the Etruscans, the Romans of 'yon small town' dispersed them and their neighbours away from their towns and began to drive the great long-distance roads north. In the rugged Ager Faliscus (see CIVITA CASTELLANA) the remains suggest only modest shacks in use, like those Cervesato saw early this century. In the rest of the Tuscia there were villa-farms, thickest and richest –

indeed most luxurious – near to Rome. Where prosperity had depended on Etruscan techniques, the system wound down. Over large areas, public safety declined; malaria took hold, in summer even in Rome itself. Some towns survived as Roman colonies – SUTRI, NEPI, NAZZANO – but most gradually disappeared: some to be re-occupied in the Middle Ages; some to be rediscovered only in the last 150 years. In Caesar's time, the Campagna was surveyed with a view to the settlement of army veterans. From Augustus' time came the massive *Lucus Feroniae* development: forum, shrine, basilica, aqueduct, baths, villas, etc., etc.

From the 3rd century AD, the population was shrinking even close to Rome. Climatic changes induced flooding; low-lying land was abandoned. In the 4th century, the Empire was collapsing under both internal and external pressures.

In 330, the newly converted Christian Emperor Constantine moved the Empire's capital east to Constantinople. Rome, now a backwater, was sacked by Alaric's Visigoths in 410, and gave up. Followed the Huns, to sack it again; and the Vandals. Italy's economy, now physically broken, subsided. Antiquity was over. The Dark Ages had begun.

The Dark Ages

The 'barbarian' tribes, always poised at the frontier and now pushed from behind by yet more barbarous nomads from the Asian steppes, descended, sucked into Italy as into a vacuum. Many were 'Germans', earlier recruited by Rome to fight other 'Germans'. The Emperor Justinian's ambition to 'give back to Rome all Rome's privileges' by reconquering Italy, failed: the Graeco-Gothic war of 535–40 left 'the Italian fields ... so ravaged that none can restore them', according to Pope Pelagius I (556–61). The people were eating acorns; there was plague; cannibalism was reported. Moreover, the aqueducts and roads had been destroyed by floods, the villa-farms of the Campagna were abandoned; Rome's granaries were wrecked.

A so-called Dukedom of Rome was established by the Eastern Emperors as an attempt at some continuation of order. A first flush of Western monasticism followed, with the foundation of rural Benedictine monasteries (the first 'Roman' monasteries had been in the houses of Roman Christians). Within Rome, increasingly the popes – most of them Romans – governed, building and restoring churches and monasteries, and responding, more or less, to the waves of invaders pouring down the roads from the north.

In 728 came the beginning of the 'sovereign state' that became the enormously powerful 12th-century Papacy. This was the 'Donation of Sutri', a deal whereby, probably in return for a gift of gold from Pope Gregory II, Liutprandt, the Lombard King, donated the town of SUTRI (50 kilometres north of Rome, which he had just conquered) to the 'Patrimony of St Peter and St Paul'. From this nucleus of official property, the popes expanded their worldly power and authority. (The Vatican today is larger than SUTRI, but not much.)

On being presented by the Emperor with two estates, Gregory II's near successor, Pope Zachary, inaugurated the system of *domuscultae*, large farming estates 'under apostolic privilege', often with subordinate farms at a distance, and even transhumance zones in the Appennines. These were organised on the same open-country model as the old Roman villa-farms, but with monastic appurtenances: church, cloister, baptistery, even sacred relics. Consequently they were vulnerable to attack, by now from Muslim Saracens, as well as opposed by the Roman landowners who considered themselves robbed: the system did not last very long. (See VEIO, GALERIA.)

The Holy Roman Empire

Some of the 'barbarians' who invaded Italy were Christians, but professing the Arian heresy (believing only in the Father's Godhead, not the Triune God). By 653 they had converted to the Catholicism of Rome because, whether Goths, Lombards, or Franks, they were hungry not for Rome's wealth, which was gone, but for the continuing dream of Rome the lawful giver of laws. The Bishop of Rome had secured pre-eminence over other bishops, and his authority had increased as that of the Eastern Empire had decayed. Pope Pelagius II (579–90), himself of Germanic origin, was elected without (Eastern) Imperial confirmation, and welcomed the northerners as alone capable of saving Italy from further devastation. The next popes looked in vain to the Franks and Lombards to help establish their power, nor over the far-flung ex-Imperial lands, but over the central Italian lands of the old Republic. The northerners went on coming for centuries, planting their names and their genes, and something of their art.

The Donation of Sutri happened in 728. Pope Leo III's coronation of Charlemagne in Rome on Christmas day of the year 800, as 'Charles Augustus ... great and pacific Emperor', represented a climax of 'barbarian' intention. The idea of a unified Europe lived on, providing a framework of disorienting magnetisms for the endless Pope versus Emperor (Guelf versus Ghibelline) antagonisms of the following centuries, as the two sides sought and fought to define the terrestrial relationship between God's Pope and God's Emperor.

Central Italy was the boundary and battlefield between the Lombard kingdoms and the Eastern Empire of Byzantium; the line ran just south of the LAKE OF BOLSENA. In the 9th century, Sicily was taken by the Arabs and Muslim Saracens began attacking all along the Italian coast: Centumcellae (CIVITAVECCHIA) was destroyed in 813 and its inhabitants dispersed; Rome itself was looted in 846; in the 10th century Saracens were fighting round SUTRI and NEPI for thirty years on end.

The open-country *domuscultae* had proved inoperable, and there followed the period of *incastellamento*, 'encastling', during the 10th and 11th centuries: the almost complete withdrawal of people living on the land, including villa-dwellers, into permanent fortified settlements. These were sometimes on new sites, always hills or spurs, often the old Etruscan places. The British School in Rome has identified a hundred of them, of which 'more than sixty now lie deserted and in ruins'.

As a result of this encastling, or along with it, came a remarkable improvement in the productivity of the land, in trade, and probably in health. With increased peasant prosperity and social propinquity came also what the French scholar Pierre Toubert has described as *une aspiration indiscutable à la garantie juridique* – 'an unarguable desire for the rule of law'. Out of this developed the system of self-government called the Communes, and the towns' growing independence of direct Church control.

By the year 1000 Italy had once again begun to flourish: seaborne trade grew with the Eastern Empire and the Arab world; technology and numeracy seeped through from the navigators, shipbuilders, and merchants; the self-government of communes resulted in a sudden building boom, both civic and religious. Whatever else, the Crusades represented a revival of spirit and capability.

There followed one of the great ages of church building: 'It was truly as if the earth itself was throwing off old rejected things and everywhere putting on a white dress of Churches'.*

The Lombards, like the Goths before and the Franks after them, had originated round the Baltic and arrived with no tradition of

**Glabri Rodulphi Historiarum, Lib. III, Ch. lv.*

building in stone. The monuments, materials, and methods they found, ancient Roman and Christian Ravennate, determined what and how they built. The building trades in Roman times had been closely organised and the Lombards continued to protect by law the interests of the hereditary builders' guild, the *Magistri Comacini*. Their expertise, together with the variety of local stones they knew how to use and of ancient buildings they knew how to re-use, ensured a certain continuity.

In Lazio, as in other parts of Italy, some new basilical churches had been going up from the 4th century. By the 7th and 8th, change was accelerating: crypts were shouldering chancels above naves; bell-towers appeared; columns no longer supported architraves in the Roman manner – though many of the columns were re-used from Roman temples – but rather arches with almost unpierced enclosing masonry above.

By the 9th century came vaults, side aisles and, instead of columns, various kinds of pier, increasingly complex on plan. Multiple apses. A decidedly fortified look externally, particularly when churches were built into the walls of the town as at VITERBO, TARQUINIA and TUSCANIA. Transverse arches spanning the nave, side aisles, or chancel. Alternations of piers and columns. Barrel vaults. Ribbed vaults; and domes on pendentives, deriving originally from Byzantium.

The churches from this time stand witness to a clarity, depth, and force of architectural intention and achievement, equalled in Italy only by the purest or lushest builders of Antiquity and of the Renaissance. Many of the buildings remain, as the Matrix at the end of this book shows. But over the centuries they have been much adapted and improved and scraped and covered in this and that. This, along with the inherent invisibility of Northern Lazio, has led to their not being much known.

The early churches contained stone-carved 'church furniture' – ambos, piscinas, pulpits, rails enclosing the choir – and some good pieces and fragments remain. Floors were covered in colourful mosaic decoration and the walls with iconographically instructive painting (the latter almost all lost).

The amazement is in the stone-carving as it developed in the 11th century: complicated and whimsical nightmares. Most of it is smallish, on capitals and door frames, but at TUSCANIA there is, large, plain, and twice-over, a most bizarre three-faced personage, a *trifrons*, on the façade of the Cathedral of San Pietro. The 20th-century beholder is in many minds about how to interpret these extraordinary images, casually ensconced in engaging plant patterns. The words 'grotesque', 'caricature', 'monstrous' spring to mind: but they are insufficient: the thing is also beautiful. For more about this and other Lombardic decorative characters, see Appendix I.

The perennial physical weakness of the Papacy could not fail to suck in first German emperors, then French kings, and eventually Spanish ones too. Yet the Crusades – the First indited by Pope Urban II (1088–99) when showers of meteors seemed to indicate the end of the world was at hand – demonstrated religious and temporal authority enough. It reached a peak in the reign of Pope Innocent III (1198–1216), whose suzerainty stretched for a while at least across most of the northern Mediterranean littoral, including the Crusader states, and across Eastern Europe, Scandinavia, and King John's England. He it was who launched the Albigensian 'Crusade' against heretical Christians in South-West France.

The distinction between physical power and moral authority continued to torment the Popes, and by the end of the 13th century Rome itself had sunk back into impotence and insignificance, due largely to the internecine feuds of the local barons and to French and German rivalry. The Papacy removed to Avignon, and exercised a dim authority through mainly French officials. The Black Death wiped out a third of the Tuscia's population; earthquakes followed; and despair. Only brigands and tyrants flourished: we tell this in more detail under VITERBO.

The great Spanish Cardinal Albornoz eventually facilitated the return of the popes to Rome in 1377, but they immediately faced schism. Although from 1378 to 1417 there was usually a pope in Rome, there were 'anti-popes' somewhere else as well, serving various national interests, French, German, and lastly Spanish. In 1420 Martin V got rid of them, but one straggler, a lay Duke of Savoy, 'reigned' in Switzerland as anti-pope from 1439 to 1449; the future Pope Pius II was his secretary.

The State and the Renaissance

The development in Europe of stable systems of hereditary power and property, of mercenary armies, of money loans to finance them instead of eventual gifts of conquered lands, and the substantial castles required for defence against them, led to the arrival of the State, the Prince, and the bankers.

When Pope Martin V arrived in Rome in 1420 the city itself was devastated and 'civilisation seemed almost extinct'. At the same time, the Renaissance was starting on its mysterious and dangerous way in most of Italy and practitioners in theology, cosmology, and superstition were together scouring Antiquity, Egyptian, Greek, and Roman, for enlightenment. There were even scattered decades of relative peace, as well as amazing intellectual, technical, and artistic achievements.

By the end of the century the Papacy had regained confidence and organisation, financial and military. Individual popes developed worldly ambitions and enmities, hired more effective mercenaries and fought wars, fathered children and ennobled and made cardinals of them, ran up debts, and figured on the European stage as princes ruling a sovereign state. On the new papal practice of having their mistresses and sons about them, Professor M. Creighton, 19th-century Anglican Bishop of London, wrote in his *History of the Papacy*: 'No-one in Italy was particularly scandalised at this state of things. It was universally recognised that the Pope was an Italian prince, and that his policy largely depended on arrangements for his domestic comfort'. Off stage, the knives of the Reformation were being sharpened.

Yet electing a new greybeard every few years, and he with two prior claims on his time – justifying God's ways to man, and manipulating the European Powers – proved no way to secure stable internal government. The short-lived Popes could be elected corruptly or unexpectedly; and their projects would start and stop abruptly. From the 15th century to the 18th, most Popes thought the best way to provide stability was, like any feudal overlord, to give towns and castles to their own nephews and sons, complete with revenues. The nobles thus installed then had to defend their lands against the nephews and sons of later popes.

Meanwhile the questioning, sometimes almost Protestant, sometimes Platonic, of the Christian religion continued bubbling away in the courts and republics of Italy. (In VITERBO, they took up Hercules). It was reinforced by increasing objection to the practices of the Papacy, and what had started as a powerful wish for reform turned into a fierce demand for reformation. In 1527, as a result in part of papal folly, the Emperor Charles V's forces sacked Rome, and other towns on their way back through Lazio as well.

From this disaster the Papacy recovered its nerve in the remarkable person of Pope Paul III Farnese, who distributed 2 per cent of his revenues in alms and re-established authority in the Papal States. Farnese government took over in the dual form of the Dukedom of Castro which Paul cut out of the Patrimony of St Peter for his son

Pier Luigi, and the Cardinal-Legatehood for Life which he gave to his grandson Alessandro along with CAPRAROLA. The Dukedom of Parma and Piacenza in the Po Valley that he also procured for Pier Luigi was the sole enduring dynastic unit of papal origin in the history of the Papacy: though CASTRO itself, a long century before its hideous end, was pretty durable.

During the 16th century a large number of rural castles, villas and palazzi were new-built or improved by people linked by blood or marriage to Farnese, Medici, or other popes. CAPRAROLA, which began as an overtly sumptuous fortress-palace, was by far the grandest. The other new buildings were not themselves flauntingly ostentatious: yet behind their gates and walls unprecedented private comfort, if not always opulence, prevailed.

Rome was slowly rebuilt, grander than before, and the matter of the rise of Protestantism was, at least for Italy, settled by the Council of Trent (1545–63). To the extent that this had started as a general search for religious reconciliation within Europe – in 1535 Pope Paul III had asked the aged Erasmus to 'help him bring St Peter's boat back into harbour' – it was a failure: it ended with Europe polarised and pregnant with the wars of religion.

Spanish power increased in Italy, and Rome became ever more a city of clerics. (In 1687 according to Pascal, Rome contained 41 bishops, 241 priests, and 630 prostitutes.) The historic Church was Counter-Reformed and sprouted saints and mystics through every pore, arduous, conspicuous, and successful: St Philip Neri, who founded the Oratorians; St Ignatius Loyola and St Francis Xavier, of the Jesuits; St Teresa and St John of the Cross, both mystics. (Northern Lazio could boast its own Saint Hyacinth: see VIGNANELLO.)

From the time of Pius IV Medici (1559–65), the Church officially deplored public display by prelates – his nephew, Cardinal Carlo Borromeo (later Saint) was the champion of the new puritanism. Provided it was theologically correct, intelligible, realistic, and a stimulus to piety, the Council of Trent commended the role of art and imagery; but these conditions were not uppermost in the minds of Lazio's villa and palazzo builders in the century between the 1530s and the 1630s. On the contrary, an extraordinarily wide-ranging inventiveness prevailed. Appendix II looks more closely at some of the complexities of the what and why.

Of the many buildings of this period, some are more or less grandiose rural castles, new-built or fashionably improved, with loggias and parterres and a secret garden or two; some are large or small town palazzi, bedecked with well-statued *giardini pensili*, some vast, some scarcely more than balconies. The variety is remarkable: CAPRAROLA, expression of many-sided action; BAGNAIA (Villa Lante), of pleasure and delight; BOMARZO, of contemplation and dream: these are three wonders and closely related. Equivocal BASSANO, and sinister SORIANO; airy BOLSENA; grand VIGNANELLO and modest GALLESE; skied CASTELNUOVO DI PORTO, and lyrical CAPODIMONTE; idyllic ISOLA BISENTINA; tragic and for ever now unknown CASTRO; the so oddly hoped-for but also vanished 'Versailles' at FORMELLO; staunch GRADOLI; the Cardinal Abbot's dark palace at MONTEROSI and the Bishop's flighty one at MONTEFIASCONE; the warlike Rocca at CIVITA CASTELLANA; clodhopper ROCCA RESPAMPANI; the pope's sister-in-law's eyrie at SAN MARTINO . . .

Most of these transformations and rebuildings were conducted by the Farnese and their network of relatives, who owed their prominence not to kingship, nor to having come out on top in the internal rivalries of any nation state, nor to blood royal legitimacy, nor to economic genius, but to their position in relation to one powerful pope and a general ability to get on together. They were not modest, but they were humane, and wherever in Northern Lazio one comes on a place which has something large, open, and strong about it, suggesting sufficiency, candour, and hospitality, it is usually due to them.

This explosion of good building and rational government was almost the last interesting thing that happened in Northern Lazio. The Farnese eclipse began with the 17th century, and in 1649 Pope Innocent X Pamphili, having destroyed their local capital city of CASTRO, took most of their lands back into the papal domain.

After the Farnese

In the Campagna and up the coast (which had not been Farnese country) neglect and indifference already prevailed, and what Montaigne described in the winter of 1580–1 was to last another three centuries:

> The approaches to Rome, almost everywhere, are seen uncultivated and sterile, either through a defect of the land, or, which I find more likely, that this city has hardly any labour force or men who live by the work of their hands. On the way I found, as I was coming, several groups of village men who were coming from the Grisons or Savoy to earn something in the season of the vintage or in the gardens; and they told me that each year it was

> their income. It is a city all court and all nobility: everyone takes his part in the ecclesiastical laziness. There is no tradesman's street, or less than in a small town; there are nothing but palaces and gardens . . .

The reforms that San Carlo Borromeo had tried to instil had, in Rome at least, substantially failed under the successors to his uncle, Pope Pius IV; he himself took off to Milan. The Spanish–Austrian Alliance that Pius V put together ensured the Battle of Lepanto was won (see La QUERCIA), but in the Papal State social and economic decay had set in.

Sheep had almost driven men off the land: lamb and *ricotta* sold better in Rome than bread. Transhumance, originally just a use of the 'outfield', was now the main use for all the land. The lives of the shepherds and *butteri* (*bovis ductor* – oxherd) on the one hand, and of the few peasants engaged in 'infield' cultivation on the other, scarcely crossed. Pastoralism and brigandage – 'outfield' and 'outlaw' – become symbiotic. Banditry had been common from the 13th century, but it reached a destructive peak in the 17th. Pope Sixtus V – great builder in Rome – made a successful attempt to improve the system of roads and bridges but his drastic efforts to check brigandage except in the short run could not but fail: malaria and social decay were to keep the Patrimony in the near-desert condition that so shocked travellers right into the 20th century.

While a mix of radical anticlericalism and economic reform began to flourish elsewhere in Italy, the 17th- and 18th-century Papacy sank back into insignificance; the economy continued to stagnate and the population fell further as malaria advanced. A few half-hearted attempts at local improvement were made, mainly sent in by the papal Camera Apostolica: what we see at ROCCA RESPAMPANI, at MONTE ROMANO, at SAN LORENZO NUOVO, at all the occasional dignified, now abandoned, *podere* buildings standing alone with their built-on chapels. A few quite grand churches – the CROCEFISSO under the CIMINO, the CIBONA in the TOLFA HILLS – recall modest miracles, excessively celebrated. Otherwise, there are some repairs – the dome at MONTEFIASCONE had to be rebuilt; and so did the nave of the Duomo at CIVITA CASTELLANA. In Viterbo in the 18th century there was some remarkably good painting.

The French Revolution, Napoleon's invasions, and his taking the Pope prisoner loosened the chains of reaction everywhere but in the Papal States; and the 'Legitimist' restoration of 1815 ensured the uninterrupted continuation of the old stagnation and poverty.

All this was recorded over and over by the northern visitors who saw it. James Skene of Rubislaw travelled the Aurelia on his way from CIVITAVECCHIA to Rome in September 1802; and what he saw was little different from what Montaigne had seen in the 1580s and what D. H. Lawrence would see in the 1920s:

> The road leads through a waste, neglected and uninteresting country, singularly depopulated and barren for so fine a climate, which does not appear to be so much the fault of nature as the effect of the total neglect and indolence of its inhabitants . . .
>
> . . . The only feeble efforts at husbandry which I could observe consisted in carelessly scratching a few fields with a wretched wooden plough drawn by oxen, where the peasant, either to add to the weight of his clumsy implement or to save himself the trouble of walking, stands upon the plough and is dragged along by the oxen . . . [See below, MARTA.]
>
> The dreary landscape wore out my patience, when at length the mountainous Dome of St Peters rose like a huge pillar of mist in the distance. . . .

Skene was a Scottish watercolourist and a friend of Sir Walter Scott (who in 1831, from Malta, sent him one of the largest blocks of lava he could find). With his boredom, his ready dismissal of what he saw, and his apparent ignorance of the fact of malaria, Skene can stand for many. (Almost alone in such a view, Shelley, in December 1818, wrote to a friend, 'we . . . today arrived at Rome across the much-belied Campagna di Roma, a place I confess infinitely to my taste'.)

When the train arrived, the iron ways followed the Tiber valley and the coast, both bypassing VITERBO and TUSCANIA by some tens of kilometres. A goods line run inland from CIVITAVECCHIA also avoided them. A later railway from the old station by Piazzale Flaminio in Rome meandered through VITERBO and many small towns, picturesque and slow. It now departs from the Termini, Rome's main station, but is otherwise unchanged.

The unification of Italy was complete by 1860, except for the Papal State. To the very end Pope Pius IX was firing anathemas at the new King, Victor Emmanuel, who became reluctant even to enter Rome. When Rome was finally included after the wars and revolutions of 1870, the inherent anticlericalism of the unified state rushed neither to improve nor to enrich an area which had been so lacking in patriotic flame. Northern Lazio remained a region of poor shepherds and absent landlords, whose sufferings continued long into the 20th century.

In 1910, Arnaldo Cervesato published a book, *The Roman Campagna*, which was translated into English in 1915. He described life in these places vividly and passionately, and contributed to the wave of public feeling and public service that had been started by Garibaldi: over the ensuing twenty years that grim area was slowly taken out of the stone age, if not yet into the 20th century.

The *guitti*, the 'dirty people' whose livelihood was the transhumance and the floods of sheep, lived in grass huts, which could be easily taken down and reassembled at the next stop. Some had their wives and children with them, others lived in huts just big enough for one person to crawl into. A village was indistinguishable from many African ones of the time: conical huts of straw or maize stalks, with a hole in the earth for hearth and no chimney. Fifteen or twenty individuals would occupy space where four might have been comfortable. Meanwhile the landowners rode out correctly dressed to hunt the fox. In all the Campagna, by which Cervesato means the 150-kilometre-long coastal plain from Circeo to TARQUINIA, there were no more than a thousand settled families, whom the nomadic hired hands outnumbered ten to one. The system was little removed from slavery: children were bought and sold, and paramilitary agents called corporals would recruit workers each year in the hills, beating drums and giving orders as though by right.

Wild horses and buffaloes roamed in great herds, moving in and out of service to man, and in and out of his breeding systems. (They were also driven into canals to keep the weeds down by thrashing around.) The men sang Tasso and Ariosto in a droning chant as they worked.

Christianity itself had only a partial role in their lives. No allusion to the thunderbolt could safely be made. Masses were said for them in the fields and on the threshing floors, but they still laid the last stook reaped from east to west as they had when Ceres was in office: the few steam threshing engines were also correctly oriented before they could begin their sacred task.

> For the first seven miles along the road out from the walls of Rome [the Aurelia], there was not one house; but everywhere along it there were little heaps of stones called *Morre*; they were the graves of those who had died (mostly of malaria), and the passer-by added his own stone.

In 1890 the German sociologist Werner Sombart had contended that mere hydraulics would never be enough, and there must be land reform. Quinine, known since the 17th century, halved the malaria after 1900; a law of 1905 began the hydraulics; the work continued under Fascism; and a wholehearted land reform in some places was undertaken in the 1950s. Today malaria is gone and the marshland is fertile, the plain is smiling once more, almost as in Etruscan times – the hills always were; many of the streams are captured for electricity; the roads are convenient enough; some towns are more than holding their own. But there are others which are becoming, or remain, ruinous; and so are their sometimes marvellous monuments and artefacts. These now risk final extinction.

To be saved, they must be known; to be known, they must be seen and visited. The purpose of this book is to encourage not only the enterprising traveller and holiday-maker to come and look, but also all those whose duty or interest it is to protect what is old and beautiful. The tourist industry of Italy is of course colossally successful, and in places it has already ruined the attractions that brought it there. This is very far from how it is in Northern Lazio: the Rosencrantz or Guildenstern, it is thought, of the performance. There is little tourism here, and with proper care it could be multiplied somefold before harm is done. Moreover fine old buildings are waiting for conversion to hotels: there would be no need for intrusive modern ones.

General

Landscape

On 3 November 1644, John Evelyn described the view of the Tiber valley, to the south, as they came up to and over 'Radicofany':

> . . . as we ascended, we enter'd a very thick, soled and dark body of Clowds, which look'd like rocks at a little distance, which dured us for neere a mile going up; they were dry misty Vapours hanging undissolved for a vast thickness, & altogether both obscuring the Sunn & Earth, so as we seemed to be rather in the Sea than the Clowdes, till we having pierc'd right through, came into a most serene heaven, as if we had been above all human Conversation, the Mountain appearing more like a greate Iland, than joynd to any other hills; for we could perceive nothing but a Sea of thick Clowds rowling under our feete like huge Waves, ever now & then suffering the top of some other mountains to peepe through, which we could discover many miles off, and between some breaches of the Clowds, Landskips and Villages of the subjacent Country: This was I must acknowledge one of the most pleasant, new & altogether surprizing objects that in my life I had ever beheld . . . [*The Diary* p. 208.]

The 'Landskips' of Arcadia are still to be found in these places, much as when they were painted and drawn by Poussin, Claude, Corot, and Turner, and all the others.* They are a particular mix of lawns and woodland, of uptumbling crag and bush-strewn cliff, of well-placed distant town or ruined tower, with a lake, the sea or the Tiber for mirror, and a suffused or slanting light.

* Nicolas Poussin and Claude le Lorrain knew the area in the first half of the 17th century, and much of the Tiber valley is unchanged since their day. SORACTE and MARTIGNANO seem to appear in Poussin's landscapes, so do the strange tall farmhouses round VITERBO, and once a town sited under the CIMINIAN HILLS like Viterbo, but as usual not quite. Classicists, both he and Claude always generalised a beauty out of particular beauties. J. M. W. Turner (1775–1851) travelled here several times, drawing prodigiously. His little sketchbooks in the Tate Gallery in London show NEPI, CAPRAROLA, RONCIGLIONE, and the LAKE OF BOLSENA.

For so small an area – Northern Lazio is about 150 kilometres long and perhaps 100 across – the landscape is wonderfully varied; never less than pretty, and sometimes, at least to our eye, among the most beautiful to be found in this continent. Even along the coast, where much is spoilt, the sea and the sea-castles – PALO, SANTA SEVERA – are not. (The weather too is various and rewarding – see TREVIGNANO.)

Near in to Rome, round SACROFANO for instance, the Campagna Romana is curly: little valleys and long crests nestle together with woods, bright green and with an intermittent enamel of wild flowers. They climb gently to the LAKE OF BRACCIANO with its almost perfect circular shape and its wooded slopes now running sharply up to the first real mountain: Monte Rocca Romana in the Sabatine Hills.

Between the Lake and the sea, to the south-west, the flat treeless plain is scoured by long straight valleys; an element of unassuming majesty begins to show. Further up the coast the wild, sheer, uninhabited hills of CERVETERI and TOLFA rise in clear repeated sequences. There are no flat valley bottoms; it is a true mountain world. Small oak and the general vegetative spread of the Mediterranean, enticing in spring and spiky in summer, are interrupted only by the occasional bare green sweep of a pasture slope. The rounded shapes already distract motorway drivers on the Via Aurelia, and tempt them to take the deserted road from SANTA SEVERA to TOLFA, which is the only town, and thence to MANZIANA.

North of the first lake comes the LAKE OF VICO, and here we are among grander events indeed. The CIMINO is a group of mountains the same height as those of Lakeland in England, and all wooded. The individual mountains group and regroup themselves impressively from different angles. The giant beechwood on the very top is a separate world.

West from the CIMINO, around VEIANO and as far as MONTE ROMANO, is an area of longer, lower hills, sometimes called Tuscia Minore; it is wooded like the TOLFA HILLS but cut with gulleys, some with cultivable bottoms, and a number of little spur-perched towns. These gulleys are the famous *burroni* that also occur in the TREIA valley.

Seawards and north of Tuscia Minore begins the Great Etruscan Plain around TUSCANIA. You travel across the rather poor and dry farmland and suddenly the earth falls away at your feet revealing a valley several kilometres long. Here the River Marta has gathered the waters flowing west from the CIMINO. The views from the high places (MONTEBELLO is the best) are vast.

Then to the north, the old Maremma and the well-named Piano

del Diavolo – the Devil's Plain. The land becomes wilder and wilder again; you cross pristine river valleys with steep slopes and miles of wood before the next town, and then, on the frontier with Tuscany, the Selva del LAMONE, a true wilderness: waterless, viewless, and but for its mysterious *murce*, featureless. And finally the fourth, lakeless, crater system, that of LATERA.

To the east, the Tiber valley is a separate world. Towards Rome the western slope is steep, sometimes no more than a tall step down from the Campagna. Then comes the ragged cliff- and stream-strewn basin of the TREIA. Level with the CIMINO, the Tiber slopes are gradual and sweeping, covered with neat nutgroves and the great palaces and castle of CAPRAROLA and SORIANO. Opposite you gaze, without much curiosity perhaps, at the more ordinary layout of the non-volcanic Appennines.

Most of the descending ridges now have or have had a town or village on top. The four or five north-west of Bomarzo are the straightest and wildest; the tops pasture with occasional great trees and forgotten olive groves, streams in the valley bottoms. Every so often you come across a flattened space, with a carpet of turf too short to have ever allowed a crop, and probably other signs of long-spent human habitation.

The culmination of these north-going sequences is the high, clear windy LAKE OF BOLSENA, surrounded by hills still riding sequentially on the echoes of their repetitive volcanic origins. MONTEFIASCONE presides, holding its unforgettable ridged and shining dome just below the crest, and its towers just on it. On some days the Lake becomes a shoreless sea; after rain it shrinks to a bright silvery coin ensconced in glittering woods, and its several castles gleam.

Vegetation

When Pope Pius II went on his journey into Upper Lazio in the spring of 1462, he wrote in his journal, 'masses of flowering broom gave much of the country a golden hue and some of it was covered with other shrubs or various plants that presented purple or white or a thousand other colours to the eye. The world was green in that month of May and not only the meadows but the woods were smiling and the birds were singing sweetly.' On his early morning rides from VITERBO, he enjoyed the fields of sky-blue flax.

The climate, obviously, is mediterranean, the 'botanical zones', maritime and appennine. On Monte Fogliano, there is a residual 'oceanic' microclimate, very moist. The Macchia Grande of MAN-

ZIANA – all that is left of the Selva di Manziana, the forest that even in the 16th century ran from the BOLSENA to the TOLFA HILLS – still has its characteristic leggy oak trees, with longer, darker, shinier leaves. On the ISOLA BISENTINA, a tiny area of its original (evergreen) ilex forest remains.

The very rapidity of the spring, the poverty of much of the soil and the variety of the rest, spell wild flowers in profusion and rapid succession. One wood is waist-deep in asphodel; another carpeted in anemones and periwinkles. A hillside is covered in strong-scented jonquils; an old track with grape-hyacinths. One field is crimson with vetch; another blue, with a different vetch. A cliff is yellow with broom; a flat field which in June is pink with a campion, in August is yellow with small marigolds. Blue-stalked thistles put a haze over one rocky slope; saxifrages and orchids and 'alpines' patchwork another; harebells dot a third with shimmering cushions. Where there is a spring, water-dependent plants will fatten and flourish delicately, some in quite idiosyncratic response to a specific chemical and thermal mix. In summer, certain fields will be as blue as Pius's flax fields; but with chicory, and only until noon, when that show closes. In the woods, the scent of vibernum, in the towns of mimosa, travel on finite breezes.

On the coast, behind the beaches, a few of the pinetas – none are truly ancient – still remain: great dark stands of umbrella pines, with laurels, rosemaries, cistus, mints between them and the sea. Vulnerable to sea-blown pollutants, many are dying; also perhaps poisoned by would-be sea-side developers. In high summer an improbably coarse, strong-scented, lily grows straight out of the sand dunes, even among plastic garbage and incomplete building sites.

On old walls, wall-flowers: often yellow, less often bronze, mauve at BOMARZO, dark red at VITERBO.

Ditches and meadows produce fragrant weeds for salads and soups (see Food); also snails. The clump of irises is there to improve the flavour of the olives. The small, often valley-bottom, patches of Tuscany-like *cultura promiscua*, where vegetables, fruit trees, nut trees, vines, bee-hives, the pig in the cave (and the sheep beyond), are all set out in neat combination, provide meals where everything but the salt comes from the same piece of ground.

Animals

Wolves

There is still a modest population of wolves in the Abruzzi, but they disappeared from the right bank of the Tiber in the mid-19th century. About a hundred years later they appeared again. The Wolf Question is: who should have his way, the peasant whose chickens and lambs the wolves still eat as they always did, or the conservationist who wants to preserve populations of such famous and virtuous creatures? For virtuous they are, in their family lives: it is only that they are still hunters and not gatherers which is counted against them. (Doves on the other hand are savage and quite pitiless with their own kind.) So when one day some peasants approached a nobleman and complained that a wolf was eating their chickens he, thinking it was sure to be a feral dog, did what noblemen, and St George, and Perseus, have always done for peasants: he took his weapon and shot the marauder. All hell broke loose, for it was unmistakeably a real live 20th-century wolf.

The question then was whether it was *Lupus Italicus*, which is national and rather small and enabled Romulus and Remus to found Rome, and which could have come back over the Ponte Felice during the snowy winter of 1956, or on the other hand *Lupus Sibericus*, which is large and Russian and altogether unmeritorious and had, as was well known to wolf buffs, been bred by a man near Arezzo in Tuscany and escaped in some numbers. The issue is not settled, but remembered. Certainly there is wilderness enough inland from the line that joins CERVETERI and Grosseto to support a wolf population of either sort without anyone knowing much about it.

Wild Boar

The main game animal – big game in European terms – is the wild boar. The infant of the species is striped and engaging; the adult less so. Their severe gaze and an expectation of tusks can alarm, though they are in fact very shy. Being extremely good to eat, they have for centuries been reared for hunting.

Bats

Both Noctules and Pipistrelles: if your bedroom has two windows, you may wake to find a pair or more speeding in, out, round, in, out, with astonishing accuracy and silence. By day, they hang upended from beams, like forgotten leather pouches. At dusk, they take over from the swifts and swallows.

Sheep

The Campagna has always been sheep country. In Etruscan times, as now, the often mounted shepherd led the flock from the front – today it may as well be from a Vespa as a horse. The sheep always stay close together and move across the ground on little flickering legs like fast shallow clouds. On the west side of the LAKE OF BOLSENA, shepherds bring their flocks down to the beaches to drink.

Dogs

The *Maremmano* sheepdog is worthy of every attention and respect. Both sexes are large, sturdy, and white; of an endearing and trustworthy aspect; intensely loyal; with memories like the elephants; and, when working, some remarkable tactics.

They are quite different from the runabout intelligences familiar in Britain. They go with the sheep and are the same colour, three or four to a flock of half as many hundred, and lounge in the middle of the flock. You do not know they are there until they take objection to you; then you know it very well. They stand up; they assume the voice and face of outraged ownership; and they will indeed attack if you come too close. This is the tactic of controlled invisibility.

The second tactic is that of misleading lethargy, the ostentatious snooze at a distance from the flock. If you take a direction the *Maremmano* does not like, he will instantly wake up and charge ferociously.

At home, on the doorstep, they can be trained to do the same and are the preferred kidnap deterrent. In familiar company, and especially with children, they are gentle, patient, smilingly comatose. Traditionally they are vegetarian (they eat pasta) and there are those who think they may have come from the Himalayan snows – which would account for their whiteness – in the company of one or other of the invading hordes, perhaps the Alans.

Cattle

Farm animals are traditionally white.* The classical Virgilian oxen are white, and the draught and milch buffaloes in the wetlands of

* The long-horned, 'White Park Cattle', well-prized in England, may have been brought to Britain by the Romans.

the Maremma (which had been introduced from Asia in the 6th century BC). The *Maremmano* cattle are also white. They have long, graceful horns and are still lowing to the skies. Unfortunately they are small and inefficient as protein factories, and are on the way out. Efforts have also been made to cross Maremma cattle with Charolais to produce an animal at once more toothsome than the native and more omnivorous than the foreign.

Birds

Some birds which still figure in the various *Birds of Britain* books, because someone saw one in 1821 and they are so beautiful, are common here: the roller; the bee-eater in small aerial dance troops flashing and turning kingfisher colour if the sun is low. Above all the hoopoe, which flies low and bobbingly, flashing black and white. And the incomparable nightingale.

Kites and harriers circle over the shores of the lakes. (See BARBARANO ROMANO for the recent disappearance there of the Egyptian Vulture, the *capovaccaio*.) And in the wildernesses and among the more 'backward' bits of the agriculture, many warblers gone from us survive.

Butterflies and Moths

Likewise with *lepidoptera*: not only the ordinary delights common in the right place but also both the Swallowtails, the Camberwell Beauty, and the Purple Emperor.

And moths, big and small, exotic and homely, glorious hawk-moths and (probably) dingy footmen.

Other Insects

Never try to squash a scorpion: they don't squash, and the vegetarians, rightly, will object. Take a broom, sweep it off the wall or wherever, and then outside. They don't slow down after a night in the fridge, either.

Cicadas, crickets, and grasshoppers of all shapes, sizes, colours, and habits – flying, hopping, planing; splashing up from the grass – are constant company in summer; as they probably were to the hunters of TORRIMPIETRA. The cicada is not often seen but, moulting, leaves a neatly sliced ghost-garb stuck to the bark of trees.

Next to the useful honey-bees, the ancients celebrated all of these insects for their cheerful 'song'. Although Ian Beavis, their historian, lists eighteen names, species were not distinguished nor was their means of 'stridulation' understood. Cicadas 'produce their song by means of the rapid vibration of two membranes or tymbals, which are situated in resonating cavities on either side of the base of the abdomen'. Some grasshoppers and crickets have a 'row of minute studs [along their thighs] which act as the bow to the fiddle-string on the fore wing . . .'. Others rasp a file on the left wing across the veins of the right wing, which hold a resonating diaphragm. For mole crickets, see VIGNA GRANDE.

The largest of the bumble bees is always about: dark blue, noisy, taking corners like a 16-year-old on a new motor bike, but quite safe. In early summer, fireflies: which are a beetle. Pliny saw them as one of the signs of *incredibilis benignitas naturae* because their appearance as little stars tells the farmer when to sow millet and harvest barley. (They were also thought to have a contraceptive effect.) In all the (unsprayed) wildernesses, innumerable further examples of the Almighty's 'inordinate fondness' for – and skill at devising – beetles, including the almost daunting stag beetle and rhinoceros beetle. The praying mantis, too, and stick insects.

By the water, all the dragonflies: blue, red, bronze-black, yellow- or green-striped. Damsel-fly nymphs climb out of the water up a reed to split slowly open and emerge, with a kind of back-handstand; and wait there, pumping up their wings, to dry.

Spring-water with a high mineral content can have a high surface tension, and then water-boatmen and such become twice the normal size. (And 20 lire pieces float.)

Reptiles

Snakes are mostly grass-snakes, some amazingly long, but harmless. A small blackish snake will take pleasure swimming in the lakes. The viper is rare, as with us, but not absent. Lizards are everywhere – *lucertola* – and geckos, who have suction pads on their fingers and toes and traverse ceilings with enviable ease. And various frogs: some like little autumn leaves (see CASTELGIULIANO).

In wild places there are tortoises, which should be let be.

Food (other than fish)

Peter Beckford's view of Italian food, at the end of the 18th century, was fairly jaundiced:

> ... what will be your penance in an Italian inn? – Your soup little better than bread and water, and blacker than Spartan broth: your Alesso, a half-starved chicken boiled to rags: your Umido, the scraps of yesterday: and your Arrosto, not a sirloin of beef, my good Sir, but a couple of linnets or chaffinches; ...
> (*Lesso* is boiled, *umido* is stewed, *arrosto* is grilled.)

Standard writing about Italian food today assumes that after the rich eating of the north – Piedmont, Parma – there is Tuscany, with all that *bistecca ai ferri*, and then there is Rome, where it's *agnello* with rosemary: and both very nice. But with food, as with art, architecture, and landscape, there is an area in between where it is also very nice, but not much known. Even Beckford went on to admit the LAKE OF BOLSENA 'well-stocked with fish, and the eels ... excellent'.

Advice

To anyone who does not already know the country, we must say in advance that in central Italy, by and large, 'fast-food' is a contradiction in terms: your pasta will only be *buttata giù*, thrown down (i. e. into the boiling water), when you order it; your fish will not be waiting around to be re-heated; no one will be wanting to turn you out to get another dose of hamburger-eaters through the system: a good meal is one of life's more reliable pleasures and is worthy of respect.

Also, if you have a dish in one place, the same name will not necessarily conjure it up in another. The best meal you can hope to have is, as we said above, the one where none of the ingredients but the salt has travelled more than a kilometre or so: which these days is rare.

We do not mention individual restaurants in this book, and if we name the *Richiastro*,* in the Via della Marocca, in VITERBO, it is because the restaurateurs are, to sensational effect, making known what peasant cooking in this part of Italy was at its best. Those not interested in discovery will also be amply provided for. The place is quite small, so telephone first – Viterbo 223609; it is only open Thursday to Sunday, and it has a summer holiday.

The main 'fast-food' exception is *porchetta*. On Fridays (nowadays:

* A *richiastro* is a small garden enclosed behind walls, green as anything because of Viterbo's plentiful water – it can be seen from the air how many of them there are; this one is particularly pleasant.

it must have been Saturdays when Fridays were meatless) you will see small trolleys at the curb-side surmounted by a full-size meat-safe, within which will be a whole roast pig, crackling and all, and it will be there for the slicing until it is finished. *Porchetta* dealers are today licensed; they will cut you what you want, weighing it on hand-held scales, and providing bread too. Make sure you get bits of the crackling and the fennelly gunge.

And the 'sweets and bits' stalls in the markets are quick food too, of course: hazelnuts in toffee, crystallised this and that, chick peas salted, broad beans, coconut slices under a little waterfall, a dozen or so different kinds of olive... Watermelons at the roadside.

The Old Food of the Tuscia

How poor was poor in pre-war Lazio? One of the principal local dishes was *acqua cotta*, 'cooked water', Beckford's black 'soup', no doubt. It would be made with whatever the shepherd out in the *incultum* could put together in the way of edible weeds or mushrooms; a bit of the *pancetta* – a kind of streaky bacon – he had brought with him; water to boil it all in. Then everything poured on to the stale or hard bread that has to be softened to be made edible. Even with a splash of olive oil, the result must often have been sour and boring. But it can be perfectly, and because of the weeds mysteriously, delicious. You add what you want: vegetables, beans, bacon, eggs, *baccalà* (the board-like dried cod that used to be important food); even lake fish; some say frogs; presumably snails.

Panzanella (stale bread soaked in water, and squeezed; available field and garden herbs, and cucumber and tomatoes, mixed in; vinegar and olive oil spattered) is another make-do, for hot weather, with much the same ingredients; you can add anchovies or tunny – still sold from the barrel – or little bottled artichokes, or ham. Both these can be delicious.

There are other uses for stale bread: particularly *crostini* and *bruschette*: small pieces of old bread, grilled crisp, with olive oil dripped across and garlic and salt. Eat like this, or have beside them to dip into a variety of cunning mixtures, strong-flavoured spreads and scrapes and drippings: grilled peppers and hard-boiled egg, black olives pounded, green olives ditto, tomato almost dried and turned to a jam, things with capers, anchovies, pounded liver, giblets, salted fish roes.

Of the field herbs, wild fennel (*finocchio*) has almost year-round uses: as stuffing, along with garlic and salt and pepper, for the *porchetta*; the spring shoots are chopped on any kind of bean – hot or cold; the stalks go under fish being grilled; the flowers are dried and rubbed, and put on anything *arrosto*. The seeds are there all the time.

So is rosemary (*rosmarino*), parsley (*prezzemolo*), sage (*salvia*), and marjoram (*oregano*). Bay-leaves are *alloro* and basil is *basilico*. Basil does not dry well, but it can be kept for winter *sott'olio* – 'under oil' – by stuffing clean dry basil leaves into a screw-top jar with olive oil in it, pushing with the handle of a wooden spoon until no more bubbles come up and the basil is covered, and the jar is full. It looks like seaweed but smells marvellous.

Among the edible weeds (the *erbarelle*) there is a mysterious little member of the Campion family, *Silene inflata*, called *strigoli* which is somewhat 'succulent', stews down to very little, and acceptably blends with a dish of scrambled egg. (*Strigoli* are Viterbese, not known by that name in the Province of Rome; elsewhere the word means 'offal'.) More interesting is the salad made from the pared and slivered shoots of *cicorione* (chicory), at that stage known as *puntarelle*: after preparation, they need to soak in fresh water for an hour or so; they curl prettily. In spring this is a crisp and delicate salad; at other times, stew it, with the flesh of a tomato added towards the end. *Agreti* are a slightly domesticated version of samphire (also called *barba di frate* – 'friar's beard'). British samphire is full of sea-salt from where it grows, and needs none adding; *agreti* do need it. (Wash well, cook minimally, hold by the root to eat hot with melted butter, cold with oil and lemon.) And there are the thistles – the *cardo*, from which the glorious globe artichoke has been developed, and *carducci*. The roots and stalks are thoroughly edible when the tough filaments are removed; in English 'cardoons'. Wild figs, stewed with garlic, oil, and fennel, make a condiment for meat. Marrow flowers, fried in batter, are eaten with sugar. *Piscialetti* are not dandelions, but a rather bitter cress. *Rafano* is a horseradish. *Ramolacci* is another kind of radish. *Gurgulestro* is a water-celery. In some places, *raponzolo* is lamb's lettuce. A salad mix of herbs from the field or ditch and the thinnings of the vegetable patch, and containing either wild or cultivated *rucola* (or *rugola* or *rughetta*) – rocket – is a *misticanza*.

Cedro is an outsize member of the citrus family, with a very delicate (edible) thick pithy skin: you slice it thinly and dress it with olive oil and salt, as a small *antipasto*. You can also eat it with sugar.

Legumes, too, of every kind and colour, and used in every possible way. One of the basics of Italian cooking is the *soffritto*: usually a mix of finely chopped carrot, onion, and celery leaves – and parsley and garlic and any number of other *profumi* (perfumes) – which you fry, and allow to catch a little, so that your eventual dish is improved with their caramelised flavours. The dullest mess of beans, if a *soffritto* is added to it, moves up from the nourishing to the delicious.

Of the mushrooms the most glamorous is the *ferlengo*, because of its mysterious connection with the transhumance routes: it is only found at the lower end of the ancient drove-ways where they come down into Lazio and the Puglie, and then only symbiotically with one of the cow parsleys. Big; to be grilled, with a little oil and dried fennel flower. There are ordinary white mushrooms, of course, and *porcini* – the much-prized autumn bolets, which then become the fragrant dried mushrooms you put in your *sugo*; and *canterelle* – chanterelles; and *cremini* – a large, ragged, creamy-mauve wedge fungus; and many others only local experts can recognise and advise on.

The Viterbese are or were proud of their purple carrots in *agro-dolce* – sour-sweet. The carrots – which used to grow wild round the LAKE OF BOLSENA – were sliced longways, dried in the July sun, rehydrated in vinegar (five days), the vinegar drained off to have sugar cooked in it (15 minutes) together with cinnamon, and then the carrots cooked in it too; after which raisins and pine-nuts and anise and anything you thought best could be added, even chocolate; finally you put the lot in special terracotta pots and serve it up with a good *bollito misto* – a dish of mixed boiled meats.

Recipes survive for every possible part of a slaughtered beast: lambs' ears – glutinous; tendons (*nervetti*), very slithery. A *coratella*, like a haggis, includes all of a sheep's innards – heart, kidney, liver, lights – stewed up with red wine, and artichokes. (Butchers' shops are highly recommended for those doing A-Level biology; for the squeamish, not.) Meat can also be preserved, salted and dried, and lasts between one season and the next. *Prosciutto crudo*, here as elsewhere, is the uncooked ham that needs to be sliced paper thin, and goes so fetchingly with melon and with black figs. (Be careful when buying figs to use the masculine form, *fico*; *fichi*, the feminine means the female parts, which is awfully hilarious.) Sometimes – restaurants in MARTA, for instance – you will find wild boar (*cinghiale*) on the menu: ham, paté, *salami*, stewed in various ways.

As to the cultivated vegetables; in the spring artichokes are every-where: the 'Roman' ones done up in huge double bunches – natural composite capitals – and lorries sell them off the back at traffic jams. The people of CAMPAGNANO believe theirs are and always have been the best: the CAMPAGNANO soil is ferruginous, as it should be ... but with the draining of the coastal marshes, artichokes now grow along the coast, round LADISPOLI. TARQUINIA has long celebrated a *Carciofata* where you have them in *acqua cotta*, in omelettes and in pancakes, fried (one excellent way is *alla Giudea*), and with various sauces, one called *pinsimonia*, which is *piquante*.

On the CIMINO chestnuts (*castagne*) have long been a staple: as *mosciarelle* – dried chestnuts – they are turned into flour, used whole in soups (sometimes with chick peas – *ceci*), added to other vegetables, eaten with meat, made into a *marmelata* – equal quantities of sugar and chestnuts stewed, covered with a layer of 'rum', and used in tarts or with *ricotta* (see below). *Castagnacci* is a fine mess of chestnut flour, raisins, olive oil, grated peel, sugar, pine-nuts, and so on, baked in a shallow pan, with oil and rosemary sprinkled on top.

A speciality would often be linked to a particular Church festival or Saint's day. *Giuncata dell'Ascensione* was a junket made in little rush (*giunco*) baskets, eaten with sugar and cinnamon. *Maritozzi di quaresima* – 'lenten husbandlets' – were little phallus-shaped cakes for the first Friday in March: they were supposed to have a ring inside. Almond-paste biscuits in the shape of broad beans were called *fave dei morti* – broad beans of the dead: and in fact Etruscans and Romans ate broad beans at funeral feasts. At Easter, there is a *Pizza di Pasqua* – different recipes and different flavours in different places – which is large, liquorous, and brioche-like, egged for a dark shiny brown surface. In ANGUILLARA it has pounded raisins on top and chopped orange peel. The poor used to make it without eggs or fat, just yeast.

Of all the bread and cakes, the *ciambella* is the most interesting. Our dictionary derives it from the Latin *suavillum* – a little, sweet cake. In Rome – and in the corner bar everywhere – it is indeed a soft sugared doughnut, standard fare for breakfast. But the historic *ciambella* is rather a dry, ring-shaped bun which one is only tempted to call a doughnut because that is the shape, even though the texture and often the size are not. And the *ciambella* is intended to last. At MARTA, where they are made huge and in vast quantities for the Barabbata, they are subjected to a prolonged double-cooking – the risen dough (the yeast is called *biga*) first coiled, then boiled (and marked with M), then baked. Presumably the shepherd and the *buttero* set off with that kind, expecting them to last for several weeks: they would soften in the *acqua cotta*. At BARBARANO ROMANO, too, they came big and the men 'wore' them on their arms, on the outing in honour of St Antony Abbot. But some *ciambelle* are indeed smaller and softer and flavoured with cinnamon or anise or lemon as well as sugar, and these have other names and are often best dipped in wine. For the question of the *ciambella* of the dog of San Rocco, see BOLSENA.

Bakers' shops very likely have the ovens in the back and lads in small white hats will be pushing and pulling great trays of loaves and rolls throughout the morning. Bread comes salted and unsalted. *Casereccio* is big rough bread, good fresh, good toasted, good (stale) for *panzanella* and *acqua cotta*. The bread rolls are *rosette*, and equally excellent. At FARNESE, a small (salt) loaf is twisted into a fat fish-like shape, with a broad tail.

Later in the day, citizens may well bring in some dish they want baked. Some bakers do the local *crostata* – fruit-tart– as well as bread; sometimes it is done in a special shop. Some do the brioches and the *ciambelle* that are for dunking: at GRADOLI, these come in an entwined shape, and go with the *aleatico*; at CAPODIMONTE, a more open entwinement, 20 centimetres across, goes with the *cannaiolo*. And then there are *tostetti*, little double-baked slices, with hazelnuts in them. . .

Cheese

The ideal very hard cheese has to be Parmesan – *Parmigiano*, *grana*, from the North – but local *pecorino*, made from sheep's milk, in much smaller cheeses, can be very fine, both for grating and for eating by itself: sharpish, fragrant. Of the rather hard cheeses, many made locally, there are several, and tasting rather different each time and in each place. If the cheese stall in the market is having a slack time, your interest will be valued, and you will be able to compare before buying. *Casciotta* is one, *caciocavallo* another. (Sometimes, they come smoked.) Of the soft cheeses, *ricotta* – a fresh sheep's cheese, properly made in flat little baskets whose shape is impressed on the cheese – is a very wonderful thing, to be cooked with, mixed with (savoury and sweet), eaten by itself, or with fruit: even with finely ground coffee, sugar, and a splash of *grappa*. *Mozzarella* ought to be made with buffalo milk, but usually isn't; even so, it is delicious fresh, and if hardened, delicious inside folded white *pizza*, with a bit of onion and oil and a lot of rosemary: it becomes *focareccia*; good too in a toasted sandwich, or on top of vegetables, or a piece of ham. At the *Richiastro* a local firm but fresh cheese called *palanzanella* is served, sliced, with raw mushrooms, also sliced, and oil and lemon juice. (The Palanzana is the mountain above the city.) Certainly there is little reason to eat most of the 'industrial' cheeses from afar: every *alimentari* will have some cheese locally made, as well as good fresh cheese – *latticini* – distributed from the big dairies remarkably fast.

Many towns have their local *sagra* each on its own day – a more or less lay festivity, in the old days with a tax exemption, to celebrate, for instance, the potato at GROTTA DI CASTRO, *gnocchi* at SAN LORENZO NUOVO, wine at VIGNANELLO, *crostini* and *bruschette* appropriately enough at tiny SERMUGNANO. Trestle tables are put out in the piazza or the street, the speciality is on sale, and wine, and everyone sits down to a splendid feast. For the locals it is usually subsidised because it used to be a charitable exercise. Visitors are normally made welcome, and should just offer what seems a reasonable sum.

Etruscan Food

How Etruscan is today's Tuscia food? There is an excellent display in the Museum of the Rocca Albornoz in VITERBO, showing what the Etruscans ate, and how they grew it and prepared it. From this it is clear that most things are there, except for the citrus from the East, and the tomatoes, potatoes, and sweet peppers from the West: your *pasta* was *in bianco*, your *pizza* could have had cheese and mushrooms; and there was vinegar to drip on your meat, and to make into an *agrodolce* – sour-sweet – sauce with honey.

The tomb of the *Rilievi* – the reliefs – at CERVETERI shows equipment for making *tagliatelle*; olives were introduced into Italy by Greek colonists between the 8th and 6th centuries BC; garlic and *peperoncini* – little hot peppers – were available in all markets; as to wine, a *moscato* called *apiana* was the favourite, but there were several others also named: *tuderana pharia*, and *talpana*; honey, particularly thyme honey (*mutuya*) was added to wine to sweeten it, and used as a condiment. (Wine was one of Etruria's principal exports.)

The diet was principally vegetarian in early days: artichokes, turnips, onions, leeks, asparagus, cabbage, carrots, cress. Broad beans. Pulses. A rich pap of calories made with *farro* – a coarse meal ground from some kind of grain, mixed with water. (Our word 'farrago' comes from it.) Various kinds of fish, including tunny. And *garum* sauce, made of fermented fish guts and brine, we have seen it suggested, must have been like the *Nuoc Mam* used in Vietnamese cooking: today's 'double concentrated' tomato purée presumably takes its place as a powerful cover-all flavour. Also quince cheese as a condiment. Boar. Domestic pigs, probably little black-haired ones, the killing of which was something of an event; pig meat also dried and preserved: did they make *porchetta*? Cattle, then as later, were too useful to be much used for food. Buffalo were introduced from Asia in the 6th century BC; and that meant cheese. Sheeps' milk cheeses too. (Indeed milk was mostly used for cheese, as it was until about 1970.) The cheese from LUNI was famous: there is tell of a mega-*casciotta* weighing 300 kilogrammes being used to feed a thousand people.

Fish (fauna and food)

When Pius II visited VITERBO in 1462 he noted that 'Fish were supplied in plenty by the Tuscan Sea on one side and the nearby Lake of Bolsena on the other'. And that is how it still is: the sea-fish, shellfish, crustaceans, squid, and such, arrive with their seaweed in time for the inland market stalls; the lake fish, some of them still swimming about in tanks, are there earlier still with the lakeside fishmongers. The tanks at BOLSENA and TREVIGNANO are fed by water coming straight out from the hill. In MARTA, the houses used to be built over and into the lake, so that their cellars could act as fish-tanks. If it is a full moon, some kinds of fish won't be on sale: the fish see the nets and keep clear.

Montaigne in Rome in 1581 found 'less fish than in France; pike worthless – they are left to the people; rarely, sole and trout; good barbehaus [probably 'barbues', brill] much bigger than at Bordaus [Bordeaux], but dear. Daurades a great price; bigger mullets than ours.' He does not seem to have come across the lake fish at all, and thus missed a treat most travellers still miss. (Aldous Huxley's poor lady in *Those Barren Leaves* who died after eating lake fish at MONTEFIASCONE had to die for the sake of the plot – nothing to do with the fish.)

There are fish in all the bigger lakes. The eel (*anguilla*, or *capitone*, when they are particularly big) and the whitefish (*corregone*) are unfamiliar to the British, the 'royal perch' (*persico reale*), the pike (*luccio*), and the tench (*tinca*) less so. And there are *lattarini* – an atherine, which you sometimes see in shoals, leaping like little rainbows from mini-wave crest to mini-wave crest.

The *Coregonus* is a wonderful genus of edible fish (which escapes notice in Britain under the name of Whitefish – n. b., not white fish, as in the old White Fish Authority, which is different, but Whitefish). According to standard guides to European fishes, etc., it is found all round the world at a latitude more or less between Siberia and say Munich, but stops north of the Alps. This is inaccurate: it flourishes wonderfully in the lakes of Lazio, and others in Northern Italy. The genus is said to be 'plastic', meaning nobody really knows whether it is one species with four forms or two species with two each, or four with one each, or whatever. Textbooks take refuge in the statement that the attempt to subdivide the genus into local forms or races serves no practical purpose. Mostly it lives in deep clear lakes and eats planktonic crustacea, but there is one form (or population) which migrates through the Baltic.

If one has to choose between the English names for the Latial *corregone*, it is neither the 'houting' nor the 'powan' but, because its lower jaw protrudes a bit beyond its mouth, the 'vendace'. In Italian it is officially the *coregono* and in the kind of book which is careful to reproduce dialect pronunciations phonetically it figures as *gurrigone*. *Corregone* is what it sounds like in ordinary speech; accent on the third syllable.

To eat, it is sweet, mild, and deeply unboring: you can eat it every day for a week and not get fed up. Convenient too: a sensible backbone, and that's it. Fried and grilled are equally good: butter, a little rubbed fennel or parsley, a squeeze of lemon. Also cold: the just-cooked fillets are spread with an oil-based green herb sauce (some of the flavours of which also turn up in local cold chicken dishes): the actual mix of herbs is a personal matter. If you have one of those portable smoking boxes from Scandinavia, the *corregone* will smoke in it even more deliciously than a trout; add fennel stalks to the smoking sawdust. You can also bake them in parsley, etc., like fresh sardines; or with garlic pigs and sage leaves. That excellent exponent of Weeds as food, Patience Gray, mentions the *Coregonus Lavaretus* – the *lavarello* – which is found in Lake Garda and in Haute Savoie; but it is different – larger, less flavoursome, and pink-fleshed whereas our *corregone* is milk-white.

The *corregone* is also a hero fish, because it eats mosquito larvae, which used to cause malaria: *Anopheles Maculipennis*, the Spotty-winged Importunate, which spend their time lying flat on the under-surface of still water.

The *capitone* is the fish that Pope Martin IV, who was French, is said to have died of a surfeit of; he liked them to have been drowned in the wine called *vernaccia*, and Dante put him in Hell as a glutton. Despite which the people of BOLSENA still send a basket of them to the Pope at Christmas. (See MARTA, for the great eel trap.)

The lake eels can, if female, grow to a metre and a half – males to 50 centimetres; the former can weigh up to 6 kilos. These of course are larger than any we in Britain know; they are also scalier; and probably much older. As with ours, the young ones, the elvers, are covered with a glutinous stuff called in English vomp (which needs rubbing off, if you want to make elver pie, say, or soup). Eels live deep when they can, hibernate, enjoy a muddy bottom, but will travel along streams and even over ground on their way to the sea. Once back in the sea they set off on a perhaps five-month journey across the Atlantic where, under the seaweed of the Sargasso Sea, they can reproduce; and whence, as vomp-insulated elvers, they must all have come to swarm up our rivers and into our lakes in the first place. Or so it has been thought since 1896. But there is puzzlement because very few elvers or eels are observed going through the Straits of Gibraltar: may there not be a nursery somewhere in the Mediterranean itself? Even this does not satisfy all Lake fishermen, some of whom are convinced that the eels they know so well are viviparous, because in spring they find eels they believe to be pregnant, with tiny slithery creatures in their bellies. Certainly it seems not unreasonable, if at one time all eels had to cross and recross the Atlantic in their lifetime, for some of them to have adapted to the sufficient depth, darkness, and warmth of these volcanic lakes, which lack only Sargasso salt. Some of the big ones, which look a bit different, may have been brought down from Comacchio, up in the Po delta, where also there are wonderful great eels.

The big *capitoni* are only caught from September to December, and may remain in tanks. The Romans, and probably the Etruscans, ate them at the mid-winter feast, and so do people still. In restaurants even in summer you will be offered the smaller eels *arroste* – 'grilled' – or *allo spiedo* – kebabbed – divided by bay leaves, or *panbruscato*, which is bits of bread toasted, oiled and garlicked – and bits of ham perhaps. If you have a grill, lay bay-leaves on the rack, and then the eel: the skin will char off. If there are *capitoni*, you can chop them into cutlets, and do the same; no basting required: eel is naturally fat, and will not drip too much. Eel also comes stewed in a rich tomato sauce, the Christmas eel: and Lucrezia Borgia had them done in pastry. If you have a smoking box, smoke the eel, filleted, for 10–15 minutes, with bay-leaves in the sawdust.

There is also a way of bottling eel and other lake fish: cooked slowly in oil; drained; placed in glass jars with garlic, peppercorns, sage and *peperoncino* and slices of lemon, covered with boiling vinegar; sealed and left for at least a fortnight. They are available at the MONTEFIASCONE fair.

The *persico reale* – perch – is usually done as egg-and-breadcrumbed or battered fillets.

Sea fish are the same here as anywhere else on the Tyrrhenian coast. A few names may be useful.

Cernia is a kind of sea-perch with white, big-flaked, flesh. A saucelet of (minimal) mixed lemon juice, white vinegar, and its own juices. *Spigola* is bass; *triglia* is mullet; *alici* are anchovies, which you may well find fresh as well as in tins, and also still salted in barrels; *sarde* are sardines, fresh (and delicious boned and baked with breadcrumbs and parsley). Fresh tunnyfish, *tonno*, is big and beautiful (but perhaps mixed up with dolphins in the catching). You may see garfish, *aguglia*, in the market, which has green bones. *Pesce San Pietro* is John Dory, and *muggine* is grey mullet. The excellent *dentice*, *orata*, and *ombrina* are not found in northern waters.

For prawns, crayfish, spiny crabs, rock lobsters and such there are various uninformative and inexact names. The prawns known as *mezzangole* are not unlike *scampi*, but with a more remarkable taste; the shell cooks darker, and the creature has a long single nose-horn; it can take a strong sauce. For the delicate, split, grilled and buttered with a squeeze of lemon or splash of brandy does nicely.

Seppie, calamari, calamaretti, polpi, etc. (squid, cuttlefish, octopus) come usually as rings in *fritto misto* or *zuppa* or *in umido* – stewed.

Shellfish appear in various and exhilarating *zuppe di pesce*, and with pasta and risottos. *Vongole* are very small clams; *cozze* are mussels; and there are cockles with various names.

A *fritti misto, di mare* or *di lago*, can be excellent, but the quality of the batter is all-important.

Wine

Etruscan wine and wine 'objects' were already widespread in Western Europe in the 7th and 8th centuries BC.

According to Pierre Toubert it is simply the ubiquity of the vine in Lazio that has prevented the emergence of 'great wines'. The 'great' French and German wines have been achieved in the teeth of unfavourable natural conditions whereas here, within certain heights above sea-level, the vine will extract nectar from every square metre of soil. The other side of that coin is that most of it does not travel well, so drink it on the spot. Restaurant-keeping is still often a personal thing: if you are there to have a good meal in happy company, your wine will be good; if you want fast food and aren't nice to your children, it won't.

The ideal way to consume wine in Lazio, indeed in all of central Italy, is in a public *cantina*. These places, getting rare but not yet very rare, consist of a big door leading from the street into a rough space, often whitewashed a good while ago, in which are scrubbed wooden tables and benches where you sit, and your half-litre is brought to you in a glass measure. This space is a vestibule to the cellar proper, which is down steps into the rock, often to a considerable depth. (The rock is likely to be *lapilla*, which is less dense and thus easier to tunnel in than *tufo*.) It gets colder and colder and the cobwebs get thicker and more glutinous and menacing. The barrels at the bottom may be very large and very old, which gives a wonderful sense of brotherhood among all those who have valued wine over the centuries. Pope Paul III liked coming to CASTRO in the summer because the deep cellars kept the wine and the melons so cool.

In 1988 we saw wine advertised at a *cantina* for 1,000 lire the litre, that is, 45p: perhaps not to be recommended. But 75p the litre should be all right. The *cantina* is the main place for long discussions among men about the usual: politics, the absurdity of life, farm prices, and the position of women. (For long discussions with women, go to either the market, or those *pasticcerie* where cream cakes are consumed with expressions of roguish guilt.)

The best ordinary wine then is that which has travelled least. When they can, people will drink their own. On the slopes towards the sea, and in the Tiber valley, it can be very good (CERVETERI, TORRIMPIETRA, VIGNANELLO). In the craters one should indeed drink the local wine, but it is sometimes a bit too impressive and it is worth going for something special. Note that a lot of Orvieto wine, which can be of the very best, is made in the hills to the south of Orvieto, so actually in Lazio.

The *Greghetto* – a lightish red wine – of GRADOLI can still be found under that name, just, but it is being absorbed by the homogenisation which has paradoxically followed the introduction of a system of *Denominazioni di Origine Controllata* (DOC), derived from the French system of *Appellations Controlées*. At this game, it must be admitted the Tuscan and north Italian wines do best. What happens is that the famous places are built up at the expense of the others, and the technologies even them all out. But wine is still a natural product here in Northern Lazio and depends a lot on how the weather has been. Another victim of the new system is the slightly bitter-sweet, slightly fizzy red wine called *Cannaiola* at MARTA, though that can still be found both there and at a *cantina* in CAPODIMONTE. It goes with special dry cakes. (The word also means song thrush.)

But the pride of crater wines in the *Aleatico* of GRADOLI. This is a *moscato* grape, and the dark, ruddy, wine used to be made in many places in Italy and the Islands. The name smacks of historical romances: pirates would quaff it. It is indeed a heroic wine, heavy, not sweet but sharp; lorry drivers drink it draught, with a slice of lemon in it. It goes well at the end of a meal. In good years it is sold unfortified, when it clocks in at 14 per cent; in other years it is fortified to 16 per cent with alcohol from the same grapes, when it travels better. The vine has immensely long roots, able to drop straight down 4 metres or more through the loose volcano dust until it finds some faint dampness. This it transforms into something deserving the effort it has made.

It is said that until the invention of the steam engine the vine was the most powerful pump known to man, quite apart from dispensing a good taste and some joy with the water. The *Aleatico* grape is Super Pump itself. The wine is made at a modern *cantina sociale*, a collective manufactory: Italian peasants are still stubbornly socialist, within limits, and that is not surprising when you learn what their life was like between the time of the Communes (around the year 1000) and recent years. At GRADOLI they say the reason why the excellent *Cannaiola* of MARTA is not a DOC is because the small private growers there have never got their act together into a *cantina sociale* and have never applied for DOC status.

As for the denomination *Est Est Est* from MONTEFIASCONE, we agree with Peter Beckford, who wrote: 'I do not think the wine at present so excellent but any drunken Bishop may pass Montefiascone in safety'. MONTEFIASCONE indeed makes very nice white wine, like everywhere else round here, but it has allowed a harmless medieval funny story to get out of hand. Perhaps in the 13th century, a German ecclesiastic travelling to Rome told his servants to go on ahead and write up *Est* – 'there is' – by the gate of any town where the wine was good. At MONTEFIASCONE he wrote up *Est Est Est*, hitting on what must be the longest lived advertising jingle in the Western world. The ecclesiastic stayed, and died of it. Since then the story has never failed to be told in every guidebook and on every bottle, and there has been such overproduction that much of it is now no good at all. It used to come only from the *conca* below, but now other wines are mixed with it. BOLSENA's wine, which is perfectly good anyhow and has a pretty picture of the ancient Roman baths on the label, is now to be described as *Est Est Est*, and so is GRADOLI's rather delicate white.

Another rule of thumb: when you find something you like, drink it while you can get it, and do not expect the next box to be like the first one.

Waters and Baths

(See also the CALDARA, CIVITAVECCHIA (for the Terme Taurine), FICONCELLA, NEPI, STIGLIANO, and VICARELLO.)

Since the region is so highly volcanic it has innumerable hot springs, and since they are there, and fun to get into, the people of Northern Lazio are firmly, but entrenchedly, convinced of the virtues of 'thermalism'. So were the Etruscans and the Romans and, after a certain date, the popes. The Romans even built public libraries beside their major baths.

There is a spatter of Roman bath ruins near where the new *Superstrada* from ORTE joins the Cassia below VETRALLA; and many others. Sometimes fields appear to simmer; at certain corners, there are permanent wafts of rotten egg from the natural sulphur.

The early Christians abandoned the ancient baths as immoral, but in the 13th century they became respectable again, after a Crusader's dream 'rediscovered' the Baths near VITERBO: the commune took them over. In the 1450s Pope Nicholas V, who went there for his gout, brought his family and had the baths 'restored ... at a great expense and in regal style' by Bernardo Rossellino, the Florentine architect and sculptor; Vasari tells us he made 'apartments suitable not only for the sick, who daily go there to bathe, but worthy of the greatest princes'. Pius II was there for the waters in 1462.

These buildings, almost an alternative 'Palazzo dei Papi', were destroyed in 1527 by the *lanzichenecchi* returning from the Sack of Rome; restored; wiped out by a great flood in 1706, and again 'restored for the public health in 1708' by the public-spirited Francesco Foscoli. The 'papal' appellation is now used for the municipal establishment, built in 1846.

The most famous of VITERBO's hot springs is the Bullicame – a real bubbling pot a few metres across, in the middle of a field into which Dante put Guy de Montfort (see VITERBO). It is on the west side of the city, off the TUSCANIA road. Within a few kilometres of VITERBO there are, as Peter Beckford noted, many 'sulphurous baths for the itch, etc., etc.', some tamed into paying establishments of greater or less comfort and some left aboriginally wild.

Besides being hot they are sometimes radioactive; until the 1970s radioactive water was bottled and sold and advertised as good for many troubles, especially deafness and sterility. We take the following word definition from the current, though undated, publication *Terme e Salute* from the Regional Assessorato (regional government department) of Lazio for Sport and Tourism: 'Radioactive waters are waters which, while not "radioactive" in the strict sense, have "emanations". They are so called when these emanations constitute a curative factor'. All radioactivity in quantities sufficiently above background to have a measurable effect on people has been found to have a bad effect. The quantities here are not sufficient for their effect to be measured. 'Emanations' is just an old-fashioned word for radiation.

Our own favourite hot spring is the place called Bagnaccio – nasty old bath – which is completely as nature produces it. 6½ kilometres on the road to MARTA from Porta Fiorentina, turn sharp back left at Roman ruin; 1 kilometre on dust road. Montaigne went there and saw 'a big spring boiling bravely . . . it stinks, pretty much of sulphur, and makes a froth, and white stuff'. The 'white stuff' hardens into a sort of feeble travertine.

The hot sulphurous water gurgles out, to slurp meanderingly down a gentle hill from one human-sized basin to another exactly as any citizen chooses from time to time to shape them out of the white gunge. No exploitation, no advertising, just hot springs in a field.

Fonte Claudia is a hugely copious spring of delicious water, bottled and drunk far and wide. To reach it, turn east immediately to the north of ANGUILLARA station. The wide low ruins had been a big Roman villa, with an exedra, and beside them are the even bigger modern bottling plant and the remains of a 17th-century garden. The great noise of the spring and the stream comes through a bamboo thicket, on the outer side of which citizens fill their bottles with the good water as it pours out of 19th-century taps and spigots.

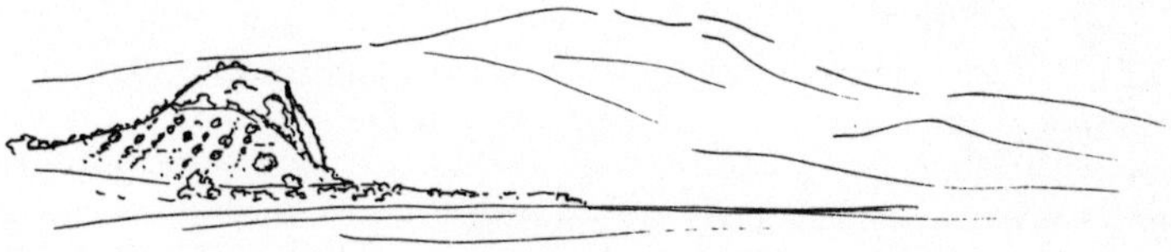

APPENDIX I: DECORATIVE IMAGES

Trifrons at Tuscania

On the façade of San Pietro at TUSCANIA is a thoroughly unusual and disturbing three-faced image, twice over, authoritative, the lower version with an entwining snake nuzzling his beard, about which remarkably little is known.

George Dennis wrote of '... grim caricatures of the Trinity'; before him, Mrs Hamilton Gray had thought these faces 'bore a greater resemblance to a Hindoo representation of a trinity, than anything not Indian I have ever seen.' Not Christian, she surmised, nor 'a monument of classical antiquity'; 'by no means rude, ... [but] monstrous'. Therefore 'Etruscan ..., probably derived from Syria, and brought hither by the Pelasgi ...'

Mostly, today's academics tend to judge it fanciful, the sort of thing people did because they could; and pass by with hints of parallels elsewhere ... Cosmatesque ... Umbrian execution ... Pisan influences ... Zone of passage. Others identify it with the long tradition, at least from the Neolithic, of three-headed or three-faced gods or godlings.

Mrs Gray was right about India: a mass of multiple-headed deities, Buddhist and Hindu, are available there, described and illustrated by Wilibald Kirfel, in his *Die Dreiköpfige Gottheit,** as well as Slavic, Thracian, Japanese, Iranian and African. But Professor Kirfel ignored Tuscania's *trifrons*.

Three-headed gods have been about in the Mediterranean from earliest times, and in Britain. One 16th-century writer (referred to by Edgar Wind) described a Sabine three-faced image with the mysterious 'triple name – Sanctus, Fidius, and Semipater', which Ovid (without elaboration) had mentioned. Janus – usually two-faced, occasionally four-faced – was Etruscan and Roman. There is a leafy *bifrons* on the Wise Virgins doorway (11th century) in BOLSENA Cathedral, and pleasant bearded ones in the cloisters at St John Lateran and at Salisbury.†

There are characters with extra heads coming out of their ears, and some with four-eyed faces, but without greenery. Again, single-faced fellows

* Bonn, 1948.

† This and much of the following material comes from G. J. Hoogewerff, 'Vultus Trifrons', *Rendiconti della Pontifica Accademia Romana d'Archeologia,* Vol. XIX, 1942–3, pp. 205 ff.

mouthing greenery are commonplace in Antiquity (in Britain, the so-called 'Gorgon's Head', at Bath); and in Romanesque art; and in the Renaissance, and after. A pretty 15th-century three-faced 'Prudence' is in the Victoria and Albert Museum; Andrea del Sarto painted a three-faced Trinity in a nimbus; Lippo Lippi had St Augustine pondering a three-faced infant-Trinity. In his *Icones Symbolicae,* of 1626, Christoforo Giarda (see CASTRO) published an engraving of *Historia,* a modest, three-faced, lady, with two great keys and a measuring rod. A little later, in the 1650s, the Trivulzi (*trevolti,* 'three faces') family tomb in Rome shows a *trifrons*: a single head with three faces – one each, moustached, bearded, and clean-shaven – for each of three Trivulzi cardinals. (Much later Daumier did a trifrontal caricature of Louis Philippe, asleep to the Past and the Present, about to be shocked by the Future; and Andy Warhol did a *trifrons* self-portrait.)

But the *trifrons* at TUSCANIA is like none of these. Most, he is like the Celtic solar *trifrons* deity, crowned and bearded, that Hoogewerff illustrates from an altar at Rheims: dignified, ambivalent, uncommunicative, in no way primitive. Hoogewerff supposes TUSCANIA's image to be an *emblema diabolica,* 'an improper – *improba* – image of the most Holy Trinity', such as Dante describes in the *Inferno* XXXIV (lines 36–42 and 49–51), *l'imperador del doloroso regno,* 'the emperor of the dolorous kingdom':

> How great a marvel it seemed to me
> when I saw three faces on his head!
> One was in front, that was vermeil;
> the other two were joined to it,
> at the middle of each shoulder,
> and joined too at the crest.
> The right one seemed between yellow and white,
> the left one, like what we see
> at the Nile's falls.
> . . .
> He wept with his six eyes, and down three chins
> dribbled both tears and bloody slaver.
> And in each mouth, his teeth like mincers
> ground on a sinner.

(Judas in the front mouth, Brutus and Cassius in the side ones.)

There are no real comparisons for the TUSCANIA characters. Their statement is plain to see, obscure to understand, and heroically large; and all over the front of a major Christian cathedral. We incline to think, despite Dante (and some earlier records of a three-headed – not three-faced – Beelzebub), that it must be the Trinity, and that the snake represents the regeneration cycle of life and death rather than the Old Testament fall from grace.

Lombardic Imagery

Lombard imagery, most of it on capitals and door jambs and chancel furniture, included recognisably Christian symbols and attributes, but there were also new beasts (whose characters were enthusiastically spelled out in bestiaries: the camel, who is luxurious but not incestuous, and always wishes to return to where he first had sexual intercourse; the stag, who eats snakes and takes their venom; the hungry fox who lies on his back with his tongue out, and grabs the rooks and crows who come to eat him); and new arrangements altogether, such as two beasts sharing one head or one tail, or starting as one and turning into another and biting each other, and animal caryatids (ACQUAPENDENTE, ALLUMIERE, CIVITA CASTELLANA, and many early crypts). And captioned jokes, like the character at San Flaviano in MONTEFIASCONE who is pointing to his beard and saying 'I am here to amuse fools'.

The identity of the very frequent character with an open mouth, pouring out vegetation, as TUSCANIA's *trifrontes* do, is not clear: he resembles both the familiar Etruscan image of 'hungry death' and the familiar Celtic leafed and bearded 'green man'. He has a half-brother, a green Man-in-the-Moon, who only appears with the Renaissance.

There are also some northern tree images, unknown in Antiquity; and symbols and characters and decorative motifs that derive straight from Roman, Etruscan, Greek, and indeed Middle Eastern practice: decent egg and dart; less decent mermaids with two tails; sciapods; centaurs (until Plato's time abominable male-only creatures who raped women, but who then became home-loving, shown with centauresses suckling baby centaurs, virtuous opponents of monsters); sphinxes; basilisks; gryphons; aspics; very occasionally a chimaera – this last all bad. All usually appear enlaced in tendrils, convolvulations, and lattices.

St Bernard of Clairvaux (1090–1153) was quite firm about it. He wrote:

> Among the brothers reading in the cloister it was asked what are these ridiculous monstrosities in which deformity mocks beauty, and beauty deformity? ... What are these monstrous centaurs, what are these half-men, what are these striped tigers? ... You see many bodies under one head and on the other hand one body without a head. Here can be seen quadrupeds with serpents' tails and there a fish with a quadruped's head, there an animal riding a horse, and there a goat pulling a cart. ... All sorts of strange and different forms appear everywhere, so you can read better on the marble than you can in the book, and some prefer to spend a whole day contemplating one of these than thinking about the law of God. My God, even if you are not ashamed of the ineptitude, surely you should worry about the expense?

The Chimaera

There is a chimaera – a rarity for the time, and female at that – on one of the jambs of the 11th-century door in the Cathedral at BOLSENA (a basilisk is on the other). Chimaeras seem originally to have come from Lycia, in Asia Minor, where Bellerophon on Pegasus saw them off. This is definitely a devilish beast, with three heads along its back – lion, goat, and dragon. It was common to the ancient Greeks and the Etruscans. The best-known is the 5th-century BC Etruscan *Chimaera wounded by Bellerophon,* placed by Cosimo de'Medici in his palace and now in the Archaeological Museum in Florence. This beast – probably all that was left of a complete Bellerophon group – was dug up at Arezzo in 1555 and Vasari saw it as showing 'to what perfection the art had arrived at among the Tuscans, in this Etruscan style'.

Over time the beast prompted some odd responses: Montaigne, in Florence in 1581, describes where

> the figure of a four-footed animal is to be seen, made of bronze, on a pillar, shown naturally, of a strange shape, the front all scaly, and on the spine I know not what sort of limb, like horns. They say that it was found in a mountain cave of the country, and brought back alive a few years ago.

Lorna Sage has recently reported* that 'among the many curiosities in the University of Bologna's collections is the Chimaera, a surprised-looking, fishy composte with a high varnish, glued together by some enterprising sixteenth-century taxidermist and sold to Ulisse Aldrovandi, who taught logic and philosophy before becoming the university's first professor of *scienze naturali* . . .'. That two such tough-minded people as Montaigne and Aldrovandi should have entertained the possibility of an animal species *Chimaera chimaera* may speak either for the new openmindedness or for continuing credulity.

A few of these strange creatures continued to appear over the next few centuries. At CAPRANICA (see the Lombardo-Romanesque menagerie on the old Infirmary door), the early 15th-century tomb of the Anguillara twins has the 'device' of one of them showing a kind of chimaera. Elsewhere, 'green men', foliating about the head, rather than mouthing foliage, were occasionally shown, sometimes in the company of fur-covered 'wild men', whose ancestry seems quite different.

The Renaissance

Many of them then reappeared in the Renaissance, with great *éclat,* some by way of *Hypnerotomachia* (see Appendix II), some in the 'Roman' decorations which Raphael derived from what he had seen in Nero's Villa Aurea, and which the Zuccari brothers further developed at CAPRAROLA and elsewhere.

* *Times Literary Supplement,* Nov. 18–24, 1988, p. 1278.

(At both BAGNAIA and BOMARZO, Amerindian detail – particularly feathered headgear – appears along with the rest.) The 'green man' mouthing foliage re-emerged (but not, we think, as *trifrons*: Renaissance *trifrontes* are respectable). And so did mermaids, mermen, sea-monsters of various kinds, centaurs, sphinxes, and so on, now often part of frescoed decoration, and shown delicate and aetiolated amid weightless architecture instead of squat, jolly, and loadbearing. They appear too as statues, mostly stone, often powerful, as at CAPRAROLA and BAGNAIA, but also lustful and sinister, as sometimes at BOMARZO and SORIANO.

The green man's face now sometimes adorns a half-moon – sometimes recumbent – as in the decoration on the front of the Cathedral at BOLSENA, above the doorway into the Palazzo at BOMARZO, on the vases at BAGNAIA, best of all on the door jambs of Santa Maria della QUERCIA. (And throughout the François I Gallery at Fontainebleau, of the 1530s.) See also the remarkable Paradise Chapel in the church of the Madonna del Rossore at CORCHIANO.

APPENDIX II: VILLAS

***Hypnerotomachia* and the Roads to Felicity**

Hypnerotomachia Poliphili, published in Venice in 1499, plays a part in a book on Northern Lazio because of its probable influence on the builders of the great villas there. On Vicino Orsini the influence is certain: what he attempted with his Bosco at BOMARZO would without it be even more incomprehensible.

The links between BOMARZO, the Palazzo Farnese at CAPRAROLA, and the Villa Lante at BAGNAIA are close. The three patrons, all related and two of them Cardinals, employed the same architects, artists, scholars, and craftsmen, sometimes on an almost industrial scale. Acting out of a shared philosophy each produced a place in which his powerful but consciously mortal human personality lives on. The prospect of the three equal gates, through one of which the hero of *Hypnerotomachia* had to pass – the Contemplative, the Voluptuous, the Active – was of consuming interest to Italian humanists. Did each adopt for himself one of these 'roads to felicity'?

What was done a little later at SORIANO (only part of what was intended) and later still at BASSANO ROMANO can be interpreted as comments on the roads to felicity chosen. 'What has been left out?' they enquired. 'What of sin and of evil?'

Hypnerotomachia Poliphili is firmly on the 'reverse side of the Renaissance medal', as John Summerson puts it. The book was printed in Aldus Manutius' clear new roman type, illustrated with equally clear woodcuts showing mysteriously exciting events and places. It has a stylishness about it which made it famous and influential at the time and still makes it glow in one's hands today. It was anonymous, but soon known to be by a Venetian friar, Francesco Colonna.

Both illustrations and text provide one of the great hunting grounds for those who feel – and it seems an unavoidable feeling – that there are missing layers of understanding which would explain the Renaissance to us. In his great book, *Pagan Mysteries in the Renaissance,* Edgar Wind took his readers by the hand through a dense Christian/Humanist/Classical undergrowth of strange and alluring triads, which is also the world of Poliphilus' adventures. 'The humanist artists of Italy strove ... to resuscitate the pagan form in all its seemingly un-Christian splendour, while reading into it a secret meaning consistent with Christian theology. Egyptian knowledge and lore – including hieroglyphs – were taken in as well, and so was Sanskrit.

Hypnerotomachia is full of this comprehensive and splendid paganism, the secret Christian meaning of which has become hard indeed to divine: illustrations of phallus-worship (which in some copies were blanked out), Bacchanalian processions, Venus adored as *veneranda et sancta*. It is a pun in Italian: *venere veneranda*.*

Colonna's language is half-way between Latin and Italian, perhaps hardly intended to be spoken, though it might be read aloud. The narrative is heavy, full of extremely precise descriptions; its meaning, as George Painter has put it, a matter of 'impenetrable clarity'. The purpose – if Colonna had one beyond any writer's – is unknown, and so is the date of writing. He was in Holy Orders, a Dominican friar in the Convent of St John and St Paul – San Zanipolo – in Venice. In later life, he was as much a pain in the neck to the Church as was that other priestly libertine, Lorenzo da Ponte, Mozart's librettist, three hundred years later; in the same ways, even in the same places, Venice and Treviso.

The illustrator is unknown: many names have been suggested. George Painter thinks he may have died young; Sir Ernst Gombrich wonders if Bramante was influenced by the *Hypnerotomachia* woodcuts or they by him. In the light of five factors – the quite stocky, Latial-looking people; the linear isocephalic arrays in many of the illustrations; the intelligent architecture, particularly the section of the circular temple; the glimpses through windows of both volcanic and lakeside landscape; and his early death – let us put a new name into the brantub: that of Lorenzo da Viterbo, a youthful genius who died in 1471 or 1472 (see VITERBO, Santa Maria della Verità.)

The first sub-title reads: '. . . where he [Poliphilus] teaches that everything human is nothing but a dream, and incidentally records many things worth knowing'. We have a first-person narrative by 'Poliphilus', this lover not only of many, as the name says, but also of Polia, who was a real girl and whom Colonna really loved, and whose name yet more strongly says 'many'. He travels a world of symbolic ruins; exchanges observations, dreams, and kisses with a number of other symbolic girls; is offered by 'Reason' and 'Desire' the choice of three gates: *Gloria Dei, Mater Amoris,* and *Gloria Mundi* (which are superscribed also in Greek, Hebrew, and Arabic). To Reason's fury he chooses the second and dedicates himself to Venus in Cyprus itself, her birthplace. He is rewarded with a brief encounter with Polia. The text ends with the date of 1 May 1467 (time enough for Lorenzo to illustrate it).

The nature of yearning, of desire, of love, of *Voluptas,* its relation with the other two 'roads', and their Christian and pagan significance, had long been central to humanist and neo-Platonist discourse. The Florentine

* The charmingly chaste pictures by Reynolds and others of Ladies Adorning Herms derive from these quite unchaste illustrations.

Marsilio Ficino had encapsulated the world view which our builders absorbed with their mothers' milk:

> No reasonable being doubts that there are three kinds of life: the contemplative, the active, and the pleasurable (*contemplativa, activa, voluptuosa*). And three roads to felicity have been chosen by men: wisdom, power, and pleasure (*sapientia, potentia, voluptas*).

Well away from Rome, in unprecedented privacy, the Cardinals and the retired soldier made their choices. The retired soldier wrote his own triads up on the walls of his terrace (see BOMARZO).

Rome's Villas and Gardens

To understand the 16th-century building 'explosion' in Northern Lazio, it is necessary to recall what the Farnese and their contemporaries were building in Rome, and why they built as they did. Many trends and influences had been coming together; one was symbolised by the book we have just mentioned. Another was the presence in Rome of the monuments and artefacts of Antiquity, and the new insights into them provided by Leon Battista Alberti. The third was the nature of the Renaissance Papacy itself. A fourth, eventually, was the crisis in the Church, and the Counter-Reformation.

The Renaissance had entered Rome in the train of the Papacy, and was funded by its, in effect parasitic, population of cardinals and clerics and bankers: the participants in the aptly-called 'Roman clerical market'.*

Taxes doubled between 1492 and 1525; the trade in offices and benefices (not excluding cardinalcies) raised vast sums, usually in gold – the value of which stayed up, while that of silver, the regular currency, dropped. With ever-mounting debts, it was like a Third World economy, and operating the Church system was the principal economic activity.

The other serious activity in Rome was the vast building spree and the unparalleled artistic explosion that accompanied it.

Nicholas V Parentucelli (1447–55) was the first properly humanist pope. He rebuilt the walls of Rome (and the baths at VITERBO), and saw to the erection of fortresses throughout the Patrimony. A scholar and knowledgeable in the arts, he founded the Vatican Library and began the transformation of Rome. He also began to remake the papal quarters into a proper renaissance palace with a grand fountained garden.

Pius II (1458–64), certainly a renaissance man in every way – when he decided to take Holy Orders, he described himself as giving up the worship of Venus for that of Bacchus – was in Rome no great builder. Yet a Bull he issued in 1462 forbade the destruction of ancient monuments; and he continued his predecessors' 'renewals'.

*For a study of the 'clerical market', see a forthcoming book, by Dr Peter Partner, *The Popes' Men: the papal civil service in the Renaissance*, Oxford University Press.

Innocent VIII Cibo (1484–92) contributed the first papal villa, on the Vatican's wooded hill: the Belvedere. Alexander VI Borgia went on building and summoned artists to Rome to paint his quarters – Pastura came from VITERBO, with Pinturicchio; and the Sangallo family began building castles and fortifications all over the Patrimony (see MONTEFIASCONE, NEPI, etc.).

But it was Julius II della Rovere, 1503–13, Cardinal at 28 and Pope at 60, and enthusiastic and successful warrior all the time, who in effect invented the Rome of the High Renaissance and its gardens. He it was who hurried his architect Donato Bramante (1444–1514) to pull down the old St Peter's Basilica, wanting, according to Vasari, 'his structures not to be built but to grow up as by magic'. He it was who had Raphael paint the *Stanze* in the Vatican and Michelangelo the ceiling of the Sistine chapel.

For him, Bramante was to connect the Belvedere villa with the Vatican palace by an internal 'garden' in the imperial Roman villa style, in which the Pope would display his remarkable collection of ancient sculpture. In the design and model he produced for the 300-by-100 metre *atrio di piacere* which was to become the Belvedere Cortile, he set out to remake the ground and manipulate space in accordance with the new principles of symmetry and proportion. His aim was to create an *architettura di percorso* – architecture for passing through – of a quite new kind and on a new scale; to bring air and earth and distance into play, developing various levels (including ramps, as the ancients had at Praeneste), as well as buildings and fountains, to create what Paolo Portoghesi has nicely called 'an enclosed universe'.

But this was not quite all. Sir Ernst Gombrich suggested (in his paper, 'Hypnerotomachiana', first published in 1951, and reprinted in *Symbolic Images,* Phaidon, 1985) that Bramante – if not necessarily Julius himself – may have had in mind for the 'enclosed universe' something more than a mere Museum of Antiques. Certain powerfully apprehended mysteries were demanding expression: a chase was on, for what was to be sensed behind or beyond appearance.

Bramante – ruthless planner and *rovinante* (puller-down) – wanted to change the orientation of St Peter's, shifting St Peter's tomb, so that the great Egyptian Obelisk should stand in front of it, to astonish us just as the obelisk in *Hypnerotomachia* had astonished Poliphilus: *incredible impensa, di stupore insensato* – 'unbelievable unthought, unsensed amazement'. Here too was the expression of the underlying humanist doctrine of 'One God, every cult'.

Professor Gombrich quotes a contemporary description by Pico della Mirandola's nephew Giovanni Francesco who, referring to the new discovered *Venus Felix,* wrote to a friend: 'Lilius, do you know Venus and Cupid, the Gods of those vain ancients? Julius II, Pontifex Maximus, has procured them from Roman ruins, where they were recently discovered and has placed them in that most fragrant citrus grove ... in whose midst stands also the colossal image of blue Tiber. Everywhere ancient Images are placed, each on its little altar ...' There was too a Cleopatra, from whose breasts water flowed, just as it had from those of a nymph in *Hypnerotomachia* (though there it flowed h. and c.). Giovanni Francesco, a Savonarolan, was moved to write a poem *De Venere et Cupidine expellendis*: 'On driving out Venus and Cupid'.

In her book on *Italian gardens* (London, 1961), Georgina Masson (Babs Johnson) quotes the Venetian Ambassador to the court of Pope Adrian VI for a 1523 account of this private garden of the Pope's:

> One enters a very beautiful garden of which half is filled with growing grass and bays, mulberries and cypresses, while the other half is paved with squares of bricks laid upright, and in every square a beautiful orange tree grows out of the pavement ... In the centre of the garden are two enormous men of marble, one is the Tiber, the other is the Nile, very ancient figures, and two fountains issue from them. At the main entrance to this garden ... there is a sort of chapel built into the wall where, on a marble base, stands the Apollo. ... Somewhat further on ... is the Laocoon ... not far from this is the Venus ...

All of which Pope Adrian, a puritanically inclined northerner, must have intensely disliked.

Eventually, the Belvedere 'universe' was completed: Pirro Ligorio (1500–83), writer of innumerable manuscript volumes on Roman antiquities and architect of the highly fantasticated Villa d'Este at Tivoli, had by 1561 built there a yet more private *casino* for the popes, the Villa Pia.

This wish for privacy developed alongside the public objection to personal display that the Council of Trent was articulating. The private *studiolo* had long been a feature of grand palazzi, where the nobleman-scholar would quietly enjoy his texts and his thoughts; but a whole building devoted to privacy was something new. At CAPRAROLA, it was embodied at first in the distinction between the public and the private sides of the *piano nobile,* and later in the distant total privacy of the palazzina up the hill. BOMARZO of course was, and represented, as complete a withdrawal from the public life of the city and of war as its owner could devise.

The Ancient Roman Villa as Precedent

The historical precedent, the villa as developed in ancient Rome, had recently been brought to mind by Leon Battista Alberti. His ideas circulated in manuscript form long before his book, *De Re Aedificatoria,* was published in Latin in 1485.* Moreover, the legible ruins of the grandiose Villa where the tourist emperor Hadrian had set up his vast compendium of world sculpture, architecture, and water systems, still filled the valley below Tivoli.

In its times of leisured wealth and domestic peace, the Empire had

*It appeared in Italian in 1550; and in an English translation of the Italian in 1726. A new translation from the original Latin has just appeared, by Joseph Rykwert, Neil Leach, and Robert Taverner, published by MIT Press. The quotations below are from the 1726 translation.

permitted farming in open country. A still familiarly enviable picture of country house life in the 1st century AD emerges from a letter the younger Pliny wrote to a friend in Como:

> How is that sweet Comum of ours looking? What about that most enticing of villas, the portico where it is one perpetual spring, that shadiest of plane-tree walks, the crystal canal so agreeably winding along its flowery banks, together with the lake lying below that so charmingly yields itself to the view? What have you to tell me of the firm yet soft *gestatio* [running track], the sunny bathroom, those dining rooms for large parties, and the others for small ones, and all the elegant apartments for repose, both by noon and night?

At his own Tuscan Villa, near Citta di Castello, he too had everything the heart could think of, including a 'hippodrome', surrounded by ivy-festooned plane trees, and beds of little box-trees clipped to spell out his and his garden-designers' names.

Such grandly luxurious villa-farming had never been available to more than the wealthy few – Virgil's First Eclogue is about two farmers, one expelled from his land to make room for army veterans – but the villa-farm was a general model as long as the Empire endured.

Between Antiquity and the Renaissance rich and poor returned to huddling behind high walls in high places. In the south, gardens were on the Islamic model, courtyards, with water and shady trees. The Emperor Frederick II (1194–1249) re-introduced them in central and northern Italy alongside his castles and hunting lodges. His rough contemporary Piero de'Crescenzi, of Bologna, wrote a book discussing classical garden design and current practice: royal gardens, he thought, should include a menagerie and an aviary, as well as thickets, arbours, and vines. Boccaccio, in the 14th century, described the gardens of Naples, filled with sculpture, and the gardens of Florence, walled, with arbours, and a fountain.

Alberti advised

> ... well-disposed Gardens and beautiful Trees, together with Porticoes in the Garden ... To these add some little pleasant Meadow, with fine Springs of Water bursting out in different Places where least expected. Let the Walks be terminated by Trees that enjoy perpetual Verdure ... [that is, box, myrtle, and laurel] and Cypress-trees cloathed with Ivy;

Moreover, he thought

> Vases of Stone ... are very fine Ornaments for Fountains in Gardens. The Ancients used to make their Walks into a Kind of Arbour by Means of Vines supported by Columns of Marble of the Corinthian Order ... The Trees Ought to be planted in Rows exactly even, and answering to one another exactly upon straight lines ...
>
> ... Nor am I displeased with the placing ridiculous Statues in Gardens, provided they have nothing in them obscene ...

A villa being 'calculated chiefly for taking the Air in', walls were allowed as a convenience against Malice or Rapine. But

> Towers and Battlements [would be] inconsistent with the peaceable Aspect of a well-governed City or Commonwealth, as they shew either a Distrust of our Countrymen, or a Design to use Violence against them.

In the Rome of the early 16th century, Alberti's pleasant arrangements began to be demonstrated on the grandest scale.

If the Belvedere Cortile (1503–13) had been Rome's first grand garden, what Baldassare Peruzzi built (1507–11) for Agostino Chigi on the banks of the Tiber was the first grand 'villa'. It was eventually bought by the Farnese (and became known as the Farnesina), who thought to turn it into an adjunct to their most grand Palazzo, by means of a private bridge over the Tiber.

The logical structure of the new Roman villa was very different from that of the ancient Roman. That had been well out in the country with its farm about it: essentially a country-landowner's house. The new high-powered cleric's villa was a relatively small, probably two-storey, house, a *casina,* built at the outer, upper, end of the *vigna,* his vineyard, or field, or wood, while his main dwelling, the palazzo, where he worked, was at the lower, townward end. The *casina* would probably include useful spaces for horticultural gear, and it would have a *giardino segreto,* a private garden (deriving from the medieval *hortus conclusus*). And it would have a loggia, where the pleasures of contemplation, solitude, and fresh air could be enjoyed, raised above the *vigna,* likely to be triple-arched, as in *Hypnerotomachia,* and with a double staircase. This pattern of ownership and construction was repeated all round the city's hills.*

The Villa Madama

The most sumptuous of all these compenetrations of garden, villa, and landscape was to have been the Vigna del Papa on Monte Mario, now known as the Villa Madama: grander than those of ancient Rome, or of modern Florence, and certainly grander than the banker Chigi's. Raphael worked it out, Antonio da Sangallo the Younger built it, and Giulio Romano and Giovanni da Udine decorated it. Work began in about 1516 for Pope Leo X Medici (see BOLSENA), supervised by his nephew Cardinal Giulio de'Medici, later Pope Clement VII. The villa, still incomplete at the Sack of Rome never was completed.

Nevertheless it was enormously influential. When Raphael died in 1520, his aura survived him: a figure of almost divine gifts and achievements.

* Shelley has Count Cenci, in his first speech, retort to the Cardinal

> Ay, I once heard the nephew of the Pope
> Had sent his architect to view the ground,
> Meaning to build a villa on my vines . . .
> (*The Cenci,* Act I, Scene I, lines 16–18.)

When he became architect to Leo X, which included being architect for the new St Peter's, he asked for and obtained the support of Antonio da Sangallo the Younger and his already successful office of relations and assistants: Vasari called it his *attrezzatissima bottega* – 'very well equipped studio'). It is from Antonio's drawings – a comprehensive plan – and from a copy of a detailed letter from Raphael that the project is known.

Raphael was even concerned that all six of the winds that would strike the building – *hostro, scyrocho, evante, et greco et tramontana et maestro** – should be taken into account – for instance unless a room needed to be hot it should not face the *scyrocho*. There was to be the villa itself, with its great view; a theatre cut into the hillside; gardens, including a 'secret garden' in the form of a raised parterre with trees on arches – described as a *xysto cusi chiamato da li antiqui* (a sports ground or running-track) – and a fishpond below; fountains with direct water; statues, including caryatids for the 'secret garden' entrances; a 'hippodrome', as at Pliny's Villa; and an easy ascent from the new bridge over the Tiber. Before deciding on the circular courtyard Raphael had gone to Hadrian's Villa and to look at the colonnaded Nymphaeum there, and to the Pantheon. (The half-built courtyard hints, misleadingly, at Pirro Ligorio's and Borromini's later concavities.) The elephant portrayed in the elephant fountain was Pope Leo X's pet, his *Benjamino*; it was white, and called *Anno*.

Cardinal Giulio let it be known that in the decoration 'dark things, as I've said, I don't want, but various, and choice'. Ovid would do; the Old Testament only in 'Our Master' [the Pope]'s loggia. There was a row between Giulio Romano and Giovanni da Udine, who were responsible for the decoration: the Cardinal was thankful when *quelli due cervelli pazzi e fantastichi di pintori siano d'accordo e che lavorino* – 'those two fantasticating harebrains of painters got on and worked'.

After the Sack of Rome, Antonio da Sangallo carried on as universal architect to the Farnese (see CAPRAROLA and CASTRO). Giulio Romano went north to build and decorate and paint for the Gonzaga family, but what he and Giovanni da Udine did at the Villa formed the taste and the techniques of several generations of patrons and artists. (Except there was no follow-up of a Venus playing with a number of baby cupids who are trying to put nappies on a rabbit.)

The name 'Madama' came from the next owner, Madama Margherita of Austria, natural daughter of the Emperor Charles V, who was married first to Alessandro de'Medici, Duke of Florence, the son of Pope Clement VII. After he was murdered, she married Ottavio Farnese, grandson of Pope Paul III; they were first Duke and Duchess of Camerino, then (following Pier Luigi) of CASTRO and then, after Pier Luigi was murdered, of Parma-Piacenza. The Villa stayed in Farnese hands and eventually went with the rest to the Kings of Spain. It was in private hands when the Italian Government took it over and began restoring it in the 1940s.

*Quotations in this section are from R. Lefevre, *Villa Madama,* Rome, 1973.

Incomplete though it was, the Villa Madama became the single most powerful model and source for a new kind of rich man's art: the patron's art of combining architecture and sculpture and fresco (in the casinos and loggias); and landscaping and garden-making; and planting of all kinds; and water engineering for fountains; and machinery for water-games (see BAGNAIA), and grotto-making, and topiary ... and no doubt much else ephemeral in the way of decorations, and food, and drink, and music, and costumes. Among those who copied the plans were Sebastiano Serlio and Andrea Palladio.

When Michel de Montaigne was in Rome in 1580–1, he visited *les vignes* – the grand villas. He described them as

> ... gardens and pleasure grounds, of singular beauty, and there I learned how much art can make use of somewhere hillocky, mountainous, unequal; from them [the Romans] draw graces inimitable in our flat grounds, and most artfully make the most of this diversity.

Moreover,

> These are beauties open to whoever wants to make use of them, and however they like, be it to sleep or to be in company, if the masters are not there ...

Such villas went on being used and built in Rome until the 19th century. Most were then destroyed: some during the Napoleonic occupation, some during the various Risorgimento battles for Rome, but most in the early days of united Italy, when Rome became the capital once again, and northerners – anti-clericalists to a man – descended, once again. Suddenly, in D'Annunzio's words, 'a wind of barbarity attempted to strip [Rome] of that radiant crown of ancestral villas, incomparable with any others in dream or memory'.

Of the few survivors some are now open to the public as museums and parks, some are embassies, some remain in private hands.* The northerners' destructive contempt is still active: thanks to their oratory in the Chamber of Deputies, the restoration of Rome's monuments continues underfunded.

The Villa as Art-Form

The villa as art-form can today be far better seen in the Lazio countryside than in poor dismantled Rome. In that same 16th century, the same prelates and newly ennobled papal families were building outside Rome, with the same architects, artists, and craftsmen, and often on the same huge scale: to the south-east in the Alban and Sabine Hills (where the Villa d'Este at Tivoli was built by Pirro Ligorio for Cardinal Ippolito II d'Este, in direct rivalry with what Sangallo and Vignola were providing for the Farnese at

* All, lost or surviving, are admirably described and illustrated in Isa Belli Barsali's *Ville di Roma* (Milan, 1970), from which the D'Annunzio quotation above is taken.

CAPRAROLA), and to the north, on the slopes of the CIMINO and by the LAKES of BOLSENA and BRACCIANO.

For Art History, an interesting point arises. In 1955 it was possible for a scholar of the calibre of Erwin Panofsky to suggest (in his *Meaning in the Visual Arts*) that while 'the Mannerist' in the representational arts could no longer be considered 'as a side line or by-product' to the 'continuous development of the "Classic" Renaissance into the Baroque', with respect to architecture '... I doubt that this [view] is necessary'. He went on: 'Mannerism, which is the rule in Central Italian painting, remains the exception in Central Italian architecture'.

May not the plausibility, even the possibility, of this opinion rest on the wholesale destruction of Rome's Villas? Rome after all is where Central Italian architecture in the age of Mannerism inextricably combined with all the other arts to reach its apogee. Today, CAPRAROLA, BAGNAIA (Villa Lante), BOMARZO, SORIANO and BASSANO ROMANO, still accurately represent that particularly Roman apogee. They are places of real glory; and the church of Santa Maria del Ruscello at VALLERANO must be joined to them in the highest category.

PLACES

Acquapendente

ACQUAPENDENTE is Lazio's northernmost town, set in a kind of lap of cliffs. John Evelyn, in November 1644, found the 'Towne situated on a very raged rock, downe which precipitates an intire river of Water, which gives it the denomination with a most horrid roaring noise'. Charles Dickens, a couple of hundred years later, reported sourly that there was 'a "Carnival" in process: consisting of one man dressed and masked as a woman, and one woman, dressed and masked as a man, walking ankle-deep through the muddy streets, in a very melancholy manner ...'

Today, ACQUAPENDENTE is an amiable, prosperous town, and what it still seriously celebrates is its liberation from Frederick II in 1166. Two peasants returning from the fields had been resting beside a wayside *madonnina*, talking about how to get rid of the Emperor's cruel governor, and one exclaimed, 'we will not prevail until this dead cherry tree blossoms!'; at which, miraculously, it burst into little white flowers. The people rose up, the Pope's forces helped, the Germans were expelled ... (There is still an unimpressive remain of an Imperial castle.)

Each year, on the next Sunday after 15 May, the union of ox-drivers presents candles to the Madonna and then processes through the town behind the *gonfalone* – the banner – carrying sticks called *bungoli* or *pungoli* (goads) decorated with flowers. By now, these have become *pungaloni* – big goads – huge, perhaps 3-metre-high, pictures, made by the women and composed entirely of flower petals, mosses, bark, lichens, dried leaves ... Napoleon suspended the festivities because 'he assumed they had particular polemic significance against foreign domination'. Quite right; and there is still today a strong political content to the pictures – the independence of the town, or apartheid, or Nicaragua, or nuclear energy. Afterwards, the *pungaloni* remain in the Cathedral until they fall to bits. The skill is amazing, the aesthetic quality social-realist; and to judge from the nursery schools' contributions, citizens start early.

The Cathedral, consecrated in 1149 and with an earlier crypt, is by the southern gate of the walls, a fine, ruddy gold building, full of good things.

The interior was damaged in the Second World War and during the restorations the ancient forms were extracted from their 18th-century baroque garb where they survived, and replaced with inappropriate white travertine where they did not. Note the 17th-century wooden choir-stalls; the elegant 15th-century bas-reliefs – St

Michael's Dragon's tail ending as an ammonite; the complicated 14th-century font; the early 15th-century marble-fronted screen in the left transept, re-erected there in 1658 and with organ-pipes above; the two fine busts.

Best of all is a 1522 glazed terracotta altarpiece by Iacopo Beneventano, in the right-hand transept. The tabernacle at the centre is a Bramante-like filled-in temple; putti and angels fly around, and hold back curtains, and adore the Eternal Father, who is fast descending upon us all, his beard parting in the rush into a cross. The predella is of the 1880s.

The crypt was there earlier; it has the dimensions and orientation of the Holy Sepulchre: hence the Cathedral's dedication. It is from the 9th century, with nine naves of columns, and of its kind very strong and authoritative, probably because there is little of the usual haphazard putting together again of pilfered Roman stuff. If the tall naves of the Middle Ages seem to take their form from the beech avenue, these multi-naved crypts perhaps take theirs from the mature hazel grove where, if it is well planted, the pattern appears to go on indefinitely. Plenty of jovial capitals here: note the single rams' heads with shared bodies making the volutes.

The town pours gently down its hillside, with fine piazzas and frequent churches and grand palazzos on the way. Of the latter the grandest is the late Renaissance Palazzo Viscontini, by Ippolito Scalza (See BOLSENA), tightly packed in its street, with high gutsy rustications. Of the churches, San Francesco, originally Gothic, has six identical 18th-century side altars, each with a pair of gallant, buccaneering Apostles – wood, 1751, Domenico Bulgarini. The pretty 15th-century building opposite is still the Hospital. The anatomist and surgeon Girolamo Fabrici (1533–1619), otherwise Fabrizio d'Acquapendente, who discovered the valves in our veins and set up the first operating theatre, in Padua, came from here.

Acquarossa

The King of Sweden and an archaeological team began work here in 1966. Their finds – which are fascinating – are now on permanent display in the Rocca at VITERBO.

Because the Etruscan town had been sacked (probably in the 6th century BC), but not razed, the remains provide a much brighter flash of detail both of daily life and of building techniques than usual. Little terracotta friezes that were used to decorate the houses have survived showing men and women at table, eating and drinking, flautist and harper in attendance, long-tailed dogs gathering up the crumbs.

Informative low walls confirm that these houses and streets for the living two and half thousand years ago were the same size and shape as those not only for the dead at CERVETERI, but also until very recently for the living, as at BARBARANO ROMANO. Note how the floors direct the rainwater away.

Allumiere

ALLUMIERE, high up in the TOLFA HILLS, gets its name from alum, a substance used to modify and make fast the colour of dyes. It was discovered here in 1462 and cut bright white from the hillside, to the enormous profit of the Papacy: supplies had previously come from Africa. Pope Paul II bought the whole territory and it was first known as the *Allumiere delle Sante Cruciate* – the Alumary of the Holy Crusades – because the money financed the Turkish wars. Exploitation now is by Montedison.

In the town, the Fabricone is interesting, 1500s housing for the alum-miners: a long three-storey building, with staircases and apartments off, as in Oxford and Cambridge colleges.

A Palio in August has donkeys instead of horses.

Anguillara

ANGUILLARA is a 'spur town' with the *sperone* rising sheer out of the clear wide waters of the LAKE OF BRACCIANO. The end cliff of the tiny peninsula is dark with trees, and terns as well as swifts and chuffs fly round the top-knot of church and castle. Black sand on the beaches.

Angularia was the Latin name: Place of Eels, from *anguilla*, an eel, seems a reasonable account; eels swarm towards the sea down the lake's outlet, the Arrone. In the Middle Ages ANGUILLARA belonged to a particularly violent family, perhaps of Norman origin, who took their name from it and whose coat of arms shows eels erect. When Pope Paul II finally defeated them in the 1470s, he took thirteen castles and a clandestine mint from them (see also CAPRANICA and FALERIA).

The way up in is steep, through a broad 16th-century gate, with curly iron work and a clock atop, probably erected by the Orsini of BRACCIANO, to whom the town then belonged: Giacomo del Duca (see BRACCIANO, CAPRAROLA, CAMPAGNANO, and VIGNA GRANDE) was working for them here in the early 1580s, in the castle, where he may have made a garden, and in the Palazzo Baronale, which is now the Town Hall. The Council Chamber still has a vigorous-coloured high frieze of stout mermaids and mermen, and babies, with bows and arrows, running right round. In what is today the Mayor's ante-room there is a small naughty fresco of an hermaphrodite flashing; they are all in a state of neglect.

Right on up through the steep, unspoiled medieval town and at last you come to the church, an Assunta as at TREVIGNANO, with a spirited 17th-century façade, a jolly brick bell-tower, and a most elegant balustered veranda from which to view the lake. There is a proper Procession of the Dead Christ on Good Friday evening.

A kilometre or so to the south-west are the Mura di Santo Stefano – the Walls of St Stephen – a great decayed tooth of a ruin, sticking up out of open rolling ground: once a Roman villa, later a *domusculta*, Piranesi drew it.

The shore to the west of ANGUILLARA is now developed and crowded. Towards Rome, the planning system has quite collapsed.

Baccano: Valle di Baccano

Perhaps the name derives from Bacchus. This used to be a crater lake, and the Romans' Via Cassia hugged its eastern shore where an emperor had a lakeside villa. At some point they may have drained it.

If so, the outlet clogged up and by the 18th century there was a famously horrid marsh that struck terror into travellers changing horses at the posting inn: terror both of malaria and malaria-proof highwaymen. In 1838 the Chigi re-drained it. Rome's once golden air is now polluted, but on a dry, clear Sunday morning, with a high wind blowing, the dome of St Peter's some 30 kilometres away can still be a wondrous sight.

Bagnaia

Of the great villa-gardens heralded in our introduction, the Villa Lante at BAGNAIA is the gentlest, calmest, and most open: formal, but not majestic; grand, but amiably; intended above all to please and to refresh.

The Commune of VITERBO had in 1202 allowed land here for a summer residence for their Bishop. About 1500 a Cardinal-Bishop – one of Pope Sixtus IV's Riario nephews – for the first time envisaged glorious improvements: enlargement of the old palace in the town, enclosure of the Barco (the Park), construction of a hunting lodge. (Pope Leo X Medici loved hunting and frequently came.)

In 1527, troops returning from the Sack of Rome were quartered in the Convent at the QUERCIA, and, all 'military discipline abandoned, [they] ... gave thought to sacking our Patria': so reports BAGNAIA's native historian, Arcangelo Carones. The men all gone to defend Rome, the women did their best. One, rushing to a high place, and 'seizing a mortar, hurled it so accurately that she deprived of life the first and hardiest of the [enemy]'. He was their 'captain', and the rest were so 'overtaken by terror and fear that they abandoned the misborn plan and gave themselves to shameful flight'. A 'semi-bust' of the heroine was attached to the bell-tower.

By 1546, Cardinal Ridolfi (nephew of Leo X Medici) had bought enough property to extend the palace and garden with loggias and little spurting fountains and spring-water brought by aqueduct. A contemporary poem has the mountain nymph hailing him:

> Great thanks to you, great Rudolf; you who drew
> Through the hard mountain's bowels my watery springs,
> That I, scarce even to the sheep well-known before,
> Might now ablute the hands and mouths of kings.

His new gardens were adorned with smart jokey fountains. 'Water games', imported from high-living Burgundy, could be awfully humorous: your guest could be showered all over; water would shoot up his ecclesiastical skirts; a female statue might stream water, milk-like from her breasts, or rudely from her bottom. (Sometimes, as at the Villa Mondragone at Frascati, 'polypriapic' events could occur: no doubt eliminated when that villa became a Jesuit boarding school in 1865.)

The town meanwhile acquired a new Borgo, between the Barco and the old town, with a run of fountains and little palazzi and churches, mostly by a Sienese architect, Tommaso Chinucci. The medieval town remained, and remains, compact within the semi-oval tract of walls its rock supports and its street system follows. (The old Palazzo Communale, newly restored, is at the furthest end: note the 'moon men' above its entrance.)

In 1566, Cardinal Bishop Giovanni Francesco Gambara, 28 years old, a Farnese relative through his mother's first husband, and wealthy, became the owner of BAGNAIA. The Villa Lante that we see today is due to him, as he fails not to remind us: his name and his prawn – *gambero* means prawn – are everywhere inscribed.

Michel de Montaigne visited in 1580. Writing in Italian (for practice), he described it as

> ... much adorned, and among other things with fountains. And in this, it not only equals, but beats Pratolino [the Duke of Tuscany's Villa], and Tivoli [the Cardinal d'Este's]. First, it has living springs of water (which Tivoli has not); and abundant enough (unlike Pratolino) for an infinity of designs ... Among a thousand other members of this excellent body [of water] is to be seen a high pyramid which throws water in lots – *assaissimo* – of different ways, some rising, some falling. Round this pyramid are four beautiful little lakes, clear, clean, swelling with water. In the middle of each a little boat of stone, with two *arquebusiers* who draw water and catapult it against the pyramid; and a bugler, who also shoots water ...

Vignola had been to BAGNAIA on Cardinal Gambara's business in 1568, and he may well have made suggestions. But what was built was not in Vignola's style, either in overall design or in the details. The texture of the two pavilions (the second, though built in part by Maderna in the 1590s for Cardinal Montalto, externally repeats the first) is in a flat, mannerist, style, the rustication and the pilasters scarcely more than inscribed (compare the entrance façade at BOMARZO). The garden works closely resemble those of Giacomo del Duca at CAPRAROLA. This is especially true of the stone ropes that mimic the water flowing over them, and the large River figures, even though the sentiment achieved in the two places is very different.

The interiors of the two pavilions or *palazzini* are complementary: Gambara's has a string of small though splendid rooms and the kitchen, and Montalto's has the grand saloon. Gambara's was decorated by the CAPRAROLA artists, with the same fantastical inventions of half-human, half-animal creatures, the same robust friezes. And the same poignant landscapes: at CAPRAROLA we have a glimpse of destroyed CASTRO; here we have a glimpse of CAPRAROLA's own lost Barco, a square lake in front and a ghostly image of its nymphaeum. Nice Annunciation by Ridolfo del Ghirlandaio.

Gambara had fully intended both *palazzini*. Perhaps it was the disapproval of St Charles Borromeo, nephew of the then Pope (Pius IV Medici) and Cardinal responsible for supervising other Cardinals' expenditures, that caused him to divert his funds for the second to a hospital. His successor built it anyway. The great saloon has a magnificent coffered ceiling with stucco groups, twenty times over, of interpenetrating putti and verdure-tailed she-angels, and much else, by the Cavalier d'Arpino; and a supporting frieze of putti and lions, and much else, by Agostino Tassi, who also contributed some little *trompe l'oeil* birds in cupolas, and fellows with wings for moustaches under their leafy Inca crowns and moon-men with Red Indian head-dresses, and so on. The Cardinal's bedroom has a scene of the destruction of Sodom, with Lot's wife just turned to salt. (Tassi is also known as having raped that fine artist Artemisia Gentileschi.)

Outside, each pavilion has its ground-floor loggia opening flat and straight on to the fountained parterre that Montaigne liked so much. Also, each is wedged into the hill to be the hinge of the design, where the slope moves us upwards, to the level of the *piano nobile* of the pavilions, and the water, which for a moment we can't see but still know and feel, is moving down to the parterre. In the box-lined paths, there are joke jets and sprays to remind us.

At our first, up-going, level, there is the tiered, whispering, hundred-small-jet Fontana dei Lumini – the Candle Fountain, where water jets presumably leapt delicately over delicately hissing flames.

Next up the vase-adorned steps – vases with 'green man' or 'Inca' or 'Etruscan' faces on them are everywhere, some with their tongues out, some with shells for mouths, and a few with lions, a few with prawns – you come to the long stone *al fresco* dining-table, one little stream running down the centre in which to cool your wine-glass or rinse your fingers, another below to dabble your toes in. In the background are the great – now darkly mossy – river gods, Tiber and Arno, brothers to those at CAPRAROLA, and perhaps kin to SORIANO's fauness and some of the BOMARZO characters, the water pouring into their basin from between the claws of a giant prawn, flanked – why not? – by obelisks.

Up again, beside the great plait of water – tripping and flashing down, again like the one at CAPRAROLA. Above that, a plateau: another formal, multi-tier, fountain. And behind, at the very top, the originating stream of water emerges from faces in a dark weed-encrusted grotto-fountain, the Diluvio, the Flood. The Flood is flanked by two elegant pavilions and between them a refreshing small rain can be turned on. Everything used to be fed by the nymph's reservoir further up the hill.

There is also a small forest of free-standing columns, on highish plinths: a *pergolata* for vines. Many of the trees are planes, now huge, crooked, and crippled: should the mind's eye replace them with straight yet shady striplings, cousins to the shadeless columns?

When Cardinal Montalto arrived in 1590, three years after Cardinal

Gambara's death, he not only saw to the second pavilion, he had several of the fountains in the park removed, and in the parterre replaced Montaigne's 'pyramid' with the group of four boys holding up the Montalto coat of arms. There was a device in it to make the water sound against little cymbals as the wind blew.

After him the Villa went to the Lante della Rovere family, who also acquired BOMARZO, and they held it until 1954. At one time it was for sale for about the price (at the time) of a good house in Wimbledon. It now belongs to the State, whose restoration has been a success story for all to emulate.

Bagnoregio

A place of substance, the shape and the history of which are not easy to seize, so much has the physical territory been washed and shaken away by erosion and earthquake. The worst earthquake was in 1695 and of the one-time nine associated *borgate,* only BAGNOREGIO, LUBRIANO, and parts of CIVITA remain.

CIVITA was the site of the ancient city: Etruscan, probably Roman, a bishopric from 599 to 1695. CIVITA was then Balneum Regis – the King's Bath – no doubt because of its nice waters; then Bagnorea; and since 1922, the 'mainland' town has been BAGNOREGIO – the name Dante used when he had St Bonaventure refer to his birthplace.

Where there used to be a saddle of level connection, erosion has created a small abyss, with the one-time centre isolated beyond. The present, late-Renaissance, rather solemn, town was set a carefully long way back from the danger zone. It is approached from the 'land' side through the now absurdly wall-less Porta Albana of 1590 – its architect probably Ippolito Scalza, of Orvieto. (See BOLSENA.) The buildings are high, the streets and piazzas straight, and the massive 1581 structure of the present Cathedral of San Nicola keeps up the solemnity. Inside, the broad, low, earthquake-surviving system was re-decorated in the 1880s in dark, almost intestine, colours which admirably emphasise the multiply superimposed pilasters (eight superimpositions?) and set off the golden busts and candlesticks. The pretty little neo-classical domed and cruciform church of St Bonaventure, near the amputated Porta Albana, is the successor to one in CIVITA, which began to lose its foundations in 1799. (It needs repairing.)

The old road to CIVITA still exists, strung about with a handsome piazza and convents of various periods and churches live and dead. Further down is the Centre of Studies of St Bonaventure; and beyond that the Belvedere, where you can have a drink in the shady garden and watch CIVITA *moritura* (or *rediviva*?), golden in her devastated landscape. A stone on the little building records that this was St Bonaventure's own convent, from which 'he took his flight to become for our example and our pride a petal of the mystic rose'. Some offensively ugly buildings here were put up as an agricultural institute in 1977 and have remained unoccupied.

Readers interested in 1930s urbanist theory may like to examine the 1825 'rationalist' sample building – the *casa campione* – in the piazza opposite the church of the Annunziata. It is one and a bit of five intended modular 'units' of 'ideal dwellings', to be erected for the refugees from delapidating CIVITA. Each unit was to house 60 or 70 people. The standard plan provided a common central staircase; two 'landings' per floor, four floors per house; and each apartment had openings front and back to allow through ventilation, as a measure of hygiene. The plan never went beyond the second unit: it seems likely that some of the 320 refugees dispersed into existing BAGNOREGIO and others stayed: CIVITA was never completely abandoned.

The third, modern town has been spreading up into the Volsinian Hills. In a small pine wood, by the VITERBO road, a three-sided basalt pyramid, a monument and ossuary, memorialises the thirteen Garibaldini who fell here in 1867, when papal troops took back the town the Garibaldini had held for a week: the attackers had two cannon, the defenders none.

Barbarano Romano

BARBARANO ROMANO is one of the many little towns of Lazio which have enjoyed vigorous and detailed examination by a local group of scholars. A massively informative book entitled *Barbarano Romano: Indagine e Conoscenza di un Paese* (*Enquiry into and Knowledge of a Village*) was compiled in 1978–9 by twelve contributors and published by the Centro Iniziative Culturali Pantheon. It would be graceless not to pass on at least some of its discoveries: most of them are typical of other places around.

Settlement began in the neighbouring cliffs in the 8th century BC. The bishopric was first mentioned in AD 649 and in 726 BARBARANO 'spontaneously submitted' itself to Church government. After that, the usual transfers of ownership and fealty continued.

In 1768, the Commune was meeting the expenses of a communal theatre. In 1849 it sought, unsuccessfully, to adhere to the Roman

Republic. The population was 1,040 in 1704, 998 in 1853, 1,223 in 1951, and 874 in 1978.

The study established that all the neighbouring 'spur' towns have their main streets oriented north-west/south-east. Almost all the houses have cellars dug into the tufo, going down $\frac{2}{3}$–$1\frac{1}{2}$ times the height of the house above ground. Cellars of houses at the cliff edge go straight down first, and then sideways to an opening in the cliff.

The common house plan was precisely that of the Etruscan tombs at CERVETERI and houses at ACQUAROSSA: a cell, with one large and two small chambers. The door frames are precisely like, too.

A once abundant bird, the *capovaccaio*, the Egyptian Vulture, black-and-white, with a yellowish ruff, has now disappeared. It used to nest in holes in the tufo cliffs opposite the town, and feed off dead sheep and even cows at the top of the cliffs, where all was pasture; but modern agriculture uses the tops for field crops, so there is nothing for a carnivorous 'head cowman', which is what the name means.

There was a recent miracle: in 1930 the pentagonal tower known as the Tower of King Desiderius (the last Lombard King) was seen to spin round three times before carefully falling in such a way as to do no damage.

There was also a regular cycle of agricultural-religious observances – January 13, St Anthony Abbot: a procession of men with *ciambelle* attached to their arms. Around April 25, a procession about rain. May 3, little crosses made of rush were put in the field with a white lily, a bit of charcoal, and a bit of bread soaked in Holy Water; *ricotta* would be eaten. First Sunday in May, a visit to the half-destroyed Collegiata of San Pietro at SAN GIULIANO and mass said there; a cavalcade and a pancake cook-up. June 13, St Anthony of Padua: the occasion of thanks for a good harvest and the donation of bread and wine for the Host, presumably for the whole year. August, the Madonna (presumably the Assumption, on August 15): grain wrapped in handkerchiefs was blessed for the next season.

BARBARANO is densely packed behind handsome walls from one cliff-edge to the other. At the tip of the spur, it is collapsing down the cliff. Immediately inside the gate is the tiny church of Santa Maria della Misericordia or delle Lagrime – of Mercy, or of Tears – which changes direction half-way up the nave. It contains a decayed but truly baroque altarpiece; putti brandish the Instruments of the Passion, hammer, spear, pliers, and torch, with full Tridentine zeal.

The Region of Lazio has set up here one of its nature reserves, the Parco Suburbano Marturanum.

Bassano in Teverina

The ancient skyscraping medieval village perched above the Tiber is fast shrinking as its cliff falls away. The single gate is locked and in the care of the Italian Organ Donors' Association. The hugely tall old tower looks down on water still running where it always did, on caves with street numbers still on their doors, and the little romanesque church of Santa Maria dei Lumi.

Bassano Romano, or Bassano di Sutri

The Palazzo Giustiniani/Odescalchi is one of the great buildings of Lazio, for its arduous and splendid construction, for its almost lost park, but most particularly for one of its frescos, which is unique: its subject is *Aeterna Felicitas* – that 'Eternal Felicity', roads to which (or whom) so occupied Poliphilus in the *Hypnerotomachia* (see Appendix II) and his followers.

The little town lies, as the name says, low. The stone is dark, the outline difficult to grasp: its streets seem to be in the basement of some geological construct. The first castle was probably of the 12th century and its partly 17th-century town plan, particularly the Borgo San Filippo Neri, has been less spoiled than many.

Giuseppe Giustiniani, of a Genoese trading family, acquired the Palazzo in 1595, when it consisted only of the present south wing. His son Vincenzo was made a marquis by Pope Paul V Borghese in 1605; and what we see here is his work.

You approach his Palazzo through a great rusticated arch, straight into its foundations; after two sharp upward bends (still inside) and a ramp, you find yourself emerging into the town's high-level piazza. One side of this is the old south wing of the Palazzo, at its third-floor level, with a line of colossal marble busts of emperors along the front of it, now hideously defaced. Behind this front are Vincenzo's new constructions, started in 1605, for which he had earth shifted and land-levels changed on a vast scale and the town street bridged.

We know from a letter that he had seen Henry VIII's long-vanished and unrecorded country palace, Nonsuch, in Surrey. 'Nonsihic', he calls it. He preferred Nonsuch's dark grey, almost violet, colour to the lighter ones then fashionable: BASSANO's *intonaco* is that colour still today.

Within the cortile, remains of frescos done in the 1570s and 80s in the style that the Zuccari brothers had introduced at CAPRAROLA are fading. Sunny dreams of architecture float on hilltops and the wind is blowing away the caryatids, but not the elements they support. More of them in the south wing, where there is also a 'view' of BASSANO before the north wing or the park were built. The 'Paradise Room' has pictures of Genoa and the Greek island of Skios, where Giustiniani possessions were already lost to the Turk.

As Vincenzo gets older, the frescos become more interesting. The *Eros and Psyche* suite is by a Genoese painter, Bernardo Castello, friend and illustrator of Tasso, and protégé of the poet Marino, whose verse swung with much the same mannered elegance as Castello's people with their tiny heads and dancing gestures.

In the north wing we are home in the mainstream: the big *Phaethon* room by Francesco Albani and the little *Diana* room next to it by Domenichino have been well known since they were painted in 1609. Albani is a superbly cheerful painter, and his *Phaethon* cycle is far from inspiring the terror which ought intrinsically to belong to this myth of holocaust narrowly averted. Domenichino's *Diana* cycle, and the *Sacrifice of Iphigeneia* that goes with it, have a goody-goody charm, but they are static and declamatory. Poussin, Domenichino's admirer, did better in the same line.

The unique fresco at BASSANO is in the Sala del Cavaliere. The artist was the Cavaliere Paolo Guidotti Borghese (1560–1629) on whom the right to use the name Borghese had been conferred by that wealthy and potent clan. Guidotti was painter (see VITERBO Cathedral); sculptor (one statue left in Pisa Cathedral); poet (his great work *Jerusalem Destroyed* is lost: it celebrated Titus's expulsion of the Jews, with the same number of verses and the same rhymes as Tasso's *Jerusalem Freed*); anatomist (he is said to have dissected stolen corpses in the remotest galleries of the Colosseum by night); musician, doctor of law, mathematician, astrologer, and inventor of a flying machine made of whalebone and feathers in which he crashed and was badly hurt. He is recorded in the *Enciclopedia Italiana* only as an early aviator. Most of what he did is lost, and this room probably tells us why.

The subject matter of this ceiling has been well explained by Italo Faldi as an image of the soul's progress through victory over sin to Eternal Felicity. The young girl in the middle of the vault, sitting on the world, holding the sun in her hand, and looking down at us with the wonderfully sweet smile which is all she wears, is Eternal Felicity. From this glimpse of the sky we are mediated through a dark neck where winged putti flutter among the signs of the zodiac into a heavy circular cornice: all here is *trompe l'oeil.* The brilliantly lit underside of this heavenly torus is ornamented with grinning male masks mostly engaged in fellatio with phallic vegetables. The accompanying fruit is also relevant, and the ring is held up by ... well. Faldi calls them *telamons*, which is something like caryatids. There are eight of them, grouped in four pairs. These naked, salt-pale men, still violently bottom-lit, look at us or at each other with sly, fixed smiles of introverted connivance, while between the legs of each three more men, equally salt-pale, writhe and embrace and hold up their simpering superman. Below them at last comes the real cornice of the room. Between the four pale pairs of *telamons* are set a series of pictures in *trompe l'oeil* frames, and between the individual members of each pair is a noble personage in full colour, seated in front of a mad column with only a pair of playful mini-putti to bear the weight, instead of a capital. The four framed pictures show the Judgment of Solomon, Judith and Holofernes, Potiphar's Wife, and Susannah and the Elders. Three of them say: flee lust.

The non-loadbearing seated personages are probably virtues. Ripe Purity with downcast eyes holds her dove in her lap. Wisdom, her feet dangling and one hand surprised, looks upward to her source. It may be Self-Sacrifice who has just torn out his own bright red heart, even this slightly phallic. Contempt for Worldly Things pins a spurned crown to the floor with his sword. It has by now become clear that it is the salt-pale *telamons*, with their turbans and their cushion capitals, who are really taking the load of all that is happening above the cornice.

This wild room is reminiscent of Giulio Romano's *Sala dei Giganti* in the Palazzo Tè in Mantua, eighty years before, a picture of ferocious and explosive downfall. But here everything is firmly held together, deadlocked in its architecture, and it is this conceptual strategy, besides the tactical oddity, which makes us so uneasy. We are to ascend to Eternal Felicity, that is clear. But the as-it-were 'scope' (telescope? microscope? periscope? even inspection hatch, escape-hatch?) we see her through is held up by those chalky stalagmites of promiscuous lust, not by the Virtues or the Biblical Examples. Is the statement that if it were not for our propensity for lust, etc., we should have no need, perhaps even no hope, of Eternal Felicity? That those two things do, and somehow must, hang together?

The usual account of free will holds that it depends on the existence of evil: our good choices can only be good because evil choices are available; if we can't choose evil, what worth is our choice of good? Alternatively, if we are dualists, Manichaeans, good and evil are incompatible, travelling on lines eternally parallel, eternally untouching, eternal rivals. Guidotti's argument seems to be that good depends on, is even created by, evil. This is a strong answer to the question of evil: evil is the necessary condition for the achievement of *aeterna felicitas,* and if we do not recognise and go through evil we shall not reach that celestial purity and sweetness: 'evil' is a fourth gate that Poliphilus might choose.

Guidotti was paid the same top rate as Albani and Domenichino and when he left BASSANO, aged 50, he went to qualify as a Doctor of Law at the University of Pisa.

In the early 17th century, wilful inversion – Shakespeare's, Gesualdo's, 'melodious discord' – in the arts and in morals went deeper than mere fashion. Here at BASSANO we may also imagine a travelling troupe come to perform, say, Monteverdi's *Incoronazione di Poppea,* which wilfully redeems the appalling murderer Nero with some of the sweetest love music ever written. A little private theatre remains intact, with a grand door for the Signoria (who sat in two tiers of wooden boxes, draped no doubt with smart hangings), and a little one, straight from the street into the pit, for everyone else. The beams for hanging the scenery remain, and double niches where the stage lights went.

From the Palazzo into the great park a private bridge steps over the town street at first-, second-, or third-floor level, depending where you start counting. The park is long and narrow, with an incidented central *viale* running a kilometre uphill to the castellated villa, the Rocca, which you could then but now cannot see from the windows of the Palazzo. The planting was laid out by species to give not only controlled massing but controlled leaf colour throughout the year.

When you reach it, the Rocca turns out to be a large, rather severe classical building of more or less Medicean proportions, triple-doored in front, and crenellated overall. The crenellated turret on top, the *altana*, was matched by four smaller ones at the corners. These were removed when the property came to the Odescalchi family, perhaps to get rid of the ubiquitous Giustiniani coat of arms, a castle rather like the Rocca itself with a crowned spreadeagle on top.*

The most probable architect is Carlo Maderna (who may also have had a hand with the Palazzo staircase), in an archaising mood and

* Another Vincenzo Giustiniani, a bishop, covered the whole façade of a small church in Apulia with the family arms: the castle is drawn in rustication, with the higher middle tower framing the actual door; the eagle's breast encloses the little round window; its wings spread out to encompass volutes; and its crown is the top, central motif. This is at Gravina di Puglia, and it was built in 1602.

providing a pleasantly castle-on-the-skyline contrast to the up-to-the-minute civilian forms of the Palazzo. Fellini's *La Dolce Vita* was filmed in the Rocca and in the cellars of the Palazzo.

The Rocca is now ruinous, and wild clematis has reached the second floor. Pigs rootle in the bracken among what were the orchard trees below its silent gold. The complexities of the park have been subsiding into temperate jungle since 1943 under a regime of melancholy neglect. Giant fallen statues lie about, of mossy heroes and dogs and bears; the basin of a great circular pond crumbles; stupendous ilexes and firs stand purposeless among the creeper. In a few years the Palazzo itself will be gone too. The furniture has been stolen. The detachable pictures have been cut from their frames. The water has come through and begun to ruin Guidotti's hell-heaven.

The little parish church in the piazza outside, on the other hand, Santa Maria in Coelum Assumpta, seems good for many years. The interior is all of a piece: nine altarpieces in *trompe l'oeil*, the reflected sheen on the non-marble of the non-columns particularly effective. The shell-shaped holy water stoups would still deceive the short-sighted.

Along the 'spine' of the town is the neat and sober Borgo San Filippo Neri and its little church all built at the wish of Cardinal Benedetto Giustiniani in the 1630s. It was he who proposed the saint for canonisation.

A little way up out of BASSANO is Vincenzo's other great construction: the conventual church of San Vincenzo, intended for the family mausoleum. The bold squarely patterned façade dominates the countryside and is dominated in turn by a colossal bust of Christ, set clear and high at the top of the façade, on a stern horizontal balustrade. A bust of Christ is a rarity, and this one with its neat beard and vaguely senatorial drapes seems the very model of a strong-willed and cultivated marquis. The interior is a Latin cross, very clean lines. It is probably Maderna again, and indeed the façade is certainly related to the five central bays of St Peter's. (Think of the glory: one's own little St Peter's, by the very same architect, and bearing the name of one's very own saint! and even consecrated by one's son's wife's uncle, the Pope! – this was Innocent X Pamphili – see SAN MARTINO AL CIMINO and CASTRO.) In 1641 the altar end began to fall, hence the interesting, indeed beautiful, buttress work added by Vincenzo's son.

We know no place in Italy the imminent loss of which so insistently challenges the way our age treats the great imaginative statements of past ages as BASSANO ROMANO. Our states skimp. Our profiteers outbid one another by millions to get what they can carry away and hide. At their gates our curators plead piteously and impartially to state and profiteer that the people should see what made them. And all the while BASSANO, which houses an acreage of great painting that no gallery in the world could buy in a decade if it were portable, is left to fall. It is to saving and revealing marvels like this that the rich of the world, whether states or munificent citizens, must turn some of their wealth.

Bisenzio

The Etruscans made sandals here with wooden soles that were hinged in the middle, and reinforced with bronze; and false teeth with gold bridge-work. You can see both, and an extraordinarily charming little bronze cart covered with small figures hunting and ploughing and wrestling, from the late 8th century BC, in the Villa Giulia Museum.

This was probably the eastern limit of VULCI's strangely unknown extent: archaeological finds, innumerable and magnificent; historical records, nil; and the acropolis not yet excavated.

The Romans had a road. Later, there was a castellated settlement; and Counts of Bisenzio. About 1650 fishermen were living among the ruins; after 1816 all was abandoned.

Today there is nothing to see but the marvellous beauty of the Lake which takes Bisenzio's name, and its islands and peninsulas, prosperous again for the first time in two thousand years.

Blera

This rather elegant little town was called Bieda until recently, but that means beetroot (and other impolitenesses), so the name was changed to 'Blera' which does not. Its gorges contain a major Etruscan cliff necropolis, with some thousand, mostly archaic, façaded tombs (see NORCIA). Recovered contents are in the Museo Civico of VITERBO and elsewhere.

From the modern bridge on the BARBARANO road, you look down a hundred or more metres to where the stream flows under a Roman bridge with one big and two little arches. The Etruscan bridge, which carried the older Clodia, is hidden in the lush vegetation.

Bolsena

Come upon from the south, BOLSENA has the look of a medieval illumination. The walls and roofs of golden grey, the castle towers ditto, the lake below and the sky madonna blue, the wooded hills above dark and bright green: all make it one of the happiest views in Italy. The oldest part, including the castle, is within an enclosure, half cliff, half wall. Beneath it is another old quarter, often destroyed, often rebuilt, and with the two main renaissance palazzi; this is physically attached to the old walls and cliffs by a system of *piagge*: steep, covered alleys and steps, and dug-out passages. It too is walled and gated. A rather newer quarter, also gated but not now walled, reaches south to the complex of churches and catacombs that surround the Basilica of Santa Cristina. Above these used to be another castle. A late 19th-century avenue of London-huge plane trees leads down to the lake and the little port, shading bosky villas. Modern developments outside and beyond are creeping as fast as the feeble planning system allows, which is too fast.

Volsinium, the Latin form of its name, was a great city of Etruria and the capital of a prosperous state. The Etruscan form was Velzna (Italian spelling). 'BOLSENA' is certainly the same name, but is it the same place? It is pretty conclusively argued that the original Velzna was at Orvieto, 20-odd kilometres to the east, and that the name passed to BOLSENA when the Romans chased the people from there to here in the late 3rd century BC. Orvieto then becomes Urbs Vetus, the Old City, and indeed Etruscan finds at Orvieto have been finer and older than at BOLSENA.

The occasion of the Roman conquest of the original Velzna, last of the independent Etruscan states, was a revolt of urban serfs, which lasted long enough for the new masters to revoke the law against intermarriage between social classes. The defeated magnates called on Rome for help, the Romans took the place and, Pliny records, walked away with more than two thousand bronze statues.

On this theory, the new Etruscan city was founded about 265 BC on a series of well-watered terraces by the Lake and in time had 5 kilometres of perimeter walls. Two little Etruscan temples have also been identified, but one was already abandoned in the 3rd century BC. So the question of the foundation date remains obscure.

Voltumna, Latin Vertumnus, the Etruscans' national deity, was also Velzna's own tutelary divinity and the Fanum Voltumnae was held at, or near, Volsinium. This was a, probably annual, politico-religious gathering of the *lucumoni,* the priest-leaders, from all the twelve states of the Etruscan Confederation: perhaps not unlike the Icelandic Allthing a millennium and a half later, which would make BOLSENA – or perhaps more plausibly MONTEFIASCONE – the Etruscan equivalent of Thingvellir, the site of Iceland's gathering-place.

Up to the east of modern BOLSENA are the remains of a Roman amphitheatre and enough has been excavated to give a sense of the Roman town. Its Baths, the Bagni di Seiano, as they were a hundred years ago still appear on the local wine bottle labels.

St Cristina and the Festa

There once was a girl lived by a lake. She was the daughter of Urbanus, the Prefect set over these parts by the Emperor Diocletian in the late 3rd century AD. One day he learned his young daughter had joined the Christians. His explanations and entreaties were vain, and so were those of his wife. Given his position, he could not ignore her conversion. He turned to threats, and at last he imprisoned her with two attendants who were to induce her once again to worship the golden images. But one of these attendants was herself a Christian, and secured the girl's secret baptism: she declared herself no longer Urbanus' daughter, but Christ's, and took the name Cristina.

The martyrdom which followed was long – her father died and it was continued by the next two Prefects – and perfectly revolting, or so the first martyrologists, sweating in the Egyptian desert, would have us believe. Among her many ordeals was having a millstone tied to her feet and being thrown into the LAKE OF BOLSENA. But the millstone knew its business, and carried her ashore to safety: you can see it to this day.

But such is the cheerful nature of the people that a most rewarding *festa* has been devised. On the evening of July 23 Cristina's image under a tall neo-classical baldaquin is carried through the town and up to the church behind the Castello, where she spends the night, and comes down again in the morning. The whole population accompanies her, at least on the upward journey.

Five times on the way up and five times on the way down she stops where a platform has been set up with curtains that open as the procession arrives, so as to regale her with a tableau vivant of the tortures she survived. (The very nastiest, though fully recorded in the *The Golden Legend*, that 14th-century saint-fancier's *vade-mecum*, are outside the canon.) People have been chosen and have rehearsed the parts, which sometimes stay in a family for years.

Among the scenes are the following:

The Saint stands by the (painted) lake, undulating slightly to show how well the stone floats.

She stands praying in (or rather behind) the cauldron she has jumped piously into, which has real flames under it, while her father Urbanus points at her in condemnation.

This unnatural father lies on his deathbed while blacked and horned devils, these days wearing kneepads for protection in the scrum, imitate bears, swoop at him, and jump on him. Finally they tip him out of bed and carry him off to hell to universal acclaim. Meanwhile a *catinaro*, or chainmaker, has been clanking chains up and down louder and louder. There are usually eleven devils, and after this scene they repair to the vestry of the nearby church and take wine and doughnuts.

In the most popular scene the Saint has snakes coiling round her neck and arms and into her hair. The snake-charmer keeps his hands on them all the time and tries to get them to bite her, but cannot; finally they bite him, and slowly he realises *he* is dying. As to the snakes, we are assured 'their teeth have been drawn', as well as their poison-sac removed, and they can do no harm. Or not much; it is recorded that once in the 19th century and once again in the 1950s the snakes bit the Cristina so badly that she bled. But this was put down to her not being a virgin as she should have been.

The Miracle of Bolsena

There once was a priest who doubted in God. In 1263, so the story goes, a certain priest was on his way to Rome: the name Peter of Prague is sometimes given. He suffered doubt whether the bread and wine really turned into the flesh and blood of Christ. As he said mass in the church of BOLSENA, the Host suddenly began to bleed. The bloodstained vestments were taken to Pope Urban IV, who was at Orvieto; he accepted it as a true miracle and instantly ordered the building of the present cathedral there to house the relic. From that miraculous mass there grew up the festival of Corpus Christi, which has been celebrated ever since all over the world. On that day in BOLSENA itself a carpet of flowers is laid on the streets from church to castle and (since 1811) part of the bloodstained stone itself is carried in procession along it; and in many other towns and villages hereabouts flower carpets are laid for the Host to be carried over.

The Walls, the Castle, and the Palazzi

Medieval BOLSENA – sometimes an independent commune – was too valuable for walls alone to deter the covetous. But on 15 August 1328 King Ludwig IV of Bavaria was besieging it, and had to give up, despite having the Empress, the Anti-Pope and the schismatic cardinals all with him, when the women of the town said a thousand Ave Marias. Ever since another thousand Ave Marias have been said on that day, which is also the Feast of the Assumption of the Virgin.

In 1377 a band of papal mercenaries, Bretons, razed a whole quarter, the so-called Borgo Guasto between the Collegiata and the Lake, which has still not been fully rebuilt.

The Castle was built in the 12th century by the Monaldeschi, one of those families of foreign origin who made everyone miserable by their brawls. It was almost totally destroyed by the Bolsenesi in 1815, to stop it going to Napoleon's brother Lucien – he obtained CANINO instead – and was rebuilt. It was rebuilt again after 1945 and its four irregular towers play a dramatic part in the townscape.

The whole aspect and character of the little town was changed with the arrival of Giovanni de' Medici in the 1490s. He was the son of Lorenzo the Magnificent, Duke of Florence, and became Pope Leo X in 1513. (He is reputed to have said: 'God has given us the Papacy; now let us enjoy it'.) A Cardinal at 14, he was made Papal Legate in VITERBO and Governor of BOLSENA at 17. He reorganised civil government, constructed the Fonte Maggiore (now the Fountain of San Rocco) and built his own official house under the Castle, which is now part of the Palazzo del Drago. (Note, as at BASSANO ROMANO and ROCCA RESPAMPANI, the decorative chimneypots: little temples, versionlets of the Mausoleum at Halicarnassus, tiny Pharoses, brick birdcages . . .)

The very grand mid-16th-century *fortezza-palazzo* at the northern end, and the five-arch loggia looking over the Lake, were added, bit by bit, by the Florentine architects Simone Mosca (1492–1553) and Raffaele da Montelupo (*c. 1505–c.* 1567), for Giovanni de' Medici's successor, Tiberio Crispi. He was Pope Paul III's stepson, and went on to become a cardinal. His Torazza, as this building was called, is well up to mannerist villa standards, with a couple of hanging gardens. The frescos – big and vigorous – are of the school of Perino del Vaga. Its northern aspect has a unified Tuscan look, but from the lakeside the whole rises in tier after tier of Roman-looking units of grey-gold stone, horizontally punctuated by the gardens and terraces. The corner tower attached to the Torazza, looking up the

Cassia to the north, contains a grand frescoed staircase. There is also a minute and perfect Vignolesque chapel between the Palazzo and the rock face, complete with dome and lantern, straddling one of the *piagge*.

Crispi's successor as Governor was one of the Farnese ladies, Costanza, Pope Paul III's daughter. She is said to have done the job with *dolcezza, pace, e giustizia* – sweetness, peace, and justice – which sounds like one of the triadic 'reconciliations' familiar to students of renaissance mysteries.

Virtually mingling with the Palazzo del Drago and below it, is Palazzo Cozza, of much the same date: it too contains fine frescoed rooms, including one small chamber shewing gentlemen in tall hats inspecting the antiquities, perhaps of the 1830s. Some of the rooms have had their fresco scheme completed over the doors with extremely stylish prancing mannerist horses by Prince Giovanni del Drago, the present owner of the Palazzo above.

The Collegiata of Santa Cristina

A Pope and a Countess went out in a boat. This was in the 1070s; he was the great consolidating Pope, Gregory VII, and she was Matilda of Canossa, Countess of Tuscany. She was his ally in war and diplomacy against the claims and invasions of the Germans, and they had a common interest in securing the lands along the Cassia, the main invasion route. They crossed the Lake to the ISOLA MARTANA, and from there brought back the remains of St Cristina, or so the story goes. The relics were to be the great attraction of a fine new Basilica in front of her little old church in BOLSENA, which Pope Gregory consecrated in 1077. They were stolen in the next century, perhaps by two French 'pilgrims', and sold to a nobleman of the Molise, who was then talked into giving them to the Cathedral of Palermo, where they still are. A small part of her poor bones remain in the Basilica the Pope and the Countess built, in a casket. (The inscription beside it is too tactful to mention these deplorable happenings.)

Giovanni de' Medici also reorganised the Basilica, giving it a façade in the new style and importing people from Florence to design and direct the work; a typically Renaissance blend of Christian and pagan symbolism. The Collegiata today is a dense congeries of ecclesiastical spaces, nine of them above ground, incorporating altogether more than three millennia of worship and art.

Looking at the façade from outside: the first little unit on the right, part of Giovanni de' Medici's new work, fronts a medieval oratory of S. Leonardo – now the sacristy. Next comes the new façade to the 1077 Basilica (originally dedicated to St George), built in 1494–6, also for Giovanni. The campanile was commissioned by one Cardinal Ranieri, in the 13th century, who was also responsible for the huge Palazzo in the piazza. Next, still moving eastwards, is the 1863 façade of the baroque Miracle Chapel or Chiesa d'Oro. Then comes the first space actually within the rock, St Cristina's Cave, the palaeo-Christian church of Santa Cristina Morta. And behind all this again, Cristina's tomb, which is where the several kilometres of catacombs start. There are also several substantial chapels scattered about.

The architects for the façade were almost certainly the Florentine brothers Francesco and Benedetto Buglioni (1462–1520 and 1461–1521) and it has been plausibly suggested that the design is a scaled-down version of one put in for the Florence Cathedral façade competition. It is a decorator's or sculptor's design rather than an architect's: the elements clumsily put together, the main door too big, the top storey pointlessly divided horizontally. But the decoration is full of charm and elegant surprises. The 'green man' is everywhere, with vegetation mostly growing out of the top of his head; he is in semi-comic schema on the four middle capitals of the lower storey; and also as semi-recumbent man-in-the-half-moon, a minor decorative motif from *Hypnerotomachia* (see Appendix II), who reappears at BAGNAIA, BOMARZO, the QUERCIA, and elsewhere. The inner pilasters on the top storey have infant herms. The glazed terracottas in the two tympana are also attributed to Benedetto Buglioni.

The 1863 façade is a modest provision by the Roman architect Virginio Vespignani (1808–82), in regrettably drab grey peperino, timed for the six hundredth anniversary of the miracle.

Inside, the Basilica once had splendid capitals, as usual for the date, and the remains of a few odd beasts can still be seen. But in 1797, during the wave of egalitarian rationalism which spread from Paris over Europe, all the volutes and other tiresome sticking-out bits were hacked off and the whole was plastered to make a sober neo-classical vaulted tunnel (taken away again in the 1930s).

Off the Basilica on the right is the Rosary Chapel, with frescos and a fine Birth of Mary (by Francesco Trevisani (1656–1746)) with chops on the grill, a servant warming the bath-towel, and a spotted setter waiting for attention. The Chapel of Santa Lucia contains a bust of Santa Cristina attributed to Benedetto Buglioni, and frescos attributed to Giovan Francesco d'Avanzarano of VITERBO, who died about 1530. The wide low architecture in the Circumcision fresco is very latio-volcanic, and the way the infant Jesus is asking his mother to cancel or at least postpone the operation is pathetic enough to constitute comment which, although the Jews had not yet been expelled from the Papal State, would have been anti-Semitic.

The marble doorcase into the Chiesa d'Oro was a gift from the Pope and the Countess. Till the 17th century it opened on to a small open space called the Piazza delle Vergini, and on the architrave are the Seven Wise and the Seven Foolish Virgins. Green men are here too (one two-headed), with luxuriously convolvulant vegetation from their mouths running up and down the door jambs. On the right is a dragon-tailed cockerel: a basilisk. Also a chimaera: this one – a female – is powerfully unpleasant (see Appendix I).

Through this magic-flutish gateway is the Miracle Chapel, or Chiesa d'Oro, plans for which began in 1693. The physical temperature drops a little, and the spiritual one rises. It is a strong coherent piece of baroque space-management – cubes and rounds – apparently mainly by the Roman architect Tommaso Mattei, a fairly distant follower of Borromini. The altar is properly grandiose; and a piece of bloodstained stone from the miracle is shown in a blue and gold neo-classical reliquary of 1980. The picture above is by Trevisani again, those in the round are by his pupils.

Now into the rock, and the light and the temperature drop again. St Michael Archangel's Chapel is the best work of art in the church: a glazed terracotta *ancona* of St Cristina and her events. It used to be attributed to Giovanni della Robbia, but now that unfamous artists are also allowed to be excellent it is given to Benedetto Buglioni. (Vasari reports that Benedetto learnt the secret of glazing clay from his wife, who was a member of Andrea della Robbia's household.) In the predella, the three tiny scenes of Cristina's martyrdom have tremendous force. The first is full of a rushing movement that marks the tragedy: the little Saint is in the cauldron and her quite young father beside her has burst through frozen horror of what he is doing into hard self-contempt. In the second the Prefect is an older man: he still points in condemnation, but the gesture is learned, it is his public duty, and he wishes it were not. She is a real 13-year-old, though as tall as the soldiers – a saint cannot actually be smaller than anyone – and four of the young soldiers are protesting; the god of love himself is falling off his column. In the last scene, only two soldiers protest; one of the others now carries a scorpion on his shield; the horse which oddly humanised the scene before now has no legs and remains a sketch or nightmare, and the creature flying through the sky bearing the palm of martyrdom is surely as much from hell as from heaven. But look up, and there is consolation: at the very top of the *ancona* there is a strong baby standing in a chalice, one brave foot raised, as if for resurrection. The whole chapel is dirty and neglected, unlike the rest of the church.

The main hollow in the rock is called St Cristina's Cave; a dark and confused space that had been a palaeo-Christian church. Here, behind a large openwork 16th-century screen, are both the altar where the miracle of the blood happened and Cristina's miraculous millstone. This is a large smooth piece of basalt, with what look like child-size footprints impressed in it. Indented stones like this were used in a Sun-worship cult of the late Neolithic; others have been found in Italy and elsewhere. This is the only known example from Central Italy.

Over the altar a tall baldaquin of the 9th century uses Roman columns and capitals, and through that is visible another glazed terracotta *ancona* by Benedetto Buglioni, this one of the miracle, again a triumph of dramatic movement. The young priest kneels in a rushing mood of renewed faith, touched perhaps with self-importance, and the seventeen members of the congregation show every reaction from rapture to outrage, from doubt to unawareness that anything has happened. The jumbled space is grandly ill-lit and holy, and the modern wish to distinguish things of beauty and interest is foiled.

Opposite is the fine piece of carved lettering by the 16th-century humanist and architect Ippolito Scalza (see also ACQUAPENDENTE) which tells the story of the miracle, in words which are supposed to have been written at the time it happened. The Latin is medieval, not humanist.

Through the arch at the end of this cave the temperature drops yet again – by now really chill – and we finally reach the Saint's main shrine. Almost everything here – railings, staircases, lamps, catafalque – is 19th-century (and admirable; the wrought iron by Pasquale Franci), but the recumbent effigy, unglazed terracotta, is Buglioni again. It is as much a masterpiece of simple calm as those others are of tragic or portentous animation. It owes much to and brooks comparison with Iacopo della Quercia's Ilaria del Caretto in the Cathedral of Lucca.

Stairs now lead down to a sort of atrium (by Paolo Zampi, of Orvieto), inaugurated in 1894, where the sarcophagus is kept in which the Pope and the Countess put Cristina's bones; it had been rediscovered in 1879 by two boy seminarists poking around in some repairs under the miracle altar when the workmen had gone home. One went on to be a cardinal.

Below this again are catacombs, unusually tall, well lit, and on three levels; the length of the galleries so far recovered is well over 2 kilometres, and there are more.

San Rocco

Under Palazzo Cozza stands the Fountain of San Rocco that Giovanni de' Medici constructed. When mass is said here on 16 August each year, the table comes from Conte Cozza's house, and when the water of the fountain has been blessed everybody runs with bottles to catch the best of it. Then they eat the doughnuts which the boy scouts and girl guides distribute free. San Rocco, or Saint Roche, for he was after all French, was born in Montpellier about 1295. According to sober acceptance he was the healer of the plague-stricken, a duty he first took up at ACQUAPENDENTE. But the Bolsenesi hold that he himself, on a pilgrimage to the tombs of the apostles, was in need of healing. He arrived in Bolsena with a nasty sore, drank the water from the fountain, washed his sore with it, and after a while was healed. On the question why the little dog brings him a doughnut, local opinion is doubtful.

Bolsena War Cemetery

The Commonwealth War Cemetery of BOLSENA is at Km. 105 on the Cassia. Immediately after the fall of Rome on 4 June 1944, the Allies resumed their advance to the north. The US Fifth Army went up between the coast and the LAKE OF BRACCIANO, the British Eighth Army up the Tiber valley and, what was harder, the Sabine Hills to the east of it. VITERBO fell on 9 June to two soldiers of the 52nd US Division in a jeep. Besides US and British, the troops engaged in this campaign were South African, Indian, French, Moroccan, and Italian. (For an account of the Campaign, see VITERBO, History.)

Down from one of Europe's oldest roads, six hundred Commonwealth dead, army, navy, and air force, are buried in familiar heartrending good order and discipline. The green lawn and the narrow herbaceous borders are a precise and determined transfer of 'England' to another, drier, soil. Most of the names are British, but a third are South African. Of these, many are also British in origin, others Dutch, Zulu, Indian, Jewish, Greek.

Bolsena, Lake of

To John Evelyn, it '... yeild[ed] a most incomparable prospect: neere the middle of it are 2. small Ilands, in one of which is a Convent of melancholy Capucines ... Pliny ... talks of divers floting islands about it, but they appeared not to us'. This is the largest volcanic lake in Italy, 43 kilometres round and 14 across. The water level is 300 metres above sea, the maximum depth half that. Its origin is partly several dozen craters run together, and partly subsequent subsidence, so that it lies in a hammock of hills. There is a part-crater under MONTEFIASCONE. The two islands are probably the remains of little volcanic cones, and so probably are BISENZIO's cliff and CAPODIMONTE's peninsula. Just south of BOLSENA an upright bunch of polygonal stones is reminiscent in miniature of Iceland or the Giant's Causeway, and beyond it a good-sized lava flow.

Live vulcanism may be responsible for the most unusual thing about the Lake: the phenomenon known as the *sessa*. The word is local only, and it describes something which seems to happen only here: a local 'tide', not of lunar origin. The Lake is a mostly shallow platter. Every few weeks, the water sloshes from end to end as if the platter were rocking, perhaps for a few hours, perhaps even for a day and a night. Each slosh takes three or four minutes, and it is most clearly visible when the water starts pouring into or out of one of the little harbours – BOLSENA, MARTA, or CAPODIMONTE. But these harbours are not exactly busy and the maximum difference in level is only half a metre, so measurement is not easy; indeed many times it must happen without anyone noticing, and there are no funds for sophisticated research into anything so unlikely to lead to economic benefit. One hypothesis was that a sudden change in the relative air pressure at each end of the Lake might cause a minute change in water level which would be picked up and magnified by the resonance of the water mass into the detectable *sessa*: but the meteorological evidence is against this. Another hypothesis proposes that there may from time to time be a series of microseismic pulses running from end to end of the crater system, every three or four minutes, and hitting the resonance as above: but equipment to detect these pulses would be expensive.

The Lake is fed, largely at the northern end, by streams and by underwater springs, mostly cold, but one as hot as 40° Centigrade. At the northern end, the water-table is only a metre or two below the surface of the soil. At the southern end, where the outlet is, it is mysteriously far down (see MARTA).

That the lake level was sometimes higher is shown by thick layers of sediment up the hillside. At other times, it was lower. There were lake dwellers here from about 1000 BC and at the place called Gran Carro, south of BOLSENA, cart ruts in the rock run straight down into the water. A pleasant short swim from the shore, and just below the surface, there are heaps of worked tufo, the origin of which is still discussed. Just outside these, 5 or 6 metres down, are the remains of a village, with pottery, pilotis, bronze pots, etc.: 9th to 7th centuries BC. The underwater springs gush deliciously hot.

Until the 1970s most of the shoreline was fringed with reeds growing in the water out to a depth of about 2 metres. On the beaches and in the groves behind these a private world existed, and in a few places still does, composed of the birds and the dragonflies and plants that you would expect. Composed also of the fishermen, though it is more draughty now. When Pope Pius II visited the ISOLA BISENTINA in 1462 he was told the fishery was disorganised and the fishermen at one another's throats. So a conference was called on the ISOLA BISENTINA of representatives of the fishermen and communes. The chair was taken by a suitable Farnese and a code was drawn up regulating catches, types of net, and fishing practices, which was agreed and seems to have won acceptance.

At MARTA, near the top of the outlet, there was an eel-trap – the Cannara. 'The Pope [Pius II] visited this place, too, that he might see with his own eyes what he had heard of.' He describes it: 'When the south wind ruffles the clear water [the eels] retreat to the end of the lake and, following the course of the river, fall into a trap. For where the river drops, the inhabitants have built a tower with a wooden receptacle at its foot which lets out the water through many small holes in the floor but keeps the eels in. Since they cannot climb up again against the force of the water flowing down from above, they are left high and dry and are caught. The tower is kept under guard and returns a very considerable revenue. [Indeed the eels used to be sent to the popes at Avignon, by sea, in water-filled barrels.] When the water rises too high it is possible to turn its course away from the tower.'

Nylon nets are now strong enough to hold even large eels, so this remarkable construction has been converted into a private house. The equipment is all still there. The canalisation and stonework are Etruscan.

The fishermen mostly now spend the winter in houses up in the towns, but in summer they are back down there in their reed huts, cooking over fires of driftwood and old fruit boxes, growing a few beans and geraniums. The boats are still the old type: hard chine, flat bottom, and high, curving bow. Propulsion was formerly by rowing, usually standing and facing forwards. Small, sober engines are now fitted for getting there and back, but the boats are still moved by arm power while the nets are being cast and taken up. The fishermen's world, which is partly shared by the lakeside peasants, is a leftover part of Europe before industry. Many of the fishing families are friendly to modern visitors: but some are not, and there are outlaw souls living among them. The words *figlia di pescatore!* 'fisherman's daughter!' are still an insult, left over from the days when they were a real under-class, like the gypsies.

The volcanic sand of the shore glitters in sun or moonlight and the water, until the wind and waves have churned it up, is still that of a *lago da bere* – a lake to drink. The storms of the Assumption (see TREVIGNANO) can whip up metre-high waves and white horses to match.

Bomarzo

Under the little town of BOMARZO, in the mid-16th century, a member of a junior branch of the Orsini family made one of the strangest places in all Europe.

Vicino Orsini was born in 1523. His father was a *condottiere,* famous for cruelty and decisiveness. In spite of a limp Vicino began his life as a soldier; he was also a lover of literature and of women; and he married the Giulia Farnese of that generation, great-niece of Pope Paul III.

The milieu in which he lived happened to be strongly Venetian, which by Roman standards meant free thinking, and even the shadow of heresy. It also meant acquaintance with that remarkable book the *Hypnerotomachia Poliphili* (see Appendix II).

Vicino twice served abroad in the papal interest: in Germany, and in north-eastern France, where he was for two years a prisoner. The anti-Spanish Pope, Paul IV Carafa, himself of a Spanish-Neapolitan family, then gave him a command in the so-called 'Campagna War' of 1557. The Spanish Duke of Alva, in response to the Pope's belief that all Spaniards ought to be driven out of Italy, was attacking northwards from Naples. Vicino was made commandant of Velletri, south of Rome, but Alva took it. Word then came from the people of the small town of Montefortino, which had already been taken, that they would defect to the Pope, and Vicino sent a company of soldiers to their support. This company the men of Montefortino ambushed and slew to a man. The Pope sent a strong force to avenge Vicino's men and after a long siege Montefortino was taken, the men were massacred, the town was looted, then fired, the fields were salted, and a church full of women and girls in sanctuary was fired and all of them burned alive. His experience of this war, and particularly this last atrocity, for which he cannot but have felt some responsibility, changed Vicino's life.

In 1558 he wrote to his friend Cardinal Alessandro Farnese (see CAPRAROLA) that although at 35 he felt he knew less of man's true work than if he had been born yesterday, yet 'in just one thing I seem to be older then Nestor: I am resolved that Epicurus was a gentleman – *galantuomo*. But: God willing, and all that'.

So Epicurus was the tutelary deity of the marvellous grove which Vicino built in the 1560s and 70s at BOMARZO. The word grove, *boschetto*, is the one he uses most often. It carries overtones of the Sacred Groves of Greek and Roman antiquity, and he intended BOMARZO to be a modern version of those.

Vicino's letters to various friends have survived, and Horst Bredekamp has published a number of them in the original Italian as an appendix in his most interesting book, *Vicino Orsini und der heiliger Wald von Bomarzo: ein Fuerst als Kuenstler und Anarchist.** They tell a lot about him, for he was a wonderfully confiding letter-writer, and something about his *boschetto*. But not much, because his friends all knew it, and knew what he was doing there, and shared with him a context of allusions and images which to us, at least intellectually, is opaque.

To Alessandro Farnese the Cardinal, at CAPRAROLA, in April 1561:

> I spend my time down in my grove to see if I can make it appear as marvellous to you as it does to the many simpletons who come here. But that won't be possible since wonder born of ignorance cannot affect you. Well, in any case, the poor little grove, knowing that it is to receive your Eminence this summer, is doing itself up as best it can, and with this I kiss your hand.

To the same in 1563:

If you ask what I am doing, turn the page.

Item: looking after my offspring, both he and she, both great and small.

* Worms, 1985, 2 vols.

Item: the harvest which, since I have no hope of selling the grain, is unpleasant.
Item: I look after my whores of whom, thank God, being now forty, I keep more than one for my own purpose. . . .
Item: granting a delay to many debtors until they come again, which seems to me no small thing.
Item: putting the fountains in my grove in order; it is a burden to be about them every day.
Item: apologising somewhat to the Cardinal of Trent [Madruzzo – see SORIANO] who I am sure will complain of me . . .
Item, item, item: but none of them matters except serving your lordship, whose hand I kiss . . .

To Giovanni Drouet, April 1574:

> As to the p–, p–, and p–, which you tell me I must avoid, your Lordship is not a good teacher when you say *pesce, porco et pasta.* I prefer to remember Trivulzi's answer when the King of France asked what was needed to regain the Duchy of Milan: 'Three things, sire: money, money and money'. So I interpret your three Ps as *potta, potta et potta* (cunt, cunt and cunt).

To the same, June 1574:

> My little wood found it a great honour to be visited by so many noble ladies and cardinals.

To the same, who has sent him a girl, April 1575:

> As for me, I am resolved that I want no more Roman gentlewomen, but will be content with my shepherdesses in the shade of a fine beech.

To the same, in the same month:

> Now I have to say that the earth has produced its flowers and done all its duty, but the heavens disagree and thwart everything, and I am in despair because I cannot enjoy the spring madness of my little wood.

At the head of the valley below BOMARZO there is a natural amphitheatre in which, as in most of these valleys, large lumps of peperino lie about, of various grades and shapes, thrown down by some eruption. Vicino had these huge blocks of stone carved where they lay, and built around them terraces and little piazzas and flights of steps. The springs that were everywhere he disciplined into fountains and cascades, and the trees he arranged or took advantage of.

He writes that he himself made drawings for the Grove; but its scheme is not now understood, nor are the names known of those who executed it. All one can say is some of the figures have a strong family resemblance to the great Fauness at the Fonte Papacqua that Cardinal Madruzzo had made at SORIANO. The name of Pirro Ligorio has been suggested* and indeed one or two of his drawings and one figure attributed to him at the Villa d'Este at Tivoli do have the broad animal slackness which marks the BOMARZO figures.

Everywhere in the grove there are inscriptions, often gnomic and obscure, and stone seats for you to sit on and think. Many of the figures are monstrous, others wild, others you could see anywhere at the time. Vicino Orsini and his circle used the old tag from Aristotle, 'in rest and sleep the soul becomes wise', and the intention behind the Sacred Grove reflects that sentiment. One inscription on the spot seems to define the whole even more precisely and nonchalantly: *Solo per sfogar il cor* – 'Just to relieve – *soulager* – the heart'.

Most of the figures in the Wood are gigantic, and the buildings small. The first event you came to on the itinerary that Vicino intended is a miniature Vignolesque church: a deep porch which seems as full of columns as the Pantheon's; a tiny octagonal combined nave and chancel, blind, with external paired attached columns; and on the drum, which has four small round windows, the purest imaginable dome. Get close and half-close your eyes: you are Gulliver looking at a great calm cathedral in a capital city. But the announcement of calm is misleading.

It was dedicated to Giulia by the widower, and there is a contemporary statement that he endowed priests to say mass for her soul there in perpetuity. This ravishing architectural statement above the green grass slope is strongly funereal in tone: like most of the best classical mausolea, it uses the classical orders rather close, just as the minorness of a minor key resides mainly in the closeness of the third to the keynote.

The mysterious little villa which you next come on is leaning sharply to one side; you may climb up and down the floors if you have rubber soles, otherwise you will stay outside and watch through its windows while others clamber at a diagonal. Was it built crooked as a jolly jape? Joy there is at BOMARZO, but not jollity.

Bredekamp suggests an altogether more sophisticated gambit.

*By the Swiss writer Jacqueline Theurillat in an unsourced book, and in an *ms.* note in the Witt Collection at the Courtauld Institute in London University, which may be by Ellis Waterhouse.

Whoever has walked round the building and gone up to its first and second floor and lived for a short time in its out of kilter rooms, and then come back into the outer world of reality and plumblines, and stumbled, will be more inclined to accept the ensuing marvels as measured and proportionate in their meaning. Bredekamp uses the image of a canal lock: the little house is a lock between the pound of reality and the pound of dream. And he quotes the opening words of the *Hypnerotomachia Poliphili*: 'This is Polia's Lover's Dream of the Sex War, which teaches that everything human is nothing but a dream'.

Influences abound and self-destruct. Two sphinxes are inscribed with their own riddle: 'You who enter here, think on each thing and then tell me, are such marvels made for deceit or for art?' which is some way from Egyptian simplicities. There are feathered or sun-rayed masks and head-dresses which could as well be Aztec as Etruscan in inspiration: Bredekamp convincingly lists the books about the Spanish conquest of Central and South America which Vicino could easily have read, and even the booksellers he would have got them from. Here were two cultures which revered the dream-world, and the sylvan dream-world at that: the Amerindian, and that of Colonna and Vicino. (There are Aztec faces at Villa Lante too.)

In *Dell'India America* by André Thevet, a contemporary writer who was a friend of a friend, Vicino can hardly have missed the chapter comparing American Indian dream culture with that of classical antiquity, or the account of how Brazilian Indians were made anxious by the forest, the secret realm of the spirits. 'In the woods', Thevet wrote, 'come many faces, and they call each one "ghost", in their language *gligi*'.

Ariosto is here too: the most terrifying of all the figures is the colossal *Orlando Furioso* – Orlando Mad – tearing a naked woman in two.

Compared with him, the grinning ogre's head called the Mouth of Hell, with the alternative version of Dante's best-known line written round it – *lasciate ogni pensiero voi ch'entrate* ('abandon care, all ye who enter here') – is just right to restore the nerves. There is a grotto inside where you can sit on stone benches at a stone table and have a picnic.

There is a life-size Carthaginian elephant, with military howdah or castle, which is raising a Roman soldier in his trunk, you think to break him like a snail on a stone; but its monumental sex organs almost divert you.

The Tortoise of the Universe with a Giantess on his back is fairly calm: she began with two trumpets to blow, either in the real Etruscan manner, or symbolising the uncertain toot of Fame, in the Florentine.

The Echydna, the two-tailed mermaid seen everywhere in Lazio from the Etruscan on, here sits upright and beautiful on the grass with her long furred and scaled tails stretched out straight.

Venus was being woken by Mars: she is like Giulio Romano's at the Palazzo Tè at Mantua, but Mars has now gone. The version of a chimaera (see Appendix I) has a woman's body, short animal forelegs, and then immediately a serpent's tail. A great wide fountain, with Pegasus above: a nymphaeum, with nymphs splashing (not many nymphs now, not splashing). A large Plain of Jars, the shape echoing that of the Stadium at Olympia: at one end Poseidon, a main-line sea-god who makes us feel secure again (unless of course the Crooked House therapy is still working, and the normal disturbs us), at the other a grandiose Ceres with a pot on her head but little faces barking and screaming at her back – climb on her lap and forget them? Sea monster. Dragon: attacked by dog and lion. A vase some 6 metres high, just waiting. Another stadium marked out by stone pinecones and acorns with little bears – *orsini* – holding coats of arms. Two colossal sirens.

And more. And more. By his insistence that his guests would do honour to the little wood by their mere presence, Vicino still invites us to make what we will of his puzzling wonders. There is no key: he did not want there to be.*

In his day the Grove's abstruse progeny of the mysterious, the perverse, and the allusive were mitigated by the amenity of stone seats and stone steps. When we first saw it in 1954, and indeed for a quarter of a century thereafter, the inhabitants of his Bosco were magnified by the wild growth of great trees and the dark low steam of undergrowth, so that to each you whispered '*gligi*' like the Brazilian. It was never 'forgotten', as is now said, let alone 'lost', just completely and fabulously neglected. (Dennis, though he describes the Etruscan remains nearby at length, makes no mention.) Though statutes had toppled, and some were broken, and the waters were dried up, it would be better if it were still like that.

The present owner, a former mayor of BOMARZO now living

* There is by now a growing literature including a long picaresque novel by the Latin American writer Manuel Mujica Lainez, called *Bomarzo*, published in translation (London, 1970), which bustles along in a simple way; the Theurillat book; an opera. Dali was inspired; Borges too; interpretative drawings have been published.

elsewhere, has by a mixture of proud solicitude and total incomprehension ruined it. All is surrounded by a chainlink fence. You buy your ticket passing perforce through a large airport-type tat-market. You pass bedraggled cage-birds in the sun. A circuit of concrete walkways directs you to miss the composed vistas, the surprise approaches, the challenges. The great native trees and the mysterious undergrowth are shaved away and replaced by blue cupressus and Finnish firs. Statues have been moved; groups of figures split up; the inscriptions picked out in dark red. In the mini-cathedral is a large inscription to his own wife. It is heartbreaking in the same way as trying to find your way round the Church of England's new prayerbooks: some of the power and mysterious glory can still be found, but it is embedded in impudent drabness.

The Sacred Grove was built also to be looked at from Vicino's ancestral palazzo-castle above. His father had begun transforming the old *castello* in the early 1500s; Vicino continued; and a later owner, Ippolito Lante della Rovere, did some more. Vicino's own contributions are not too easy to disentangle and it seems odd that the best views of his Grove from the Palazzo should be from the handsome staircase in the south-west corner: there is no loggia. The frescos Vasari tells us Annibal Caro advised him on (see CAPRAROLA) are no longer visible: may they be hidden under the present wall surfaces in the room where the town council meet? They would like to think so, but haven't the money to look. Off this chamber is a chapel under the altar of which is the embalmed body of a 17th-century saint 'not known to the Vatican', but here revered: San Moderato – St Moderate.

Vicino's most conspicuous contribution to the Castello is the forced symmetry of shallow fenestration and rustication impressed on the entrance façade. It is mannerist in the Peruzzi mode, the stone carved into almost gelatinous shapes. Peruzzi's name is locally mentioned – but he died in 1536.

Vicino also constructed two open terraces from which to look down at the wood. That above the appliquéd façade is a kind of inside-out chamber: niches, blind window-frames, several inscriptions. On one side: *ede, bibe, et lude/post mortem nulla voluptas* – 'eat, drink and be merry: after death there is no pleasure'. On another: *sperne terrestria/post mortem vera voluptas* – 'spurn the worldly; after death is true pleasure'. A third reads: *medium tenuere beati* – 'blessed are they who hold to the middle way', which in this context looks less than easy. (Perhaps San Moderato succeeded.)

The second terrace is bare save for a stone bed set under a curiously gothick arch, composed of two giant inturned volutes leaning against each other, with a flare of acroteria – formalised honeysuckle. Where nothing is meaningless, what does this mean?

From here, the view is straight down to the tiny façade of the 'chapel', now called Santa Maria della Valle. It bears the arms of the Lante della Rovere family and an ordinary – but huge – later chapel-body is tacked on, askew. Its properly pedimented façade has eight free-standing columns, each raised on its own plinth – as in the Bosco church; and the whole is too small for its proportions. The façade is today unwindowed, and oddly shot through the middle by the pediment-framed door: the two central columns simply dispersed by its presence. Was it a screen of Vicino's imagining? Do the door and its frame belong? What was behind?

All round the Bosco is a wall and just before the head of the valley, a fine gate in it, with all-over rustication so deeply incised that each stone appears poised in shadow, unattached; unformed capitals of unexpressed pilasters look loosened; the keystone, in Giulio Romano's Palazzo Tè manner, has dropped. Within the volutes, the acroteria have developed prehensile tentacles. Beyond, the huge stones still lie about, unworked, fruit trees and vegetable patches among them.

The Town

The old town was rebuilt in the 13th century, and of Lazio's medieval towns it is one of the neatest and best lived-in, as well as most convoluted: a rich pudding from which emerge a few Vicinian plums. The old church was the tiny one dedicated to BOMARZO's own saint, St Anselm (Bishop), whose body is now in the big church. On that, an inscription records that Vicino's wife Giulia saw to its completion while he was away at the wars. A pretty curved double staircase leads up to the main door and the proportions of the nave and two aisles suggest mannerist dress on high medieval bones. The tall square columns have characteristic Bomartian capitals. The Saint, with a fluffy beard, lies under the altar, and his original palaeo-Christian sarcophagus is against the right wall. The great medieval bell-tower has a Roman base.

Officer Fosci of the Urban Vigils, with the approval of the town clerk, showed us round: the name is that of the family in whose house, 'one of the best', George Dennis stayed.

Polymartium

Two *burroni* away to the north is the site of old Polymartium, an important Etruscan settlement, where fine things have been found. At the end of the spur, some dozens of caves are exposed. George Dennis claimed to see in one of the tombs the first instance of Florentine 'rustication'. And in a painted tomb he saw on the wall 'water-snakes uprearing their crests and gliding along in slimy folds'. The usual exploiters and exporters were at work and it was from here that the British Museum obtained its remarkable temple-shaped sarcophagus with many curious creatures and snakes 'in knotted coils' on its roof.

Bracciano

BRACCIANO claims most conspicuously to be the ruler of its circular LAKE, so firmly does the great Castle appear to straddle the ridge. Yet the military doctrine it embodied had already been overtaken by new weapon systems: it was never as invulnerable as it still appears.

Inside the massive 15th-century outer shell an older, probably 12th-century, castle of the Prefects of Vico is still detectable. From them it had gone to the Commune of Rome in the 1370s, and then in 1419 the Pope enfiefed it to the tempestuous Orsini clan. The present colossal structure was begun about 1470 by Napoleone Orsini, chieftain of the clan.

What Napoleone conceived was Pharaonic in scale and solidity, and he and his son Gentil Virginio completed it. The curious shape – a sort of bashed-in trapezoid with a 'handle' at the town end and six great towers – was forced on them by the lie of the rock. The east (town-side) range embodying much of the earlier castle and the beetling north (lake-side) range are Napoleone's; the south-west range Gentil Virginio built, in the 1480s. (Although he was a little milder than his father, 'Gentle Virgin Little Bear' was not an apt name.)

BRACCIANO is among the last and largest of the archery castles of Europe. Already by the 1460s artillery castles, designed to resist cannon with squat, angled towers and low walls on sloping taluses, were replacing the archery castles with their high curtain walls and soaring round towers. Napoleone and Gentil Virginio can hardly have made their archaic choice on military grounds: perhaps they just wanted a colossal and theatrical version of the familiar symbol of power when it came within their financial reach.

Napoleone operated skilfully through the treacheries and wars of the 1470s among and between Florence, the Pope, and the Kingdom of Naples, and in 1478 he was actually host at BRACCIANO for three months to Pope Sixtus IV, the Franciscan Francesco della Rovere, who stayed in the new north range. Sixtus came again in 1481, to stay with Gentil Virginio.

Orsini loyalty to Sixtus did not continue towards Alexander VI Borgia. At Christmas 1494 King Charles VIII of France, then rampaging up and down in pursuit of the perennial northerner's dream of control over Italy, stayed in the castle. Alexander excommunicated Gentil Virginio, and in the Borgia-Orsini war of 1497 the papal army brought up the artillery the great Castle had not been designed to withstand, stationing it half-way up the high street, and blew the tops off the tall towers.

The Borgias also pursued a naval war. A *brigantino* was launched on the LAKE from which Cesare Borgia presumably hoped to capture the lakeside villages, cut off the town, and starve it into submission by a maritime blockade. Giovanni Borgia was attacking TREVIGNANO at the same time, but on the water the Orsini were a match for the Borgia: the papal fleet was taken and burned by an Orsini cousin, Bartolommeo d'Alviano. In the end, in 1501, the castle had to yield.

The Orsini gradually regained control of their estates and were readmitted in stages to papal favour. In 1560 Paolo Giordano Orsini, recently elevated Duke of Bracciano, grandly married Isabella de' Medici. Then in 1576 he fell in love with a Roman beauty called Vittoria Accoramboni, the wife of one Francesco Peretti. With characteristic Orsini self-confidence, he first strangled his own wife, Isabella (for alleged infidelity), and then (probably) had Vittoria's husband murdered.

In 1585, Peretti's uncle, Felice Peretti, Franciscan Cardinal of Montalto, was elected Pope (as Sixtus V) and set about restoring the badly dented civil order of the Papal State. Paolo Giordano and Vittoria fled to the Veneto; Paolo Giordano died the same year (perhaps even from natural causes), and one of his cousins, Lodovico Orsini who was arranging the division of the estate, had Vittoria murdered by an armed gang.

She, of course, was the Vittoria Corombona of John Webster's play *The White Divel* (*sic*; first produced about 1608, a mere twenty years after the events) and Paolo Giordano was his Duke of Brachiano, a not incorrect older spelling. Her story has as many forms as she has biographers: Webster gives her a court hearing on a charge of adultery before her murdered husband's uncle the Cardinal, in which, under monstrous provocation and heckling from the judgment seat and before a jury apparently composed of the Ambassadors in Rome of the principal European powers, she cries out:

> Sum up my faults, I pray, and you shall find
> That beauty, and gay clothes, a merry heart,
> And a good stomach to a feast, are all,
> All the poor crimes that you can charge me with.
> In faith, my lord, you might go pistol flies;
> The sport would be more noble.

Paolo Giordano II, successor to Webster's duke, industrialised BRACCIANO, building an aqueduct from the hills by MANZIANA: four water-powered forges, a paper mill, and a printing works were the result. Where the modern road to TREVIGNANO drops lakewards, the workshop where the mechanic still makes sparks is a relic of one of the ironworks.

The Orsini power decayed and the Castle was auctioned in 1695. It was bought by the family of Pope Innocent XI Odescalchi (he it was who introduced the sensible rule that no pope should make more than one nephew a cardinal). They had been successful drapers in Como. They built an extension of the aqueduct to bring water to the town as well as to the industry, and they still have the Castle today. (See also BASSANO ROMANO, PALO, SANTA MARINELLA, and VIGNA GRANDE.) Debt forced them to sell BRACCIANO to the new family of Torlonia in 1803, but the marriage of Prince Livio III in 1861 to the Polish heiress Sophia Branitska, who was as rich as she was energetic and optimistic, allowed the whole interest to be redeemed.

The interior of the Castle is impressive for sheer size, but interesting and even endearing as well. You go in (conducted tours) up a magnificent ramp to Napoleone's main gate of about 1475; the architecture that curves round the huge tower is later work, by the Sicilian Giacomo del Duca, and probably for Paolo Giordano I's 1560 wedding to Isabella. The courtyard contains two renaissance elements, each magnificent, but together sitting uneasily round what seems a cramped triangular parade-ground. Napoleone's north wall loggia speaks an old language; the strong diagonal staircase – almost a *profferlo* – makes it look like a major scene in the streets of Viterbo. (Note how Etruscanly the beams under the roof lie on their columns.) Gentil Virginio's two-storey loggia recalls some cortile in Florence; its harmony and civilian grace cry out for a rectangular setting. Through the vaulted tunnel opposite are the massive protomilitary forms of the old castle of the Prefects of Vico.

The first-floor rooms of the north range, although colossal, convey a sense of greater ease, because the forms are steady and rectangular. Here the Torlonia interlude was disastrous: doors were lost and furniture sold (or perhaps that was during the debts before) and most of the frescos were catastrophically restored. When the Odescalchi returned with Sophia's wealth, their agents dashed hither and thither in Europe, buying everything they could lay hands on, especially in Belgium and Bavaria, most of it good, some of it bad, much of it appropriate, much not, and hardly any of it big enough.

The grandest fresco, the overall painter of which was Antoniazzo Romano, in 1491, is now in the Sala dei Trofei, the Hall of the (hunting) Trophies. It was originally in the vault under the entrance tower and moved here in 1964, the two scenes it shows (from the life of Gentil Virginio) had been separated by a window. They have now been put together, and the bottom of the mountain was the window area, painted in after the removal.

One scene has Gentil Virginio's nephew Piero de' Medici coming, in 1487, to a BRACCIANO that never was, on his way to Rome to marry his, Piero's, sister to Francesco Cibo, the son of Pope Innocent VIII. On the left is shown Gentil Virginio's cavalcade when he was invested General of the Neapolitan Army in 1489. The fact that Antoniazzo employed a large number of assistants, that he was a sort of wholesale art contractor, accounts for some of the execution being as pretty as anything of the date and some absurdly bad.

The marble busts by Bernini in the next room are of Paolo Giordano II and his wife. He figures as a baroque fop with a wonderfully silly moustache. There are other good rooms, including one full of guns – note the 17th-century model cannon. Also a 19th-century Bavarian knight-and-lady flying through the air with some lit-up antlers; or so it seems.

The cycle of eighteen frescos in the so-called Pisanello Room (an attribution not now favoured) shows women in scenes both everyday and mythical. They are of about 1500, horribly restored, hard edged, as if by a Victorian Lichtenstein. One shows *Ypolita Amaçorum Regina* (*sic*), and another a battle scene showing women with bound breasts in the supposed Amazon manner. The defence of the Castle in 1496–7 was at least in part undertaken by Gentil Virginio's sister Bartolommea, the wife of the successful lake admiral Bartolommeo d'Alviano. A 16th-century book about the Orsini describes her as 'manly, and worthy of the most outstanding fortune'. The art historian R. Siligato has imaginatively suggested that this series of frescos was Bartolommea's idea, and celebrates family and female valour in the siege.

As well as the Amazon scene, the girls go out in a canopied boat (Fellini effect) and play their lutes; they have a picnic; they catch crayfish in the lake (now no longer found); they beat olives out of the tree; they splash naked in a fountain; they play the lute again under a canopy; they have another picnic; they ride in a canopied cart; they practise juggling in the dining-room. The atmosphere is more domestic than heroic; and quite a little nostalgic.

Some rooms in the more amenable south-west range are still used. Two were decorated by the Zuccari brothers for Paolo Giordano I, also perhaps for his marriage to Isabella. One contains the tiny *Psyche* cycle by Taddeo, which Vasari thought his best work: Psyche trying to hold Cupid back by his leg as he flies off into the air after the light has been turned on (not very well preserved).

The 'secret garden' at the south-eastern corner, more a terrace with a vast view, was laid out for Paolo Giordano and Vittoria by Giacomo del Duca, with a fountain coming out of the native rock, a carved scene of a boar and a hound, and a blind portal against the round tower. All this is lost.

The immense half-cellar rooms under the north wing remind us that at least 150 people used to live in the castle. During the Allied bombardments in the Second World War, several hundred people again squashed in.

The Town

The parish church, Santo Stefano, has a 19th-century painting of the Stoning of St Stephen, taking place by BRACCIANO's own LAKE. Not illogically: the 'Sea' of Galilee is much like it.

Just beneath the walls, Sophia built herself a small villa, to look up at the castle from. (It became the town hospital.) Behind her graceful façade, she took in a pre-existing chapel with a really fine Antoniazzo: painted with his own hand alone.

On the road down to the LAKE, Santa Maria del Riposo which contains (in the eastern apse) a realistic circumcision scene, not usual for the date.*

* But see BOLSENA, where there is one in the Cathedral. When Montaigne was in Rome in 1581, he attended a Jewish circumcision and described it in detail; so sixty years later did John Evelyn.

Bracciano, Lake of

The Lake – *Sabatinus lacus* to the Romans – is nearly circular, its shore 30 kilometres round, its surface 160 metres above sea-level, and its deepest place just at sea-level. It looks like one great crater with a few little craters intersecting it, but in fact is several. The soil at the edge is wonderfully fertile and for the first tens of metres out the shallow bottom is volcanic sand and chunks and dollops of thrown lava; wet-foot alders and willows; a few weeds; then a sharp weed-hidden lip, and a precipice to untold depths, where the giant eels have their home. Kites. Kingfishers.

The Lake is much fed by underwater springs, and the sudden chill as you swim over them may explain the golden Soldier of Bracciano. Is he a belief, a yarn, a treasure? Is he Etruscan or Roman? Better not ask. He is a presence. He lies on the bottom like the Narnian Lord in the '*Voyage of the* Dawn Treader', and his cold golden gauntlet fingers could easily pull swimmers down, perhaps especially children.

The normal clockwise current of circular water masses in the northern hemisphere is quite perceptible as you row home on calm evenings. Romans will tell you of the extreme dangers of swimming or sailing: they can bear to watch, but only just. Why is this?

We have long thought modern Romans' horror of lakes may be a survival of their forebears' horror at the annual ritual regicide they found at the small volcanic Lake of Nemi, south of Rome, home of the Golden Bough. Official murder of the king was an abomination to all good Romans, and the lakes remain contaminated. Seashores are different: Venus herself foam-born, the sea ours, *mare nostrum*, for trade, and conclusive victory.

The coast is developed for 100 kilometres north and south of Rome and our three lakes are almost unspoiled, BRACCIANO, nearest to Rome, being naturally the most affected. The spread of BRACCIANO itself has been planned to avoid spoiling what the people come there for. The same cannot be said of TREVIGNANO or of the strip west of ANGUILLARA. The west coast, where all is still princely hunting woods, and the east, where enlightened agriculture is holding its own, remain Arcadian.

In 109 AD the Emperor Trajan constructed an aqueduct to carry BRACCIANO's waters to Rome. His underground ring collector begins somewhere above VIGNA GRANDE, and descends clockwise, picking up springs and streams as it goes. No one knows its whole course, though there are *spie,* stone beehives marking the original digging spots, still used for maintenance and ventilation. It picks up the surface gravity flow of the Lake's natural outlet just north of ANGUILLARA, the origin of the River Arrone. Thence, often on magnificent aqueducts, to Rome, where it feeds the Vatican fountains and the Fontanone on the Janiculum.

This enormous system decayed in the Dark Ages but Pope Paul V brought it back into operation – hence its present name, the Acqua Paola. A later Pope, Pius VI, restored it yet again. A deeper extraction from the Lake is being added and a ring sewer is near completion, with twenty-one pumping stations on the way; the purified effluent goes into the Arrone. The streams no longer float nameless suds into the Lake, but the reedbeds are already mostly gone.

Various ideas for making money out of the Lake have so far come to nothing. During the 1960s it was proposed that the polluted waters of the Tiber should be diverted into it as a vast settling pond. During the 1970s a concentration of faceless capital registered in Lichtenstein was believed to have proposed (it never published anything, even its own name) to turn VICARELLO into a massive holiday development. The first can be regarded as dead, but there is no guarantee that the second is.

Calcata (and Narce)

CALCATA is one of the best preserved of the miniature medieval hill-towns. Views both from below and from above are spectacular, and so is the entrance through its double medieval gateway part-cut through the tufo. Also it is a fine place for that particular Northern Lazio pleasure, looking down through medieval arches at the bright green of the valley far below.

The parish church is dedicated to the Holy Name of Jesus. It contains portions of his foreskin, which Mary's midwife saved; her son, a perfume-seller, preserved it in a phial of oil, which was the very oil that Mary the sister of Martha anointed Jesus' feet with. It was in Rome in the early 9th century and the reliquary is dated 1064. Stolen during the Sack of Rome in 1527 by one of Charles V's *lanzechenecchi*, it was fortunately rediscovered in a cave and placed in the church whence, on the Feast of the Circumcision, it processed through the town. The expression of doubts would summon up thunder and lightning.

In the late 1960s John Betjeman said to us: 'Let us go on an expedition. I don't mind what: a small industrial town perhaps?' We took him to CALCATA because that was the only industrial town within miles, the industry being hazelnuts. Grown in wonderfully tidy groves in the TREIA VALLEY below and harvested in summer, they used to be brought up the rock on donkeys; there to be sorted, plucked, laid out on marked-out places, and turned, by very old men and women in faded black. In due course they were sold northwards, to the chocolate-makers.

Old CALCATA is now week-end inhabited by middle-aged ladies in furs and their smooth sons in designer jeans and shades. And antique shops, one called *Arsenico e vecchi Merletti* – 'Arsenic and Old Lace'. The marked-out place for nut-drying is now marked out for cars. Even so, it remains one of the great scenes of Italy.

The precipitous hill immediately upstream is the site of Narce, a place inhabited – along with LUNI SUL MIGNONE and SAN GIOVENALE – from the 13th century BC. The TREIA has often shifted its bed, many layers of human occupation have been uncovered and one piece of pot has the earliest representation of a centaur to be found in Central Italy, probably *c.* 650 BC.

The Caldara

'They say its voice is the devil's voice for it stops neither night nor day', or so we were told about this wide low crater. And certainly there is a constant little chatter or buzz as innumerable bubbles sizzle and twitch and burst and bounce through the fine mud or the delicate gravel or the cracks in the pinkish lava. Trains of bubbles move in the water like shimmying caterpillars. Some single bubbles make coloured circles in opaque water; others make opaque circles in clear water. Some muds are bright dark red, and there a different little reed grows, and a different forget-me-not. Old footprints show bright green but not hellish. Reed-cutters. The place is on the scale of the Solfatara outside Naples, but wild and gentle where that lowers and stinks. There are smells here, but they smell healthgiving.

To reach it, take a dirt track left off the road from MANZIANA to SASSO, some 2 kilometres after the end of the oak wood and immediately before a bar on the right: 700 metres along the track turn sharp left after a gate along an orange track. In summer, it is a fine place for a splash; in spring for a picnic.

Campagnano Romano, or Campagnano di Roma

The stateliest of the small towns yet caught in the tentacles of affluent Rome. The bouncy little hills around are now dotted with the villas of those who have paid high to leapfrog the apartment-block suburbs, to obtain cleaner air, a nostalgic hectare of orchard and vineyard, and a paddock for the decorative horse.

The name may come from the Campagna, but the bell – *campana* – it suggests appears on the solid, rounded Porta Romana that leads into the 18th-century town; on the splendid dolphin fountain in the main piazza (Vignola, despite the date?); on the ingeniously angular Cathedral tower of 1602; on the Cathedral's polychrome wooden ceiling and on its organ case; even in the shape of some of the newish street lights. The Corso is long and wide, its many fine doorcases signifying wealth and importance.

The Cathedral of San Giovanni lacks definite character, being much rebuilt, on ancient, possibly Etruscan, foundations. Its glory is a brilliant wooden ceiling which Giacomo del Duca made for the BRACCIANO Orsini. The choir stalls, classical, masculine, and firm, are also his.

The nave part of the ceiling fell during the Second World War and was renewed in 1971. The combination of dark green, oxblood, and dark gold with the large, deeply incised and pendent patterns makes for very glorious refulgence. In the chancel, where all is original, the Evangelists expatiate beyond the frames of their corner roundels; at the centre, superimposed on the quadripartite/cross pattern, a triangle-nimbused God the Father leans out to bless from a deeper roundel, in minatory glory. The John the Baptist, in the nave part, appears stylistically earlier and hardly meant to float horizontally: those uncarved soles to his feet were surely for standing on.

Below the Cathedral, beyond a nice early 16th-century aediculed fountain, the town runs out into shacks and pigsties and feral cats. Among them, a tiny romanesque church with a minute 2-column crypt at ground level.

Canale Monterano

The people of MONTERANO found refuge here.

The church of Santa Maria Assunta, built by Mattia de'Rossi (1637–95), may have been designed by the great Gian Lorenzo Bernini.

Canepina

The picturesque little town stretches up and over a well-wooded hillside. CANEPINA became an autonomous commune in the Dukedom of CASTRO and danced neatly between two stools: the people refused to pay old taxes to VITERBO or accept new mayors from CASTRO. Rancour was finally quelled by Girolama Orsini, widow of CASTRO's first duke and founder of the Convent delle Duchesse in VITERBO.

The nave and (over-chipped) colonnades of the parish church, Santa Maria Assunta, look 12th-century, but there are remains from a much earlier structure. The apse and the façade were tidied up in the Sangallo style.

The ex-convent of the Carmine now houses a 'Museum of Popular Tradition', with bygones, and not-so-long-gones: yesterday's tools and tableware not much different from the Etruscans' – overnight, into museums gone.

On the hill opposite, a very short pilgrimage away, stands Santa Maria delle Grazie, smart in new paint. It is a circle in a square, in pure and most minimal renaissance manner. Behind, almost hidden, is a much earlier place of worship, cut into the tufo. As we wandered, three women came and rang the bell: 'We always do that when there is a visitor'.

Canino

Outside the convent building at the upper end St Francis planted trees. Later, Franciscans from the ISOLA BISENTINA retired to it from over-arduous island life. The pleasant, modestly frescoed cloister was built for them in 1484 by Francesco Gabriele Farnese.

Pope Paul III Farnese was born here in 1468, in the little *rocca* his father had re-fortified and made comfortable: the great Collegiata stands near the site. According to Paul III, *se vuoi vivere in eterno/ /a Gradoli d'estate a Canino d'inverno* - 'if you want to live for ever/ /GRADOLI in summer, CANINO in winter'; and it is an amiable place. The Farnese contributed the handsome fountain (perhaps Vignola), and the little castle by the southern gate.

Napoleon declared his sister, Elisa Baciocchi, Queen of Etruria. Ingratiatingly, perhaps, Pope Pius VII allowed Napoleon's brother Lucien Bonaparte to buy land here, and later made him 'Prince of CANINO'. 'Luciano' he became, and lived and was buried here. As principalities go, CANINO was small: yet it had wooded hills to the north and fertile plains to the south, a mountain of its own, and an old abbey, which Luciano used as a summer residence, at MUSIGNANO.

When Napoleon arrested the Pope, Luciano and his family hastily embarked for America; captured by the British, they were imprisoned for four years. After 1815 they returned and Luciano improved the agriculture, embellished the town, exploited the mineral waters, and cared for the poor and the afflicted. Suddenly, in 1828, a plough broke through a thin volcanic crust, straight into an Etruscan tomb: first revelation of the vast and hitherto unknown necropolis of VULCI, much of it in his land. He dug for loot, not understanding: as each tomb was despoiled, it was refilled with debris, and cultivation resumed. When the Prince died the Princess carried on. Later the newly rich Torlonia family bought it.

CANINO's principal church, the Collegiata, had been majestically enlarged and rebuilt in the 1790s and today it is unexpectedly cosmopolitan. The Bonaparte Chapel contains monuments to Luciano's (and Napoleon's) father Carlo; to Luciano's first wife, Christine Boyer; and to the first child, Giovanni, he had with his second wife Alexandrine, all dated 1806–7. Each monument is tender and cool: neo-classicism at its restrained and poignant best. The English will recall Flaxman, but this is grander. Alexandrine's tomb for Luciano, of 1840, combining neo-classic drapes and neo-gothic business within a renaissance wall-tomb frame, fails.

Other good things were introduced by the Bonapartes: a late 15th-century Nativity (painter unknown), skyed and unframed, the composition mysteriously just off centre; a Pastura *Pietà*; other renaissance pictures; a strange and beautiful aedicule; a nice collection of rustic reliquaries; a font; an 18th-century ciborium; and a swirling wooden Madonna rising on a crescent moon. Outside, the piazza is filled with large cedars.

Capena

CAPENA's main claim to fame is that it was the home town of an Italic, Latin-speaking tribe, the Capenati. A splendid 3rd-century dish, now in the Villa Giulia Museum, showing a battle-elephant followed by her baby, came from here.

Modern CAPENA is south-west of ancient CAPENA and a 1452 tryptich by Antonio da Viterbo the Elder, the father of 'Pastura', is in the parish church.

CAPENA's lesser claim to fame is that its lake is, and by far, the least interesting in Northern Lazio. Sometimes it has been known as Lago di Puzzo – 'Stink Lake' – and some of the people of CAPENA wrongly think it does not exist.

Capodimonte

From 1385 CAPODIMONTE belonged to the Farnese, and the beautiful Giulia, facilitator of the family's papal fortunes, was brought up here.

> O that Capo di Monte is such a beautiful thing! Indeed for that little palace, for that little peninsula bathed by that lake, beautified by those little islands, adorned with those gardens and surrounded by that shade, I would give more Tempes and more Parnassuses than ever were.

Thus Annibal Caro, cultivated secretary to the younger Cardinal Alessandro Farnese in the 1560s. And apart from one thuggishly misplaced church and one enviously misplaced 19th-century palazzo, it is still 'a beautiful thing'.

The renaissance Castle is octagonal, embracing a square medieval one. Antonio da Sangallo the Younger, the Farnese family architect, was responsible for most of what we now see.

The main rooms of his wonderfully elegant building look out over the Lake. They are arranged round a square courtyard, which backs on to the older fortified castle, and is entered by a high bridge over a moat: this is the formal front, where the suave upper parts emerge bud-like from the fortress base.

Inside, the hugely thick medieval tower wall has a tightly packed little chapel inserted right into it, behind great wooden doors. A special internal staircase from the courtyard was installed for popes to ascend on their white mule: sunlight reflected from the lake glitters on its ceilings. The uppermost room of all, aptly called Paradiso, was at first an open loggia, catching the cool of the evening and the beauties of the Lake and the islands and the hills and mountains beyond. Only one fresco remains: of a Farnese being presented by a pope with certain honours he had dearly hoped to have been presented with but actually was not. Others were whitewashed in the 1830s after an outbreak of cholera – its waterborne character was still not understood.

The thuggish church was built in 1763; perhaps the architect never saw the site? It has pleasant things inside. The Palazzaccio – 'Horrible Palazzo' – that somewhat damages the view from the Castle was put up by the Poniatowski family, who had been kings in Poland, when the then owners of the Castle refused to sell it to them.

As for the beautiful Giulia, who was born in 1474, she had been promised from a baby to Orsino Orsini, Count of Pitigliano and Lord of Bassanello (today VASANELLO), who was related to the

Cardinal Rodrigo Borgia who became Alexander VI, and whose mother had brought up the Cardinal's daughter Lucrezia and his other children. Giulia and Orsino were married, she 15 with long golden hair, and he 18, and the Cardinal, who was nearly 60, was irresistibly smitten. She became his mistress, and her long relationship with him as Pope did wonders for the Farnese: her brother Alessandro was made a Cardinal at an early age and (though mocked as 'Cardinal Petticoat') went on to become Pope Paul III. Pope Alexander was possessive and at one point objected to Giulia returning to CAPODIMONTE where her elder brother was dying; her husband tried to reclaim her; she shut herself up at CAPODIMONTE; and when she finally set out for Rome, she was captured by the troops of Charles VIII of France and imprisoned at MONTEFIASCONE. Ransomed by the Pope, she was released and returned to Rome.

Eventually Alexander, near 70, began to show greater interest in the doings of his elder children: Lucrezia he left in Rome in 1501 for a time actually as his deputy, and Cesare's advancement had become one of his principal aims. Giulia then returned to VASANELLO. Alexander VI died in 1503; Orsini also died; Giulia married a handsome Neapolitan; and died in 1524. Her brother put her naked on his tomb in St Peter's – representing Justice. It is said that she always took things calmly.

Capodimonte has one of the best remaining *cantine* – the wine cellars cut deep down into the cool rock. This is one of the few places where you can still find *Cannaiolo,* a soft sweet wine to drink most comfortably with the local half-leavened biscuity doughnuts.

Capranica

Drive up the Cassia from Rome and at the end of the SUTRI narrows CAPRANICA suddenly rears up, almost over your head. The road sweeps you up, almost into, and then away from, the town. The last thing as you rush by is the calm, severe façade of the church of the Madonna del Piano, probably by Vignola, with two chaste colours of stone. (It has a fine ceiling and some good pictures.)

This was part of the territories of those lords of misrule the Anguillara family: Petrarch stayed with them, and praised the climate, the landscape, and the fauna, but objected to the bandits, who caused even the shepherds to carry arms.

There are in effect three towns: the modern one; the rather grand renaissance *borgo*, full of palazzi from the late 16th century when Cardinal Altemps was papal Governor; and, led into by a narrow bridge and a towered gate, the oldest part. The church of San Pietro at the south-eastern tip of everything may have been the church of the 10th-century fortified village.

The enormous 19th-century churches of San Giovanni and Santa Maria replace earlier ones and both display so much crimson velvet, so many and such powerful chandeliers, such heavy, gilded, overall opulence, as to make them outstanding survivals of a fashion now heartily reversed.

In Santa Maria, there is a good triptych of the school of Pastura in which San Terenziano shows a cool thigh. Other, later, frescos show even more doubtful holy activities. The Duomo (San Giovanni) on the other hand has a waxwork of a beloved priest, with one poor boy, barefoot, hands together, gazing up, and a smaller, rich boy, in a sailor suit and nice shoes and socks, pointing the poor boy out to the priest.

The plum of the middle town is the basically 13th-century Franciscan church of San Lorenzo. (The staired front is 1920s.) A regular five-bayed nave-and-two-aisle church of moderate height opens through a round arch into a (probably later) pro-chancel of the same width but much taller, which in turn opens into a perhaps 14th-century chancel with a lower vaulted ceiling on romanesque columns. The effect is mighty fine. The nave has been turned into an exhibition hall where the vaguely sexy clichés of a provincial art show and photographs from the town dress shop do not go so very well with the remaining frescos. But on the end wall is an intriguing (and magnificent) early 15th-century monument to two Anguillara brothers, the twins Francesco and Nicola. According to the art historian Rosella Cervone it is by the Umbrian, Paolo da Gualdo, who also did the part-dismantled 'Briobris' monument in VETRALLA. Thick-winged angels hold back the curtains of a big and intricate *baldacchino* to show the two soldiers, armed and armoured, tilted diagonally so that we should see both. Between plaited and twisted columns, are the brothers' 'devices': very peculiar variations on the eared eels of the Anguillara. On the left, note the hand emerging or protruding from three and a half coils-worth of eel; and on the right, chimaera-like, the little monk's head protruding or emerging from the winged forehead of a bearded face with pigs' ears, and the eagle's claw coming round the ear, and the turned-up tail coming from somewhere else. Twisted rods are an Etruscan symbol of death; the Etruscan genius of death is winged; chimaeras are Etruscan (see Appendix I).

In the same piazza, the white marble doorway to the one-time hospital came from the earlier church of San Giovanni, and before that perhaps from a destroyed abbey. The carving is obscure and entertaining: man-headed birds greet each other in the foliage; a vine-leaf gnaws a vine-stalk; lions have Ronald Colman moustaches.

When Mazzini passed through among the spent volcanoes and the Etruscan tombs, he said he felt he was walking in the dust of the centuries mixed with the ashes of ancient heroes. He could have liked the children's rhyme recorded here:

Thumb says I'm hungry.
Forefinger says there's no bread.
Middle finger says what shall we do?
Fourth finger says we'll steal some!
Little finger says oh no we won't; if we steal we hang.

Elevated moralist that he was, Mazzini would not have found the paternalistic message of the Duomo waxwork sufficient, and would have gone on: 'Big toe says best have the revolution'.

Caprarola

The Palace of CAPRAROLA is one of the great achievements of the Renaissance. Setting, palace, *palazzina*, decoration, gardens, fountains, and parks add up to an explicit philosophy of how life may be lived through the whole gamut from near-royal public grandeur to near-heavenly privacy. St Charles Borromeo, one of the first and most puritanical of the Counter-Reformation saints, said of CAPRAROLA '*che sara il Paradiso*'. Or, as Vasari put it, 'though . . . in a place where it can give but little pleasure to the generality, [the palace] is marvellously situated for one who wishes occasionally to withdraw from the worries and tumult of the city'.

In 1504, Cardinal Alessandro Farnese the Elder (who in 1534 became Pope Paul III) had bought CAPRAROLA intending in time to build there. The idea of a huge, probably pentagonal, fortress prevailed and plans poured forth, from Baldassare Peruzzi, from Antonio da Sangallo the Younger (already working for the Farnese on their palazzo in Rome, and elsewhere in Lazio), and others. A substantial beginning was made on the Sangallo plan, but work was slow.

Paul III died in 1549. In 1537, he had cut the Dukedom of CASTRO out of the Papal State for his son, Pier Luigi and, though distant, CAPRAROLA was included. In 1545, he advanced Pier Luigi to Duke of Parma and Piacenza and it was his grandson, another Cardinal

Alessandro Farnese, who came into CAPRAROLA and made of it what we see.

The Building

His grandfather was long dead, the Counter-Reformation was on the way, his own papal ambitions were thwarted – times had so changed by 1558 that Alessandro discontinued the giant fort. Antonio da Sangallo too was dead and the commission went to Jacopo Barozzi da Vignola (1507–73), who had by that time succeeded Antonio as the family architect. He was the most substantial of the mannerist architects who worked in Central Italy. He had worked for King Francis I of France at Fontainebleau with Primaticcio for three years, where a remarkable grotto remains, with the usual three openings and rusticated giant caryatids. He later built the revolutionary church of the Gesù in Rome for Cardinal Alessandro. CAPRAROLA was now to be more a palace than a fortress, but at the same time it should declare the unarguable grandeur of the Farnese. All this Vignola performed.

Mario Praz, in his 1940 *Garden of the Senses*, saw renaissance villas as essays in the art of keeping cool: where in France and England grand builders took their cue from silence and nature, in Italy and Spain 'summer was our teacher.' Everything at CAPRAROLA was to glorify and heighten that sweet moment when you come indoors from the noonday sun, and the equally sweet moment when you step out into the evening cool, to the sound of water, and to build glorious fantasies upon both.

This; but not only. What the Cathedral at Chartres is to the European Middle Ages, when every modestly decorated parish church was the poor man's Bible, so, Praz is right, is CAPRAROLA to the High Renaissance: 'a supreme formulary of our cinquecento', 'a breviary of proud cardinals', a 'bible of the rich'.

The form was given by the part-built fortress. Vignola gently converted the five bastions into an enthronement for the vast matter we see today. Within the pentagon, he placed the circular court Antonio da Sangallo had first suggested, a harmonious, inside-out *tempietto*, reminiscent both of Raphael's proposed circular cortile at Villa Madama and of Giulio Romano's at Mantua: Heinrich Woelfflin thought it 'possibly the most magnificent [cortile] in secular architecture'. At the top, canted inwards, it concludes with a wide, domestically urban terrace all round, the uppermost storey opening squatly and intimately on to it. To reach the upper floors, Vignola built the huge single spiral staircase inside one of the angles. It derives from Bramante's staircase at the Belvedere in the Vatican, perhaps from some ideas of Leonardo's, and from the one Vignola himself had put inside a dovecote at Minerbio.

The approach began 25 kilometres away, at MONTEROSI, whence Vignola built a new road to provide as many views of the Palace as the lie of the land allowed. He gave the town a new gate* and rebuilt much of it, driving the present long main street straight through and up, sometimes on legs over the old winding lanes, and dividing it into two parts known ever after as Corsica and Sardinia.

The last lap consists of the two oval horse-staircases with a triple-arched space between; the great windy brick-paved piazza; and last of all, sharp, scissoring, staircases up to the drawbridge over the moat, and the main, narrow, entrance. (Behind all this sequential complexity may lie thoughts about the Roman Temple of Fortune at Praeneste (Palestrina), the ruins of which architects at the time were trying to reconstruct, as well as what Bramante had part-built, in the Belvedere cortile (see Appendix II)).

The triumphal route has been uphill all the way, and the great building dominates town and countryside with utter confidence. SORACTE alone punctuates a view that reaches almost to Rome. High and mighty, this is a civilian royal palace, built to proclaim not only the uttermost in cultivated splendour, but also that its owners had once fought and conquered, and would do so again if necessary. The institutional propriety of a cardinal of the post-Tridentine Church acting so royally in a territory that had been part of the Patrimony of St Peter was not open to question.

The Fabric

When Vignola took over, he found – or himself hewed – an annular cave in the tufo under what was already built, leaving a central mushroom stalk to hold up the whole palace. This space (with the kitchens off it) was lit through overhead grilles. The structure above modelled the hierarchy of the occupants: first standard-sized rooms for knights and pages, on the two floors above the cellar; then two floors of state rooms (in front and gigantic) and private apartments (behind and semi-gigantic). As well as the distinction between state and family, there was another between summer and winter rooms, facing north or south. As the Cardinal-builder combined spiritual authority with temporal, a sombre and magnificent circular chapel

* Pulled down since Turner sketched it.

occupies the eastern of the two front angles, articulating the passage from *The Labours of Hercules* to the *Deeds of the Farnese* – the fresco subjects of the adjoining rooms.

The Curia and the Nobility went – or were transported – up the glorious spiral staircase, enjoying a frescoed allegory of the *Creation of the World by Mathematics*. Whence they emerged into a circle set within its tangential pentagon. (The servants, invisibly, spun up and down spiral staircases within the thickness of the walls.)

Vignola died in 1573, and a new architect was not immediately appointed: the great stable and coach-house block to the west was built to Vignola's design ten years later.

Gardens, Parks, Buildings, and Fountains

The overall system is that to which the great families and cardinals in Rome were building: the palazzo; the formal gardens; a wood or park; and last the *palazzina*, or villa. Throughout, fountains, statues, and surprises. At CAPRAROLA there was also a *barco* – deerpark – lower down the hillside, with its own *casina* – hunting lodge – and a small lake and nymphaeum (pictured in the Villa at BAGNAIA).

Behind the palace itself are two square, parterred, gardens which are 'secret' in that they could only be reached or seen into from the private rooms. Above them comes a tract of planted wood, with careful paths laid through it: the *barchino* – the little park, as opposed to the *barco*. This in turn leads up to another formal, wondrously fountained, Giardino Grande, which forms the approach to the Palazzina del Piacere – the 'Little Pleasure Palace'. The Giardino Grande and the Palazzina were made and built mostly in the 1580s, and share certain modular dimensions. This supremely elegant and habitable composition, designed after Vignola's death by Giacomo del Duca, was for the Farnese Cardinals' privacy behind the grandeurs in front.

The first fountain, the Lily, is a single jet in a wide, low, smooth bowl, a mirror of water chanced upon in a glade. To its left a large male figure on a plinth, with watery hair, puts his finger to his lips – Silence; to the right, a female holds artichokes between her breasts – Prudence; between them the steep and spectacular ascent to the Palazzina takes off.

It is first glimpsed, a long way up, far behind two great lounging river gods (with attendant creatures) on either side of a giant calyx or beaker, at the top end of a dolphin-rope of twisting water; on either side are flamboyantly ascending and undulating steps and side walls; at an indefinable distance beyond, which it seems to fill, is the Palazzina. It shows first as an unexpectedly classical, single-storey structure: the perhaps over-fragile, triple-arched loggia seems to be flanked by unpierced walls and superscribed by a short stretch of cool attic roof: a garden house perhaps . . . or a screen?

Just before we reach the upper piazza, the walls and steps round the lounging river gods have opened out into an oval space, complex and atilt, with beasts and giant masks and heavy squat rustications and earthquake baroque pilasters. The finish is various-sized pebble-dash; and there were all round (and will be again when repairs are complete) the flashing textures and sounds of falling, rising, streaming water.

What we had glimpsed from below was the loggia on the upper floor of the Palazzina. Beneath this (quite sexily) frescoed loggia are the three dark arches of a portico – *Hypnerotomachia*'s Roads to Felicity – and on either side a single distant window on each floor, set in the smooth ashlar. This is a fully habitable place and the pleasures it is to be devoted to are, as St Charles foresaw, the personal pleasures promised in Paradise. A letter of 1584 to Cardinal Alessandro from Cardinal Gambara at BAGNAIA proposes that among these would be watching the fountains below while they dined – as befitted their age – in the pleasant shelter of the loggia.

Around 1620, Cardinal Odoardo Farnese had the effect completed with the *Plain of Caryatids* across the front of the Palazzina, and the wood-surrounded, parapeted garden behind. The caryatid herms, he and she, huge, variously garbed and variously occupied (hugging a rabbit, blowing a conch, holding hands and gossiping), edge a great clipped box-decorated area, each with a vase, or pot, or tub, on his or her head, for tumbling plants – or perhaps flambeaux.

At the back, the Palazzina is one storey high and the three-arched loggia – now glazed – is level with the still rising ground. All appears today in relative *déshabillé* – green lawn instead of figured box around the stone seats and fountains and parapets. At the distant top a modest, rusticated gate holds up three great Farnese lilies. Note a curious swaddled-caterpillar motif on the not quite pilaster jambs.

Gerolamo Rainaldi completed this upper part of the gardens and also designed the two pavilions, with their crisply nodding rustications, beside the first fountain and the 'dolphin' skein; these had perhaps been part of Vignola's original plan. The statues were done by Pietro Bernini, father of the great Gian Lorenzo.

The whole of this vast construction is *architettura di percorso* – 'architecture for moving through' – and time has made it into one of its own supreme achievements: meaning dressed as grey stone rises straight out of matter dressed as green grass. Make of it what it will make of you.

The Interior

Mario Praz called the inside of the Palace 'a busy factory of post-tridentine allegories'. The entire surface of all the state rooms and of all the grand private rooms is frescoed. So are some of the rooms below the *piano nobile*. The team leader for this vast work was Taddeo Zuccari, the elder of two brothers whose work, or the work of whose school, is in a dozen other villas in Lazio.

Vasari quotes an enormously long letter from Annibal Caro, the Cardinal's all-important secretary and agent. After describing what in general is required for the 'bedchamber of an illustrious lady', Annibal gets down to some of the detail:

> At the top of the oval, Dawn. This can be done in several ways, but I will select those which I consider to be the most graceful for painting. We will have a girl, as beautiful as the poets sing, composed of roses, purple, red, and similar charms of colour and flesh-tints. Her habit should possess three distinct colours, white, scarlet and orange, corresponding to her three conditions, and I would give her a white diaphanous shift. [And so on, with her other garments. Moreover,] the shift and the tunic should be moved by the wind and flying in folds.

Tithonus, her husband, is to seem to be in his second childhood; her lover Cephalus to have his dog at his side; a woman representing Diligence to be obscuring the Sun's rays and to be wearing a

> helmet surmounted by a cock flapping its wings and crowing . . .

The letter – several thousand words on the one room, and with a bow in the direction of the painter's 'imagination' – eventually ends:

> I cannot think now of anything else except that you should consult our illustrious lord upon everything, and add or remove anything as he may suggest, and endeavour to do yourself honour. Farewell.

The painting comes in two styles: a large forthright one for set pieces, where Caro's instructions prevailed, and a delicate straight-limbed one for decoration, derived from the ancient Roman, via Raphael, to which the name Zuccaresque is often given.

In 1566 Taddeo died. His brother Federico took over, but was soon dismissed for dallying in Rome. The job went to Giacomo

Bertoia but the change was not for the better: Bertoia's work is cold and formal compared with the joyful and fecund Zuccari; he brought with him from his native Parma a heavy weight of Correggio. Federico later worked on the gory *Last Judgement* in the dome of Florence Cathedral.

The staircase vault was done, at least in part, by Antonio Tempesti. Other names show up in the documents: Barthel Spranger, Cesare Rosetti, Pietro Bernini, Giovanni de' Vecchi, Raffaellino da Reggio. But it is hard to know which did what: it all amounts to a major museum's worth. A good account comes in Faldi's book.

Generally the picture in the middle of the ceiling is what the room is about: summer, angels, Hercules, wool, philosophy, justice, etc., and above all the exploits and merits of the Farnese family and their modestly adopted deity, Hercules. In the Hall of Hercules – the Salone dei Fasti d'Ercole – which contains a large indoor fountain in grottesque work, note the half-finished temple of Hercules: the older man in front is Vignola, the younger Bertoia. Note also, in the vault, Hercules creating the LAKE OF VICO by plunging his staff in the ground and pulling it out again. Here *fasti* means labours.

In the Salone dei Fasti Farnesiani on the other hand, it is better translated by its normal meaning: pomps. Between Hercules and the Farnese, standing in the eastern bastion, is the Chapel – circular, sombre, nearly but not quite oppressive. How the richness is obtained can be calculated by reading the thirty-six horizontal lines or layers, of either decoration or architecture, downwards from the top of the dome. There are full-length pictures of all the apostles, eight in fresco, four in stained glass: why St John is a woman is hard to guess. In the little vault above St James the Great is another portrait of Vignola.

The Farnesian Pomps show Farnese Dukes marrying Austrian and French princesses and Cardinals hobnobbing in a military manner with Francis I of France and the Emperor Charles V, and socialising with the Queen of France, Catherine de' Medici, and the King of Navarre, and the Constable, and the Dukes of Guise and of Nemours, and others. King Philip II of Spain is there. And Pope Paul III is seen in the act of excommunicating Henry VIII of England.

In the picture of an earlier Farnese riding with the Emperor into Paris to meet Francis I, the men holding the two right-hand supports to the canopy are the Zuccari brothers, and behind is their father. There is also a poignant picture of now vanished CASTRO, the capital of the Dukedom.

In the corners of the Council of Trent Room, the *trompe l'oeil* columns were painted by Vignola himself.

When you come to the Summer Apartments of Cardinal Alessandro, overlooking the northern garden, everybody is at once more naked. The first room illustrates Philosophy, including Diogenes in his tub. The Tower Room still smells of the cedar of its handsome ceiling. West-facing are the Winter Rooms, where the subjects are biblical and the principal personages at least have put their clothes on again.

In the Judgement Room we must pause. The subject is all about us – good judgements, Solomon, and so on – but the interest is the decoration. Everywhere at CAPRAROLA the main 'examples', the set-pieces of painting to illustrate the theme, are in simulated frames, some very large, all held together by a network or trellis of decoration. This varies from the genially space-filling to the profoundly related and mysterious. In this room the decoration reaches an apogee of beauty and mystery.

In general the decoration here is not erotic, as it might have been before the Council of Trent. In this Winter Room, there is something happening which you would expect to be erotic or unpleasant or both, and mysteriously is neither. Everywhere the forms are slender, but so etiolated that they become, in one of Faldi's admirable phrases, 'filiform and insubstantial'. Proto-rococo colours of mauve and pale green appear. Unspeakably elegant string patterns hang straight down (or rise straight up, come to that) carrying (or supporting) architecture of a kind never seen and never to be seen. Airy follies and domes are suspended from four threads or held up by four spider-thin legs: one does not know which. Willowy golden-brown girls stand in cages through which the winds of time and heaven are gently blowing. A woman is taking her clothes off and they are being handed down by heraldic attendants to gnomes below, though an objecting matron rushes to put a stop to things. Other women are hanging by their hair from slender beams which float in the air. In the next scene, the beauty in the cage has won and is seen quite naked; the gnomes have presumably fought off the objecting matron. The golden-brown suspended people are still pendant.

The puzzle is deeper than the iconography. Are all these people enjoying an alternative gravity? Are they being marvellously upheld by the long thin curly tails many of them have instead of legs? The effect throughout is weirdly cheerful; no one appears to be suffering. An alternative world? Drugs? If so, a charming trip. (See also

BAGNAIA, where decorations of the same miraculously off-beat kind enliven the Gambara Pavilion.)

The World-map Room invites comparison with the Vatican's. The shapes of the world, of Europe, of Italy, of Central Italy, as known and felt in the 1570s and 80s were mostly not very different from today's, but the details of the differences are interesting: the anticipated Southern continent, the Arctic Ocean full of ships. The cartographer was Giovanni Antonio from Varese. Huge figures, America blacker than Africa, symbolise the Continents, coevals of those in the grand passage in the Palazzo del Drago in BOLSENA.

How was life in such rooms? Mario Praz quotes the 17th-century Lorenzo Magalotti, writing to a friend in northern Europe:

> You come in at midday all heated; you have taken in more heat through your eyes from the reflections of a sun which scalds whatever it touches than you get all over your body from morning to evening in your country; you come into a ground floor room which after it has taken the cool of the night has been caulked up with curtains, with mats, with window panes, with shutters, and with fine muslins soaked in water or scented vinegars ... [There are] bowls of galingale on all the tables, the scent of which cools the air and restores your spirits through your sense of smell.

The Town

Under the great straight street, the old town continues to twist and climb as best it can: its cathedral is of little interest, but the nicely coherent late-16th-century church of Santa Maria della Consolazione – or of San Francesco – not only has a galaxy of verdant mermaids and green men and a windy Annunciation and the Father Almighty in a small bush on its door but a very glorious coffered and gilded ceiling with Franciscan figures in high relief.

The handsome palazzo at the corner of the final piazza (now the Town Hall, and little more than a front for old buildings) has been attributed to Vignola. A plaque on a fine house in the straight street recalls a visit there by King James III (the Old Pretender) and Queen Clementina in 1725.

Santa Teresa

On the next fold of hills to the south, and to be part of the Palace's view, Cardinal Odoardo Farnese in the 1620s founded the church dedicated originally to St Silvester, but now known as St Teresa, and a convent. At right-angles to it stands the Palazzina del Cardinale. On its wonderfully neat mini-façade, a flourish of Farnese lilies ensconced within triple festoons recalls the rich decoration of the contemporary church at VALLERANO. Its door is perhaps the last and most sophisticated version of the so-familiar shouldered doorway that we know from the earliest Etruscan tombs. (But see also the Viterbo Gate at SAN MARTINO AL CIMINO, reputedly by Borromini.)

Inside are three of the grandest-ever coffered wooden ceilings (the best of them in abominable condition) and several fine plaster ones.

The church itself is the masterpiece of Gerolamo Rainaldi (1570–1655). There is no middle view of the complete composition – it can be glimpsed and read only from the Palace opposite and from its own little cliff-top piazza: rich, no mere piece of scenery from close to it is equally satisfactory. Note the faint suggestion of absent herms in the shallow downward-shrinking pilasters superimposed on others.

Rainaldi had worked in Northern Italy and there is a Venetian feeling about the interior, with its strong all-round cornice and balconied windows. The High Altar, very much in the Palladian manner, has a well-lit space round and behind. There are several fine paintings, including a Lanfranco and a reputed Guido Reni, of heroically gory subjects. In the Convent, the remarkable, if damaged, painting of Jesus at table being waited on by angels with folded napkins. Also a collection of vestments of the time: the designs open and lavish, huge blown roses, tulips; carnations and lilies; gold, green, yellow; dark blue; a fine mauve.

The Barco

A few kilometres downhill the ruins of Vignola's villa-like hunting lodge on top of a little knoll remain in the wild woods, and there is still a roadside chapel to the Madonna del Barco.

After 1649

In 1649, Pope Innocent X Pamphili destroyed CASTRO and took its territories back into the papal dominions except for CAPRAROLA, which the Farnese, along with their Roman glories, were allowed to keep. In 1731, on the death of Duke Francesco Farnese, all passed to the Spanish Bourbons, through the last Farnese, Elisabetta of Pavia, wife of Philip V, King of Spain. In the early 20th century, it belonged to Prince Alfonso Doria Pamphili, who lent it to the mother of the remarkable Gladys Deacon, who for a while was

Duchess of Marlborough and was able to compare living at Blenheim with living at CAPRAROLA.

Finally, the Palace has passed to the State. Most is now open to the public and massive works of restoration are in progress: admirable but for two things. One is the outside colour, a garish orange: it was, and we hope will be again, a mild russet gold. The other is the introduction of rhododendrons: enough is known of the *verde storico* – the historic vegetation – for this kind of solecism to be avoided.

Carbognano

The Selva Carbonaria, from which the name comes, was the whole wooded cover of the CIMINO. (Much of it was devoted to the production of *carbone* – charcoal – by *carbonari*.) The Farnese erected the Rocca, on top of the previous castle, and the beautiful Giulia (see CAPODIMONTE) is supposed to have liked it. There is a large neo-classical parish church and below the town, a tiny church of San Filippo Neri: '1636', furnished with all the idioms of the day, amiably interpreted.

Castel Cellesi

The history is unusual: it was built from scratch as an embodiment of social doctrine.

The Papacy was shewing its (infrequent) interest in the possible improvement of agriculture, and permitted the sale, in 1663, of a small castle and its land to one Girolamo Cellese, Count of Pistoia, who wanted it for an agricultural settlement. So he built a little town on a plan which, according to the architectural historian Mario Munari, expressed 'a consciousness of the real relations between social classes' and the 'potential antagonism between them'.

Quite so: there was a rectangular piazza on to which the Cellesi family's palazzo and the other genteel houses gave, and a long triangular section containing two very narrow streets' worth of peasant houses; between rectangle and triangle came the church. The peasant houses, though new-built, were medieval in size and convenience, signalling that no social or political improvement was to be expected. The piazza was entered only through a fine gate, outside which the poor man kept his station.

Castel d'Asso

CASTEL D'ASSO was rediscovered in 1817; Mrs Gray and George Dennis visited it. Then it was forgotten for a hundred years except by the landowner.

Like NORCHIA, it is a solitary and beautiful spot full, in the spring, of asphodel and grape hyacinth and bird-song. Lines, almost streets, of great ravaged tombs along cliffs face the site of the Etruscan town across the valley. Traces of gates, cisterns, and cuniculi have been found, and terracotta tiles from the same matrix as some at ACQUA-ROSSA, showing Hercules fighting the Cretan Bull, probably from a 6th-century BC temple. Axia was the Roman name; there was a castle-village in the 9th or 10th century, a bit of which still sticks up.

Castel Sant'Elia

The ancient places are down in the spectacular gorge. The upper village has a nice 18th-century approach, but its castle is only great old red molars worn down almost to rock level.

The main interest on top is a tidy pilgrimage and conference complex, today run by Polish monks, formerly the Franciscan Convent of Santa Croce in Sassonia, founded by German Franciscan friars in the late 19th century.

You may from within it walk down to the cave called Santa Maria ad Rupes, St Mary of the Precipice: 144 steps in the rock cut by an 18th-century hermit who lived there for 37 years. It is now a museum of vestments and church gear: 12th- to 14th-century.

On down from the cave (but you may go another way, by road), you come to the ancient Basilica of Sant'Elia. The walls of the gorge glow red-gold; its cliffs, tradition claims, were sacred to an Etruscan rock god, Falacrus. Here the Romans built a temple to Diana, which in turn became a hermitage for the early 6th-century Frankish Saint Anastasius. The first church was built in the 8th century, and the present Basilica dates from the early 11th century – simple, tall, and cool. Bits of the earlier church are incorporated over the doorcases and bits of the Roman temple have been found round about.

Inside, two light colonnades carry the ornate festoons of re-used Roman capitals. The classically, almost Greekly, proportioned baldaquin is wide open and airy, like the ones at TUSCANIA: the effect is an enthronement of the table by bright lines of light, utterly different from the heavy closed crowns that were to come later.

The Byzantine frescos are interesting for being signed by Giovanni and Stefano and their nephew Nicola, in the late 11th and early 12th centuries.

A place calmly grand.

Castelgiuliano

From BRACCIANO, a long road meanders south to the 17th-century village of CASTELGIULIANO: three parallel streets, built by the Hospital of the Holy Spirit as a new agricultural farm settlement. The presiding field-palace, a most conclusively placed civilian castle, stands high on a sloping talus. Screened off within the Castle's enclosure is a three-sided service cortile; and a church which embodies an earlier building – see the outside of the apse. Its façade, inward-facing, has nicely modish downwards-diminishing pilasters. The main building has a (later) staircase as magnificent as any of its date in Rome.

CASTELGIULIANO belongs to the Patrizi family and by a chance of family fortune its pristine *piano nobile* was never inhabited from the day it was finished in the 17th century, until the present owner married a few years ago and at last moved in. The garden is one of the best in the loose style known in Italy as 'English'.

Beyond and below a good track continues along the stream to CERVETERI, past a waterfall (much of it now taken for electricity), and an ancient ruined bridge; here and there, signs of Etruscan water workings. In some of the pools in the stream, the surface tension of the water is such that 20 lire pieces will easily float, and the water-boatmen – *Corixidae* – are able to be unusually large (see also CELLERE). Where the stream runs through tunnels of foliage, wet leaves on the wet rocks will suddenly hop into the water: tiny frogs. As in the haiku,

> At the sound of one jumping in,
> All the frogs
> Jump in.

Castelnuovo di Porto

The main street drops straight into the Palazzo Ducale. This, a rebuild of the late 1500s, is hugely high on the town side, with flanking but enclosed towers, and apparently symmetrical, a great stair zigs up right, for half the height of the podium; then zags left, and only at the top of all this is the entrance to a vastly elevated ground floor. The *piano nobile* (probably with Zuccari-type decorations) is a floor above that; then there is yet another floor; and on the sky-line, two little bells. On the Tiber side, all the symmetry has merged into a cascade of tiled roofs.

It was not long ago a prison, '*all'Italiana*, where the prisoners came and went as they wished, and did the shopping (and cooked) for the deputy governor's wife', according to Zeppegno. Today it is sinking into irreparable ruin. It belongs to the Commune.

Castiglione in Teverina

Below the town, a grand chapel, Santa Maria delle Neve, St Mary of the Snows. MDVIIII, says the doorcase.

Up in the town, the remains of a Farnese castle and wide streets. The church – 1630, says the door – contains two very winning, Caravaggesque, 'Mary' pictures: well-dressed and sociable.

Castro

Qui Fu Castro

The CASTRO that here once was, was the capital city of a hundred-and-ten year long Farnese dukedom. It was to have been for the Farnese what the earlier Pienza (near Siena) was for Pius II, an ideal city where everything would please the eye, gratify the heart, and redound through time to their credit.

If you read the triumphant and abominable message HERE WAS CASTRO where it is carved on its stone, you are in a dank valley bottom west of the little town of FARNESE, a mile or so off the road that goes on to Manciano (in Tuscany), on which you will have seen the sign to the Rovine di Castro. There is a stream, and woods, and a track up to the right, which you follow. The ruins of CASTRO are in the wood that lies across the field before you as you emerge over the shoulder of the first little rise.

The Etruscans – and earlier people – were at CASTRO: necropoles have revealed chamber-tombs, trench-tombs, and at least ten columbaria. One with some 400 'pigeonholes' is further along that same track where it goes down to the now broken bridge over the Olpeta. Beyond that bridge, the Etruscan road – the old Via Clodia – was cut straight through 81 metres of tufo: its walls are up to 20 metres high.

Between the columbarium and the bridge, Belgian archaeologists in 1967 uncovered a 4-metre-long bronze and oak *biga*.* The CASTRO

* *Biga* = bi *juga* = two yoke = a two-horse (and two-wheel) chariot; there were trigas too, and quadrigas still top arches all over Europe.

biga was probably made about 530–20 BC, probably at VULCI; and certain details of its axles are still seen in Tuscia farm carts. There are *bigas* on the ACQUAROSSA tile decorations, but only one other has been found, at Monteleone di Spoleto, now in the Metropolitan Museum in New York. The CASTRO *biga* and the skeletons of two horses found by it are now in the Villa Giulia Museum in Rome.

Other Etruscan finds from here are in the little museum at ISCHIA DI CASTRO: winged monsters, lions amiable and fierce, panthers, horses, pots galore. Also nearby is an unexplained 13-metre-long altar – the *Ara di Tufo* – with a cornice and rams' and lions' heads, dating from the sixth century BC.

The Romans used the place too. Then it was a bishopric, with a cathedral probably not unlike the church of Santa Maria Maggiore at TUSCANIA.

By the early 16th century the local branch of the Farnese family were coveting CASTRO and in 1527, while the Emperor Charles V's *lanzechenecchi* were sacking Rome, Pier Luigi Farnese, who had become a Captain of the Imperial Forces, persuaded the inhabitants to accept him as their protector. Pope Clement VII Medici, who had escaped to Orvieto, ordered Pier Luigi to leave CASTRO, and his relative Galeazzo Farnese, of the LATERA branch of the family, to inflict exemplary punishment and sack the city. This Galeazzo did, admitted by traitors and using Corsican mercenaries, on 28 December 1527. But Galeazzo's was not the sack that coined the phrase.

Ten years later Pier Luigi's father, Cardinal Alessandro Farnese the Elder, had become Pope Paul III. CASTRO was conveyed to Pier Luigi in exchange for Frascati, and Farnese lands, of which CASTRO was to be the capital and Pier Luigi the Duke, now covered large parts of the Tuscia from the Tiber to the sea-coast, from the foothills of Monte Amiata in the north to RONCIGLIONE, NEPI, and the MARTA river in the south. Always excepting VITERBO: where the Pope appointed his grandson, another Alessandro Farnese, Cardinal-Legate for Life. Paul III even hoped that with Antonio da Sangallo's help, they might find some way to repopulate the Maremma.

According to Annibal Caro (see CAPRAROLA) in 1532, CASTRO was a *bicoca di zingari,* a gipsy hovel, where the bread was black and the wine was *acquarello.* The people lived in caves and the town needed to be completely rebuilt. So the Pope, Vasari tells us, 'sent Antonio to design the fortress that the duke began, the palace called l'Osteria on the piazza, and the mint . . .'; and also 'palaces and other buildings there for various natives and foreigners, who incurred incredible expense without reserve, all these structures being ornate and most convenient.'

Building began at once, material from the sacked medieval town and from earlier settlements right back to the Villanovan being tossed over the cliff, where it has now been examined by local archaeologists. The ancient cathedral survived and the little picture of CASTRO at CAPRAROLA shows the cliffs barbered, the lawns manicured, the valley bottom tilled. When Annibal returned in 1543 he was delighted: '... it rises now with so much and such sudden magnificence, that I am put in mind of the rebirth of Carthage'. A phrase of ill omen.

The journey from Rome was a mere two days and Pope Paul and his companions enjoyed the boar-hunting and the games in winter and the melons and the cool wine from the *cantine* in summer.

Antonio da Sangallo was 54 when he was given the job: he was not only the Farnese family architect, he was also an innovative military architect and given CASTRO's hideous experience of assault in 1527, the destructive power of new weapon systems, and the continuing threat from the barbary pirates (Barbarossa, in particular), the new city's fortifications were important. His family made up what was perhaps the first international architects' office; his cousin from Florence, Aristotile, worked admirably on the walls but never managed to address his betters in the correct Roman manner, and Francesco, another, oversaw the work at CASTRO, while Antonio himself was in Rome reinforcing the walls for Paul III against the Turk.*

* The Sangallo family of painters and architects:

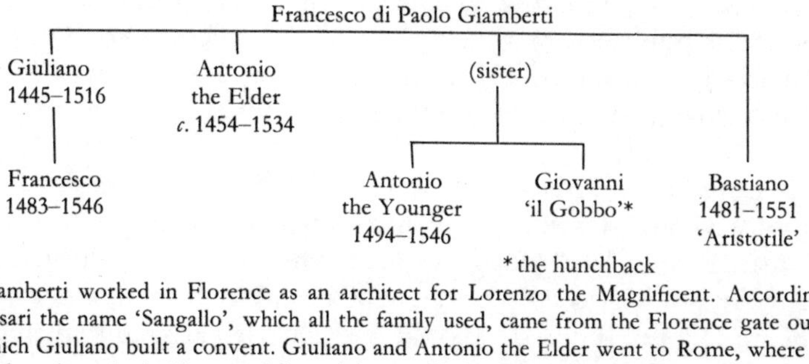

Giamberti worked in Florence as an architect for Lorenzo the Magnificent. According to Vasari the name 'Sangallo', which all the family used, came from the Florence gate outside which Giuliano built a convent. Giuliano and Antonio the Elder went to Rome, where their nephew Antonio the Younger followed them and helped the old and paralysed Bramante with his drawing. His first building there was a non-ostentatious palazzo for a respected lawyer: it already shows that clean, almost quakerly, restraint, which comes in fact from his absolutely convinced use of simple proportions. He later became the family architect and built for the Farnese throughout Northern Lazio.

When Antonio died in 1546, some of the fortifications were more or less complete, including a pentagonal fortress outside the main city gate and two small forts designed to protect the 'hollow' (Etruscan) road. Several grand private houses were well on the way. (One of Antonio's clients was being provided with bathrooms *en suite* to each bedroom, a fitted kitchen, and an underground larder; another, who had the postal concession, wanted houses in CASTRO, GRADOLI, ISCHIA, and MONTALTO.)

The main piazza promised to be a very gem of renaissance town-planning: a stage-set within which to conduct life, business, and pleasure. On one side stood the official *osteria*, with a thirteen-arch, 65-metre-long, arcade and grand apartments: the Farnese themselves stayed in it while waiting for the Palazzo Ducale to be built.* The market piazza was reached through the thirteenth arch of the main piazza; the Mint was at one end and the palace of the Podesta, here the Duke's representative, was at the other.

Antonio produced several drawings for a convent and church. Moreover, unlike most cities of the time, there were real drains, and a regular water supply, apparently to be pumped up into cisterns from the river below.

When Antonio died work at CASTRO had already slowed down. Paul III was in his eighties and in 1545 Pier Luigi had exchanged parts of his Castro Dukedom for Parma and Piacenza, of which he then also became Duke. He moved the Mint to Parma in 1546, and handed the Dukedom of CASTRO over to his second son, Orazio.

The original vision of a city compact and representative of the time's best in artistic and military achievement was short of fulfilment. But with Antonio's Uffizi drawings and the admirable booklet, *La Citta di Castro e Antonio da Sangallo* which reproduces several of them and is published by the local Gruppo Archeologico 'Armine' (from nearby ISCHIA DI CASTRO), we may at least enjoy a well-furnished imagination as we clamber about this now desolate little hill.

Pier Luigi was murdered at Piacenza in 1548, and the ancient Paul III took CASTRO back into the control of the Church. He died the next year. Pier Luigi's younger brother Ottavio rebelled, managed to provoke war between France and Spain, and was excommunicated by the next Pope, Julius III. CASTRO was shuttled around, returning

* Drawings for this survive in Antonio's hand at the Uffizi: at once powerful and rich. The building may have been started, but where it stood is still not known.

to another Farnese Cardinal in 1653, and then to his Parma/Piacenza kin, who, heavily indebted, mortgaged it.

In 1641, Pope Urban VIII Barberini, insolvent through excessive generosity to his own family, occupied CASTRO, and there followed a war between him and the then Duke Odoardo which lasted until 1646. Peace was then made, the French and the Republic of Venice intervening, and CASTRO was restored to the Duke, but he died without paying his creditors, and was succeeded by a 17-year-old, Ranuccio.

Pope Innocent X Pamphili in 1649 sent to treat with Ranuccio a Monsignor Giarda (a well-known student of antique iconography) who was to be the new bishop, although unacceptable to Ranuccio; or perhaps rather to his Cardinal uncle. Giarda was murdered on his way, near MONTEROSI; Innocent chose to hold Ranuccio responsible; and with crusading zeal (his Bull was to be read 'in all the Churches of Christendom') he ordered the destruction of CASTRO. After a siege which Ranuccio, away in his other dukedom, was unable to raise, but in which the town, though starving, was not taken, CASTRO surrendered on 2 September 1649, 'on honourable terms' and with guarantees of life and goods, to the captain of the papal mercenaries, Count David Widman. The Pope went back on his captain's word and CASTRO was destroyed utterly.

The fortifications and the Cathedral were mined and blown up; smaller buildings were dismantled with pickaxes, and the costs were paid by a levy on the other inhabitants of the Duchy. By November everything was gone except one Crucifix, some bits of church furnishing now in the church at ISCHIA DI CASTRO, and a picture now at GROTTE DI CASTRO. The Crucifix, despite the efforts of the papal soldiers, kept re-attaching itself to the wall of a humble shrine outside the Gate of the Ghetto.

The loathing of the Pope's redoubtable sister-in-law Olimpia Maidalchini Pamphili (see SAN MARTINO AL CIMINO) for the Farnese – one was reputed to have seduced her son out of his youthful Cardinalcy into marriage – contributed to the Pope's ferocity, which shocked all Europe.

Survivors escaped to neighbouring villages, some to GROTTE DI CASTRO above the LAKE OF BOLSENA, some outside the Papal State, but they and their descendants continued to return on the eve of the first Sunday each June to hear mass before the Crucifix at the Ghetto gate and at dawn to view the site of their deleted city. If they entered its ruined walls, they risked excommunication. After two hundred years the Church authorities relented: in 1847 a chapel for the miraculous Crucifix, on the main road towards FARNESE, was erected on the order of the local bishops and with the agreement of the Pope; not until 1907 did the Bishop of ACQUAPENDENTE and BAGNOREGIO organise the first 'guided' pilgrimage to it.

'On no site', wrote Dennis of CASTRO, 'does Nature more completely regain her dominion over Art – or the Past becloud the spirit with a deeper awe'. Crosses were at first erected where the cathedral and the twelve churches and their cemeteries had stood; but the vegetation won and the single Crucifix stood for all the windblown parishes. Today, bits of worked stone lie about, and steps and pavements can be traced, especially at the old cathedral, and a collapsed cistern. Some walls remain up to first-floor level.

Two things survive undamaged; a phrase, and the shudder that goes with it. QUI FU CASTRO rings in Italian with a more than historic sound: it rings for utter perfidy, cruelty, and destruction wherever and whenever they disgrace the human name.

Celleno

Celleno for a well-balanced journey back through time.

The 1950s town is flat, drab, and built of small blocks, rather far apart. A kilometre beyond, two to three centuries back, a large, handsome convent, now a well-heeled community centre: 18th-century saints smile on 5-year-olds racing trikes round the cloister; voluminous old choirstalls in the rather grandly restored church.

A rudimentary tile and brick Via Sacra, down the hill. At the bottom of which, the second village, where the people moved after the 1593 earthquake: 16th- and 17th-century.

So far, it has been downhill all the way but now, arranged to slow up but not deflect your horse, a wide, tall bridge rears steeply up, to land you in a high ruined medieval piazza: the first and earliest town, and one of Italy's least known magic places.

It is like a moonlit opera set all day: two churches, some small renaissance houses, a miniature Orsini/Farnese castle which you reach over a flat little bridge halfway up its façade. The tufo here is warm middle brown, the door- and window-cases are bluish peperino, the ravine is bright green below, and all around is a global view of the CIMINO and the Tiber valley.

Wait for night, and we do not doubt you will be rewarded with a Gatti grandee from VITERBO, baritone, his granddaughter, Atalanta Gattesca, perhaps, soprano, her husband, Ottavio Colonna, tenor; the male chorus doubling as Guelf knights or Ghibelline hangmen.

Don't stay if the clouds cover the moon: the place is real, and not all good.

Dionysius of Halicarnassus, who came to Rome in about 30 BC to research its provincial beginnings, is said to have said that CELLENO was founded, in memory of his daughter Cilenia, by Italus, son of Telegonus, descendant of Enotrius, who came to these parts from Arcadia. In the light of which, Benvenuto Cellini, sculptor, metal-worker, romantic and self-trumpeter, claimed CELLENO for his ancestors: 'Julius Caesar had a foremost and valorous captain, called Fiorino of Cellino. . . .', after whom Florence took its name.

Cellere

Cellere is a messy place, with only grubby remains of a Farnese castle. But below the back road stands the church of San Egidio, by Antonio da Sangallo the Younger, which anticipates Palladio. It is small, bright golden, its framing pilasters smooth, the rest of the fabric tweedy tufo. On plan it is a square with an apse and an inscribed round nave; in elevation the three (non-apse) sides rise as square pedimented frontispieces, with the apex of each reaching as high as the drum which supports the low dome; all four angles are filled, and roofed at half-drum height, and nicely flank the frontispieces. It is all in cheerful Ionic proportions and nothing could be neater. (The back, with the apse, is (1988) in foul and dangerous condition.)

Nearby, springs, on which coins will float, feed the stripling Timone.

Cencelle

High walls and a dozen or so towers surround the grass of a smooth low hill, up the valley from the sea, across from the TOLFA HILLS.

Centumcellae was originally the Etruscan, then Roman, port town on the site of today's CIVITAVECCHIA. Despite the efforts of Pope Leo III (795–816) and Charlemagne to defend the place, it was taken in 813 by Muslim raiders. The people took to the hills, for forty years, until on the strength of a dream, Pope Leo IV (847–55) provided them with a stone-built town, on a defensible hill, to be called Leopoli. And so it was, but the old name re-attached itself. The pastoral economy of the new town failed to compare with the commerce of a major port, so, according to legend, there was a 'glorious return' to the Old City in 889, to 'Civis Vetula'; whence CIVITAVECCHIA.

CENCELLE, as the inland town remained, kept its bishopric for a few centuries but then lost it; got into debt with the moneylenders of TARQUINIA; and finally sold itself to VITERBO in 1220. The sale included all its 'woods, meadows, lands, pastures, castles, waters, cliffs, willow-groves, rocks' and everything else it had that was useful, on land or sea. A pope then bought it back; but from 1416 CENCELLE appeared in the salt-tax lists among the 'lands destroyed and uninhabited'.

What remains is an ideogram of the medieval.

Centeno

This, the frontier of the Papal State with Tuscany, is now notable only for the great old customs house with its deep arcades, a reminder of bureaucracy in the hot sun. (The round, multicoloured stones it is built of are a reminder of the Sabine Gulf.) Peter Beckford wrote here, 'you enter the territories of the Pope, where you will be stopped, questioned, and your baggage visited.... You leave a country where a *commercio libero* – "free trade" – is permitted, and enter one where it is not ... The public advantage of a *commercio libero* unlimited and unrestrained, as at present permitted in Tuscany, is a doubtful question....'

Ceri

The name and population of Caere (see CERVETERI) moved over the hill to this minute plateau in the 13th century. Caere became CERVETERI, Old Ceri, and this tiny but perfect hill-town, CERI NOVI.

All the local rock is blood-red, and the road up to CERI is ground into and through it. The church of St Felix the Pope is up steps along the edge of the ravine: a rewarding miniature, with a fine Cosmatesque floor. At the altar, 17th-century painted theatre curtains reveal an aristocratic Madonna holding her experienced 3-year-old for us all to see. Spirited frescos celebrate the life of Pope Felix II (355–65). Others, remarkable, have been uncovered in a newly excavated right aisle; one an almost Michelangelesque Crucifixion.

Cerveteri

This was the great Etruscan city of Kysry, Latin Caere. One of its many necropoles, the well-excavated Banditaccia, is truly a city of the dead, with grandiose buildings standing above ground so that you walk through streets and piazzas.

Caere grew where the fertile and well-wooded outer slopes of the Sabatine volcano abut both the coastal plain and the metal-bearing

TOLFA HILLS. By the 7th and 6th centuries BC, it was one of the most populous cities of the Mediterranean basin and its ports of Alsium, Punicum, and Pyrgi (see PALO, SANTA MARINELLA, and SANTA SEVERA) traded with that entire world. Its ancient history was like TARQUINIA's, with which it shared commercial and political dominance over the surrounding lands.

The ancient city spread back over CERVETERI's present site, occupying an area some fifty times greater than today's townlet without its post-1950 sprawl. Today, the townlet is built of dark orange tufo, while the necropolis is mostly grey. The remains and the finds – bits of walls, gates, *cuniculi,* deep-cut roads – speak of a great city indeed. Pliny records that the paintings in the Etruscan temples which still stood in his day were among the oldest in Italy, and modern excavation has produced the remains of no less than eight of them. In Rome's early days, young men of noble family were sent here for a polite education. The quality and richness of what was found in the Regolini-Galassi tomb in 1836 – gold, silver, wafer-thin ceramics – suggests why. (Those finds went to the Gregorian Museum in the Vatican.)

Under Rome it declined in the usual way, and some nearby baths became more famous than the city. In the 5th century AD it was abandoned in the face of raids and invasions from the sea, and fell to ruin. Eventually its fine site restored it to life and by the 10th century it was enough of a city to take others, to be retaken, to massacre, to manufacture, to build a basilica. In 1236 malaria and Saracen raids forced the people inland to New Caere: now CERI. Eventually some trickled back, and life resumed: there is now a building explosion.

The necropolis on the hill called the Banditaccia is perhaps the greatest collection of 7th- and 6th-century BC ashlar buildings to be seen in Europe. Excavation did not begin till the middle of the last century, by which time TARQUINIA had been well known and largely pillaged for centuries, and VULCI for decades. It is now amply visitable; and many splendid tomb objects are in the town museum. (The principal collections from here are in the usual places: the Villa Giulia in Rome, the Gregorian Museum in the Vatican, the Louvre, and the British Museum.) Both tombs and objects date largely from the 'early' or 'orientalising' phase of the Etruscan culture, so like and yet so unlike the early Greek ones.

To visit, a map is essential and Mario Moretti's *Cerveteri* is an intelligent and well-illustrated guidebook. (Moretti was in charge of the work here for some years after 1950.) A visit even of half a day will place CERVETERI in the same part of the consciousness as the Pyramids, Luxor, Athens' Acropolis, and Baalbek, though the scale is smaller.

We are here in a city built as it seems for the dead alive, with streets, houses, piazzas, and domed and sculpted buildings with many doors. In one of the piazzas it is possible to sit down under a great tree and feel surprise that no waiter comes to offer a drink. In most Etruscan necropoles the dead were provided with well-thought-out rooms, or at most small houses: here they have a whole amiable town.

Most of the streets between the buildings are carved down into the native tufo, and the buildings are then built on upwards with blocks of the same stone. Some of the tombs, those that are more underground than not, are complete houses with several rooms on more than one floor, and staircases and corridors to walk about them. One, though 4 metres underground, even has what appear to be windows. Others are arranged in long streets above ground, with differing degrees of unification into a terrace with, say, continuous cornices. (One of these streets is clearly the model for the street of tombs in Highgate Cemetery in London.)

The most spectacular are the great round tombs under domes, each of which contains three or four apartments, with separate entrances, and looks like a small version of the Pantheon. It was indeed from here that the Romans got their ideas for it and some say that colossal saucer dome was meant to be covered with grass, just as these were and still are. (Grass-covered graves are of course still general throughout Europe, but grass-covered temples can now only be seen in Iceland.) One of the tumuli is built of alternate courses of dark tufo and pale gold macco; it is the ancestor of the cathedrals of Orvieto and Siena and all the horizontally striped buildings in Italy.

The interiors are not, or are no longer, frescoed like those at TARQUINIA: only patches of ornamental painting remain, picking out carved objects here and there. Some rooms are splendid tents with weapons hanging, carved from the rock; others are stables or kitchens, with harness or knives and pans; others again are ceremonial halls with beams. Again and again the burials themselves were in niches: behind columns, between columns, perhaps with stone pillows plumped up. One has two stone chairs for guards by the door, or perhaps to sit on when you came in from the heat in the other world.

The silence, the unsprayed verdure, the unimpaired bird and insect life, the dreamlike, almost Boullée-like, grandeur and perfection of this ancient city must be as close as one can now get to the experience of antiquity our ancestors had before cars and buses.

Thousands of tombs are known. Thousands more are expected to be found sooner or later, only a few hundred have been opened, and only some of these are now open to the visitor. CERVETERI's other necropoles are not arranged for the convenience of the visitor.

The town museum is in the small 13th-century castle: a good collection and well-arranged, but badly lit. (Also unprovided with loos, informative keepers, or even postcards.) There are two very grand *olle*, cinerary urns, shoulder-high on their stands, one of bronze, one of terracotta, larger pots successively stuck into the necks of smaller pots, six all told, and a larger one at the bottom. A half life-size Charon in tufo. A graceful boy reclining on an urn lid. The lips on jugs and the spouts on pitchers are animals, or flowers, or snakes, or cabbage leaves; the handles are gymnasts ...

That so many Etruscan things are domestic, pretty, inconsequential, punning, is what separates them from the Greeks', which, though sometimes funny, do not pun and are always consequential. Even the Villanovan pots here strongly suggest hats on rather stout people.

Across the piazza is the church of Santa Maria Maggiore: a double one in that the 1959 façade leads into a (characterless) nave, with across the end the smaller old basilica of nice reddish tufo, with variegated ancient columns. Alongside, is the 16th-century Palazzo Ruspoli, obviously of Orsini construction.

The great towered ruin to the south, the Granarone – 'Big Granary' – was also once a Ruspoli palace.

At the bottom, on the PALO road – still in D. H. Lawrence's time the merest farm track – stands a little renaissance church, Santa Maria dei Canneti ('of the Reedbeds'), surviving in the middle of a roundabout.

Cesano

A fine tract of aqueduct from the Acqua Paola survives, and a small piece of Trajan's earlier one (see LAKE OF BRACCIANO).

Chia

The old church has fallen down and the tiny rock-top is abandoned except for someone's hopeful personal eyrie. People from the newer village still go up there to sit.

To the south, in the walled ruins of another settlement, is the Tower of Chia, famous not only for its tall grace but because Pier Paolo Pasolini bought it, and chose the nearby stream, the Vezza, as the setting for the baptism of Christ in his film *The Gospel according to St Matthew*.

Cibona, Santa Maria della

The grandiose sanctuary church of Santa Maria della CIBONA stands beside the TOLFA to CIVITAVECCHIA road that avoids ALLUMIERE, and the façade dominates the entire countryside. It is by Domenico Castelli, 'il Fontanino', of the papal Office of Works (d. 1657), of pale pinkish-yellow tufo and brick.

If it is still there, look at the twisted cloth motif used in the decoration: it hangs between the volutes of the Ionic capitals, from ramshorn to ramshorn, and down the side of the door jambs.

The Cimino Hills

We saw Old Father Time here, freewheeling downhill on a small motorbike, beard flying, unsheathed scythe across his back.

This group of hills includes the highest in our area, Monte Cimino, and LAKE VICO, the smallest of the three main lakes. Most of the hills date from vulcanisms some hundreds of thousands of years ago, but the eruptions the lake and its Monte Venere emerged from happened a mere 60,000 years ago. The legend about Hercules pulling his stick out of the hillside and causing the lake to form suggests the sequence may always have been understood.

To the very ancient Romans, the vast Ciminian forest was impassable and supernaturally terrifying. Once they lost this dread, the Etruscans' fate was sealed. The Romans then built their great safe roads; the elder Pliny visited the forest – worse than the German forest, he thought – and saw the *sasso menicante*, the 90-cubic-metre 'trembling stone', still near the top of Monte Cimino.

The altitude here is above 1,000 metres, which allows the great crown of beeches to flourish incomparably; hugely tall trees, steep slopes, great mossy boulders ensconced in millennial dead leaves: a survival from the ancient forest.

Below the beech wood, away from the lake, the CIMINO's natural scrub-oak and chestnut cover has been converted to great chestnut groves in parkland: chestnuts are the local industry. Lower still are olives with neat-mown grass in among the boulders and the squidgy-looking lava flows. Lower still, among the woods and ravines, come the new hazelnut plantations, all rich in geometric regularities of trunk and shade. The descent provides misty, Claude-like views over the foothill towns of SORIANO with its great castle; VIGNANELLO and VASANELLO, a serpentine cliff of masonry above the natural cliff; smaller places gathering round a castle of sorts; the occasional tower in a dark wood: beyond, the invisible mist-strung Tiber.

The western slopes merge into those of the Palanzana above BAGNAIA and VITERBO. Then, always wooded at the top, the hills curve southwards, with vineyards and olive groves, past SAN MARTINO with its French Abbey church, towards VETRALLA whose mayor marries the forest on Monte Fogliano every May. (Here there is a surprising, residual, 'oceanic' microclimate, very moist, a 'botanical monument'.) Far to the south bunch the TOLFA HILLS, the light of the sea beside them.

On these well-watered slopes, innumerable religious communities grew up and disappeared, sometimes leaving a little chapel. On Monte Fogliano there was the convent of S. Angelino (where the singer Gigli would go to rest). A hermitage built as late as the 16th century by someone from Siena. There was a palaeo-Christian basilica at S. Eutizio, over 3rd-century catacombs. And the little roofless church of S. Rocco at the top of the Cassia Cimina, in two shades of tufo. And an infinity of others too modest or too decayed to mention. Best of them all, the old, old, field-church of SANT'EUSEBIO, near RONCIGLIONE.

There is also a shatteringly ugly disco in open country high up on the main road.

Civita Castellana

Nearly three thousand years ago, CIVITA CASTELLANA was already a city: its high, stream- and cliff-protected position shows why. The best individual thing there now, the portico of the Duomo, went up a mere eight hundred years ago. For several hundred years after the Romans destroyed it the town was deserted. Today, newly bypassed and newly prosperous, it still shows the long centuries of alternating neglect and attention.

The first city on the splendidly defensible, 1,500-metre-long plateau was Falerii, one of the two chief places of the Falisci (the other being Narce; see CALCATA). The Falisci had been in this rugged area – roughly the TREIA basin – since the second millennium BC, allied and intermingling with the peoples of CAPENA and Veii (see VEIO). Tradition held the town's founder to have been Agamemnon's son Haliscus, escaped to Italy from Greece. The Roman historian Strabo described the Falisci as a distinct tribe, but their language was close enough to Latin to count as a dialect: the Romans called it (and others) *sermo rusticus*, while they called Latin *sermo urbanus*: country talk and town talk.

The original city, one of the Twelve in the Etruscan League, covered all the site of the modern town plus the hill of Vignale, not now built on. Of the city wall, a few substantial tracts remain: one is seventeen great courses high, and among the highest anywhere. A network of *cuniculi* has been discovered, encompassing the city's entire length from east to west.

In the 4th century BC, the 'Hellenising' painted pots the Faliscans produced for export in almost industrial quantities were very highly prized. On the spot, impressive terracotta temple decorations and innumerable votive offerings, including anatomical ones, have been turned up by excavation: the Villa Giulia Museum in Rome houses many of them. (The new Museum of the Agro Falisco, here in the Rocca Borgia, has some too: see below.) Necropoles and temples have been found all round in the cliffs and valley bottoms.

The Romans first destroyed Falerii in 394 BC and then again in 241 BC. This second time they expelled the people, requiring them to build the less defensible FALERII NOVI some 6 kilometres away. The old city became Falerii Veteres: New and Old Falerii. The local cult of Minerva was transferred with the people to FALERII NOVI, but the most important of the temples, those in the sanctuary of Juno Curite, 'Juno with the Spear', remained and indeed were restored and improved by the Romans. They were to the north-east – and their ruins are still there – at Celle, below the hill of Vignale, in a bowl dramatically enclosed by ruddy cliffs where several ravines meet, with streams, a waterfall, and fine smoothed spaces for the ceremonies.

Ovid (born in the 1st century BC, died in the 1st AD) described to a friend how he and his Faliscan wife came to the famous games and festival being prepared for 'chaste Juno', at *pomiferis* – 'apple-bearing' – Falerii. Understanding the rite was a great prize: *Aspice; concedas numen inesse loco* – 'Look; admit the gods are here'. Great trees, clouded with incense; prayers and offerings; the sound of solemn flutes. The ancient altar, made without art, and snow-white heifers brought (Maremma cattle then as now?), whitened, it is said, by the local grass. And hornless calves. And the flock's leader, horns curved back over his hard forehead. Piglings. Only the she-goat is unwanted by the Goddess. In the rites, Ovid saw the Greek heritage of his wife's people: white-veiled, the sacred vessels carried on their heads.

A *via sacra* was made from FALERII NOVI, and Celle remained a place of veneration until the end of the Empire. Today the substantial remains of precinct and buildings are still being uncovered from a huge inflow of river sand and pebbles. A narrow medieval bridge athletically spans the stream. These beauties you reach ten minutes walk down a steep and ancient track – Ovid complained it was tiring – sharp left out of the town on the way down to the Via Flaminia.

The Roman roads, the Flaminia and the Amerina, had made the area, though not the town, altogether more accessible. Gradually some of the people of FALERII NOVI, the better to protect themselves against barbarians from the north and then Muslim raiders from the sea, returned to Falerii Veteres, and fortified it. This was when it took its present name of CIVITA CASTELLANA, Castle City. (Today FALERII NOVI is known in the vernacular as Falleri, with the accent on the first syllable. The nearby village now called FALERIA was never any kind of Falerii and used to be called Stabia.)

By 727, there was a cathedral and under the raised presbytery of today's cathedral there is still the ancient crypt, of nine naves. The pilasters against the apse wall, with their interlaced thong pattern, look even older. (One pilaster is part, upturned, of a Roman inscription.) At the turn of the 12th century, Pope Pascal II made a papal fortress of the town; after which it went for its pains to the Prefects of Vico. Eventually it returned to the Papacy, to be fortified again and again.

The Cathedral – Santa Maria – had been rebuilt in the great age, and the portico of 1210 which extends across the whole front of the church is among the very best of its kind. A tremendous central classical arch with roofed extensions on either side, the whole set on slender classical columns and rising from an equally broad basement of steps, constitutes a sort of variegated and externalised pronaos. The decoration is 'Cosmatesque' mosaic, from the name of the Cosmati family, the Roman marbleworkers Lorenzo, his son Iacopo, and his grandson Cosma. This cool and luminous structure with its mosaics and its relief sculpture, their masterpiece, is a reminder that the language of classical form was never out of season.

The interior, a Latin cross, was remade in 1736–40, big, dark, and elegant, but its glory too is the Cosmatesque floor, surviving from the earlier church. Also Cosmatesque are two marble *plutei* in the Old Sacristy: altar-rails is probably the closest English word, but *plutei* normally have solid panels. Each of these is supported by two beasts; one by two lions, one of these in turn having his chin supported by a well-hung little fellow who wears the lion's beard like a crown, and the other by a lion and a sphinx, the latter beaming surely the fattest, homeliest, and least inscrutable smile ever attributed to that equivocal creature (see Appendix I).

In about 1490 the castle, the Rocca (at the western, naturally least defended, end of the town), came into the hands of Cardinal Rodrigo Borgia, who became Pope as Alexander VI in 1492. The elder Antonio da Sangallo rebuilt it for him as the Papal State's northernmost stronghold, and to meet the revolutionary new technology of firearms. The main body is pentagonal and large; among the innovations were a high talus and very little curtain (the vertical is where cannon balls could do most damage), two ravelins, and no machicolation or crenellation. (Compare this with the magnificent dinosaur the Orsini had just built at BRACCIANO.)

The younger Antonio da Sangallo was then employed by Pope Julius II, Alexander VI's next but one successor, to put up the octagonal keep and to complete the remarkably grand fortress with a severely elegant courtyard. Later, the Zuccari decorated some of the apartments, and various popes or their associates spent time there in lavish entertainment. The visitor first enters a circular, domed antechamber with a chimney piece rounded to follow the wall, and an equally rounded door. Further in, by way of a deep, closed court, like an impressively formal prison yard, you come to the octagonal keep (now offices, though from the top the view is stupendous), and beside it the wide two-tiered cloister or quadrangle. All is in pinkish-dark peperino and the effect, as much of each part as of the whole, is of weighty and powerful perfection. The cloister started to collapse while it was being built because, contrary to Antonio's instructions, rubble was used in the piles; hence the arches' supporting ring of brickwork at ground level.

In the early 19th century the Rocca became the principal prison of Northern Lazio, the papal Bastille, and to it were consigned many who later became national heroes of Italy. One was Pietro Missirilli, whose story Stendhal wrote up under the name of its other protagonist, Vanina Vanini, a tale of passion, guerrilla revolution, and betrayal which runs at a speed just short of the headlong to its chilling denouement in the chapel of this prison.

Another prisoner, who never quite became a national hero, was the brigand Gasparone or Gasbaroni. He was sent down for half a lifetime of extortion and murder, mostly committed in Southern

Lazio. The papal government had declared a general amnesty, a priest made contact with the most famous brigand of them all, and Gasparone and his band gave themselves up in good faith. But they were double-crossed and imprisoned.

Dr Evory Kennedy*, formerly Master of the Rotunda hospital in Dublin, visited Gasparone in 1859 while travelling in Italy and from him bought a manuscript, which remains in our family, written and drawn by fellow prisoners. This 'Historical Collection of the Most Famous Acts of Brigandage by the Well Known Antonio Gasbaroni . . .' is in a minute, regular, hand, and every page has a different decorated border. The illustrations are stiff and *naïf* and show personages in tall hats robbing and murdering each other: 'Gasbaroni is wounded by the Force', 'Gasbaroni takes the son of a rich man hostage', 'Gasbaroni kills a spy'. This last puts it mildly; he has cut off his head and all his four limbs and is holding up his liver and lights with a puzzled expression. The narrative combines listless endorsements of civic virtue in general with passages of pedantic and sometimes revolting detail where the writer thought the authorities had got the facts of a particular crime wrong.

After the Second World War the Rocca was used to shelter refugees. Restoration, begun in 1952, is well if a bit antiseptically done, as is the way of national departments of antiquities the world over. Apartments round the courtyard now house the Museum of the Agro Falisco, certainly one of the more brilliant local collections. The forms a pot or a dish can take are not infinite, so we should not be surprised that many of the solutions reached by these people are the same as our own. But we are surprised, and delighted: art nouveau, even Tiffany, forms are perhaps the most unexpected. For the rest, the ingenuity is endless. Little people sit on a lid and bang two or three different drums. There are enormous ornamental hooks and eyes, and forty similar glossy bowls in *bucchero*.†

In 1798 there was a battle. Two years before, Napoleon had gone to Egypt, leaving behind him a republic in Rome. Queen Maria Carolina of Naples, who was Marie Antoinette's sister, persuaded her husband King Ferdinand IV that this would be a good time to attack the French, and he tore himself away from his hunting long enough to lead an army on Rome which, to everyone's astonishment, not least his own, he took. The French army evacuated the city, but

* My great-grandfather. W.K.

† The black ceramic is so called not from the Etruscan or Latin but probably from the Spanish word for something like it made in Spain and exported to Italy in the 16th century when this Etruscan ware was beginning to be admired.

fought some Neapolitan units which were trying to consolidate the conquest in Northern Lazio and, under Marshal Macdonald, defeated them here at CIVITA CASTELLANA. Ferdinand tore back to Naples, seized his wife and, properly attended by the British Ambassador Sir William Hamilton and Lady Hamilton, fled in one of Nelson's ships to Palermo. His later life defined all that democracy and socialism in Europe came into existence to clean away.

The town has a somewhat neglected look, though not decayed like its neighbour NEPI. Although the medieval is never far out of sight, the centre is tightly packed with streets of fine buildings: many date from after the Flaminia was brought closer in 1606. Pope Clement with his splendid bridge of 1709 poured it straight through the town.* The central piazza is mainly of the 17th century, with streets sent out from it under arches, so the traffic is abominable.

When George Dennis was there, the population was down to a mere two thousand souls but the place has now learnt to do very well again out of its sands and clays, which allow it to produce fine industrial ceramics for export, just as ancient Falerii did. Today it is bathroom suites.

In the 1820s, Corot stayed here and did some thirty paintings, including six of SORACTE.

Civita di Bagnoregio

St Bonaventure was born here in the 13th century: 'I will not establish new orders. I will not load others with chains or new or heavy burdens. I will only proclaim truth, which it is not permitted to pass over in silence'.

CIVITA is famous for being *la citta che muore* – 'the dying city' – because for centuries it has been crumbling away into the valleys below. It has now stopped dying because of the great fame of its moribundity, and those of its houses which have a chance of surviving into next week are again inhabited.

Several little towns on the Tiber side of the 'Volsinian volcanic apparatus', as it is called, were built on rafts of tufo floating on a kind of macro-sand, which flood and earthquake have sucked and rattled off and away down the river. CIVITA was the oldest of the settlements and had the cathedral. Most are now gone into whiteish scree; CIVITA itself still perches on a bit of crust; LUBRIANO and BAGNOREGIO have had a dress-circle view of the fate of the others.

It was in the 18th century that earthquakes and erosion finally

* The architect was Filippo Barigioni.

isolated CIVITA in the dramatic way we see today. There was talk of an iron bridge of a kind thought to have been used successfully in England. But in 1821 evacuation to Bagnorea, as BAGNOREGIA was then called, began in earnest, with carefully devised new dwellings planned for the refugees.

A narrow path on concrete legs now swoops up to what is left. The gate is part-Etruscan, cut in the tufo, and the street through it goes into the piazza, the site perhaps of a Roman forum; and of the bishop's quite humble palace. Until 1699 the church here of San Donato was the cathedral of BAGNOREGIO and, like most cathedrals, many centuries contributed to it: the 12th the tower, the 15th the façade, the 16th some frescos.

Dusk is the best time, when the brown-gold of the town stands out against the disaster-scape behind.

Civitavecchia

An immensely ancient port, so battered it seems no longer to understand itself or what it was for.

It became important when other Roman ports silted up, and in 106 BC the Emperor Trajan built himself a villa and baths up the hill behind, to watch in comfort the building of a new harbour. (The ruins of the baths are well-preserved: the very splendid Terme Taurine – a corruption of Traiano, nothing about bulls.)

Trajan's port had an outer basin between two moles, protected by an 'ante-mole', and an inner basin reached by a channel; to the south, the arsenal; to the north, a basilica; in the centre, a monumental arch and temple; and two arcaded levels of workshops. The younger Pliny described it in detail and much survived until the Second World War. The ante-mole still protects the harbour entrance, and still has an old, old, lighthouse standing where Trajan's did, halfway along. That, and the so-called Forte Michelangelo, give the place continuity.

The Roman port was called Centumcellae (see CENCELLE); the name carried on into the Middle Ages, and at one time this was the Byzantine Emperors' only port on the Tyrrhenian. The Saracens attacked and burnt it in 828, and then used it as a base to attack Rome from. Although the people returned, and even though the hinterland's economy revived, CIVITAVECCHIA never caught up again with the other trading ports – Amalfi, Pisa, Genoa – where wealth and technology flowed in.

The Pope's man, Cardinal Vitelleschi (see TARQUINIA) secured it in 1431. Pius II repaired the castle and the walls, and great works to protect the whole port began under Julius II in 1508. In 1535 Paul III came to bless the papal fleet on its way, with the Genoese, Imperial, and Spanish fleets, to fight the pirates of Tunis. Then the Roman Arsenal was restored; and Clement VIII had the ante-mole restored; and then a great new Bernini Arsenal went up. The alum trade from the TOLFA HILLS and shipbuilding caused CIVITAVECCHIA to flourish, and in 1748 it became a free port. Through it came all the overseas trade of the Papal State, little enough, but including iron from Terni, brought down by railway.

Most of that two thousand years' worth of port buildings are now gone, and their ruins are shapeless as sore gums. New buildings stretch over and around them; filth belches. Today CIVITAVECCHIA's trade is mostly petroleum products.

Almost alone, the great 'Michelangelo fort' survived; and is well restored. Bramante probably produced early designs for Julius II, but Antonio da Sangallo the Younger, the better military expert, took over; it was finished about 1535. It is a large, leisurely building, 100 metres by 80, with a great round tower at each corner, and one yet grander, and octagonal, the *maschio*, at the middle of the northern side, 23 metres high, its walls 7 metres thick. (This last is the part attributed – probably wrongly – to Michelangelo.) Between the two rounded mouldings that go all round the exterior, the stone is bevelled outwards, top and bottom, and smoothed, so that it looks like a belt over the rougher stone above and below. It is a bone-coloured thing, designed to stand and be scoured for ever in salt wind. The interior is a vast courtyard now lived in by sea-going officers' families and unmarried seamen of the Italian Navy. The decoration is smooth and flat, with drawn-looking pilasters and window frames.

Although the fortifications proved effective in 1527 against Charles V's *lanzichenecchi*, in 1798 Napoleon's forces took it and in 1835 the Pope began dismantling Sangallo's outer bastions.

Small pleasures: in the Museo Nazionale, Roman and Etruscan sculpture (good gold ear-rings) and also a metre-high bronze lion-head doorknocker of 1516, from the Arsenal. The church of Santa Maria dell'Orazione or della Morte – St Mary of Prayer or of Death – is an 18th-century oval construction with tunnels and chapels, and restored frescos in the dome. The Campo Santo, the cemetery, on the road north, is full of house-sized tombs: ostentatious fortunes laid down in the face of death as with CERVETERI Etruscans. Also a vast crenellated papal prison. And a Vanvitelli fountain in the dockyard.

North along the coast, petrochemical works and tank farms. The giant new power station is all symmetrical suavity, enamelled colour, glittering labyrinths of metal steps. Pylons stride off into smog-veiled countryside. Tucked away down in, restored sea-castles; Torre Valdaliga and Torre Marangone.

Stendhal spent ten years here as French consul, and wrote the *Chartreuse de Parme* and some dramatic short stories. He also described the groups who came on archaeological 'expeditions', hunting Etruscan tombs as they might wild boar; and the soldiers in the papal guard at MONTALTO who used painted vases for target practice.

Although a gentleman could until quite recently travel from CIVITAVECCHIA to Sardinia and expect a cabin for his manservant next to his, the harbour was not deep enough for the British Royal Yacht when there was a recent State Visit.

Civitella Cesi

Like other little places it was abandoned in the Middle Ages but one Cardinal Cesi rebuilt and repopulated it in 1554. It is a miniature of the usual: castle, church, gates and all, with the charm of a toy.

A wild, bad, picturesque road will lead you to ROTA.

Civitella d'Agliano

A tremendous square tower dominates everything. The piazza is scenic and out of it goes Via Cacciaglialtri – Drivetheothersout Street. Here they honour San Gorgonio.

Civitella S. Paolo

The 'Monks' Castle' was immemorial property of the abbey of San Paolo Fuori le Mura. Small and thin, it is now the gate into the village. A butcher's shop is incorporated.

The Commenda

A *commenda* is a place where the Commendatore of an order of knighthood resides. This, the COMMENDA dei Santi Giovanni e Vittore, on the southern slope under MONTEFIASCONE, is a rundown collection of large buildings, the remains of a large estate held by the Knights Hospitaller of St John of Jerusalem, later the Knights of Malta. The wood for building and rebuilding MONTEFIASCONE usually came from this 3,000-hectare estate. A lawsuit between the Knights and the Commune of MONTEFIASCONE about cattle grazing lasted 129 years.

The buildings are ranged round three sides of a garden open to the south, full of great trees. One contains a tremendous medieval vault.

The view over the Great Etruscan Plain is wide and townless.

Corchiano (including Ponte del Ponte)

Notable churches here.

The romanesque parish church of San Valentino was pulled down by the State in 1880 to make a piazza inside the still tightly lived-in medieval town. The present parish church, Santa Maria del Rosario, has one portal dated 1423 and another dated 1499 brought from elsewhere. Frescos will probably be uncovered. Among the *ex-votos*, a musket.

On the FABRICA road is San Biagio, where wallfuls of frescos have already been uncovered, by Pastura, Antonio da Viterbo, and possibly Lorenzo da Viterbo. Those attributed to Lorenzo, though a bit washed out, are excellent (though in a for him rather unlikely Sienese manner); and so is Antonio's *Annunciation*. A *Deposition* – people crawling over the crucifix in an almost Flemish manner – has been restored by the authorities with a crudity beyond belief, whereas a pair of little 17th–18th century pictures, which the priest and parish had restored at their own expense, are fine. Two ancient and comical capitals from San Valentino now form part of the altar, and confirm its destruction is to be regretted. A 15th-century tabernacle, also from elsewhere, had been cut out of a large marble column and the fluting is there behind.

Corchiano's great glory is on a back road in the valley, hard to find for so huge a building: the Madonna del Soccorso o del Rossore – Our Lady of Help, or of the Blush – a 16th-century votive chapel of gigantic size, presenting most interesting puzzles for the art-history buff. In front of the grandly plain, uncompromisingly square façade are four free-standing columns at the top of a wide flight of weed-covered steps, indicating a never finished portico (to be compared with both Santa Maria in Gradi in VITERBO and Santa Maria della QUERCIA). The only decoration, on the jambs of the doorcase, includes two naked pregnant women, *Bonae Deae*. Everything a light grey peperino, crisply cut.

The inside is breathtaking for size and power, and for the high-stepping rigour of the two arcades. A fresco-cycle on one wall tells the story of the foundation: a husband and wife dream that the Madonna commands them to found a convent here, and the Pope dreams the same. (Appalling restoration by fairly recent monks. Bottom right, note the concealed portrait of the Devil, dated 1581.) The impressive altarpiece, of 1616, is all gilt and pale blue paired columns; the central Madonna has been stolen.

A space between columns in the right-hand aisle is filled with a mysterious, and mysteriously-named, 'Paradise Chapel'. It is evidently rather later than the church, with Zuccari-like frescos. The carved decorations on the enclosing pilasters are very fine work, but obscure, verging on the occult. They are not unlike those round the QUERCIA's middle door: a winged serpent whose knotted tail has a head at the end; a squatting, open-legged person with wings; a vase with cloths hanging from it on a tripod; two lions tied by the neck to a something . . . This cascade of unlikely events and images appears on the easternmost pilaster; on its westernmost mate, there is the 'green man', with his leafy tongue or beard, and a beautiful basket of fruit at the top. And papal insignia. (The parish priest has the keys to both these churches.)

The Ponte del Ponte, or del Pontone

The 'bridge of the bridge', or 'of the big bridge' is a nearly 30-metre-long aqueduct over a stream. It was built presumably about the 5th century BC, by Faliscans (see CIVITA CASTELLANA), to bring water from a spring through *cuniculi* from one side of a torrent, the Rio della Tenuta, to a settlement on the other. The waters of the torrent itself were rerouted through another, lower, *cuniculus*, under and within its own south bank. The name is locally forgotten, though the big stones spanning the *burrone* are not.

Within a thick mass of temperate jungle, and invisible until you are almost on it, the 'bridge' is substantially still standing, to the impressive height of 10 metres. The visitor unequipped with strimmer, secateurs, and perhaps rope-ladder will have to be satisfied with that: the various *cuniculi* in the rock faces are hard for the amateur to identify, though the experts from the British School at Rome have done so.

To reach this remarkable structure, leave CORCHIANO by the VIGNANELLO road; 2 kilometres beyond the Campo Santo turn right immediately after a railway bridge; travel some 800 metres along a dust road, and again turn right, under another railway bridge; right again, and almost immediately left; another 800 metres along another dust road; up a little ramp on the left; along a track between a vineyard and an olive grove, to a small agricultural building, and leave your car. Walk round to the left, and on a bearing between the second and third oak trees from the left go down the grassy field to the jungle at the bottom, in which is the *fosso* of the Rio della Tenuta. There is a way into it by the telegraph pole; here enter, turn left, and persevere.

Il Crocefisso

Perhaps the grandest of the CIMINO's pilgrimage and field-churches. It dates from 1747 and stands on the road between VALLERANO and FABRICA.

It is an immensely tall building, saved from pomposity by its height, and decorated throughout in *trompe l'oeil* marbling – yellows, pinks, and mauves. Its three almost equal units – narthex, nave, presbytery – are in detail different, the middle one has a cupola, the first and third have saucer domes.

Perhaps earlier worship took place in the little cave beside it.

Fabrica di Roma

Pier Luigi Farnese bought FABRICA in 1539, and the castle, not quite gone to ruin, shows something of the family style.

The Collegiata of San Silvestro contains rewarding frescos by the brothers Lorenzo and Bartolommeo Torresani (of Verona, *c.* 1500–60). They still have some of the delighted assertion that went with the first mastery of perspective: belated overtones of Piero della Francesca.

Faleria

The Castle is large, old, ominous, ruinous, and built of funereal brown tufo.

The town's oldest part is abandoned, falling off the sharp end of its spur; the 13th-century church and the 14th-century castle straddle the middle bit. The historical name was Stabla, or Stabia, from a Roman road station, Stabulum, on the nearby Flaminia. It was changed in 1872, though there is no connection with either historical FALERII NOVI or Veteres.

The Castle has the erect eels of the Anguillara family everywhere and it must have housed scores of people in its huge up-ended maw. There are windows of all sizes and periods on seven or eight visible levels, and no knowing how many cellars or dungeons; and a couple of haphazard loggias; arches to go under; a once fine internal courtyard; wiring, live and dead, slung about.

Girolama Farnese, sister of Pope Paul III and of the beautiful Giulia (see CAPODIMONTE), wife of Giuliano dell'Anguillara, was murdered here by her stepson Giambattista in 1504, while dining, in circumstances said to combine passion, criminal ambition, duplicity, and poison. Her daughter Sabella was removed to safety and Giulia took away her body to bury at VASANELLO. There was a trial at Magliano Pecorareccio (as MAGLIANO ROMANO was then called). Giambattista lived on.

Maddalena Strozzi, wife of Flaminio d'Anguillara, had a *casaletto* here in the 1550s, with friezes and landscapes, as her *luogo di delizia* ('place of delight'); she was arrested by Pope Julius III for coining.

Falerii Novi or Falleri

In the spring of 1462 Pope Pius II came here and recorded that

> this is a very ancient monastery situated on a level plain, but there are no monks or other inhabitants. It has very high walls built of square stones without mortar and the great rocks are so cunningly fitted together that the joints can hardly be detected. The area surrounded by the wall is extensive enough for a large town but there are no buildings inside – only the church in the middle still intact, though the monks' cells and the offices are in ruins *and the church itself was for a short time used to stable horses – such is our age's reverence for religion* [his italics].

The roof of the church fell in, in 1829, but little else has changed.

The wall that Pius observed is one of the finest examples of Etruscan or Roman town wall. Built near enough to 241 BC, of darkish tufo, it is over 2 kilometres long, 5 metres high, and in places 2 metres thick. It had fifty internal towers and four principal gates; and the individual blocks are roughly 100 by 30 by 40 centimetres. It is still mostly still standing, 'bannered with oak saplings, and battlemented with ivy', as Dennis found it. The way in today is from the west, through the fine peperino Gate of Jove, whose head (if, beardless, it is his, and not Apollo's or Bacchus') surmounts the arch.

The Falisci were dumped here after the Romans finally wiped out their great city of Falerii (see CIVITA CASTELLANA). New Falerii had a regular plan, straddling a crossroads. Both Roman and Faliscan tombs and necropolises have been found, and a theatre inside the walls and an amphitheatre still visible outside. The *via sacra* to Celle (see CIVITA CASTELLANA) probably started from the east gate.

The once-defensive ditch along the eastern wall is now a long glade-like hollow, in spring all daisies in the sun and blue and white anemones in the shade. At the south-eastern corner, the tower still outreaches the trees and round beyond it is the heavyweight Porta del Bove.

In time the people returned to the old site, FALERII NOVI being finally destroyed by Normans. The church of Santa Maria di Falleri was built in the 12th century, no doubt on ancient temple foundations (perhaps Minerva's), using Roman columns and material. The ruinous 'monks' cells and the offices' that Pius saw in ruins were replaced by large and dignified convent buildings, probably in the 16th century.

Thirty years ago the wide nave and elegant aisles and apses where Pius II saw horses stabled were being used as an ace pigsty and more recently for drying tobacco. The convent buildings are in farm use, the church is fenced against all but 'authorised persons', and dilapidation continues.

Farnese

Which got the name first, town or clan, seems not known. A *farnia* is some kind of broad-leaved oak – *quercus* either *pedunculata* or *latifolia*. Oak-folk?

The town has good things, and one bad loss: the Park of the Palazzo Farnese, sold for speculative development. There is a medieval nucleus, but the place is convoluted rather than muddled.

The parish church, San Salvatore, has several good pictures: Orazio Gentileschi's *St Michael*, slaying a very human Dragon with minimal batwings; a *Solemn Mass of Paul III* by Antonio Maria Panico; a *Virgin of the Rosary*, with fifteen little pictures from different dates; and a fine, damaged, almost Michelangelesque picture of – perhaps? – St Antony.

The Palazzo Farnese has long been in multiple use. Its big, Vignolesque entrance gate is at once grand and cussed in the way its leather-like rustication attaches the columns to the fabric and frame. It leads into a covered *androne* which in turn sends steps up into a tiny courtyard; then more staircases, more courtyards, doors grand and humble. The reputed chapel could be anywhere. The Uffizi-like, roofed and windowed viaduct, whose great legs over the piazza used to carry you to the Park, started from a small terrace-garden with a classical end-piece, on an upper floor.

The road from the south-west, and *magazzini* on either side of it, are cut deep into the (greyish-gold) tufo; and above them are three or four airy little streets of terrace houses, the tufo the same, their roofs stepped to the slope. Above all this, the convent of San Rocco. From outside, it looks ordinary 17th-century, but the simple interior is grandiose and full of light. (To would-be pacers and measurers it seems to promise delightfully exact proportions.)

Here too a picture: *St Antony* is praying to Heaven before an altar, on which the boy Jesus, naked and aged about 4, has suddenly appeared; and is reaching out his hand into Antony's breast to take his heart. The Boy finds it all a great joke, and his smile is casting brilliant moonlight over the altar cloth and over his own body. This picture is framed by an ebullient late 17th-century altarpiece, all-over children and others jumping and singing. Its fellow, different in every detail, is opposite, and both are splendid.

Above the main altar is a 16th-century wooden Crucifixion which seems to speak more of the early 15th or of the pietism of the 18th century, so full it is of lamentation. Elsewhere, San Rocco, himself with a small cheese, and his dog with its usual bun.

And away down in the *burrone* is Santa Anna, small, lavish, very Farnese. It is square-domed, with an eight-sided light on top, and papal crowns; inside, frescos; and very distinguished plaster work. Note the heads facing out in the place of capitals in the frame of the central picture; the flat, shoulder-like, volutes below; and the laid-back, elongated angels in the spandrels. The little building is almost standing in the stream; in the bank, three man-made caves suggest nave-and-two-aisles: an earlier cult perhaps, officially taken over?

The CASTRO Crucifix is kept in a smartly drab sanctuary close to the road west.

La Farnesiana

With good springs, a high heart, and plenty of time, you can make a 30-kilometre drive, down north from ALLUMIERE round Monte Sassicari, glimpsing CENCELLE to the west, passing the isolated Charles Addams-style railway station of ALLUMIERE on the old CIVITAVECCHIA–Terni line, and come upon this very odd affair.

It is a mid-19th-century church, fully pinnacled and crocketed but reviving no known Italian Gothic. Pink; unroofed; in a small ilex grove. Inside, the all-over fretwork pattern and little 'pointed' apse could have come from an English copybook. What was it for? Summer picnics with 'our uncle, the Cardinal'?

Ferento

On the VITERBO side of Ferento there is a place with the name Carnaiola, because in 1160 there was a carnage there. Or in 1172. Or some other time. This was FERENTO's history: destruction, finally utter and complete, by the Viterbesi. When excavation of the Roman remains began in 1901, the medieval rubble was metres-thick.

The Etruscan settlement, ACQUAROSSA, to the south, was sacked in the 7th or 6th century BC. Roman Ferentum started in the 3rd and came into its own in the 1st century BC when its elegant theatre, and much else, was built. The Via Ferentiensis – a Cassia–Clodia link – ran through its rectilinear lay-out, and Vitruvius made mention of its public buildings: forum, amphitheatre, Augusteum, baths, artificial lake, portico with statues; and the theatre. Flavia Domitilla, wife of Vespasian and mother of Titus, was born here.

The theatre was known and studied in the 16th century, and is now substantially restored. Some of the original statues are in the Archaeological Museum in Florence: eight of the nine Muses, made of Greek Pentelic marble, a head of Apollo, and a copy of Scopas' pretty statue of Pothos (Eros's brother, 'Desire', a member of Aphrodite's Court of Love), all possibly brought from Greece in the 1st century AD. They should eventually go on display in the Rocca Albornoz in VITERBO.

The bumpy well-grazed grass covering medieval FERENTO looks fit to burst with things long buried.

Fiano Romano

From below the walls the castle (built probably by Orsini in the 15th century and vigorously restored) is seen to tumble upwards in a most romantic and military way, every inch the Castello Ducale. To its piazza, it presents a decorous renaissance front.

Two things in the church: the Orsini monument with its oddly spaced-out succession of storeys (Nicola Orsini, who had it made in his lifetime, can only be seen from heaven); and, in a side place, a most graceful and abstract marble font. In the town, two life-size memorials: one, an Iranian patriot in the act of being shot – powerful and unpleasant; the other, Enrico Berlinguer, the leader of the Italian Communist Party who took it away from Stalinism, complete with folded copy of *Unità*, the party newspaper.

Ficoncella, Terme di

The people of CIVITAVECCHIA drive up here to splash around in a jolly open-air, blood-warm spring. Roman proles did the same. The Emperor Trajan built his own baths a little further round the hill. (See CIVITAVECCHIA.) At FICONCELLA (the name means Little Big Cunt) there is just a series of white walled enclosures down the steepish hillside, each with its own different shaped water basin in it, and perhaps making use of ancient stonework. Showers are bits of piping with holes punched in.

Comfortable citizens and their children slosh, or just loll reading waterproof paperbacks. On the fence enclosing this scene of happily thronged immersion are notices saying 'It is absolutely forbidden to come inside the fence' and 'Bathing forbidden'. Another says: 'Help us to keep the Ficoncella clean'. That one works.

Filacciano

A theatre set, commanding the Tiber valley.

The road has hairpinned down and now flattens obediently before the impressive pair of squat towers – or pavilions – or lodges – that flank a deeply recessed first gate. Through this, a second gate can be seen, which conducts the road up and through the basement and ground floor of the castle, and on into the medieval town beyond.

The Castle itself has a high frontispiece, rusticated for the flared lower half, which carries on above the perforation to a fine square top, with a couple of expressive saints and a bell between them. Leading up to all this, confining, even blinkering, our view of it, are two elegant runs of neatly detailed, two-storey, service buildings.

It is probably a 1690ish dramatisation of existing medieval elements: some of the walls made use of are much thicker than others. The architect of the remarkable ensemble has been forgotten, and is proving hard to rediscover: the tower smacks vaguely of Carlo Fontana.

Formello

The name comes from *formae*, meaning water conduit: the Etruscans took water from here to Veii (VEIO).

The town is within the Rome commuter belt and is mostly ugly suburb, but it has a medieval walled village in the middle. The condition of its handsome and ancient palazzo is lamentable, but restoration is promised. The church, San Lorenzo, uncomfortably abutting it and unpleasantly restored, is by the architect of the façade of Santa Caterina dei Funari in Rome, Guidetto Guidetti; it and another church still have fine early towers.

Outside FORMELLO are the remains of a villa that Cardinal Flavio Chigi built in 1670–81, and called 'Versaglia' after Versailles, than which it is smaller. The architect was Carlo Fontana, and he provided a monumental entrance, a square tower, and an axial arrangement of buildings down the slope, including an elliptical chapel: all set crossways in a small valley, on an exposed and bumpy hillside.

Galeria and Santa Maria di Galeria

SANTA MARIA DI GALERIA is a broad and handsome farm settlement of uncertain age round a wide square, open at two corners. Behind a Protestant-looking 1900s-ish façade stands the church of Santa Maria in Celsano, ancient indeed, though over-reinvented when the façade was put on. It is broad and low, with three arches each side: four granite columns in all, with bashed-about, Corinthian capitals, presumably Roman.

GALERIA is about a kilometre and a half beyond. The last stretch you go through a tunnel of greenery and out into a butter-rich glade with cowbells tinkling and the stripling Arrone purling away: a time-warp.

Here was the ancient Careia, Etruscan and then Roman. They quarried paving stone basalt. Refounded in 780 as a *domusculta*, destroyed by Saracens, GALERIA somehow survived to become an important place, but was abandoned in 1809 during a sudden spread of malaria. A town gate, the remains of houses of the 16th or 17th century, some arches over the streets, and the church tower still stand. The ravine is shrouded in impassable temperate jungle, through which you hear the waterfalls growling. Wellies till mid-June, then machetes.

Gallese

From its rocky spur, GALLESE commanded a long-used route from the CIMINO to where the Tiber was at once bridgeable and navigable. Pope Gregory III bought it in 733, the second of the Holy See's acquisitions, after SUTRI. In the 9th century, three natives of GALLESE became pope.

It became in 1558, with SORIANO, the place of banishment of a nephew of Pope Paul IV Carafa, the 'hermit pope'. Mistakenly, he had appointed his three nephews to positions of great power: Carlo, a cardinal and his chief minister; Giovanni, Duke of Paliano and

Commander of the Papal Forces; the third, a marchese and Captain of the Papal Guard. All turned out dissolute, villainous and corrupt, and all three were variously banished, Giovanni to these small acres on the CIMINO.

In 1560, here in the castle, Giovanni strangled his pregnant wife Violante Diaz, on suspicion of her having an affair with Martino Capece, the Captain of the Guard; Martino, he tortured into (probably false) confession, and then knifed to death. Alternatively, perhaps her brothers strangled her, as a matter of honour: the family was Spanish. Carlo Carafa meanwhile failed to be elected Pope on the death of his uncle and the successor, a Medici, Pius IV, immediately opened an inquest on the deaths. Giovanni went into a depression and Violante's brothers were executed. Stendhal made a story of these and later events, *La Duchesse de Palliano* (1838).

The castles of GALLESE and of SORIANO then went, in 1562, to Cardinal Madruzzo, Bishop of Trent (see SORIANO). He left both to his nephew Fortunato, who was married to Margherita Altemps,* and through the Altemps family GALLESE came to the present owners, the Hardouins, Dukes of Gallese. The present Duke's aunt was married to Gabriele d'Annunzio.

The Ducal Palace we see today, with its towers and high walls, is a late 16th–early 17th transformation of an earlier 16th-century castle which handsomely replaced and partly incorporated a medieval one. The usual architects' names are cited – Vignola, Giacomo della Porta, Carlo Fontana. The result is pleasing but not marvellous. On its far side, an arcaded loggia frames the Tiber valley.

Up in the town, the cathedral is unexpected; a huge, cool, airy, structure of 1796. Below, is the ancient church of San Famiano, 12th-century or older. The tower is oddly placed, and behind an agreeable full-width arcaded portico comes a complicated series of busy spaces – a fourth nave and an off-centre altar in a deep pit. Frescos are many and various, and a 15th-century tapestry half fills the chancel arch.

Through the fields and *burroni* to the south, about 3 kilometres downhill, the tufo gets creamier and the flowers ever more delicate and brilliant and there is a tiny other San Famiano, this time San Famiano a Longo – 'at a distance'. It is no more than a field chapel, anonymously post-Tridentine, but embraces, or embodies, something very old indeed. There is a spring; the tufo is ground

* The name Altemps is a Latinisation of the Austrian town of Hohenems, now home of the Schubertiad.

away, and two lots of rough, foot-worn steps lead down into a minute and ancient compound, flush with brilliant, water-dependent plants. Here is somewhere to feel the very beginnings of holy places: the water that people have always brought thanks for. The names of God change. The little spring is still flowing.

Gradoli

Unmistakably Farnese, the Palazzo dominates GRADOLI, half-way up its steep valley. Commissioned in 1513 by Cardinal Alessandro Farnese (the future Pope Paul III), Antonio da Sangallo the Younger here tapped coolness and fresh air by placing an austere and purposeful building on a rock-top medieval fortress. The Pope believed GRADOLI the healthiest place to spend the summer – CANINO for the winter.

The 13th-century capsule is still inside and the horse staircase which goes to the top is indicated externally by the 'yoked' windows of the north façade. As at CAPRAROLA, Sangallo carried upwards some of the battered fortifications, but the base here was so narrow that it began to shift and within ten years he buttressed it at three corners, an effect which still produces a gasp today. The big *salone* runs right through the building, a Venetian effect to improve ventilation, and above the already elevated *piano nobile* a large frescoed loggia, now glazed, took up the whole north-east quarter of the top floor. The *salone* was decorated (later) with grotesques in the CAPRAROLA manner; of which something remains. Some of the other frescos are by Perino del Vaga. The sea battles, a genre Paul III liked, are outstanding – for human expression it must be said, rather than sea-likeness, let alone seamanlikeness.

After the Farnese it was used by Philippine fathers, of the teaching order founded by St Philip Neri, who organised song and dance performances with the children, to which men and women were invited separately: these were so popular that the men came again dressed as women and vice versa. Later it was a school and the *salone* was used for basketball, which did surprisingly little damage.

Above the ravine the whole edifice piles seven storeys high. On the town side, where small streets and *piagge* were pulled down to secure better access and solidity, the Palazzo's fourth floor is level with the piazza. Here a wide neo-classical façade fronts the 17th-century church of Santa Maria Maddalena. Architecturally, the interior is unassuming, but the furniture and decoration are full of baroque swank; the side altars getting baroquer and baroquer as you go east, the shiny black confessionals with wonderful topknots, the pulpit with a fantastic feathered bottomknot as well, and the high altar and galleries resplendent with gilding.

The *passeggiata* is intense in the late afternoon. On Ash Wednesday the whole town brings its knife and fork to the Purgatory Dinner, and sits down to dine for the good of the dead. It used to be a silent and penitential meal, but they have thought better of that.

Graffignano

Open and airy. The Castle has one fine fat round tower and the remains of another. A fillet of delicate machicolations circles all.

Grotta Porcina

A 6th-century Etruscan site, on the old Via Clodia, between BLERA and NORCHIA, known at the turn of the century, then lost except to tomb-robbers until 1965. The monuments are unique but hard-to-read: a large, drum-shaped, perhaps-altar, with a single associated tomb; another largish drum, with what appears to be a procession of animals – *una teoria di animali* – carved on it and a little perhaps-auditorium around it.

Teoria in Italian means 'theory', 'procession of similar things' (as here: a theory is after all just a procession of ideas), and even 'embassy', because embassies used to go with mule trains.

Grotte di Castro

One of the teams in Pius II's 1462 boat-race (see ISOLA BISENTINA) came from 'Crypte San Lorenzo'. Afterwards he went there,

> through green fields and a lovely valley watered by clear streams ... [a place] steep and protected by very deep valleys. The townspeople have dug out caves in which most of them live.

All this sounds like GROTTE.

When Pope Innocent X destroyed CASTRO in 1649, many of the people came here: hence the later name.

The church stands castle-high above the road. Because its densely packed streets are parallel, the whole smoky-grey town looks combed back along its spur. It has many fine solid buildings, with smart windows, and a building pattern of two rows of brick to three rows of smooth-cut tufa.

The elder Rainaldi, Girolamo, started the church in 1625; Andrea Selvi completed it, with the great oval dome, in 1672. The huge golden 'glory', of 1713–14, is particularly magnificent, and should be seen when the sun is low in the west, but the whole interior is rich and interesting. The *Crucifixion*, school of Guido Reni, with a gold and mauve Mary Magdalene, is reputed to have come from CASTRO.

Some Etruscan tombs and colombaria are visitable. It is now a flourishing place and its lights are part of the nightscape of the Lake.

Grotte di Santo Stefano

Fossils of *Elephas Italicus Antiquus* and other great beasts were found here. The people came from destroyed FERENTO, and were living in caves until recently. San Venerando, than which a saint could hardly be more generalised, is commemorated on the church façade – a Roman soldier.

SS. Salvatore

A wild drive of some 5 kilometres brings you to a *sperone* and a ruined village, its church probably 12th-century. Across the gorge, a few hundred metres, is impressive and lonely MONTECALVELLO: by road 10 kilometres or more.

Ischia di Castro

This is a small bustling town, pouring along its *sperone*, with a lively medieval quarter and a fine 18th-century church full of good things (the 1538 font, or ciborium; Lombard enlacement work, recalling the predecessor church; and among the pictures a miraculous Madonna from a nearby hermitage – see POGGIO CONTE). Also several piazzas, a huge unfinished Farnese palazzo dramatically wrapped round the medieval castle, other palazzi and churches of various dates, a good local Antiquarium (the POGGIO CONTE frescos, material from CASTRO), and generally encouraging cooking smells.

Its amenity society, the 'Armine' (from the ancient name of the nearby River Fiora), conducts archaeological research, publishes excellent scholarly and popular booklets, and organises expeditions to local sites.

ISCHIA is where in 1395 several Farnese brothers were killed by infuriated peasants, in a ruckus over a woman; only two brothers survived, one of them Paul III's grandfather Ranuccio, who hid in a well; luckily for the Papacy and for Lazio. Already in the 9th century there had been a 'Ranuccio de Iscla'.

Pope Pius VII made the sculptor Antonio Canova Marquis of this

ISCHIA in 1816 for arranging the return to Italy of works of art removed by Napoleon.

Isola Bisentina

In the oceans of the world stand the continents of Eurasia and Africa: mediterranean to them lies a sea, peninsular to which uprears the land of Italy, among whose dead volcanoes smiles the LAKE OF BOLSENA, in which stands the Bisentine Island, where a watercourse broadens into a lakelet, where Jack, if he were small enough, could build a micronesia of twigs and sand. And Tom Thumb could continue with the fractals.

It is a place of Christian oratories and neat, paganising temples; of sombre Florentine proportionality and a little Edwardian opulence; of primeval ilex forest where there is no sound but the wind, and where, through the trees or at your feet, there is always the blue or silver light of the water. It is a place to garden, or await the last trump, or remember it.

The easiest access is by public boat from BOLSENA, which goes cheaply and pleasantly to the four other harbours on the Lake: ISOLA BISENTINA, CAPODIMONTE, MARTA, and ISOLA MARTANA. Turn up at the harbour by 9.30 any morning in summer.

The island presents a gothic crag to the north, sheer into clear deep water. Down the east coast are the quarries the buildings were taken from: the Lake washes into one. But the boat normally rounds the north-west bay where the wooded rocks decline gracefully to vertical clifflets and fine underwater tables of flat rock for standing on, and various caves with daylight showing through, and trees growing in the water: also a free-standing lion carved in the rock, with a blue, Hanoverian eye. As you round the low-lying wooded, western point, the southern point comes into sight; gothic giving way to classic. A miniature *tempietto* called the Rocchina stands atop a small, sharp cliff. And as the ship swings into the Elysian cove, a view opens up of the pink and gold cathedral, all to scale, the feathered dome floating above treetops. You land. Surprisingly you are in an Edwardian roofed dock, with sphinxes on guard among the oleanders.

Until recently you saw Etruscan sarcophagus lids among the lakebed boulders: this has always been both an Isle of the Blest and an Island of the Dead. The sarcophagi and the columbarium below the Rocchina suggest the Etruscans of Bisentium – BISENZIO – on the cliff to the west used it as a necropolis. When Pope Pius II visited the Island in June 1462 the ruins of a Roman Bisentium were still visible. He enjoyed his visit and recorded:

> Friars Minor [Franciscans] live there who, because they strictly observe their Rule, are called Observantini; they are exemplary men devoted to poverty and abstinence. Ranuccio Farnese built both a church and a convent for them, and he gave them the fields of the island, which they diligently cultivate with orchards and corn and olives and beans. There is plenty of meadowland. A part is left to the rabbits, very many of which hide among the brambles; hunting them often enriches the friars' table. They cut a path with sickles among the thorns and the rocks across which they stretch nets a cubit high; with sticks and stones they beat the spinney and force the animals to come out, which are then easily held in the nets. A third of the island is wild and rocky, but there are olives and almonds there, and no lack of vines, and ilexes grow on the peak. There are many oratories there which you reach by steps cut in the rock. Pius ordered a new one to be built on the summit, and endowed it with spiritual graces.

Another day there was a boatrace.

> After lunch, the captains of the boats ... presented themselves, and also lusty young men who were the rowers ... All were extraordinarily confident and boastful. Everyone despised everyone else and exalted himself, and the more they had to drink the more they lauded their own exploits.... The boats were to have four oars and a coxswain.... The coxswains ... wreathed their heads with white linen and poplar leaves, and so did the oarsmen, who were naked but for loincloths, and glistening with oil ... They were followed closely by a fleet of smaller boats full of spectators shouting and applauding one crew or another and making the air ring with their cries till the hills re-echoed ...
>
> Although the Pope was in a quiet spot some way from the harbour discussing politics with the cardinals, still he watched the boatrace with pleasure and amusement.
>
> Among those present was a certain Guicciardo related to the Pope and for that made Prefect of Bolsena.... He cried: '... our men are made strong by exercise and by drinking unwatered wine. I snap my fingers at [the others]. Award the prize now and declare us the winners!' The judge answered: 'If the palm belongs to heavy drinkers, I do not deny your clients are famous for that.

[They will not win] unless you have seen to it that they can get a drink every time they smite the water with their oars.'

The coxswain of the Marta boat cried 'What are we doing, boys? We're lying third; shame on us, we're used to being first ... Row up! Row up! Save our nation from this outrage!'

[Three boats passed the Bolsinians] for by now the dry lips of the drinkers were panting and the men were streaming with sweat which there was no wine to replace....

The Martani came in far ahead of the others ... The Bolsinians, left among the last and dreading reproaches and abuse, did not come into harbour at all.

Nowadays, Marta produces motor-boat champions.

On the Island, nothing much has changed, except that there are now pheasants, and a number of more or less formal walks and, it grows on you, a sense of carefully devised, even orchestrated, vistas in the 18th-century English 'landscape' manner: nature and art so well married their progeny ever smiles.

On the mountain, 'Mount Tabor', there are seven oratories, in different stages of disrepair, with frescos in different stages of erasure. Four of them were built between 1431 and 1462. Up the east side to the top they make a real *via sacra*, and from the top down to the south-western corner a contemplative and cool wander. The first is a chapel of the Crucifix, with several scenes in fresco; the third on the way up has a fresco of the *Transfiguration*, which is still legible and is of a striking design. Benozzo Gozzoli had been in VITERBO painting a cycle of the life of St Rose and the painter here could have been one of his assistants. The design was possibly Benozzo's.

The classical *tempietto* so visible from the water is one of a pair planned by Antonio da Sangallo the Younger between 1516 and 1522 to stand on the northern and southern peaks of the island. The Rocchina, for half its height, is accurately built in the grey mainland peperino Antonio was using elsewhere at the same date: above, the execution is rougher, and uses island tufo. The second *tempietto* on the high north peak never got built, or was built different, or has been superseded by a later building. Vasari says both were built, which is hard to square with what remains.

The Rocchina is so named because it was built on the foundations of a little medieval fort. (The razorback climb to it is another giant effect in miniature, like the view from the water.) Cut into the rock straight under it is an Etruscan columbarium – a chamber with some hundreds of funerary pigeon holes. And at water level a cave is hollowed through the rock from coast to coast: a poolside scene with everything reversed. You sit and sip under cover in the breeze, 30 metres under a tomb two and a half thousand years old and a renaissance temple, in a crypt with a view, and take your dip in a sunny 115-square-kilometre pool.

The tall church of St James and St Christopher down on the flat probably dates from 1586, long after Antonio's death. The cloister (in process of re-erection) was presumably attached to the previous church. It may also be related to the cloister that Antonio drew in the 1520s for Santa Maria in Montoro, below MONTEFIASCONE.

With only a fine wooden reredos and tabernacle, the empty church is spacious and peaceful. Its contents were removed during the Napoleonic vacuuming of Italian treasures and only Ranuccio Farnese's tomb by Isaia of Pisa remains from the older church. He was the Farnese brother – see ISCHIA DI CASTRO – who hid down the well. He is spelt Rhamnutius in the bombastic way of the first humanists, perhaps hopefully suggesting Egyptian ancestry. Other Farnese tombs are now all gone. The convent building beside (no miniature, this) is probably of between the mid-15th and mid-16th centuries, as are various other buildings which add to the magical harmony of this place.

In 1599 the last 'Rector' of the friary on the Island preached in BOLSENA during Lent about the economic plight of the friars, and after a public debate the Town Council agreed to give them the church and convent of Santa Maria del Giglio above the town. Various other monks and hermits tried it, among them Evelyn's 'gloomy Capucines', but none stayed long. In 1893 the Church sold it outright and it has since had several owners. The convent building was restored around the turn of the century and a pair of splendid mock 15th-century fireplaces was installed at either end of the refectory. The tall open ironwork vault over the little dock – boathouse is not a princely enough word – is a prefab bought at the Milan Fair in 1914. The Island is now lovingly cared for by Prince Giovanni del Drago.

Isola Farnese

A volcanic neck overlooking VEIO, with a village close enough to Rome to have changed from total decay to total repair in recent times. Not an island, and only briefly Farnese.

Isola Martana

The Island of Marta is a narrow porcupine of a rock; vertically corrugated and downwardly striated; smaller and wilder than the ISOLA BISENTINA.

When the Gothic King Theodoric died, his daughter, the widowed Amalasuntha, whose broad calm gaze we know in the Palazzo dei Conservatori in Rome, became regent on behalf of her son Athalaric. She tried to bring him up with her own attainments (she was trilingual in Gothic, Latin, and Greek) but the men took him away to a martial education, and he died of drink at 18. Her heir was then her cousin Theodahad – Thomas Hodgkin called him 'a student of Plato and a practitioner of every kind of low chicanery' – whom in 534 she invited to share the kingdom. Within a year he had imprisoned her on this desolate island, perhaps as a hostage in negotiating with the Emperor Justinian, and then had her murdered. Theodahad was deposed the following year by the Gothic Council, and killed by a hired assassin.

During the Saracen raids, of the 8th century, mainland shepherds and farmers, who rowed to work each day, lived on the Islands, and both became free communes. In the 1070s, Pope Gregory VII and the Countess Matilda were lucky enough to find the bones of St Cristina here (see BOLSENA).

Under Farnese ownership, religious communities came and went. Benedictine nuns had renamed it Isola Maddalena when Pius II sailed around the Island, attended mass, and kissed the

> bones of St Mary Magdalene who washed the holy feet of the Lord ... These are said to have been discovered recently by a miracle and attract crowds of worshippers.

Amalasuntha's prison is not known. At the miniature private harbour, a single 19th-century house stands in fine trees on an apron of soft moist grass. An old pump, if vigorously worked for long enough, will produce a naturally chilled mineral water.

The rest, in Pius's words, is 'a high rock difficult of access'. Some way up, the rock provided natural fortifications for the former town gate. The scale of the walled enclosure suggests a settlement of several hundred people. At one point, from a gash in the hillside a tunnel runs diagonally down to the back of the Island at water level. At the very top the remains of a small church with Lombardic apse are clearly legible; a square tower beside it, sheer above the lake.

Swallowtails of both kinds bounce around together up here and everything is more amiable than the view from the water suggests.

Ladispoli

The worn stump of the Torre Flavia stands out in the sea: a papal tower from which the coast has retreated. The fine beach prompted Prince Ladislao Odescalchi, in 1890, to found a resort town. He also wished to shift peasants out of the courtyard village attached to his castle at PALO.

LADISPOLI has grown prodigiously. A grid town: come live in a noisy street nearer the sea than your own noisy street. Today, there are several thousand Soviet Jews here: Israel would welcome them, but they want to go to the US. But with *perestroika* they are no longer political refugees which to enter the US they must be. Yet the US insists the Soviet Union prove its bona fides by letting them leave. Catch 22.

Lamone, Selva di

The River Fiora rises in Monte Amiata, flows south to the sea, and from the beginning of human time people lived beside it. It and the Olpeta (see CASTRO) bound the SELVA DI LAMONE, the great wilderness that straddles the Tuscany/Lazio border and runs seawards from the LATERA crater. Metalled roads encircle it, but only dust tracks wind through; there are indicated 'walks', but Annibal Caro was not exaggerating when he described it as frightful – *spaventoso*.

It is a waterless scrub forest: the biggest trees are oak. There is also maple, a bit of ash, and thorn, and never a clear view of more than 120 metres; which adds claustrophobia to silence, solitude, and heat. Truly intimidating are the *murce*: technically 'parallel cumuli of basaltic masses', to the rest of us long, piled-up heaps of dense, dark grey boulders, somewhat pitted; they are broken or split and obviously volcanic, but the heaps are formless; deposited, you feel, not pushed or rolled, but no one knows how. The stunted trees grow straight out of them. They cannot be walked among or over. The flora and fauna – 240 species of vertebrates – are remarkable, and mostly undisturbed.

Signs of human presence – worked stones on the right bank of the Fiora – go back to the earliest times and some 100 Bronze Age sites of the 26th to the 10th centuries BC have been identified. By the 12th century BC there was a 'spur' settlement near the springs of the Fiora's tributary, the Nova, with ovens in a separate zone from the habitations. Elsewhere there were fortifications of a sort, making use of high places and building up dry-stone walls between the *murce*. A site called Crosteletto, which was destroyed in 1972, was inhabited for a thousand years and seems to have been a small capital, with identifiably 'monumental' structures. Near the Ponte San Pietro (see POGGIO CONTE) there are signs of a water cult where a torrent disappears into the rock.

In the 10th century BC, the settlements suddenly ceased: did everyone move to VULCI and become Etruscan townspeople? It seems not unlikely because before the 10th century there was no one at VULCI.

During the Middle Ages innumerable little towers and fortresses were put up and destroyed along the river: here ran the borders of the Patrimony of St Peter with both Siena and the County of Pitigliano. Romantic ruins remain.

The LAMONE was always a famous refuge for brigands: Domenico Tiburzi was one. Born at CELLERE in 1836, he was fined 20 lire by his employer – then a substantial sum – shot the overseer who tried to collect it, was convicted, broke gaol, and lived his life an outlaw. He blasphemed against God, but respected the Virgin Mary. During the Second World War partisans and escaped prisoners of war followed his haunts.

Latera

In 1987, the middle school collected information about LATERA: 608 men, 578 women; 45 per cent *inabile* – economically 'inactive'; 18 per cent of school age; 37 per cent 'active' – among whom 18 per cent in agriculture, 7 per cent in industry, 5 per cent in commerce and 5 per cent 'other'. Geothermal power may improve things.

In 1394 LATERA was handed over to a *condottiere*, Jan Tedesco, for him to pay his troops with. In 1408, a Farnese obtained it and in 1452 another became first Duke. (It was his descendant who sacked CASTRO in 1527 on the Pope's orders.) Pope Paul III left it intact when he established the nearby Dukedom of CASTRO and if ever LATERA flourished, it was then. In 1668, it reverted to papal rule.

The oldest part, tight, tear-drop-shaped, is behind the bastions of the north gate. Many houses have *profferli* in the VITERBO manner. There is of course a 16th-century Farnese palazzo, small but powerful, now nearly ruinous, and the 17th-century church of San Clemente (also Farnese) has pleasant pictures of the time.

The rest of the town slithers pleasantly down into the bottom of the volcano of LATERA, the third, and latest, of the three volcanic systems that together make up the complex of the Monti Volsini (the others being BOLSENA and MONTEFIASCONE). Until recently, steam escaped and gases stank. The Madonna della Cava – of the Quarry – where the processions went, stood by an old sulphur mine. Greenish-blue piping now zigzags across the flat fields and a quarry produces bright white potassic feldspar.

Lubriano

A robust and well spruced-up baroque chapel welcomes you to this rewarding little town: Santa Maria del Poggio, where San Porcolo (St Piglet, unknown to standard hagiographies) is venerated. The fan of up-sweeping steps, the lusciously calculated curves and scoops of the façade, could well belong in some splendid Alpine *Sacro Monte*.

From its terrace you look over to poor estropiated little CIVITA, and the rest of a chain of dwindling summits, down to the Tiber. Some have a remaining bush, or a ruin, at the top and the line your eye draws from one to the other shows the original surface, which the streams have been sucking away at for millennia.

Ancient decorated stones in the fabric of the parish church of San Giovanni Battista show it is old, and there is also a fine framed piece of 16th-century fresco. The subject is obscure: an angel turns towards us while swiftly pulling a small child along, out of a cave, and out of the frame, to some undefined safety.

Most unusually, there is a wealth of good modern artefacts, many of them commissioned by the present parish priest. The excellent altar carvings and some others are by Luigi Fundi. The not big, but powerful, wooden Crucifix on the east wall is by Aldo Belocchio. There are also new Stations of the Cross, and silvered bronze altar furniture. In the 1930s, the east wall was successfully opened up to reveal through tall arches a number of receding chambers at different levels.

The agreeable 18th-century façade shares the piazza with a delicately mannerist palazzo: the ground-floor windows are neatly rusticated over rustication and the *piano nobile* ones appear secured to the string course by little flaps. The palazzo's west-facing side presents what passes in Italy for Rococo: gentle plaster curves, light pilasters superimposed in groups, feathery ironwork. A former formal garden behind.

The Field-Castles: Santa Caterina, the Castello delle Seppie, and la Cervara

In the Middle Ages all this countryside was dotted with 'field-castles', controlling the route across from the coast to where the upper Tiber could be forded. A few remain, now mostly as towered farm buildings.

Santa Caterina, in the valley beneath LUBRIANO, is a dark tower in a solitude. It was rebuilt in or after the Renaissance, rugged and tall with neat string courses and careful detail. A pair of farm sheds give an appearance of balancing pavilions.

The Castello delle Seppie – *seppie* are cuttlefish – further up the same valley, had been Lombardic, and probably Roman: now converted to a house.

La Cervara on the other hand, Place of Deer, over the rim towards the LAKE OF BOLSENA, is derelict and dank.

Lucus Feroniae

Here just above the Tiber flood-plain was the sanctuary of the goddess Feronia, addressed equally by Faliscans, Latins, Sabines, and Etruscans: an ancient Italic personage concerned with crops, waters, health, and fertility. Along with the place she was taken over by the Romans in the usual way and they paved the Via Tiberina all the way from Rome.

Hannibal sacked it in 211 BC. It was rebuilt more grandly, as the Colonia Julia Felix Lucus Feroniae and the shrine lasted as long as the Empire. Votive offerings take the form of human parts, including internal organs. (At one of VEIO's sanctuaries, most of the votive offerings were genital organs, indicating perhaps a local medical specialism.)

The site was only identified in 1953. It is a wide slope, nicely mown by sheep, dotted with unexcavated bumps and here and there the low walls of satisfied archaeology. The best thing is the mass of sumptuous mosaic floors in what remains of the villa of the Volusii Saturnini, a senatorial family, which was the centre of a large agricultural estate.

Luni sul Mignone

Home to early pastoralists (from the fourth millennium) and a place for cheese in Etruscan times. One of nature's fortresses.

Magliano Romano

The name has been changed from the excessively expectoratory Pecorareccio, to that of a town on the other side of the Tiber.

In the piazza, we saw a flock of long-haired sheep pouring past a smart silver Mercedes, led by their shepherd on his mule, his umbrella furled across his back.

The castle good-looking, irregular, appears to grow out of its rock.

Malano, Selva di

A landowner has reported finding, beyond Santa Lucia, in among the near impassable vegetation, three megaliths, along with shaped walls and worked blocks, that put him in mind of those of Brittany and Britain.

Malborghetto

The Arch of Malborghetto is a fortified *casale* built around a four-sided Roman brick and travertine arch, which became a refuge for brigands.

Before his nearby victory over Maxentius, Constantine had seen a luminous cross in the sky, inscribed 'IN THIS LIES VICTORY'. In the words of Lemprière's *Classical Dictionary* of 1788, this 'reminded the monarch of his superstitious adherence to the heathen religion, and he immediately became a convert to Christianity'. The arch celebrated the victory.

It was filled in probably in the 6th or 7th century. Restored in 1567, and recently turned into a house.

Manziana

This pretty town was planned by the Collegio del Santo Spirito, and new-built in the second half of the 16th century for the exploitation of *Pietra Amitiana*, a fire-resistant substance found here. The work-force was brought in from Tuscany. At that time, the Selva di MANZIANA stretched right to the TOLFA HILLS: the forest that remains is still very grand. (And smells of sulphur.)

Before the new town, there was a castle with the name of Santa Pupa (St Breast, St Doll, or St Poop) and two little old towers from it are embedded in the 16th-century palazzo built for the Barons of the Holy Spirit who managed the development. The well-disposed piazza, with its well-designed fountain of 1733, enjoys a distant glimpse of the LAKE OF BRACCIANO.

The church of St John the Baptist, perhaps of the 1790s, holds a surprise: where you would expect aisles behind its wide, low façade, there is a shop on one side and the priest's house on the other, all under the one roof.

Manziana is a grand place for early figs. When they were making Spaghetti Westerns nearby, this is where the Red Indians would stop for coffee.

Marta

The village used to stand in the LAKE OF BOLSENA, where the river of the same name leaves it. It is not an aristocratic place: the Farnese, who of course owned it, left their usual mark, but modestly.

A fine chunk of 13th-century castle, even a fortified zone, still dominates the town: a 'clock-tower', square below and octagonal above, and crenellated, which signals Marta all across the Lake. (Ordinary families have long lived in it.) Lower down is a small Palazzo Farnese and, under various tunnels, the medieval quarter, with a tall neo-classical parish church shoe-horned in. The church of San Biagio, out of the old centre, is a holy cupboard, where lanterns for night processions are stored – they are like flies' eyes – for the parish banner, which is a skull and crossbones. (Not for piracy on the Lake but for the *Buona Morte* – Good Death. Big lads wearing T-shirts saying *Buona Morte* are not aggressive: it is a charitable society with an annual dinner for the poor.) Over the altar the Crucifix has all the Instruments of the Passion on it – hammers, tongs, spear, mallet, pincers, whips, thorns; no Christ. It is a place to submit oneself for a short time to the late 17th-century sensibility which has somehow survived here among the peasants and fishermen.

The promenade beside the Lake was made only half a century ago. Before, the substantial fishermen's houses were 'amphibious': their fronts on the street and their backs standing in the water. Their cellars were open to the lake waters and used as tanks for breeding and rearing fish, with watertight doors between cellar and lake. A curious geological freak allowed the water to disappear into the earth's bowels when the doors were closed. Old photographs show the calm and noble repeated structure of these houses reflected in the Lake.

Marta's main fame is the extraordinary *festa* called the Barabbata.

There is an oral tradition of a former ceremony called *Va a Pigliar Barabba* – 'Go get Barabbas'. A man would be Barabbas and hide in the *macchia*, and all the other men would go after him by night with staves. When they had him they would 'kill' him.

Another possible origin in the reported exclamation of a bygone cleric: *Ma questa e una barabbata!* – 'But this is a shambles!' (Barabbata is not a dictionary word.) This could well have been the Cardinal-Bishop Barbarigo of MONTEFIASCONE, who in 1704 tried to suppress it. Such opinions are not unheard even today, but recent parish priests have been glad to encourage any homegrown sprout of religion which is neither sacrilegious nor indecent, let alone so marvellous a one as this.

The tradition recalled is common: a baker's girl was collecting firewood up the hill and the Madonna appeared and told her she needed a shrine. The men put the girl in an oxcart to carry her down in honour, and the oxen dug their heels in at a certain spot, so the church called Santa Maria del Monte was built, to which the Barabbata now goes, or rather at which it charges, each year since.

At four o'clock on the morning of 14 May the men go round the town beating drums and knocking on windows and the church bells ring. They then go, or are supposed to go, to mass, in their own parish churches. After that they get properly dressed: white open-necked shirt, straw hat, checked kerchief, black trousers. Next the carts or floats are brought down to the lakeside gardens and finishing touches are carried out, mostly by the women, who have also made most of the floats in the months before, while the men have an energy-conservation programme. There are hundreds of visitors, of whom almost all are from neighbouring villages. No foreigners in the sense we foreigners use the word.

There are twenty or thirty *trofei* or *fontane*: floats. Some are pulled by men, some by oxen still, some little ones for children by donkeys, some even littler ones by the children themselves, and quite a few by tractors. For their structural ingenuity, their knowledge and sense of renaissance architectural style, the playfulness of their design, the imagination with which natural materials – flowers, reeds, wheat, maize, fish, foliage, flowers, flowers, and flowers again – are combined, for the diligence and adroitness with which they are made, these spring chariots not only preserve those of the high renaissance 'triumphs', they also show a generation that never knew what peasant culture can be. In former times it was part of the pride of the rite that there should be out-of-season produce: olives, mushrooms, grapes, and soft fruit in spring. This was achieved by secret means 'handed down from father to son for generations', which refrigeration has taken the marvel out of.

There is a large boat with fine lines, made entirely of *ciambelle* (see Food). Boats and houses made of reeds. An altar-piece made of reeds and barley with flowers correctly draping the baroque columns. A papal triple tiara made of huge carp. Little fish left where they were caught like stars in the nets which are now spread out for the night sky. Little trolleys for children with yet littler fish upon them. A giant chalice made of reed. Floats carrying entire agricultural cycles, some of them with fountains on board (hence the name *fontane*), the closed-cycle water now driven by an electric pump, no longer by a pump handle: among them vintage, maturing, drinking; sowing, reaping, threshing; the fisherman's net, the paraffin lamp for night fishing, the cleaning knife. Loaves a metre long and half a metre wide. A *ricotta* cheese the size of a Jumbo's wheel. Children's carts with a tiny church or house above and a separate compartment below with a cock and two rabbits in it, looking staid. A vast sacred heart done in purple flowers and dressed with fish all round. (And what fish: not only the standard *corregone*, perch, eel; but green lake trout and giant carp and tench from the bottom that you never see in the market.) Plenty of *vomeri*, the Etruscan-Roman wooden plough that you stand on behind your ox, to push it down.

Under the two *Ceri*, the elected Captains of the Festival, each of whom carries a big candle, the men are divided into two overall classes: the *casenghi* and the *bifolchi*. The former were originally those who worked about or for the castle and the Farnese: the carriers and the mounted cowherds called *butteri*, the overseers and stewards and craftsmen. The latter were and are the peasants themselves. They divide into the *villani*, who are general farmworkers, the *sementerelli*, sowers, the *vanghe* and *zappatori*, spades and hoes, the *pescatori*, of course, the *pecorai* (only since the 19th century, when the new cheese factories made them producers), and the *mietitori*, the gleaners, who still don't count for much, and are not allowed to take part in the *passate*, which we shall come to in a moment.

All these then, when the moment comes, climb on board and start reaping or drinking or whatever, or mount and caracole along, or start walking beside their *trofeo* or indeed beside their infant son, the smallest *buttero* of them all, complete with straw hat and kerchief, to make sure he doesn't fall off, and the procession goes up through the town. It is men and boys only. The women and girls on the balconies scatter yellow broom petals, laughing and vying to scatter best on the best-loved unmarried men, who caracole below with careful nonchalance. Each team stops from time to time and the men take off their hats and wave them, shouting very cheerfully and loud: *Evviva il Santissimo Sacramento della Madonna del Monte!* – 'Long live the Most Holy Sacrament of Our Lady of the Hill!' and other suitable sentiments, and laughing half in satisfaction and half to distance themselves from it.

There is also of course the village band, as there always is and, as there very often are today, the drum majorettes. (How did these uniquely privileged girls in their absurdly incompatible rig get here? From the United States, of course: but how did they get to America?) How startled Benozzo Gozzoli and Botticelli would have been by them, though by nothing else. At the rear come the clerics, the *pretonzoli* as some voices say among the crowd – that is the rude word for them. The bishop is quite old and very regal-looking; he blesses the multitude with assured satisfaction. He is also delighted with the youngest *buttero* of them all.

For the last few metres of the ascent to the shrine, the cars drawn by manpower or childpower go shouting at a run, while the oxen and tractors wait respectfully. The men do not go into the church for the mass which is being celebrated. They rumble and lumber up the lane on to a crowded ledge in the hill behind, where they start cooking. And they cook and cook, and pour and pour, and give food and wine to the multitude for a long time, in a sort of counter-mass of their own.

After the mass some of them do go in. They take goats with them, but nothing bigger. At the door they shout: *Viva il Santissimo*... etc. as before, and then, in a low voice, they mutter (if that is who they are) *Casenghi*, *Casenghi*. Then they kiss the Peace, which is a bit of the Virgin Mary's robe in a reliquary, and make the *Passate*. These 'passes' are a matter of walking three times out of the church by a side door, and three times back in again by the main door, shouting the while about the *Santissimo*, etc. During the third, they thresh a token quantity of wheat before the people on the paving stones outside, and that is the culmination of the festival. Then they take the loaves and fishes home to eat, and in the evening if it is fine they all get drunk and play the fool.

You can make what you like of the Barabbata. Some see pre-Christian rites in it: and indeed perhaps the months of work on the miniature gardens and vineyards do descend from the Adonis gardens of the classical world: the first windowboxes. More attention than is needed has been lavished on the 'Get Barabbas' aspect, which no longer exists, because it seems to belong with the regicide rites

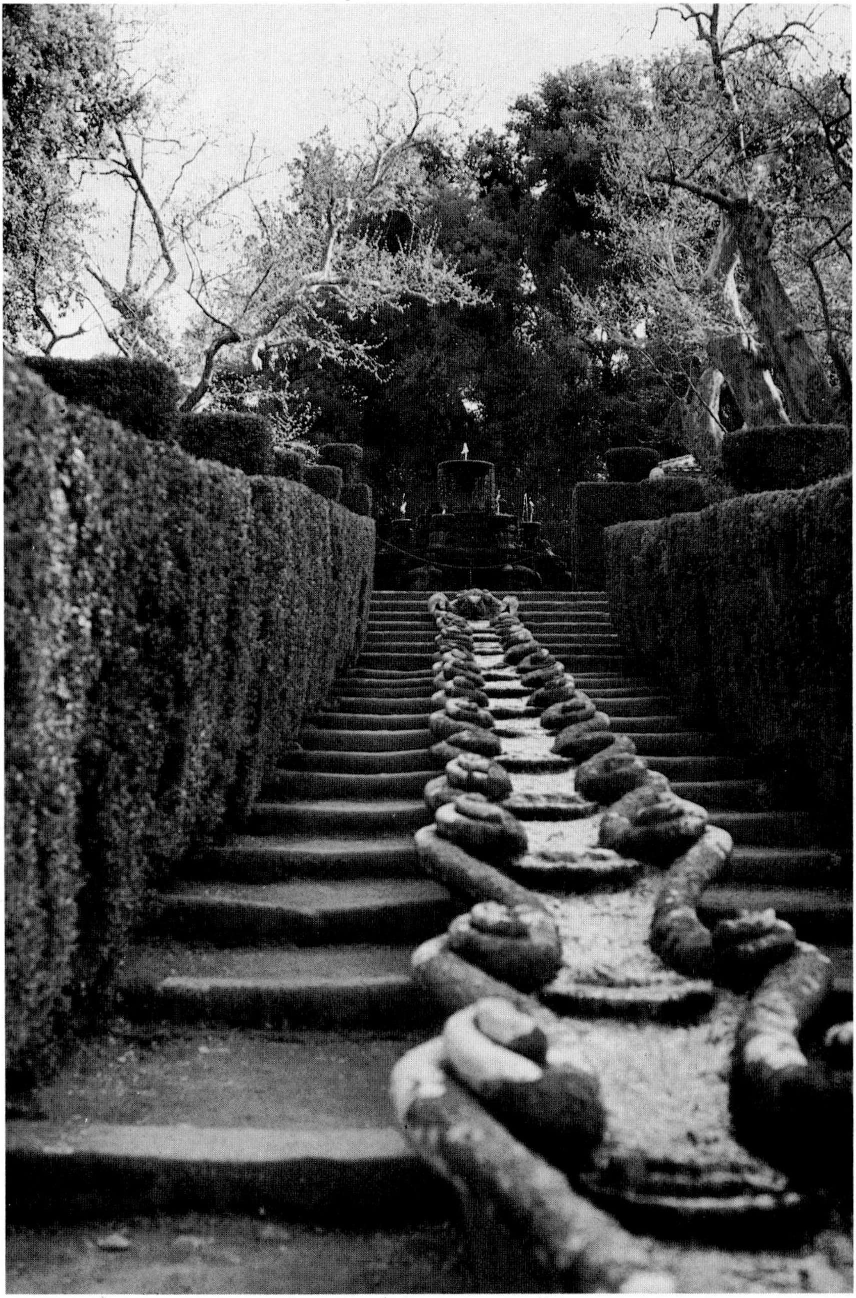

1. Bagnaia, Villa Lante, the water-rope

2. Etruscan art nouveau, Tarquinia, Museo Nazionale

3. Tarquinia, wall painting, Lioness tomb

4. Civita Castellana Cathedral, little fellow with lion

5. Civita Castellana Cathedral, sphinx, 11th century

6. Tuscania, San Pietro, *trifrons*

7. (*right*) Capranica, San Lorenzo, the Anguillara tomb

8. Monterano, ruined convent

9. Bassano Romano, San Vincenzo, with bust of Christ

10. Tarquinia, Santa Maria in Castello

11. Viterbo, San Sisto

12. 15th-century house near Viterbo

13. The *festa* of the Barabbata at Marta

14. Caprarola, the Great Garden

15. Cerveteri, Etruscan tomb, interior

16. Castle of Santa Severa

17. Castle of Onano

18. Tolfa

19. Bracciano

20. Calcata

21. Anguillara

22. Caprarola, the Judgment Room

23. Viterbo, Chiesa della Verità, Mazzatosta Chapel, *The Marriage of the Virgin*, Lorenzo da Viterbo

24. The Bagnaccio, near Viterbo

25. Cellere, Sant' Egidio, Antonio da Sangallo the Younger

26. Bomarzo, the Sacred Grove: the Echydna

beside the other Latial – but not Tuscian – lake at Nemi which provide the framework for Frazer's once almost infinitely influential *Golden Bough*. Others see a begetting-and-conceiving festival, and of course there is something of that in any Spring rite, but the little dolls included among the flowers and leaves did not look very phallic or philoprogenitive to us. Some were clearly of the Pope. Again, a good and careful book has been written by a Gramscian scholar, Paola de Sanctis Ricciardone, which makes it a manifestation of class defiance by the have-nots against haves of the priesthood. Whatever it is, it is extremely beautiful and cheerful.

Martignano, Lake of

You approach by a track off the Cassia cut 6 metres deep through the rim of the BACCANO crater, presumably by the Etruscans. The meagre remains of a 13th-century castle, abandoned in the 14th, are incorporated in the farm buildings which now stand alone in the crater. The land is private, but careful walkers are not made unwelcome. Cars are, and should continue to be. The place is of a rare and shining beauty, straight out of Poussin.

Mazzano

MAZZANO is three villages: the very old, the rather old, and the modern. The very old is packed on to a neck of rock, high above the rushing TREIA and goes back at least to 945: an example of *incastellamento*.

The church has fallen in, though its walls remain. The one-time *castello*, very small, shows two arches' worth of 16th-century loggia: enough for a smart impression? A single donkey-wide passage threads through mostly abandoned houses; a gothic-arched window or two; thin cats; old *conserva* tins growing nettles instead of the basil of yesteryear.

A little girl warns us that rats come out of holes between the paving stones at five o'clock.

The views are magnificent.

Mezzano

In the big dry crater of LATERA, the tiny Lake of Mezzano standing in for any previous lakes. The River Olpeta, its outlet, circumfluctuates almost the whole crater before going off west to join the Fiora.

The Lake is now 36 metres deep, very blue, and at the centre of an agricultural estate with not a metalled road on it. Everything is clean, farming methods are modern, and apart from the essential *Maremmano* dogs announcing arrivals, silent. In among the prosperous farmhouse buildings is a small chapel, with monuments to the Counts of Brazza-Savorgnan, one of whom gave his name to Brazzaville.

On Monte Becco, the tree-quiffed hill to the south, Swedish archaeologists have found (but not yet explored) a 4-metre-diameter Etruscan well. It may be a *mundus*, a safety vent to keep this world and the Underworld in good touch (cf. C. S. Lewis, *The Magician's Nephew*).

Montalto di Castro

Vulci's port, Regas, was near here and after defeat it became a Roman military camp. Vulci minimally survived, had an early bishopric and transferred to Montalto, probably in the 8th century. The hill is extremely modest and the castle probably began as a fortified convent.

Formerly Farnese, it now belongs to the Guglielmi shipping family, of CIVITAVECCHIA. The long strung-out red brick structure manages to look as if most of it were curtain wall. Nice crenellating of neighbouring buildings continues the effect.

A post-modernist cemetery is being built on the CANINO road. Those who like colour patterns in the soil will enjoy the undulating Piano del Diavolo.

Nearby on the coast is a Brobdignagian power station which was built to be nuclear, ran into fiery green opposition, was changed to coal, oil, and natural gas, was subject to further economic analysis, and is at the time of writing to be for oil and gas only: it is already a monument to expenditure and dissension.

Monte Romano

MONTE ROMANO is a smallish place on the main road between TUSCANIA and TARQUINIA. It is made up of handsome but disjointed urban elements of the 17th and 18th centuries.

The castle had been regularly destroyed and rebuilt, and at one point the Church sold it to arm a fleet against the Turks. Then in 1644 the Ospedale di Santo Spirito, sometimes called Arcispedale – Hospital of the Holy Spirit, or Arch-hospital – decided to follow up its enterprise at ROCCA RESPAMPANI by establishing a substantial 'agricultural colony' here as well; all of which required detailed permission from Rome.

A Papal Brief allowed two substantial new residential 'nuclei' at the eastern end of the village, with houses for 'vassals' and leaseholders, away from the existing nucleus. Then a *centro monumentale* was attempted in the gap between the two ends, with a prison (1731), a church and a palazzo (both 1767), a clock-tower (1768), and several fountains, all on the south side of the main road.

Nothing jelled: these were the *membra disjecta* of a town. So, the long Borgo Calino was built (between 1766 and 1776) on the north side of the road, in three sections – two residential, one a granary – made up of repetitive modules, in a clever attempt to impose visual continuity and linkage across the now straddled road.

The effort is there: grand, but still a spatchcock. The visitor has a haunting hope that everything may suddenly fall into pleasing relationships.

Whose might the effort have been? Dr Munari, the architectural historian, has observed that early drawings show the Borgo 'indefinite in its longitudinal development', but not related to the 'real situation of Monte Romano' (i.e., whoever was responsible for the plans had never actually been there). Vanvitelli and Ferdinand Fuga had both been producing a string of hospitals and prisons within the Papal States at about this time, and Munari is willing to attribute such 'august paternity' to the Borgo. Not implausibly.

Monte Virginio

High on the rim of the BRACCIANO crater, but facing the TOLFA HILLS, is the Eremo – the Hermitage – del Monte Calvario, which Discalced Carmelites took over in 1651.

The place has a feel of ancient holiness – Bona Dea? Sylvanus? The views are splendid; the wide low buildings of 1668 generously cared for. The church is small and handsome and its many fairly good pictures are ascribed by tradition to a Fra Luca Carmelitano – Brother Luke the Carmelite. The central cloister is a great garden, and all is wide open to visitors and the warm winds.

Montebello

A farmhouse, rightly named, built for the Camera Apostolica in 1769.

Montecalvello

The courtyard of the Castle, which could only expand along and round the rock it was built on, was redone in the 16th century, and the two little half-streets in the 17th, when the Pamphili had it. That is all there is. Inside, renaissance friezes in empty, airy rooms. The painter Balthus has worked here for many years.

Montefiascone

MONTEFIASCONE presides so authoritatively over the Etruscan Plain that George Dennis believed it must be 'the site of the Fanum Voltumnae, the shrine at which the "princes of Etruria" were wont to meet ...' He admitted that 'to prove the fact with the *data* we have is impossible'. The present data are no better; the site remains stupendous.

Before any Etruscans, about 1800 BC, people were ranging the wooded plain and slopes, hunting and raising beasts: Rinaldone, south-east of MONTEFIASCONE, gives their culture its name. They buried their dead one above the other in grotto-like tombs, with big stones on their bellies and amid small fossil shells. Their wounds and weapons show they were fierce fighters; some were 2 metres tall.

The Etruscans certainly used the place, though not necessarily as a town: it could have been a sanctuary. Their stones are in the lowest levels of the Duomo and the Castle; and a complex of large *cuniculi* (2–3 metres high, $1\frac{1}{2}$–$2\frac{1}{2}$ broad) has been found under the city.

The medieval town developed as people from the plain withdrew behind walls against the barbarians. (The name's derivation is obscure.) In the mid-13th century the Popes, finding the Romans intolerable, moved to VITERBO; and when the Viterbesi also became intolerable, the Popes almost made of MONTEFIASCONE a great fortress: a first powerful tower was indeed erected in 1262. But then they were hijacked to Avignon and only functionaries (mostly French) remained. It became a bishopric only in 1368.

In the Renaissance the castle was adapted to the age of the cannon in the interests of Cesare Borgia, and various great names are mentioned – Bramante, Michelangelo. The younger Antonio da Sangallo certainly worked here (see Santa Maria in Monte d'Oro, below) – being paid in fish and wine (and once elected Captain of the People). Pope Paul III Farnese, Cardinal-Bishop here for twenty years, found the people troublesome and gave military preference to Perugia.

The Old Pretender, James Stuart, supported by the Papacy as James III, true and only King of England, was married here on 1 September 1719 to Pope Clement XI Albani's 18-year-old goddaughter, the dashing and wealthy Maria Clementina Sobieska of Poland, whose grandfather, King John Sobieski, had chased the

Turks from the gates of Vienna. Clementina had been kidnapped while travelling incognita to Italy, escaped disguised as a boy, and then crossed the Brenner on foot when her carriage overturned. There is a picture of the wedding by Sebastiano Conca, in the Bishop's Palace. Bonnie Prince Charlie, the Young Pretender, half-Polish, quarter-Italian, part-French, hero of Scotland, seems to have been baptised here.

MONTEFIASCONE today is a rather grand place, its buildings enigmatic, its views broad and distant. Also rewarding vistas within the town: the steep main street up through the 1744 Porta di Borgo; the street winding from the Bishop's Palace and the Cathedral to the Seminary, which gets quieter with your every step; the few great buttress-like walls of the Castle, seen from underneath; the Bishop's garden and its gate in the Castle wall; the two towers of the Seminary church peering over its own wall.

San Flaviano

In 852, there were three Benedictine monasteries and six churches here and San Flaviano was one of them; in 862 Pope Leo IV was recommending it to the Bishop of TUSCANIA for restoration. It was first dedicated to the Virgin Mary, as many of Minerva's temples were. (Flavian was a Roman prefect, tortured and killed in the time of Julian the Apostate, perhaps down the hill at Monte d'Oro.)

The church has now been restored for the umpteenth time and the clean golden timeless façade beams and squints. The Etruscan (then Roman) high road to the north – the Via Cassia – ran at an upper level behind and the way in was there. Now, for centuries, both Cassia and way in have been at the lower level. (The little covered balcony in front is where popes used to bless the people from.)

Today, the surprise as you enter is to look up through the ceiling into another complete church. Earlier, the surprise was to look down into a complete church through the floor. This is in fact two churches, one above the other, oriented in opposite directions.

In Italy today baroque is what generally gets thrown out during a restoration, sometimes with disastrous effect. But here the recent restorers have done a good job of not choosing one time at the expense of another. Bits of fabric from the most ancient temple remain, some columns and capitals reworked perhaps in the 6th or

7th century when the first church was restructured from it. What S. Flaviano's bones are in is probably a Roman sarcophagus.*

There was another rebuilding, beetle-shaped on plan, in the 11th century. And yet another in the early 14th century. From these times there are Dark Age capitals (beasts eating people, a fellow holding tight to some unruly volute ribbons, another fellow making a joke), columns thickly twisted, lots of fine frescos including a loyally over-touched-up S. Flaviano on his white steed. Later too, including a *Slaughter of the Innocents* by Pastura, and in the same chapel the remaining one of a pair of monochrome female centaurs, blooming flowerpot on head, and winged. There are also the pretty ghosts of a couple of baroque altars. And throughout odd, powerful, irregularly rhythmical arches, spaces, ceilings, and proportions; luminous *gris-clair* above, rich and mysterious below.

In a side chapel is the now illegible tomb of the medieval ecclesiastic who died of drink (see Introduction: Wine). As a better version of the moral the fresco by the door: two knights out hunting have a vision of two skeletons, and St Macarius the Hermit tells them *pensate quod estis et quod non vitare potestis* – 'think what you are and what you cannot avoid being'.

The Duomo

The Cathedral, dedicated to Saint Margaret, Virgin, of Antioch, was already in 1330 'ruined with antiquity', and it took more than three centuries to get it fully rebuilt. In 1498 Bramante was perhaps to do it; and perhaps it was he who determined the giant scale, the octagonal shape, the unforgettable position on the edge, not the top, of the hill, and the consequent form of the great undercroft. By 1506 little more than the foundations of the octagon were complete, but Pope Julius II was able to say mass. Michele Sanmichele is next mentioned; he was at Orvieto between 1509 and 1527 working on the Cathedral, and here perhaps in 1519 Antonio da Sangallo is said to have assisted him. Still nothing much happened, even though Alessandro Farnese the Elder set aside money. Then he was succeeded by a 9-year-old, there was the plague, there was war, Rome was sacked by Charles V's *lanzechenecchi*. By 1534 only the first cornice was reached.

In 1583 a papal official, the Sacred Visitor, noted that although its

* Most of them, that is: his skull is in the silver bust in the Duomo.

> rude walls sought to defy the weather, only the blue dome of heaven covers the grandiose octagon which the genius of man and the piety of a people have erected to the celestial patron Saint Margaret Virgin of Antioch.

The church lacked even a bell, and to call people to church two small boys were sent round sounding *piccoli tintinnabuli.*

In 1602 the new cardinal, P. E. Zacchia, took things in hand. He ordered 32,000 bricks from BAGNAIA, 5,000 measures of stone and 10,000 of sand, 2,000 measures of lime, 200 oak beams from the COMMENDA, and 2,000 oak blocks from elsewhere, and by the time he died three years later the church was finished.

But disaster struck: Biagio Gentili, a lawyer of the city, was there and recorded it for posterity:

> In the name of the Lord, Amen. On the 4th April 1670, the night of Good Friday, the cathedral church of St Margaret in this city was burned. It began with a fire in the organ of the said church which was caused by some coals left by Mr Francesco Velesi the organist who was using them to melt glue to mend the organ. The ornaments of the said organ fired the vault and the door of the said church. The fire was uncontrollable because of the north wind that was blowing that night, and when the people ran up nothing could be saved but the most holy Sacrament. In order to get this from the altar, Anzovino di Venanzo went three times into the flames and each time he returned without it. At last he wet himself thoroughly with water and, putting all fear behind him, he reached the place of the said Sacrament and took the whole tabernacle and carried it to safety without harm. As for the rest: all the pews were burned, all the confessionals, the big pew of the magistrates, the credenzas of the priests where they stood adorned in front of the altars to the number of 17, the two big credenzas of the Rosary, the two stands for the relics and the preacher's pulpit, the episcopal chair and the whole choir, which was very beautiful and which had cost 900 scudi to make, together with four big pictures which were worth 400 scudi each, with all the choir books, the lecterns, the big credenza with the veils, two pastorals and other furniture, all the brass candlesticks more than half melted, the little metal bell with all its handle melted. The altar pictures were saved half burned, and all that was left was the most holy Crucifix which was saved with great diligence since it was set on fire three times, and the curtain was burned which was in front of it, and a little bit of the left arm of the said Crucifix,

which was a miracle that it was saved. All the roof fell, all the great and small beams, so that not one was left standing. The said beams in falling broke into four funeral vaults in which the fire lasted several days.

The sacristy was saved by great diligence: to get at it, they had to unwall a window at the top of the staircase that goes up to the bells and many people went through there and they thought they could not save it because of the great fire which they saw inside the said church which seemed a *mongibello** so they filled many sacks with books and all the best things and threw them out of the said window. They also took away the holy relics which a few days earlier had been moved from the usual place because it was raining, and they put them in the sacristy and I think it was a miracle of God because if they had been in their right place it would have been impossible to save them . . .

I think that that church burned by God's will because there were so many unfortunate circumstances: first the sacristan that was used to sleep in the sacristy could not sleep there because in the closet or little room of the said sacristy there was a young girl of Bagnorea in custody who was the daughter of the parish, and as soon as he had sounded the Ave Maria he gave the keys of the church to Don Quinto Magni, and the same evening being Good Friday they did not ring the bells and the said sacristan did not ring the Ave Maria for the quick or the dead; but if he had gone there he would have easily noticed the fire. Secondly, the said sacristan that evening wanted to begin to decorate the church for Easter Saturday morning and he could not find Don Quinto who had the keys of the undercroft of Santa Margarita where the stairs were, but if he had begun to decorate it that would have kept him there until the fourth or fifth hour of the night by which time the organ had begun to burn and he would easily have kept the church from the ruin which followed . . .

Let us pray to the Highest that He has now made an end of our punishment and that he will show the most eminent Lord Cardinal Paluzzi our Bishop and all the clergy and people of the City how to rebuild and restore this holy temple; so let it be. Amen.

Which the Highest did, and the glorious dome, and the great cathedral beneath it, and the amazing crypt beneath that, and the baptistery at the very bottom are His reward.

The Cardinal-Bishop, Paluzzio Albertoni Altieri, nephew of Pope

* Italian *monte* = Mount Etna: Arabic *djebel* = mountain.

Clement X, promised his own money to rebuild, and the Roman architect Carlo Fontana produced plans. They were at first for a lantern in the Borromini manner, with the dome *in* the drum. This was abandoned, and he decided to put the dome *on* the drum, its thickness equal to that of the walls. (At this point, it was without furrows.) Work began on 10 September 1670, the church was open again for mass on 16 December 1674 –

> ... and the Te Deum was sung with a great crowd of priests, musicians, people and much firing of mortars ... and fires were lit all over the city, and rockets were fired off and thunderflashes ... [Gentili again]

It was all finished in 1680. (All, that is, except the façade, which was completed in 1840, abominably, with wretched little turrets attached, by an architect purportedly 'in the Palladian tradition'. Fontana's work was then criticised for being too much influenced by Borromini's *lachrimevole magnificenza* – 'tearful magnificence'.)

The dome of course was heavy (though Fontana claimed it was no heavier than allowed by architects from Vitruvius to Scamozzi) and the great earthquake of 1695 damaged the fabric. Cardinal Barbarigo (see MARTA) gave the architect of the Seminary (see below), Giovan Battista Oricono, the job of repairing it. He 'excavated ribs, removed the decorations, and inserted strong tie-rods inside'. So for the glorious *cupola ondulata*, the furrowed dome, with its defining stripes of shadow throughout the day and from any distance, we have Oricono to thank.

In 1893, the interior was restored, by Luigi Fontana, and no-expense-spared frescos and statuary were provided, some with an inappropriate touch of *Kaiserstyl*. There are nice things from before: the marble St Margaret attributed to Arnolfo di Cambio, the supporting columns of which are said to have been brought from FERENTO; a large glazed terracotta *ancona*; and some pleasant pictures and tablets. The space is vast and nebulous, on the scale of the Pantheon and reminiscent of it, but extravagantly over-*embourgeoisie* by that last doing-over.

The famously rich 'Treasure' is for safety's sake now invisible: sad not to see the silver busts of the saints, St Margaret and St Flavian of the 16th and St Felicità of the 15th centuries, with their real skulls inside their regal, sexless, heads. These were no doubt some of the 'sacred relics' saved from the great fire: St Margaret's in theory put out any fire it was pointed at.

Out, round, and down many flights of steps, is the entrance to the great tenebrous crypt, an octagon 12 metres high with 10-metre sides, a great ring-arcade of pillars round the central altar, all half buried in the bowels of the earth. It has been given by some to Bramante, or to his widow, and is said to have been constructed – excavated rather – in 1483. Used and misused over the centuries, it was cleared out and cleaned up by Bishop Boccadoro in 1962, and it is now resoundingly numinous. The Stations of the Cross (of 1986) are life-size sculpted figures pinned out from the walls to be alongside you in the shadows; the Henry Moore altar (now so miserably out of place in Wren's lyrical St Stephen Walbrook in London) would here be truly at home.

Other Churches

These include the tiny and very old S. Andrea, where whizzy lizards chase and bite each other all round the Romanic capitals. Beyond S. Flaviano, S. Maria delle Grazie makes a pleasant picture below a new roundabout, its early 18th-century façade framed by two advancing houses.

Other Buildings

Opposite the Cathedral is the Bishop's Palace, a long lowish building, up a flare of stepped piazza. Behind it is his long stepped garden, worked out by Cardinal Aldrovandi in 1736 to make the most of a steep space slung along the contour below the castle wall. (Until the bombing of 1944, the Palace of St Peter, from which the Patrimony had sometimes been governed, was at the far end, and the garden was shared.) It consists of several parallel walks, cunningly engineered at the several levels, between tiny or tall box hedges, some tracts under fruiting pergolas, some with a line or two of olive trees in front of the walls; lilacs for shade, and little fountains, and occasional flights of steps to permit a change of company or view, all punctuated with white statuary. This was never distinguished, but all the godlings and goddesses are affably pleasant, and did not deserve to be knocked about as they were by republican Franciscans in 1798, expressing their disapproval of the then Bishop, Cardinal Maury, supporter of Napoleon. Many are still lying there.

The Castle, whose remaining high parts crown the town, has been in part converted and houses exhibitions in some of its still noble spaces; but most of it is ruin. Cardinal Barbarigo it was who permitted the general dismantling of what was still standing in 1700, and the use of door-cases and fireplaces in the new seminary building.

There had been a cortile, awkwardly wedge-shaped, but with a three-by-five arcade ingeniously worked out (by Antonio da Sangallo?) to give an impression of proportionate breadth.

A few of the cortile arches remain, but nothing of the loggia above; some tall, Albi-like buttresses; a bulwark associated with Michelangelo; rooms, some with Etruscan-cut stones under much later floors; indications of another loggia overlooking the lake, and of a little chapel.

All this is on top of the world. Below, the Seminary and its church and the topmost city gate wrap round the steep southern tip of the town to overlook the plain, the hillocky crater lip, and the surprisingly high lake. They were all built at the end of the 17th century.

The Seminary had at one time its own printing press 'with characters for printing Italian, Latin, Greek, and Syrian in every size and great number'. Today, at the end of its long street and behind its high wall, with a mere handful of seminarists, it is half deserted: a mixture of linoleum and grandiose fresco, vast views and deal furniture. The little old library is slowly being catalogued; in the tall cold church the bust of Cardinal Barbarigo looks out coldly from over his tomb. It would make a wonderful hotel.

Santa Maria in Monte d'Oro

From the high places, the road south drops out of the town to a slope called Montoro or Monte d'Oro. Half-way down, a tall, incurious, octagonal building stands as a dignified reminder of an intended convent; there are splendid designs in the Uffizi in Florence, by Antonio da Sangallo the Younger, for an octagonal church, the circular choir enclosed within the fabric of the convent and rounded staircases leading up hill to the cloister. After the horrors of 1527, there was no money.

Monterano

When Napoleon's troops sacked MONTERANO in 1798, malaria had already sent much of the population to CANALE DI MONTERANO. The rest then left the castle, the church, the aqueduct, the walls, and the convent at the end of the *sperone* to dilapidate at their leisure, which they still do, in utter quiet, among spring flowers and summer butterflies and year-round whiffs from the sulphur springs below, where people de-flea their dogs. Access is difficult: an 'island' site. But persevere.

Villanovan hypogea have been found, and an Etruscan cuniculus-like tunnel which has been travelled (by a smallish person) right up from the river-bed below.

When the Lombards destroyed Forum Clodii (see SAN LIBERATO) around AD 500, the bishopric moved here. Later, the medieval castle was smartened up with something of a loggia and, below, a very handsome fountain, reputedly by Bernini; with water gushing out from under a straddling great lion, to tumble in steps down a heap of mixed boulders and outcrop. Nothing remains but the outcrop beneath brambles. The small church beside is a shape of walls, roofed with ivy; a fig tree for reredos.

Along the saddle of cropped, used-looking grass, there was another fountain, and at the far end the convent – now a substantial ruin. Its church must have been fine indeed, low and wide-doored, domed, its pedimented façade between substantial twin turrets in the Borromini Sant'Agnese manner. The convent was behind, commanding a wide view of the woods and the TOLFA HILLS.

Monterosi

Dennis considered the little lake 'dreary', but the American Philosophical Society in 1970 devoted a whole issue of its *Transactions* to its geology, limnology, vulcanology, history, ecology, botany, fauna, and chemistry. We found it full of frogs and waterlilies and a curling-leafed lotus. In May, its slopes display a characteristic wild rose.

This is where Frederick Barbarossa refused to hold Pope Adrian IV's stirrup, which caused a nasty incident. It is also where Monsignor Giarda was murdered, which triggered the tragedy of CASTRO.

The original town was at the top of the hill. Gradually it moved down to the old Via Cassia, at which level there are two churches, both 18th-century: S. Giuseppe, a miniature, with onion-topped bell turrets, and Santa Croce, the parish church, tall and disciplined. The ruinous palazzo is from 1690, the end of the great age, the Palazzo Abaziale.

Morlupo

Morlupo was 'Castrum Mori Lupo' in 1038: Castle Wolfdeath.

Pope Martin V destroyed the castle in 1425, along with other Orsini castles, but they rebuilt it, pretty and low, in 1598, and tell you so: the lintel of every window is inscribed ANTIMO ORSINI, in case you forget between one and the next.

Mugnano

This conspicuous village with a great (dilapidating) round tower was possibly the ancient Maeonia; the so-called BOMARZO Tazzetta, which for the first time showed Greek and Etruscan alphabets together, was found nearby. The golden sand beneath its golden rock is being washed away.

The Palazzo Orsini is exceptionally grand considering the surrounding neglect – MUGNANO is not described in the TCI guide. It is a sober seven-bayed affair (Baldassare Peruzzi might, it is said, have had a hand), with alternate round and pointed pediments to the *piano nobile* windows and a tremendous rusticated doorway. 'Carlo Orsini' say the window frames; 'percussus eleanor' says the motto in the arms over the doorway which is about the wife of Orsino Orsini, of Pitigliano, whom he punched out of jealousy, and who perhaps came here to be away from him. 'Gabr. Ursinus' whispers the tiny building next to it.

On the inward-facing side, the building appears complete. But on the Tiber side, an outer layer appears, with an Ionic loggia, tall and deep, of seven bays, opening above a great battered and windowed basement that bends with the cliff it is built on. Outer and inner construction do not mesh and the outer is unfinished. Behind the chicken-netting and the washing can be seen the still-bright frescos of the loggia.

The tiny church of Santa Maria has a *Madonna and Child* over the altar, the baby doing a pretty *ciao*; and to the right of the door, a ghostly *Calvary*: the single cross empty and four figures almost in silverpoint.

When these Orsini died out in 1587, they left MUGNANO to the BRACCIANO Orsini; but the papal authorities would not allow and litigation went on until 1705. This pace endures; the letterbox says *Regie Poste* – 'Royal Mail' – and therefore dates from before 1946.

Musignano

(See also VULCI and CANINO.)

George Dennis wrote:

> Among the videnda [sights] of this neighbourhood, Musignano, the villa of the late Prince of Canino [Luciano Bonaparte], and the residence of his widow, claims a visit.... The son-in-law of the Princess showed what vases and other relics the Princess's cabinet at that time contained. Few of the treasures of this unrivalled mine

of Etruscan wealth are retained on the spot. The finest vases are bought by the Pope for the Gregorian Museum, or find their way into foreign countries, for the Princess has agents in many of the capitals of Europe....

The 'villa' had been an abbey, whose monks built castles against the Saracens, here and at VULCI's Ponte Abbadia. The castles fell to Breton mercenaries during the Schism and Jan Tedesco, their captain, was given MUSIGNANO – another time he got LATERA – to pay his troops with.

Luciano's heirs sold the house to the Torlonia, a wealthy Roman family, ennobled in the 19th century.

Nazzano

NAZZANO has been continuously occupied since at least the 8th century BC. It is now a delicately coloured medieval village; the single street spirals up to a tall 13th-century castle with a great round tower of 1457. The wallscape with sparse, high up, windows is very splendid.

The ancient church of Sant'Antimo stands in trees, beyond the walls, near where in Imperial times there was a circular temple, with comprehensive dedications to Diana, Magna Mater, and Bona Dea. Nave and two aisles; a 10th-century white marble area for the choir – a sort of holy swimming pool – which takes up most of the nave and from the sides of which rise bebobbled *pergami*. The Ionic capitals are set square-rigged, not fore-and-aft; which happens in romanesque churches because it can finish tidily at the wall end.

The 15th-century frescos are by that grand colourist, Antoniazzo Romano. Note the blue on blue of the Annunciation top right; and the curly *angeli musicanti* with their nicely recherché instruments.

From here the views over the valley and into the snowy Appennines are idyllic. The other way, the less said the better.

To the north-west the mostly empty buildings of the perhaps 16th-century Convent of San Francesco, visible from the *autostrada*, set among ilexes and cypresses.

Nepi

The countryside round NEPI, Dennis rightly said,

> ... is one of the few portions of central Italy that will remind ... an Englishman of home. Those sweeps of bright green sward – those stately wide-armed oaks scattered over it, singly, or in

clumps – those cattle feeding in the shade – those neat hedge-rows, made up of maples, hawthorns, and brambles, with fern below, and clematis, dog-roses, and honeysuckles above ...

But NEPI itself is not at all English. It is now one of the handsomest and least spoiled of towns, decayed but cheerful and with many good things. The gigantic scale of the castle, the Etruscan walling and surrounding ruins in which the townsfolk keep hens, ducks, and rabbits in little lockups, and hay in lofts, and the stream which runs through all this, make the entrance from the west both pretty and spectacular. Dennis thought the Etruscan wall there, nineteen courses – 13 metres – high, might well be the very one that Camillus Furius and his troops scaled to take the town in 386 BC.

Throughout history, NEPI, with SUTRI one of the 'Gateways to Etruria', has stayed modestly important. In the Dark Ages it was a bishopric and one of its dukes, Toto, made his brother Pope (and kept him Pope for a year in the 760s) as Constantine II. Parts of the Cathedral crypt are from these times.

The still spectacular Castle was built by Rodrigo Borgia, when he was Cardinal-Governor before becoming Pope Alexander VI. He gave it to his daughter Lucrezia in 1499, and she spent time here when not being married off or unmarried again by her idiotically unscrupulous father, or acting in Rome as his regent. She finally married the Duke of Ferrara (by whom she had a son who became the cardinal who built the Villa d'Este at Tivoli), and travelled to her wedding through NEPI with two hundred horsemen.

NEPI was included in the Dukedom Pope Paul III Farnese created in 1537 for his son, Pier Luigi, and the Castle was then reworked by Antonio da Sangallo the Younger. He also started on a Ducal Palace: this is now the Palazzo Communale, and on top of his rusticated basement it now sports a heavily majestic 18th-century affair, with a big balustrade and a whoosh of sail belfry in the middle. (The attached fountain has been attributed to Bernini).

There is a Sangallo air to some of the private palazzi, and Antonio could well have had a hand in them. There are also drawings of his in the Uffizi for a church here, San Tolomeo, which was never built: a remarkable (and prescient) façade, with a square tower on either side, surmounted with corner and central obelisks, all to frame a tall dome on an octagon behind. (In the 1540s the Bishop was writing that Antonio must be *made* to come to NEPI: 'I have no time to winter here; it begins to get cold ...')

The French burned the town in 1798. The 1831 rebuild of the

Cathedral keeps the outline and plenty of the stones from the 9th- and 12th-century church. The wide portico across the façade is from the 12th. The inside, a basilica, is painted throughout in *trompe l'oeil* marble and hangings: the effect with the tall central barrel vault and the ancient low colonnades is almost bizarre. The chancel is raised over a grandiose crypt, 12th-century and earlier; from which palaeo-Christian catacombs run out.

At the end of the left-most aisle is a Giulio Romano triptych; the separate small panels at the top of each side panel make an exhilarating Annunciation across the breadth of the main picture. The figures are low, energetic, almost crouching: the angel sends his message with an urgently outstretched hand, and Mary reaches out both her hands to catch it as if it were a ball. The golden section is in play.

The front of the high altar, right forward *coram populo*, is an *alto rilievo* sarcophagus from Bernini's studio: three angels and a woman reach across a bishop, San Romano. All smile.

Many of the churches are ruined; quite a few houses and streets are approaching ruin; yet the place gives a strong sense of potentiality, as though at last something nice might be going to happen. There is a new influx of wealth and enterprise, and let us hope that because it comes with experience gained elsewhere, it will be wise and modest. NEPI is much too good to spoil.

Terme dei Gracchi

Three kilometres from NEPI on the road towards Settevene, a small track to the left by an old bridge, down into the woods and rocks, is signposted Terme dei Gracchi. This is where very delicious NEPI water is bottled: 'green label' as it comes out of the rock, 'red label' with extra of its own gas put into it, extracted by an artificial bore from the same layer. One of the conditions of the licence granted to the bottling firm by the Region is that the local people can take as much as they want: there is a convenient tap, and they come with their crates of empty bottles.

Automation began in 1961, and several thousand returned green bottles now arrive at the back of the establishment in yellow plastic crates, to be extracted by the dozen, five dozen at a time, and sent on their rattling, nudging, ever more glistening way, to be washed, disinfected, observed, sterilised, filled, inspected, capped, labelled (neck and torso), put back by the dozen, five dozen at a time, in now clean yellow crates, to fill up the lorry that has just brought in another load of empties.

Steam; a great whirring undersound, and the mainly women workers wear red pom-pom ear-covers. Underfoot is wet. Inspection is by ultra-violet against a back-lit screen and demands intense concentration: no more than half an hour at a time.

The Gracchi were virtuous Roman brothers who sought justice and land reform for the people: their mother considered herself the happiest of Roman matrons for having given birth to them. Their connexion with the springs or baths here is obscure.

Visitors, by appointment, welcome.

Norchia

Because it presents so dramatic, so melancholy, and so solitary a picture, no traveller should willingly fail to visit NORCHIA. Although Nature is taking her time over dismantling its remains, NORCHIA is hard to find, and hard to find one's way about, so come in spring.

The almost island site was occupied from the Bronze Age and the Etruscans dug a trench to island it completely. It lay half-way along the BLERA–TUSCANIA road, where that crossed a TARQUINIA–ORVIETO road, and so was central to the Etruscan road network. The Romans bridged the trench, and their Via Clodia ran the whole length of the town, to carry on westwards through the still visible (Etruscan) cleft in the tufo. In the Middle Ages, and perhaps to the Etruscans, the name was Orcla.

The thickly wooded cliffs are honeycombed with tombs. Some groups of them are excavated, others are unexcavated, even unknown, in among the cave dwellings of the medieval town.

These cliff-tombs – some very grandly façaded – are more or less unique to this area, the hinterland of Caere (CERVETERI), Tarquinii (TARQUINIA), and Volcii (VULCI); there are tens of thousands of them. Nearly all of them come from two periods: the Archaic (6th to 5th centuries BC) and the Hellenising (4th to 2nd centuries BC). The gap between the periods is indicative of the crisis and decline that had set in in the 5th century, when some settlements, like ACQUAROSSA and BISENZIO, disappeared altogether from the Etruscan map. The earlier tombs appear in the upper reaches of the two southern rivers, the Mignone and the Bieda; the later ones in those of the Marta. A movement northwards is indicated.

The tombs mostly consist of a façade cut in the cliff with relief moulding and in the centre a pretend door. Beneath this, there is usually a small room with benches and perhaps more pretend doors; under this and reached by a corridor, the *dromos*, perhaps stepped, is the real sepulchral chamber, not decorated, within which the sarcophagi were placed, with recumbent figures on top.

George Dennis described his visit to NORCHIA:

> At length we turned a corner in the glen, and lo! a grand range of monuments burst upon us. There they were – a line of sepulchres, high in the face of the cliff which forms the right-hand barrier of the glen, two or three hundred feet above the stream – an amphitheatre of tombs!

He compared the scale to that of the Colosseum and judged this was 'the most imposing spot in the whole compass of Etruscan cemeteries'.

In his day it was still possible to read the decorative detail of these tombs, and his friend Ainslie's engraving helps us to accept his account of heroic figures on the remains of the tympana and on the inner walls of certain porticoes, all that way up the cliff, which we can no longer see.

Of the medieval golden stone emerging from the dark wood some is the 12th-century apse system of the perhaps 9th-century church of San Pietro, and the rest is castle.

A daily tide of several hundred nibbling, shoving, pellet-dropping sheep and their attendant *Maremmano* dogs wears the sward along the valley bottom quite smooth. Bee-eaters perform gleeful aerobatics overhead; smells are pristine; and great golden walls of cornices and deep-cut openings and perilous staircases glow through the temperate jungle.

Olgiata

There was a rich 18th-century villa, but now the newly rich of the 60s and 70s, struck by the danger of being murdered for their money, live here huddled together in big houses behind electrically operated crash barriers manned by a private police force. Estate agents actually advertise *una vita olgiata*, which refers to *una vita agiata*, 'a life of ease'. The reality is like a South African township in reverse.

Onano

What must be the sharpest and highest quoin in all castledom soars above as you make to enter the little town. The Castle's huge façade on to the piazza is a balance of small apertures and blank spaces, impressive and illegible. It has three entrances at ground level, the centre one with steps up to it which go on within, the left with a weighty entablature, the right strayed from some farm building. There were Dukes of Onano, who died out in 1712. And yes, the name does mean the same in Italian.

Oriolo

The town was founded in 1560 by Giorgio III da Santacroce, of VEIANO, who brought in 1,500 settlers from Tuscany and Umbria. The grand converging vistas of its three streets fail to quite converge on the piazza, down from which, however, there are converging balustered ramps. The ideological glance is at Praeneste. Nothing quite sings.

The late baroque interior of the parish church of San Giorgio, across from the ramps, also shows what happens when conceptual complexity outruns animation.

The Palazzo that closes the piazza was enlarged by the Altieri family in 1674 at the time of their Pope, Clement X. In the 1960s the family had dwindled to one heiress, who also inherited a palazzo in Rome, so Oriolo went to auction, and the State bought it and its furniture by *prelazione* – pre-emption. And then sold the furniture.

The outside creates its harmony, unItalianly, by the repetitive use of small features and motives. Behind, wings enclose a cortile which extends into a small garden, beyond which there was, and perhaps still is, a great wooded park. A stretch of its avenue survives at the MONTE VIRGINIO end, but the rest has been bought, apparently without any house, by a Roman lawyer and is kept as closed as Wormwood Scrubs.

Inside the Palazzo there are some fine frescos. On the ground floor, seven historical scenes of ancient Rome foreshadow Piranesi. Four of a suite of five quite small but splendid rooms show Old Testament stories by a pair of artists: a big loose-wristed fellow does the scenes and a delicious neo-Zuccaresque fellow does the decorations. Dotted about various rooms are little views of VICARELLO, ROTA, MONTERANO, etc., places which then belonged to the Altieri, by Giuseppe Barberi. The chapel's altar picture is Caravaggesque.

A famous Gallery of Popes is in the east wing: portraits mostly given by Clement X, more or less identical from the year dot to about 1500, since when the run has been continued. Clement X's are not good, and they have got no better, present Pope included.

The State is now making amends and restoring the fabric, unfortunately with the heavy uniform *intonaco* it so much loves.

Orte

ORTE's volcanic neck is excelled only by Orvieto's. The name may come from the Etruscan root *hort*, high place, sacred hill, and the related Horthia, goddess of fate and fortune. *Hortus* is Latin for garden. From ORTE came a Roman patrician clan, the Gens Hortensia, and from them all the Hortenses in the French-speaking world and, after one of them, all the Hydrangeas.

The Tiber was long navigable this far and excavation shows that the Roman port had quays at three levels, for different states of the river. In the Middle Ages marble blocks were brought up on horse-towed barges. As late as 1581 Montaigne, who called it Corde, saw the stones of the bridge, washed away in a flood in 1515, wherewith Augustus had sought to attach Sabines on that side of the river to Faliscans on this. Today Orte Scalo is down here, a railway town in origin, now industrial.

Near the top, in front of the large 17th-century Cathedral (its façade is 1901), a public wash-house is dug deep into the tufo, its roof held up by two little classical columns of uncertain age. The water is warmish; perhaps it was once a holy spring?

Mainly ORTE is medieval. The little church of San Silvestro, built in the 12th century on the ruins of a Roman temple of Peace, is now the Diocesan Museum, and outstanding of its class. (Key from the parish priest.) The pictures are mainly from the Cathedral, and the most interesting historically is the 13th-century portrait of St Francis, which may well be the oldest to survive: not long posthumous. A clear impression of the sort of face comes across: round, large-eyed, intense, harmonious, on top of a small man. The oldest is a mosaic of the Virgin Mary watching Salome washing the infant Jesus, which came from the oratory of Pope John VII (705–7) in Constantine's Basilica of St Peter's in Rome. (Who is to say that Christianity was not more fecund when belief was less uniform?) There is a nice 15th-century *Eterno* blessing the earthly globe, perhaps by the 'Maestro of Castiglione': no America.

The cycle of scenes from the Life of Sant'Egidio, St Giles, 15th-century Viterbese, is good art and good story-telling – one of the best stories in the *Golden Legend* (a 14th-century compendium of often hair-raising tales of the saints and martyrs).

On Good Friday there is the 'Procession of the Men'. The several confraternities gather after dark in the church of Sant'Agostino, cleaned out and lit to show off the altarpieces and the great baroque Bier of Christ, which the men will carry. (The women will stay here till the men come back.) The town lights are all turned out, the procession moves off in the cold dark. Candles shine wobblingly through glass flies' eye lenses, in silver-crowned lanterns. First is a confraternity in white robes and black capes with torches, thirty or forty men; a few children in correct garb. All the confraternities are hooded. Then red-robed men, barefoot and led by children; the chains on their ankles rustle on the cobblestones. A company of white children. Men in black with a forest of crosses, 6 metres high and nobbly in the baroque way: perhaps fifty of them. One is even higher, carried by one man but with rigging held by other men. With luck the moon comes out.

Up in the piazza in front of the Cathedral they form a great circle with their crosses and their glittering lanterns, the rest of us behind them. They sing, raggedly. The Band arrives, playing a slow not uncheerful march, and then the Bier of Christ, all great flickering candles, borne by fourteen men who alone with the priests are not hooded. The Christ on the bier is black. The Mater Dolorosa follows on a podium, and the lanterns are lowered.

At half past ten, the Cathedral bell strikes twelve. One of the tubas in the band plays a whole tone lower than everyone else throughout the evening; he has an E♭ crook in his F instrument. The others seem not to notice. Or perhaps he is the mayor.

Palidoro

A Roman bridge is embedded in the proportionable *casale*, built at the order of Sixtus V, road- and bridge-builder Pope in the 1580s.

Palo

The Castle of PALO, of ideal symmetry and washed by the sea: neat by sun; high romance by storm and whirlwind.

The remains of CERVETERI's port of Alsium are buried under the sand. The basic shape is from the 15th century, when the string of sea-castles was renewed against Moorish raiders. Civilianisation began with Pope Leo X Medici, great rider to hounds, who made it a hunting lodge (despite the Moors), and was completed by the Orsini in 1662, who demolished a great round tower and also completed the present tidy square. It passed to the Odescalchi in 1682.

During the Napoleonic Wars, when the port was already drying up, two English privateers attempted to board French and Neapolitan merchant ships which were within it, and the papal artillery bombarded them from the Castle.

In the late 19th century Prince Ladislao Odescalchi (see LADISPOLI) returned the castle to its 15th-century appearance with four round corner towers and crenellated wall between. It can now serve as the ideogram of the European castle. Inside, wide spiral staircases lead to wide halls from which no land is in sight.

The great wooded park where Pope Leo hunted is now a World Wildlife Fund 'Faunistic Refuge', where badgers, porcupines, and marsh turtles may live in peace. Orchids too.

Here were shot the Garden of Eden scenes in John Huston's film *The Bible*: the Tree of Knowledge was a great beech painted red and giraffes and other beasts wandered freely. Paul Getty II rented the castle in the last years of his life. It is not open to the public, but it can be seen from the beaches to the south, its magic unreduced by distance.

Pescia Romana and the Maremma Coast

Behind the narrow sandy beach, the land reform has paid off: the irrigation works, the eucalyptus has taken, the unmistakable houses are enlarged and choicely painted.

Pianiano

A tiny place, with proper walls, gate, and church. It became 'unpopulated' in 1736 so the Camera Apostolica sent in a colony of Albanians from Scutari. Whence the 'Via degli Albanesi'.

Piansano

PIANSANO's mini-crater contained the Lagaccione – Nasty Great Lake – famous for breeding malaria mosquitoes. An underground channel now drains it, as probably happened in Etruscan times.

The town's Palazzo Communale sports a multi-secular concoction of medieval bears and ho-ho lackeys slapping their knees.

Pisciarelli

This tiny hamlet, beyond MANZIANA, has a late mannerist church whose broad façade rises smiling over the low bowl it stands in.

It contains a magnificent picture by the Viterbese Vincenzo Strigelli (1713–69): the Virgin Mary and two young saints are enjoying the religious tradition they stand for as much as the painter enjoyed the artistic tradition of which he was a master.

Poggio Conte and Nearby Hermitages

POGGIO CONTE is a dark round hole up in a cliff-face, with a second, more elongated, dark hole beneath. The name means 'Earl's Hill'.

Nature has provided a more-than-half cylinder of space, 30 metres in diameter by 50 high, contained in a wall of tufo, with a sandy bottom, and a stream dropping the full 50 metres at all seasons. (It was once a whole pool; a side fell out.) A little below and beyond, the River Fiora runs. A little above and behind, are the Colli di S. Columbano, called after the Irish saint. A monastery there bore his name.

A hermitage, a cell of that Monastery, consisting of a complete miniature church and a tiny living space beside, is here, carved back into the tufo cliff. The dark round hole is the 'rose' window, 30 or so centimetres across; the other hole is the 'west' door, its threshold slowly rising as the interior fills with the detritus of nature. The 'church' has two spaces: a 'nave' about 4 metres across, with a cupola-shaped ceiling above a drum and a pretty little quatrefoil – an Irish four-leaf clover for St Columbanus? – at the top; and a 'chancel' with a cross vault. Arches are pointed, and there are little apses in the right place for a Cistercian church of the 12th or 13th century, also decorated with floral and geometric patterns. The drum, divided into thirteen pseudo-niches with columns between, was decorated with fresco figures of the Saviour and the Twelve Apostles dating probably from the same period, robed and haloed characters, in soft shades of ochre and white, red, and blue, with the blue used for outlining and features.

'Was', scandalously, is the right word about the frescos: the panels were stolen, cut from the walls, in the summer of 1964. Some were recovered shortly after by the police and went on show in the Exhibition of Recovered Art in Florence; returned only in 1988 to the local museum in ISCHIA DI CASTRO. Six others are known to be in the 'possession' of a 'noted Swiss collector', without objection from the Swiss authorities.

This hermitage and others in the area are unfindable without a guide.

Hermits and anchorites tend to leave few traces: most made do with something less elaborate than this – a natural cave, an Etruscan tomb. But some hermitages have been as elaborate, and a kilometre or so up the Fiora there is another cut in the tufo, which is socially, if not architecturally, more complicated than POGGIO CONTE. This is Ripatonna Cicognina (which we have not seen), almost a little monastery with excavated spaces connected internally and identifiable zones for study, work, rest, prayer, and cooking.

Ponzano Romano

The village stands on a cliff, with a castle of course, some really bad modern buildings, and a view of the double bend in the Tiber, the Bottiglia – the Bottle – where it just doesn't break through and create an oxbow.

On a slope just above the valley floor, east of the motorway, is the tall old abbey church of Sant'Andrea in Flumine, St Andrew by the River. It belongs to the *Pro loco* ('for the place') Association of PONZANO, who have put it to rights and have the key.

There was a church already in the 5th century. Pope Paul I gave it to Pepin the Short in 762, the better to attach him and the Franks to the Papacy. The present church is mostly 12th-century, but with varied textures: note a face, under the eaves. The tower was one of three built for defence: the castle shape shows clearly from below. The farm buildings alongside were in the 14th and 15th centuries a newly restored 'palace' and monastery.

Inside it is a garbled basilica. The fine Cosmatesque floor is unreconciled with a big screen – an echo of screens in northern cathedrals, and the columns of which may have come from a now vanished crypt. Within the (raised) presbytery stands a (further raised) tabernacle, Carolingian in design. It is hard to make out how much of the fabric is original, but the effect is dazzling.

Proceno

As well as the Turkish crescent on its coat of arms (some citizens were gallant at Lepanto), Proceno has everything without that being very much. The best thing is on the way up: the church of the Giglio – the Lily – a fine tall space, with nice frescos.

Quercia, Santa Maria della

The resplendent ceiling displays part of the first cargo of gold ever to reach Europe from the Americas.

In 1414 the Madonna was sighted in an oak tree; the event was commemorated in a painting on a tile by one Maestro Monetti, which was placed in the tree.

People tried to take her out of it, but she always returned. She saved the Viterbese from the plague in 1467, and the Sienese from an earthquake, and many other people from many other fates. In

1467 the cult was made official and 30,000 people came to celebrate. Money flowed in, the oak tree was encased in a small chapel, and the Dominicans came to run things.

The cathedral-sized wayside shrine we see is an altogether glorious building, with its steps and its great free-standing bell-tower. It also has two convents attached, and a fragment of planned town.

It was built at the expense of various VITERBO guilds and groups between 1470 and 1525, in open country. Pope Julius II came in 1505. The overall architect is not known – both Bramante and a Sangallo have been mentioned, implausibly – but an anonymous 'plan' was in existence until the 16th century, perhaps the work of one of the local Dominicans. The building was 'guided' by a Maestro Danese of Viterbo, contractor also for the 1466 portico at VITERBO's Santa Maria in Gradi. If a portico was intended here, as the free-standing columns suggest, Santa Maria in Gradi's is what it might have been like. (See also CORCHIANO.)

Everything was done in the new Florentine manner, and craftsmen were brought in from far and wide although the middle portal, where the decorations are strange and vivid and include several versions of the recumbent 'moon man', is given to Giovanni di Bernardino of VITERBO. (The door itself is later, 1620.) The lunette terracotta is due to Andrea della Robbia of Florence; the bell-tower to Ambrogio da Milano with help from Marino di Basilio of Naples (again, strange and vivid capitals, some appearing to derive from the capitals in the Cathedral of VITERBO); the rosy peperino façade is given to Carlo di Mariotto and Domenico di Iacopo, again of Florence; the design of the coffered ceiling to Antonio da Sangallo the Younger and its construction to one Giovanni di Pietro, also from Florence. Its resplendent gold is said to have been given either by the Emperor Charles V to Pope Paul III Farnese, or by the Queen of Spain to a cardinal, but the story of the 'first cargo' runs through the records.

Over the main altar the splendid marble *tempietto* enclosing the holy oak itself and the miraculous image was made in 1490 by the Milanese Andrea Bregno; at the back, the Cult of the Image as performed in 1467 is illustrated. Behind the altar are 'the remains of twelve bombs dropped by English aeroplanes on the 20th January 1944'. The intarsia panels (incorporated in later choir stalls) and the huge lectern for reading choir parts from a distance are early 16th-century.

In the Sanctuary, the big painting of the *Madonna del Carmine* by Bonifazi came from the former Carmelite church of St Joseph and St Teresa in VITERBO (now the Law Courts).

A side-chapel houses a museum of *ex votos* – little thank offerings to the Virgin for miracles performed, often with illustrations of the event.

The convents have their respective cloisters: the big one is of the 1550s; the smaller, of *c.* 1480, is 'Gothic', in the manner of VITERBO's Santa Maria in Gradi; its neat well-head is of 1508. The 'Gothic' cloister is vividly frescoed with more official illustrations, done in 1671, of the Madonna's miracles. Among these was the victory of Lepanto, of 1571, and a Turkish pennant 7 metres long is in the church behind glass; it was taken by some Knights of Malta from a Turkish warship. The miracle had been that the Madonna appeared to the Pope to announce the victory at the very moment the attack commenced. The flower of the papal nobility took part in this crucial battle, in which 8,000 'Turks' and 7,500 'Christians' died, and Christian Europe held its own at sea. (In fact the Turkish Janissaries were all the children of Christians.) It ended as an infantry battle fought on the decks of the ships.

Pope Paul III drove the straight, tree-lined road here from VITERBO, and his grandson, Cardinal Alessandro Farnese the Younger, provided the fruit-swagged fountain half-way along.

Every fortieth year the Madonna herself goes to VEIANO, where they carpet the streets in leaves. On her most recent trip she travelled in a small van.

Riano

A tiny medieval town and castle so perched on their volcanic neck they seem afloat on the surrounding new town.

Rignano

RIGNANO, neither important nor beautiful, is full of character. The castle is a great estropiated chunk of 14th-century masonry, improved with travertine in the 16th; the piazza contains a colossal, early 16th-century bombard, curly metal tongues emerging flame-like from its muzzle, with bits of two Roman columns to prop it up.

The local friable, very white stone is called *capellaccio*, and innumerable statuary yards supply a strong local demand for cherubs made of it, and eagles perched on balls, gnomes, Venuses, small Michelangelo Davids, all of which citizens display on their gate posts.

The cemetery has catacombs and a round 18th-century chapel with a whoopsy on top, dedicated to the Roman matron S. Teodora. In the valley below, beyond an ever-smoking rubbish dump, a tiny, picturesque, ancient church, stands on the podium of a perhaps Roman temple and incorporates bits of it. It is dedicated to Sts Abbondio and Abbondanzio: Abounding and Abundancy. The distant, melancholy, ruin, with the forlorn sail belfry, was a convent of Our Lady of the Graces.

Rocca Respampani

Field palazzo extraordinary: quiet, gigantic, unfinished, alone.

There were people surnamed Spampini or Pampani (*pampanoso* means like a big vine leaf, useless) who came from this constantly disputed, and as constantly devastated, piece of country. In 1456, Respampani – so named – finally went to the Ospedale del Santo Spirito, with MONTE ROMANO part of the same holding, and Pius II encouraged them to set up an agricultural colony, which failed.

The old site was abandoned (the ruins can be glimpsed a ravine or two away) and in 1608, a new building was begun, to contain everyone and everything from the old castle and village; and probably more: a new kind of *incastellamento* – encastling. Square on plan; surrounded by a moat; a full-size palazzo forming the main front; and reaching back at its either end, equally large blocks with habitations above and farm spaces beneath. The side-blocks were never finished and the corner towers seem possibly wrong – was something crenellated intended? Note the decorative chimney pots, in the manner of BOLSENA, BASSANO ROMANO, etc. The internal courtyard has a central well, and a raised chapel-cum-pigeon-loft in the middle of the low rear wall. On its courtyard side, the Palazzo is arcaded at ground level and has a full-length gallery along the first floor, reached by an internal horse-staircase. The main rooms, off the gallery, face north over the scarred plain. The middle one is a huge *salone* – it may well have been frescoed – with a fine great ceiling. Its fireplace, inscribed 'Stepano Vaio, Vescovo di Cirene, 1648', has modishly peculiar decoration: on either side, girl-headed volutes lean over the shoulders of bearded, draped, and hooded caryatid prophets (?), who are fish-scaled from the waist down and perch on the points of their fish tails.

Also modish are the *feritoie*, little embrasures opened in the brickwork under each of the *salone*'s large windows, with internal ledges, for firing cannon through. Sir John Hale's opinion is that 'embrasures under windows in single "fortified" palaces in the C16 were (France, Malta) chiefly decorative', rather in the manner of castellation in the 19th century. 'I don't know an example of their [military] use; they are generally too high in the building and too restricted in their field of vision to have been practical.'

ROCCA RESPAMPANI is now a Maremma cattle centre belonging to the Commune of MONTE ROMANO, and you see the great white beasts in their hundreds taking a proper time to get from one place to another.

Ronciglione

RONCIGLIONE still has the feel of a very small capital city. It is built high, wide, and grand on a steep slope among precipitous ravines, with a grand boulevard, grand palazzi, and a very grand cathedral. Farnese, of course: and for a while joint capital of their Duchy of CASTRO. They no doubt chose it because of the industrial potential of the Etruscan outflow tunnel from the LAKE OF VICO (see below).

In the Middle Ages it passed like other towns from Guelf to Ghibelline, murderer to murderer. In 1465 it passed by conquest into the church's direct possession and eventually Clement VII Medici gave it to his protégé, Cardinal Alessandro Farnese. He, as Pope Paul III, included it in the new Duchy of CASTRO he established for his son Pier Luigi. Under him and his successors, this main road village (the Cassia came over the mountain in those days) became the major industrial centre of the Patrimony: iron, copper, brass, flour mills, a mint, paper mills, and by 1609 a printing press. Also an academy: the Accademia dei Desiderosi – of the Desirous Ones – founded by the Farnese. The iron ore was mined on Elba, landed at Porto Clementino (see TARQUINIA COAST) and brought here in ox-carts, to be smelted with wood from the CIMINO. In the early 19th century RONCIGLIONE still produced most of the Papal State's steel, and the Papal State had most of the iron production of Italy.

In 1641, when CASTRO was expunged, RONCIGLIONE passed back with the rest of the former Duchy to the Papacy. In 1799 the town was largely burned by the French invaders, and three hundred people were killed here in the Allied bombing of 1944.

The principal sight is the long street, which was designed, probably by Antonio da Sangallo, to keep traffic out of the medieval town and to give a grand aspect to the second city of the Duchy. It consists of four stretches of straight boulevard on a slope, articulated at three angles.

The first part, which was opened in 1558 by the second Duke, Ottavio, starts very broad at the church of Santa Maria della Pace

(1581, and full of good pictures), and then tapers slightly towards Vignola's excellent Porta Romana.

The next straight leads into what is locally known as the Piazza della Nave, after a former inn. The broad space was made with characteristic Farnese verve: a 50-metre-deep *burrone* was filled in with several thousand tons of earth, thus obliterating the gap between the new road and the existing medieval town.

After this (elegantly palazzoed) resting place, the boulevard or *corso* swings right, to go steeper uphill past several handsome churches (all now closed or turned into municipal conference centres) and more fine palazzi of the 17th and 18th centuries.

Lastly it turns left, and up again, to shrink a bit as it approaches the rim of the crater. The church here is San Francesco, built in 1628; it contains a good 1581 picture of the Immacolata with angels, by Scipione Pulzone: a Capuchin convent is attached.

The medieval town is nearly untouched. Near the bottom, its own piazza, Piazza Madonna degli Angeli, is packed tight with comfortable houses of the 15th century: an unusually complete late medieval scene. At the end of the little *sperone*, the church, now Santa Maria della Providenza, is basically 11th-century: it was the cathedral until part fell into the ravine. It was baroqued (1742) and de-baroqued (recently) and has a little Sangallo porch from elsewhere attached to its terrace wall. On Good Friday, the terrace is a small Calvary, or even Golgotha, to which growing grass-tufts in pots are brought. From it, you may look down over on to arcadian smallholdings and the clear stream of the Rio Vicano.

Sant'Andrea is the 'clean ruin' towards the top of the medieval quarter; it was the second cathedral. Its conspicuous little 15th-century tower now presides over a concreted enclosure. A few columns remain and determined former parishioners come in the afternoon with flowers, altar cloth, crucifix, and candlesticks, to say the rosary.

What is left of the castle stands where the old town merges with the new, up near the present cathedral: like others it has fallen into final disrepair only in the last twenty or thirty years. Across the piazza, the Chiesa del Popolo – the People's Church – is now just a vast medieval shell up a vast number of steps. It is private property; the State somehow found it impossible to prevent it falling into ruin, a process hastened, we are told, by the use of private pickaxes on the frescos.

This Piazza in front of the Cathedral, and the streets out of it, are all of them from the Farnese time. The splendidly upstanding fountain is by Vignola: its three unicorns share the central column for their non-existent hindquarters. The street in which the Oratorio of Santa Rosa, or the Rosario, stands, left of the Cathedral, and the rest of that quarter were all won from the ravine. The Rosario (1626) is arranged inside like the chapel of an Oxbridge college, which is unusual. Busts; a pretty organ case and gallery in a single curly unit.

Where the Farnese wanted a very substantial Cathedral there happened to be nothing but thin air. The Roman architect Pietro da Cortona began the great substitution, and the main visible architecture was done by him and continued by Carlo Rainaldi, the latter between 1671 and 1695.

The interior is colossal but feels abbreviated: the nave arcade has only three bays, and the eye demands four, perhaps five. But that would have taken all the air there was, right across to the hill opposite. The high altar has bishops and saints stepping out from between its columns, a mass of cherubs in the broken pediment, and some angels in conversation above. The altars are real marble – the transept ones very fine – but behind them all is *trompe l'oeil.* Three pictures are noteworthy: a *Madonna, Child and Saints* from the studio of Giulio Romano, over the high altar, and in the transepts, an *Assumption* by Francesco Trevisani and a *Rosary* by Giuseppe Ghezzi.

The spaces beneath the church might be called crypts in the sense that elephants might be called mice: first down is the Duomo di Sotto – the Lower Cathedral. It runs under the whole length of the Upper Cathedral, and has the same plan and only a little less height. Because the forms here are unornamented, the effect is of overpowering size, and utterly dramatic. This was the funerary chapel. Beneath is yet another vast chamber, this time standing only under the dome: the cliff makes its presence felt. This is the region's second piece of macro-infra-architecture: the other being at MONTEFIASCONE.

A handsome bell-tower of 1734, not quite as tall as the gigantic dome, is attached on the north side. On the south side, where the ground drops sharply, and perching on the slope, is the mouse-sized belfry for the funerary chapel, a strange miniature with all its parts in proportion.

RONCIGLIONE's carnival is somewhat famous. It includes a genuine *corsa dei barberi* such as used to be run in Rome, when wild horses race riderless down the main street; it is why Italian high streets are called the Corso. These *barberi* were a favourite piece of psychotheatre throughout Italy until recently: the one day in the year when the polite urban artery is cleansed by a deliberate injection of the wild and dangerous.

The Emissario

This is the artificial outlet from the LAKE OF VICO, whose water appears, rebaptised as the Rio Vicano, at the bottom of RONCIGLIONE's ravine. It is a *cuniculus* about 300 metres long which drains water through the hill at a level lower than the lake's natural surface. That the Etruscans dug it is known because a Roman road, which dates from Augustan times, runs below the original water level, and the Romans were not keen tunnellers. The Etruscans of course cut their *cuniculi* by hand: they are normally just big enough for a small man to work efficiently with a pick. How they overcame the problem of opening this one to the flood at the last moment, we can only guess; it must have been appallingly more difficult than diverting a stream into a *cuniculus*.

The actual outlet is not particularly easy to find. About a kilometre along the low lane beside the stream, past all the industry and up towards the crater, you enter a deep hemicycle of vertical grey volcanic cliffs, 30 metres high perhaps, 200 in diameter. There walk and scramble, following the sound and then the sight of fast-running, now canalised, water. It was over the rim of this hemicycle that the water poured naturally, if not usually voluminously, before the emissary was dug. The actual exit from the rock has been destroyed by copious pouring of concrete, the closer to canalise the stream. It had been restored by Pier Luigi Farnese in 1540, and was surely worthy of more respectful conservation.

The Vicano flows down through green pasture, wilderness, allotments, a one-time fish hatchery now stable to a single horse, and soon comes to the industrial zone. Better than at BRACCIANO, though still with effort, one can trace the shapes of the renaissance mills and forges with their stabilisation tanks for the head of water (ducks in them now) and their furnaces for the chestnut wood. Until the Second World War the old water hammers rose and fell to thump woodpulp into paper, night and day. It was a comforting sound, and signified all was well with the world. That is, so long as you knew what it was: for its effect if you did not, see Don Quixote.

Sant' Eusebio

A very ancient field-church, of great natural holiness.

The key is with the parish priest of Santa Maria della Pace in RONCIGLIONE. Three kilometres along the Cassia towards Rome, turn left at a green gate between two cypresses in a long row of umbrella pines. A green track brings you up through an oak grove to a green field, and there, standing at the top under huge trees, is this small, infinitely old church, quite alone and in utter silence. A Roman military man, Flavius Eusebius, was buried here, and his tomb was taken for a saint's. Later a correction was made; the saint the church is now dedicated to is the real St Eusebius who was Bishop of SUTRI in the 5th century.

It is reputed to have been built in the 7th and 8th centuries by monks who had fled – nothing changes – from Palestine, and then it became part of a *domusculta*. It has a graceful, careful, façade of the time of the monks, with a slightly overwide renaissance doorcase added, and a little arch and a proper typanum above; one aisle is broader than the other. Behind: remains of the bell-tower and other ruins. Inside: good capitals; old frescos; Flavius Eusebius' marble slab; cool and rather moist. A view of the Tiber valley over the tree-tops. It is easy to believe mass has been said here uninterruptedly for a millennium and a half.

Rota

In this unspoiled countryside, ROTA most truly of all the places we describe offers Italy's 16th-century appearance. Below run the swift River Mignone and the road that accompanies it along its always green valley. The wild TOLFA HILLS are steep and grand all round; white long-horned Maremma cattle hardly move; and there is no inhabited place within five miles in any direction. The distant towers of TOLFA on its mountain top stand up against the sunset, when steam is seen to rise from the hot springs in the valley. (It is true that in the last couple of years a single house has been begun and left unfinished on the hillside opposite: it is an outrage against a unique and uniquely precious landscape and a disgrace to any planning system. Perhaps a flash flood may wash it away.)

A very few people have always lived here: Etruscans, Romans, the occupants of the field-castle in the Middle Ages. In the mid-17th century salt-tax returns show 200–250 souls, probably living in two regular streets like the present single one.

The big house today consists of three sides of a square firmly planted on the irregular top of the little height. The main range is a never-completed but still substantial palazzo of the 1570s, arcaded at ground level on to a properly flattened cortile, and reached through a gated arch and steep ramp under the fabric. The name of Martino Longhi the Elder, of Varese, is mentioned as a possible architect – his grandson of the same name assisted Rainaldi at S. Teresa at

CAPRAROLA – and the owners were a branch of the Santacroce family (see VEIANO). The west range, built on the very edge of the precipice, tapers to a beetlingly narrow end. Opposite is a scruffy 13th-century range – a barn, and a tumble of ancient buildings, the stump of the castle. The fourth side is open to the pure view; the whole makes an utterly harmonious Ark in the middle of a limitless Arcadian sea.

Indoors, the as-it-were ground floor has been modernised, but the *piano nobile* is unchanged since the Lepri family came into the place in 1709. This too is virtually unique. There are frescos contemporary with the building, Zuccari-like, and later: a *Creation* with an extraordinary bird of paradise resembling a feathered spacecraft with long legs; a *Flood* with an Ark of Vignolesque proportions and some of the people who couldn't get in clambering back in despair on to the shrinking shore, with their horse; the *Children of Israel* in the desert, with manna falling conveniently into pots on the ground (some of the children are a bit thin, but all are extremely well dressed). The Ark is on such a scale that it makes one remember the Renaissance was when art, natural history, and engineering first combined into the kind of realism that is still with us. Its superstructure looks like some grand old *casale*.

The tiny baroque church has an unusual chancel arch: two big inverted cornucopias with their tails twisted together at the top close the arch and their open ends rest on the piles of apples and melons they have spilled on to the tops of quite ordinary columns. An allegory? On the pillars of Church and State rest the fruit and veg. which, in the words of Pope Gregory the Great, 'belong to the people by right, not charity'.

Sacrofano

Historically this was Scrofano and the arms over the gate show an unmistakable sow – *scrofa*: 'Sowsville' has been bonified to 'Holyshrine'. Dennis approved because he identified its hill, Monte Musino, as Etruscan and important: it has terraces 30 metres broad and the remains of a circular building.

Twelve miles from the centre of Rome, among the rolling hills of the Roman Campagna, SACROFANO's medieval nucleus is unchanged, the castle remains lived in to the hilt by country people.

The church of San Giovanni Battista has a 12th-century tower, but was rustically rebuilt in the 15th century, with a bend to the left halfway up. The town hall has some flat, Lecce-like, rococo architecture applied to it. Outside the gate, the 1704 church of San Biagio (archaic for the date) is quite odd.

San Giovenale

One of the King of Sweden's digs, kept accessible under a nice roof. (The Etruscan and Greek finds are in the Rocca Albornoz in VITERBO.) Fourteen layers of occupation have been found.

Bronze Age people from the north built cabins. (See also CALCATA and LUNI). The next ones, from the TOLFA HILLS, made sheep's cheese and span. About 700 BC, Etruscans dug the huge defensive trench and a town well 10 metres deep, and had necropoles in nearby hills. About 200 BC, the rich left for Rome, and the poor scattered, to work the vast estates for their absent betters. About AD 900 they returned to the protection of the little eminence and rebuilt. The place was finally abandoned in the 15th century. The tufo here is bright orange with black cinders.

San Giuliano

(See also BARBARANO ROMANO.)

A fine Etruscan site islanded among 'horrids'. In the Chiusa Cima necropolis, the 6th-century BC Cima Tomb is a great domed drum, like at CERVETERI. One chamber, in the 'orientalising' manner, has a shell vault, then four pilasters fluted in a Chinese box pattern, supporting a beam-and-rafter-simulating vault.

San Liberato

Far up in the hills between BRACCIANO and VIGNA GRANDE stands the perhaps 9th-century churchlet of SAN LIBERATO: an elegant arcaded interior; Roman fragments. In 1888, Prince Baldassare III Odescalchi excavated, and Roman columns, statues, and inscriptions were taken down to VIGNA GRANDE. (q.v. to discover their fate.)

San Lorenzo Nuovo

SAN LORENZO NUOVO is a rational solution to a precisely-defined problem. In the mid-18th century the people of San Lorenzo were living unhealthily beside the lake, their houses crumbling, and they began to leave. But the fields continued fertile, and the papal government intended Alto Lazio to be Rome's granary. Therefore, 'salubrity having been frustrated...', a healthier place should be found and the peasants moved to it. The decision was taken in 1771, the new town built, and in 1778–9, 98 families were moved. Conclusively, the roofs were taken off their old houses. Faint traces of a tower remain to show where.

The new town lies like a saddle cloth along the spine of the lake's containing hills, and the Via Cassia cuts across, through the piazza. The architect was a Roman, Francesco Navona, and according to the historian Mario Munari, the design of the central octagon closely resembles that of the Amalienborg Square in Copenhagen, built in 1749. On site, a VITERBO engineer called Filippo Prada was responsible. The almost neo-classical church of San Lorenzo dominates the octagonal piazza, the housing is divided into four neat sectors, and the whole is inscribed in a tidy rectangle. The Capuchin church and convent of the Assunta (1779) closed the town at the south end.

Down below, in the fields called Val di Lago, are the remaining walls of a little octagonal church of San Giovanni. The Saint appeared to a small boy on 5 June 1563 and told him he wanted the church he had once had there rebuilt. This was done – was the architect a Sangallo? – and a great fair was inaugurated, which now happens up in the new town, on 24 June. The new town's own feast is about *gnocchi*, and happens in mid-August.

Turner did a sketch here, looking south over the lake to MONTEFIASCONE and the CIMINO, with the two islands just discernible.

Santa Marinella

This was the Etrusco-Roman port of Punicum, the 'Carthage' port. Roman remains have been copious. It was an agreeable resort in the late 19th century because of its mild winter climate, with prosperous villas behind walls and tall trees. Even after the Second World War it still had the feel of a plush oasis in the wild. Today it is engulfed in anonymous shoeboxes and *villette*.

The greenery-draped, pine-girt castle you see today, out on the point, is on the site of a Roman villa and includes parts of several later castles. It is now Odescalchi property.

This Santa Marina (= Marinella) is reputed to have been an Alexandrian martyr for whom some Basilian monks built a quite small chapel on the deserted beach in about 1000. But according to the *Golden Legend* (see TREVIGNANO), Santa Marina's tale was quite different (if less suitable for a nice seaside resort). She had been dressed as a boy by her widowed father and received with him into a monastery, as Brother Marinus; 'he' would plough and fetch wood and one day 'he' was accused of getting a girl pregnant and was driven out; 'he' cared for the baby so well at the door of the monastery that the monks readmitted 'him', to perform the most menial tasks. On 'his' death, they discovered the truth. The girl who had accused 'him' became possessed by the Devil; confessed; and when she was led to Marina's tomb was made whole again.

San Martino al Cimino

In 1202 Innocent III gave the 'four walls' of an old Benedictine convent to the Cistercians of Pontigny in France, and by 1305 a complete Cistercian abbey in the French manner was spread out on the hillside. The imported style influenced building in VITERBO and TARQUINIA.

Although there were then some ninety Cistercian abbeys throughout Italy, this one had shrunk by 1426 to one monk and the abbot. In his 1462 travel diary Pope Pius II commented that owls were singing instead of the monks of old.

That San Martino is still a fine abbey, that approaching from Tobia you still get a sudden and dramatic view of what you can hardly believe is not a piece of France, is largely due to the sister-in-law and *ispiratrice* of Innocent X, Donna Olimpia Maidalchini Pamphili. He gave it to her in 1645 and she died here of the plague in 1657. Even the two apparently characteristic bell-towers and the ceremonial apron in front of them, were added by her as buttresses. The great west window, whose tracery on closer examination turns out to be a nice essay in interacting cogwheels, was a perhaps 15th-century, perhaps later, substitute for an original rose.

Inside all is cool, pointed, and familiarly northern: the nave with its hardy regular arcading, the steady rhythm of the alternating piers and columns and of the stone vault, the light from the huge clerestory windows. Donna Olimpia provided grand furnishings, all marked with the Pamphili doves-with-olive-twigs and lilies. There is a shapely wrought-iron cage for the font; and a splendid 'standard', a two-sided picture, rather faded, by Mattia Preti. In the north transept, a gold and silver bishop.

Donna Olimpia came from VITERBO, born in 1594 to a family of many children, all of whom but the eldest were put into monasteries and convents. Unamused, the tale is, she escaped by accusing her confessor of impropriety – he was later rehabilitated; found herself a rich husband who died; and then another, the brother of a Cardinal Pamphili. The Cardinal, under her guidance – he wrote to her from Spain, 'away from you I am like a ship without a rudder' – became

Pope Innocent X at the age of 70. She is said to have been responsible for many of the beauties of Piazza Navona, including the River Fountain, and for the Villa Pamphili on the Janiculum.

It was perhaps by her will that the ancient Pope had CASTRO wiped out in 1646 because, it is said, she believed the Farnese had tempted her son, a teenage Cardinal, away from the glorious future she intended for him in the Church and into matrimony with one of their relations, Olimpia Aldobrandini.

At SAN MARTINO she also built herself a serviceable, not immodest, palazzo beside the church, and a new town. On plan it is almond-shaped, with a gate at either end and two main streets, the outer houses windowless at the back to make do as town wall. It runs down the slope like a mining village. For population she is said to have obtained released prisoners and reformed whores. The Porta di Viterbo is held, not implausibly, to be by Borromini: it is a powerful shape, strongly Etruscan. Nevertheless, she did not succeed in having the Via Cassia rerouted through her town.

Another story goes that once when her brother-in-law the Pope came to stay, roasted chestnuts were put back into carefully opened husks still attached to the chestnut trees. There were shouts of amazement, the Swiss Guards were set to find them, and the Pope *Prese non Mediocre Piacere* – 'took no mean pleasure' in the joke.

San Michele in Teverina

The village goes straight up the hill, a long, straight street lined with long low houses; below, a long ornate palazzo, of about 1726, across a little bridge, with its church beside it.

Sant'Oreste

SANT'ORESTE is a big, poor village that has perched on SORACTE's shoulder since at least the 8th century: whence, probably, its name. Easy mistake: one of our children thought the mountain was called Sir Harold Acton. The outwardly gaunt 16th-century Palazzo Canali was prettily re-decorated on its shallow inner side in the 18th. Vignola's correspondence mentions work at the church of San Lorenzo, and the lower part of the façade looks as though it just might be partly his.

Santa Severa

SANTA SEVERA is the grandest of Northern Lazio's sea-castles, its corseted towers a solitary and unmistakable shape in the sweep of the coastline.

Here was the Etruscan port of Pyrgi, serving Caere (CERVETERI), which became rich on trade with Greece in the 7th and 6th centuries BC. It was also a religious centre, and Aristotle records that its sanctuary of Leucothea – the 'White Goddess' – was sacked in the 4th century by Dionysius of Syracuse. From the 3rd century, it was a Roman colony and port.

Virtually all this coast was abandoned during the Saracen raids. A castle of SANTA SEVERA is first mentioned in 1068, built on the remains of the Roman fortress, probably a lookout tower little different from the Etruscan ones for which the Greeks called them the Tower People. A small garth was added, then a large one, which followed the outline of the Roman settlement. The Orsini rebuilt the Castle in its present form, apparently as much for defence against the people within its perimeter as against attack from the sea. In 1978 the Region of Lazio bought it, and let holiday flats.

You enter through various curtain walls, finding a fountain of 1791, a church of 1595 restored at the end of the 18th century, a little chapel with 14th-century frescos, a few shreds of medieval village, and finally the Castle itself. The 100-metre length of the north-west wall, 3 metres thick and 4 high and made of huge blocks of stone, presumably comes from the Etrusco-Roman foundation of the 3rd century BC. Out to sea you can scramble over more giant blocks which used to be the harbour wall, now scattered by time, storm, and war.

Eastwards along the beach the Sanctuary of Leucothea has been excavated: two temples and some other public buildings. The Greek sources speak of Leucothea, while the Etruscan inscriptions speak of Uni, whose name in Latin became Juno. White Goddess enthusiasts can thus elide her with the wife of Jove, and conclude that he obtained his kingdom by legal marriage.

Sasso

Magnificently placed in a pass through the Colli Ceriti above the sea, under its crag (*sasso* is rock), the tiny self-walled village (the houses are, externally, the walls) and small but perfectly formed palazzo enclose a rectangular piazza. The church is 16th-century and the palazzo was rebuilt then (and at other times) round a 12th-century tower. The box garden below was made in 1928.

There is a drawing of Sasso by Claude in the Louvre.

Sermugnano

Few places are smaller, and the walls curl neatly all round the top of the hill. The old town is inside them, steps corkscrewing in shafts through the masonry. There are signs – two windows on an upper floor – of a minute castle from the great age, and a minute chapel with a memorial to Karolus Orsini. The Sagra is *crostini* and *bruschette*: small food.

Sipicciano

The gate of the town is widely spread-eagled, hearsay Egyptian perhaps, with a complicated polygonal house or one-time towerlet on each side. A grand (18th century?) tunnel staircase leads to a high piazza in a tumbledown medieval quarter. A sad church of S. Maria, long gone, has a frescoed 16th-century chapel one would have travelled to see.

This is wine-country, within the Orvieto appellation.

Soracte

For Byron, SORACTE

> ... from out the plain
> Heaves like a long-swept wave about to break,
> And on the curl hangs pausing ...

And we may properly plant SORACTE among the waters of the long vanished Sabine Gulf, but as island, not wave.

Its stegosaurus back and more than diagonal sides rivet the eye, even though it is less than 700 metres high. It is calcareous – a palombina limestone. Its striating caves are both natural – where Bronze Age potsherds have been found, and artificial – war materials were stored here. The Fuji-like aspect from the north is quite misleading – it is not volcanic – but like Mount Fuji, floats on mist at dusk and dawn.

At the very top, a place of wind-whitened rock and shiny shrubs, Apollo Soractis was served by priests called Hirpi, who could walk unharmed on burning coals. Some of his temple's columns adorn the crypt of the little (reputedly 6th-century) church of San Silvestro, the saint of summits, who has inherited the site, and is perhaps the successor of Silvanus, the Roman god of the wild places. Or more likely, the 4th-century Pope, Silvester I, who came here to escape persecution by the Emperor Constantine. St Benedict of Benevento, missionary in Poland, lived here as a hermit during the perilous year 1000.

The old, old church has been a receptacle for columns, odd capitals, bits of pergama with leafy and lop-sided patterns (perhaps from the other churches and hermitages), frescos of many dates – one shows a flayed martyr with his skin tidily folded over his arm. Recent restoration has left everything neat and concrety. The lower church, Santa Maria delle Grazie, at 656 metres, no beauty, has a grand statue of St Silvester the Pope.

The views of course are stupendous.

The road from SANT'ORESTE, though vertiginous, is passable by car. In May, 'Soracte in flames' is celebrated, with great fireworks.

Sorbo, Madonna del

A Sorbo is a sorb apple, and the Madonna here holds one, perhaps for the same reason the Madonna at Paestum holds a pomegranate: that a predecessor goddess did so. The pilgrimage church stands over a gorge between two wooded hills, 22 kilometres from St Peter's, and the only sounds are wind and bird-song.

A shepherd boy from FORMELLO was approached by the Madonna: she needed a shrine here. He ran back to his village to tell them, but no one believed him. So he ran to CAMPAGNANO: they believed him and built it at once. The people of CAMPAGNANO make their pilgrimage on Easter Monday, and those of FORMELLO think it wiser to come the next day. Both eat and drink round bonfires, and there is a small fair.

Approach (from FORMELLO) through Arcadia; twinkling stream, cool caves in the rock, stock-rearing of a Virgilian kind all round, seasonal sheets of flowers.

On this road we were once held up while two peasants, their cars stopped side to side, discussed an arrangement. We could hear nothing, but watched the dialogue of the two left hands through their respective windows. Provisional agreement was reached and approval indicated by two raised thumbs; doubts recurred, indicated by flat hands wagged; an objection was overriden; provisional agreement was re-established with thumb-to-index satisfaction; a final reassessment – perhaps of third-party risk? – was proposed and accepted; and Almighty God was called in witness to the deed by a forefinger pointed to the sky. At last another peasant stopped his tractor and pointed out that they were holding up the traffic, viz. us. The agreement was ratified and, half the repertory of Roman rhetoric having been deployed, the two hands finally clasped. We all drove on.

The main doorway of the church carries the date 1487, but much of it has been rebuilt. The robust little tower is 17th-century. The rambling convent buildings have mostly fallen over the cliff, but bits of fresco remain in the chambers and corridors that still stand. Restoration proceeds in a leisurely manner, with the glum grey *intonaco* which is now the curse of Southern Europe.

Soriano nel Cimino

The place is a fine and rousing sight, an unmistakable profile on the lower slopes of the CIMINO. But also problematical on two counts. One is the huge 13th-century Orsini fortress, sitting high and unblinking, like a giant spider holding in her young, which is an unvisitable (and unimaginable) prison. The other is Cardinal Madruzzo's extraordinary Fontana Papacqua, the 'Popewater' Fountain, which is a piece of 16th-century ... No word to describe it comes immediately to hand: a 16th-century piece.

It is the castle's very symmetry that seems menacing: an expression of conclusively organised power. It is said to have a steep annular approach system within, and two high courtyards, from one of which the great squat tower emerges.

The town's main church is the Collegiata, with, unusually, an 18th-century brick front. (Inside, do not miss the 15th-century St Antony, with his little pig between his feet, and a jauntily combined mitre and halo.) Under the awful fortress, within the old walls, Sant'Eutizio is an 18th-century rebuild of an earlier church: everything curls and dodges in an almost over-affable manner. Close by, the Fontana Vecchia is partly an old capital, pierced for spouts, and water comes out of human faces. On the CIMINO road the great gate recalls to posterity CAROLUS ALBANUS, an 18th-century owner: a full-size classical gate, extended upwards excessively, like a court wig. Also on the CIMINO side, mostly in desolate and looming decay, is a gigantic piece of 19th-century religious industrial plant: the combined bulk of a church (of 1818) and a one-time Dominican convent.

As for the Papacqua. Pope Pius IV had given Cardinal Cristoforo Madruzzo (he called himself Madruccio) the revenues from SORIANO and some other places, free of tax, in thanks for his work in setting up the Council of Trent (he was Prince Bishop of the city) and chairing it for many years. Madruzzo rebuilt an existing house, and between 1560 and 1578 constructed what we now see and admire, even as we lament that it was not finished and deplore present neglect. (It is all in private ownership.)

The steep hillside is north-facing and there are gates at three, or more levels. The main buildings are two large palazzi, one probably begun in 1562 to a plan by Vignola. Vignola may also have sketched out what was built later, and much that was never built at all: signed drawings survived here until the 18th century. Possibly Giacomo del Duca, who certainly worked at CAPRAROLA and may have worked at BAGNAIA, had a hand in it.

Behind and above the second palazzo, and attached to it, is a pleasant-looking, rather later, three-wing palazzo, with park beyond and balustered terrace facing west; this has a Vignola-like rusticated aperture in the wall beneath.

Above the entrance level of the two earlier palazzi, a number of formal clipped box gardens and built structures, including two churches, one of them round, ascend the steep slope: they seem to adhere rather than to grow or stand on it; like antimacassars. All of these are now in ruin or decay.

Below the two palazzi, as it were among their roots, the water descends as a single splash into a wide basin that nature and art have designed to receive it. Note the 'dripping' rustications round the cellar, or dungeon, windows; they foreshadow Ledoux' oozing keystones at Salines.

At the very bottom, a flat space seems carved out of the rock, with a sheet of still water that mirrors the cliff above.

It is at a mid-level, at the end of a formal, heavily balustraded walkway round two sides of one palazzo, that the Cardinal's mysterious imagination took charge. Through a pair of gateless gateposts with little tongue-out faces *all'etrusco* (or à la Rolling Stone) for the water to pour from, you are sharply turned towards the hillside; as you go, you pass a row of fifteen (different) gargoyles spouting into three long basins which are attached to the end of the first palazzo, and come, still at right angles to the hillside, on a quite classical tripartite fountain. Here Ceres is in a niche on one side, and Venus at the other. In the middle, Moses, deep-carved, is Striking the Rock. Thirsty Jews are tumbling forward to get at the spring, and among them a curiously classical woman, not tumbling, with a pot on her head. If it were empty, she'd be holding it; who is she? What is her pot full of?

We now turn to face the rock of the hillside, and face the Fontana Papacqua. The main figure is a giant fauness with three baby fauns clambering over her (the one that was at her breast has lost its head); behind her is a twisty-phallic satyr with an owl on his wrist, and three goats; at her feet, a giant frog spouts water (or should) into the trough beneath; and behind it is a giant snail. Between them and the goats, there's a snake – on leave from duty in the Garden of Eden?

Further into the rock we now see that what can only be the Lord of the Underworld is emerging, huge, horned, with 'cruel sensuous nose and lips', and that with a wide and quite ambiguous gesture he is pulling back a curtain; but from what we cannot see. Above him, in a niche that he is also supporting, is a small figure of Pan.

Today the fountains are dry. The row of gargoyles and the 'water ropes' between them – miniatures of the big ones at CAPRAROLA and BAGNAIA – should all be purling and glittering away; the Moses group should be murmuring excitedly. But apart from the frog spouting, it is hard to guess what the water might be doing with the fauness and her neighbour, the great Devil.

The fauness has a steady, atavistic, look and at noon in high summer the sun catches most of her torso, but no more. That none of this is intended for clear viewing is obvious from your being sun-blinded as you come round the corner. The moral – for few renaissance scenes were without a moral – will no doubt be discovered or guessed in time. One thing is certain; the sculptor of the fauness was also the sculptor of the most striking figures at BOMARZO. Vicino Orsini's *boschetto* was, in his own words, *per sfogar il cor,* to lighten the heart. His friend Cristoforo Madruzzo's purpose was perhaps just the opposite. But why would he have wanted that?

Stigliano

Low between the Sabatine and the TOLFA HILLS was Vicus Stigianus, a place for baths since ancient times. (Five springs: 35° to 70°C). There had been a castle, and in the 1670s the Altieri of ORIOLO made something of it. The Baths of STIGLIANO are now a 1900ish hotel in the later stages of decay as a spa: opening times scrawled on a bit of cardboard, immemorial vegetation creeping over the formal gardens, cattle lowing around the disused restaurant. It could be revived for walkers and riders.

Stracciacappa

A twin crater to MARTIGNANO: until the last century there was what Dennis called 'a lonesome little lake'. This was drained into the Lake of MARTIGNANO, so there is now a lonesome depression, made memorable by the tall and most lonesome 13th-century tower that dominates it. The name means 'Tearcloak'.

Sutri

SUTRI's coat of arms shows a man on a horse – Pelasgius, perhaps, Jupiter's son; or Saturn, his father – and whichever it was founded SUTRI, perhaps about 1000 BC. The great Pope Innocent III gave it the title of Antichissima in the early 13th century.

Arriving from the south, you see Etruscan and Roman tombs among the roadside bushes; and the great worn-looking amphitheatre, through its narrow gate; then to the right darkish cliffs merge upwards into the town's walls, pocked with Etruscan drain-holes. Larger caves and incoherent ruins merge into the nearer undergrowth; Etruscan roads cut through the rock. (Nothing to show for the Muslim bands that occupied the territory in the 10th century.)

Deemed by all 'strategic', SUTRI was probably first walled by Veii (VEIO) Etruscans. The Romans seized it in 383 BC; as a gateway to 'Hetruria' (as the inscription on the northern town gate puts it), and commanding the Cassia, it was important ever after.

For some centuries the boundary between the Byzantine Dukedom of Rome and the Lombard invader kingdoms ran here. In 728 the Lombard King Liutprandt gave SUTRI, which he had just conquered, 'to the blessed Apostles Peter and Paul' – the famous 'donation', perhaps in return for a present of gold from Pope Gregory II (715–31). SUTRI thus became the first nucleus of the Patrimony of St Peter, from which grew the temporal power of the Papacy, and many later claims. Pope Zachary (741–52), realising land would give a more solid return than castles, secured the Valle di Sutri detta Magna – SUTRI's own rich and winding valley bottom.

The buildings in between SUTRI's three hills started as hospices for pilgrims on their way to Rome. The main hill, fortified at the west end, has the Cathedral at the east. There was a bishop in the 5th century; and the Cathedral has early, probably pre-Christian, foundations. It is basically Romanesque, but redone, and again redone (including the dashing baroque porch) in the mid-18th century. The elegant 11th-century crypt is now encumbered with concrete pylons to support what is above, including the 12th-century tower. There are good pictures of the school of Pastura, a fine 15th-century wooden Christ, and a Bernini-esque statue of the patron saint, Santa Dolcissima – Sweetest.

The town itself is above the through traffic; it has some fine palazzi, a good piazza (the fountain a copy of one removed to Rome by a greedy cardinal); internal walls; and towered gates. One of them is called Porta Furia, after the Roman general, Camillus Furius, who regained the town the day it was lost.

But SUTRI's main beauties are outside. The hill opposite has mostly kept its ancient character as a city of the dead (though there is now one gardened villa on top). The whole volume of the amphitheatre, 40 metres by 49, is cut out of the faintly glittering rock: rather than seats, it has steps, and so may have been for standing-only *ludi funerari* – 'funeral games'. It is probably Roman, 1st century BC.

The hill is a warren of chambers. One is now Santa Maria del Parto, a hypogeum probably cut by Etruscans in the 7th or 6th century BC. It will have begun as a tomb, with space for bodies along either side of the slightly rising, arcaded central aisle, parallel with the cliff. In late Roman times the followers of Mithras probably used it. In the Middle Ages it was adapted as a church, and the name *parto*, as in parturition, derives easily from its womb-like character. The Child in the Nativity fresco is swaddled like a little chrysalis. In the make-do narthex, frescos show the legend of St Michael in the Gargano, the spur of Italy; the Archangel battled with the Devil in a holy cave there as had Apollo before him. Note one non-clerical pilgrim going uphill on his knees: pilgrims to the Gargano shrine still did so only a few years ago.

The hills and woods around are full of more or less abandoned churches and chapels. Santa Fortunata, almost opposite the amphitheatre, has spacious catacombs behind. In the valley, the tower of San Paola has a nice pointed gothic door frame. A group of caves and buildings, implausibly called the 'Castle of Charlemagne', is where Charlemagne's disinherited sister Bertha is said to have given birth to Orlando, or Roland. When Charlemagne recognised him, he made him Paladin of France and Governor of Brittany.

Tarquinia

There are three things to see in TARQUINIA today: the bare site of the great Etruscan city, whose walls were 8 kilometres round (VITERBO's medieval walls are 5); the Etruscan necropolis, where their own pictures are still there on the walls; and the medieval and renaissance town, the golden-towered city you see as you approach from the north, which has some of Lazio's best churches and pictures, and its best Etruscan museum.

TARQUINIA was the Etruscan Tarxuna, or Tarxna, from which came Macaulay's 'great house of Tarquin': enemies of Rome, kings of Rome, and subject of the best narrative ballad in the then uninvented language of some foggy northern islanders twenty-three centuries later. Chiusi, in Tuscany, is the Clusium Lars Porsena came from.

The traditional founder was Tarchon (same name), the brother (or son) of that Tyrrhenus who (according to what Herodotus heard) led the Etruscan migration from Lydia. Artefacts and burials abound from the 11th century BC, and in the 9th TARQUINIA became one of the principal proto-Etruscan, or Villanovan, settlements of Italy. In the 8th to 6th centuries it grew rich on trade, both in raw materials and in manufactures, between Greece and Sicily and the Etrurian towns. It was also well sited to control, militarily and commercially, the coast road, the Tyrrenian sea, the minerals from the TOLFA HILLS, and the Etruscan Plain behind: the River Marta was then (and in the Middle Ages) navigable.

In the 6th century, there were Tarquin kings in Rome, but in 510 BC they were driven out, and in 474 the Etruscan fleet was defeated by the Greeks of Sicily. After losing control of the seas, the Etruria that TARQUINIA dominated turned increasingly inland; the LAKE OF BOLSENA was the Tarquinian Lake. In 307 BC, the Romans conclusively defeated TARQUINIA; and twenty-odd years later, VULCI and Volsinii (BOLSENA); and then built the Via Aurelia.

In the 4th century TARQUINIA was a bishopric. Why the town moved from the Etruscan to its present site is obscure: against malaria and invasion it hardly seems better. Maritime trade eventually revived and TARQUINIA became rich enough to build walls in the 9th and 10th centuries, and field castles and, mostly in the 12th and 13th centuries, several splendid churches. Also to entertain popes. The Castle, of which little remains, may have belonged to the 11th-century Countess Matilda who made a great bequest of Tuscan lands to the Patrimony of St Peter.

Its most noticeable medieval personality was Giovanni Vitelleschi, Pope Eugenius IV's *condottiere*, whom he made a cardinal in 1437. Vitelleschi destroyed the Rocca Albornoz in VITERBO, to dislodge the last of the Prefects of Vico (and had him beheaded at SORIANO), and secured Eugenius' return to Rome and his control over the papal dominions. Eventually suspected of treason, he was put in the Castel

Sant'Angelo in Rome, where he said of himself, 'One who has done such deeds as mine either ought never to have been imprisoned, or can never be released'. Shortly after he died, either of wounds or poison. In TARQUINIA he had begun to build the splendid palazzo which now houses the Museum; and was later roundly celebrated on the walls of the Palazzo Communale.

TARQUINIA then went definitively to the Church. It was occupied by the French in 1798, and the British in 1809. Its Etruscan riches began to be uncovered in the 19th century. Its Etruscan extent and population were several times today's expanding town.

Etruscan Tarquinia

The Etruscan town until the 8th century BC was probably where the necropolis now is. Then it moved to the hill still called Civita, 3 kilometres east, and the bases of many buildings, gates, and walls remain there, showing its vast extent. The most substantial is the so-called Queen's Altar, an ashlar podium 77 metres by 35, on which one or more temples would have stood: at one end it had a great stairway, at the foot of which the winged horses now in the Museum were found.

The 5-kilometre-long hill called now Monterozzi, Rough Hill, from its hillocky appearance, then became the necropolis. It contains some 6,000 tombs, including 62 fully, and many others partly, painted.* This is by far the greatest number of all known Etruscan painted tombs and, since Etruscan painting has fared better than Greek or Roman over the centuries, it forms a massive part of what survives of ancient European painting. Also it is the most direct and vivid experience we can have of the Etruscans and the way they lived.

The room-shaped tombs are dug straight into the ground and are reached by modern steps. The 'furniture' is for ordinary use in death as in life, and the paintings are to remind the dead of life.

The impression is strong and pleasant. Here are these people, red-brown men and white women, all dark-haired, doing many of the things we do, the later ones depicted in this very light and delicate style of painting which is the elder brother of the Roman, and the ancestor of the Raphaelite and Zuccaresque and of the English 'Pompeian' of the Adam brothers and of Wedgwood pottery. (Josiah Wedgwood called his factory town near Stoke-on-Trent 'Etruria'.)

* The number open to the public and the visiting hours vary according to the condition of the tombs and the state of the finances: usually not more than ten.

They wrestle, dive off rocks into lakes, ride leggy delicate horses holding a little whip behind their backs, knees-up impetuously, go fishing and wildfowling, play on a double pipe. They also hand one another eggs, husband to wife and wife to husband, held between forefinger and thumb, and recline at meals where they are waited on by naked youths.

There is a bit of preaching too: in one part of a frieze a man and a boy engaged in buggery are about to be charged by a man-faced bull, while in another a man and woman making love are guarded by a man-faced bull lying peacefully on the grass with its face turned to us as if to say: that's better. There are also many real creatures: leopards, lions, bee-eaters, dolphins; and invented creatures: sea serpents with horses' heads, demons, chimaeras, and naked men with wings. And patterns, geometric or with natural motifs, round or between scenes, and vigorously developed.

In 1925, Aldous Huxley sent his cultivated derelicts in *Those Barren Leaves* to the TARQUINIA tombs. One of them tries the translation of an inscription. Another answers: 'But for all you know *flucuthukh* in Etruscan may mean soda water ... "When *Fulfluns flucuthukhs* the *ziz*" may be the translation of "When Bacchus drowns the hock with soda". You don't know.' On the other hand, D. H. Lawrence's description of the tombs in *Etruscan Places* (1932) is one of the modern world's finest laments for the lost directness of the ancient one. He also goes straight to the spatial meaning of Monterozzi when he sees that the 'dead lying buried and quick, as seeds, in their painted houses underground' are a sunken version of 'the living Tarquinians in their gay wooden houses'.

The Town

TARQUINIA's stone is *macco* – unmetamorphosed cousin to marble. It is rather paler than Bath stone, but absorbs and holds the light in the same way and it enlivens the whole town.

The descriptions that follow are listed more or less geographically; the city is not big: best to park and walk.

The Palazzo Vitelleschi, which is now the Museo Nazionale Tarquiniese (not *macco*) was started by the Cardinal-Condottiere in 1436, and not finished for two generations. Perhaps the Florentine Michelozzo Michelozzi had a hand in the original design, but both construction-wise and stylistically it is a confusion. It is embedded in the old city walls, it straddles the Gothic/Renaissance architectural transition and it switched ownership – from Vitelleschi to the Camera

Apostolica, the papal authorities. In January 1944, it was badly damaged by bombs; restoration continues.

Its own interest – particularly the cortile, staircase, loggia, and the series of grand windows – is considerable; but it is outshone by its contents, perhaps Italy's best Etruscan collection after those in Rome and Florence, and better displayed than either. The famous Winged Horses are the collection's glory. They are of the 4th or 3rd century BC, about half life-size, of painted earthenware, attached to the shaft of their *biga* (see CASTRO). In a room to themselves, they are now fixed on a wall rather high up for comfort. But then so they were: they come from a temple and perhaps Apollo was driving the *biga*. Never was alertness so combined with noble calm.

Elsewhere in the collection, as well as grand pots and dishes with the familiar stories and dances, are decorated ostrich eggs from the 7th century BC, a pretty she-Janus with fringes, tiny gold dolphins leaping over golden waves, 'art-nouveau' ewers, a toby jug with an African face, a man doing a back bend with his beard sticking straight up in the air, plump birds riding on wheels (from before the time of wheeled traffic) ... Fine great sarcophagus people stare out from behind the cement mixer in the cortile.

Santa Maria di Castello is the great golden compilation of castle ruins, city walls, church and tower which you have seen from below. You reach it from the city down a dusty lane, through gates: one of the most perfect romanesque churches in Italy. The eye is first captivated by the relation between the clear, slender, separate, tower, conclusive triumph of less-is-more, and the façade, which as instantly breaks up into its component pierced flatnesses. It was begun in 1121 and consecrated in 1208. Round the outside of the dome – which is not visible from the front (and which fell in an earthquake of 1819 and was put up again) – is a pretty collar of colonnettes.

The inside repays long contemplation of the kind which starts by working out what holds up what, and how many of them there are, and what proportion that is of the number of something else, and what holds up nothing, and why, and ends by speculating on the nature of reality and spirit. Note that collar of colonnettes repeated crown-like inside the dome; and the lightness of the side aisles, which is achieved by the repeated intersections of almost semicircular arches (which are lumpish enough when they appear alone); the alternate round and square ribs in the vaults; the rose window, on the south-west side, and its echo on the north-east; the (in parts) fine mosaic floor; and also the distant effect of the raised chancel and its stone furniture. Smaller events: the curving petal motif in many places;

the familiar and mysterious bearded man's head set alone in the north wall just below the dome; some fine (if altered) capitals of 1209 by Giovanni di Guittone. Also an octagonal font, perhaps made of pieces of an ancient tomb, and much other work of tidy antiquity.

The Franciscans came to Tarquinia about 1230, and soon afterwards built another very large church at the top of the town, San Francesco, where they have been ever since. Where at the earlier Santa Maria di Castello rhythm is imposed on light by dark incidents, here it is the other way round. There is much the same pattern of pilasters and cross vaults. Transept and sanctuary arches pointed, nave to crossing still round. In the chapel on the right of the high altar, a coruscation of baroque *stucchi* benefits from really nice baby faces; winged 12-year-old she-herms are sticking out their tummies in mild ecstasy. An 18th-century side chapel is covered in cool Corinthian curlicues: soft brownish-beige grisaille on the palest pinkish-brown and green background.

The big free-standing tower of 1612 plays pleasingly with earlier forms: the square main body is a variant of the normal 13th-century pattern of an increasing number of openings as you go up; the hexagonal domed toplet is from Bramante. Beside are the convent buildings, perhaps a little older than the church, and enlarged a couple of centuries later with a large, plain, pleasant cloister. Popes stayed here. On the other side, big farm buildings with low pitched roofs like the church and the same tiles. A vegetable garden-cum-orchard.

San Martino stands in the northern quarter of the town, where poor medieval houses are now giving way to poor new houses. 12th century, and still encrusted with houses. The regular interior has six pairs of 'peperino' columns (some are painted to look like peperino) and all gigantic for so small a church. On the first capital on the left St Martin's horse is walking away from a pious pelican and a bear is coming round the corner to meet it, but the bear is beginning to be eaten from behind by a dragon. The sail belfry is rigged for-and-aft.

Further up and into the quarter is another small church, the Annunziata, attached to its convent by a bridge. 12th–13th century, the façade frontispiece with a rose window and plenty else going on, including black and white zigzag – Siculo-Norman, it is said, and squat Lombardic apses; baroqueries were recently put round the corner; the new table a slab on a handsome 200 BC Corinthian capital.

At the northernmost edge of the town, above the Marta valley and apparently about to fall into it, San Giacomo Apostolo is what remains of a single-nave 13th-century church, in an enclosed cemetery. The low hemispherical dome, of a Byzantine or Arab sort, is like those found in Southern Italy. The façade is 17th-century.

San Salvatore is shed-sized, rough and inexpert; chevrons; shelly stone; a tiny apse with a Celtic serpentine feature built in. And there are other churches fast falling into ruin: perhaps more than in other towns of the size.

San Giovanni Battista, or Gerosolamitano – of Jerusalem – was built about 1230, near the centre. Good façade, with the usual rose window, and two sarcophagi as ornaments; at each end, a nonchalant shepherd. The large apse is buttressed outside, and supported inside by side apses, so the ceiling appears 'bat-winged'. The mainly gothic interior is much redone, but note: the way the windows in the (pointed) side chapels interpenetrate the vault; the pointed arch between the chancel and the sanctuary sporting dogtooth and zigzag (a solecism in Anglo-French eyes); above all the romanesque apse. Frescos.

The Palazzo Communale stands beside and above the well-be-columned church of the Suffraggio; the church of San Leonardo is opposite, on a kind of wide podium; and there is a handsome fountain: all this makes up the Piazza Matteotti, which enjoys a really grand arrangement of street-surface planes. The oldest bits of the Palazzo are 11th-century and it goes on, a spatchcock of masonry and apertures of many dates, some of the earlier windows cosmeticked up as late as the 17th century. The external staircase is constructed as three great Viterbo *profferli*, trying to keep up with the ever-rising street, and reaching rest in a fine four-arched loggia. Inside are frescos depicting the city's 'legends and facts', probably of 1629–31, by Camillo Donati and others; recently restored, and before that restored in 1734, when the inscriptions were 'redone'. They show the Etruscan Kings of Rome; Frederick II's massacre; Gregory V deemed of Tarquinian origin. Cardinal Vitelleschi is celebrated as the 'Third Founder of Rome'.

Downhill, the busy façade of the church of the Suffraggio – the word means 'prayer for the dead' – has become monochrome from over-cleaning and restoration. For the style, 1761 is late.

The façade of San Leonardo, opposite, is flat, but the oval interior is a fine exercise in Roman Baroque. A huge black and gold 'Empire' sarcophagus. Dashing modern glass, coloured, over the altar.

San Pancrazio, in behind, is odd: the interior reads like the truncated last three bays of a very large nave-and-two-aisles 12th-century church, with pointed arches, the last bay raised and constituting a very spacy *presbitero*. It is now a concert and exhibition hall.

Santa Maria di Valverde is a 13th-century building (rose window, nave, and two aisles) under the town wall: no longer now the Greenvale of the name. On the 1450 marble altarpiece appear the Four Patron Martyrs of TARQUINIA: St Secondian, St Theophania, St Lithuard, and St Pantaloon.

The Cathedral of Santa Margarita was rebuilt in 1656 after a fire (and the façade renewed again in 1933 by Pietro Magnani): only the chancel from the smaller previous church survived. But it contains the best work of the VITERBO painter known as 'Pastura'* and one of the finest fresco cycles of Northern Lazio, his *Life of the Virgin*, painted in 1508–9. Four (newly restored) frescos on the vault: three of *Prophets and Sybils* – King David, Hosea, and the young Isaiah, each turning regretfully away from his Sybil, and she from him. The fourth panel shows the *Coronation of the Virgin*, and she is Latial in the same way that Perugino's girls are Umbrian: they looked like that then and they still do. The dove ascending between Mary and her son-spouse-king cleaves the air with flame of incandescent pyrotechnics.

On either side below, the big pictures: on the left, the *Birth of the Virgin*. In a strongly 'earthquake'† *quattrocento* loggia, the newly delivered Elizabeth lies naked under her sheets, though with a headcloth, while the baby is washed in a basin on the floor. The archangel entering left is rehearsing for the Annunciation, which will be performed in the manner of Botticelli, later, elsewhere. What arrests the eye and the heart is the mysterious and emphatic young woman, dressed in heavy renaissance dark red, who is facing out on to a view reminiscent of Perugino. She stands with her back squarely to us, her left arm out straight, in a gesture of imperious permanence. What is she doing? In her hand is a flat dish, of the sort Etruscans hold in death: is she handing it to St Elizabeth, is it something for the bath scene in front, is she showing mother – or child – to God, who is present in the blue trees outside?

Opposite is the *Marriage of the Virgin*. As in Lorenzo da Viterbo's Santa Maria della Verità fresco, a strong feel of portraits and self-

* Antonio Massari, son of Antonio da Viterbo the Elder. His dates are approximately 1460–1516. Pinturicchio, with whom he worked in Orvieto Cathedral, took him to Rome to work on the Borgia Apartments.

† The Tuscia, unlike Florence, has regular experience of earthquakes; for this reason the architecture tends, like the Baroque of Central America, to be squat and powerful, and this is the sort of architecture Pastura painted here.

portraits hangs about it. Two boys behind the main events break sticks over their knees while looking up to heaven; Eros and his brother Potros, perhaps, breaking their bows? (Raphael's 1504 *Marriage of the Virgin* has just one youth breaking a stick.) Behind is Tuscia's volcanic landscape, with little towns and cathedrals akimbo. In the distance the sea, or perhaps the LAKE OF BOLSENA, with the proper sunset clouds. Pastura's colours are surging forward to Mannerism: mauves in particular, and soft oranges. The frieze above shows mermen winged and harping, on the curl of whose defiantly leafy tails sit winged and two-legged young mothers, suckling their babies.

Elsewhere, some splendid tombs and a pretty late 17th-century *Visitation* with a blonde Madonna. The large side chapel in the left aisle is a startling example of how people brought up among the good may commission the bad; note also how the impregnating ray of divine light from the hand of the archangel in the *Annunciation* goes with attention-demanding prudery to Mary's head.

There are many *festas* and processions: on Easter Day, a half-ton wooden Christ from Canova's workshop is carried by sixteen *facchini* while guns are fired; on spring Sundays there is the *carciofata*, the artichoke feast; and also in the spring *butteri* from far and wide gather for a rodeo, when the young cattle are herded, caught, and branded.

At some point, TARQUINIA became 'Cornietum', Italian 'Corneto', which does not have an entirely serious ring, being too close to *cornuto* – horned, cuckold. Aretino: ... *non me acceca tanto il vino che non vegga ch'io son da Corneto* ... – 'the wine does not so blind me that I can't see I am from Corneto'. So it was changed back, to Corneto Tarquinia in 1872, and to TARQUINIA in 1922.

Tarquinia, Coast of

Marina Velca is a new seaside resort, north of the River Marta.

Tarquinia Lido is an older and larger resort, south of the Marta, with a long esplanade and shoebox blocks overlooking a broad sandy beach.

Just south of this, in and under a modern holiday development, are the remains of ancient Gravisca: an Etruscan and then a Roman port, with an inner basin and two channels to the sea. It dates back at least to the 7th century BC and had a commercial temple area, *sanctuarium emporicum*. Excavations began only in 1969 and Attic pottery and Etruscan artefacts have been turned up. Until 480 BC, the inscriptions were all in Greek.

Virgil described Gravisca as *non salutifera* – non-health-bearing – perhaps because Etruscan drainage arrangements had already been abandoned. George Dennis discovered an enormous arched vault nearby, with voussoirs 'from five to six feet in depth', which he surmised was 'the mouth of a sewer or a stream' . . . 'not inferior to the Cloaca Maxima or about 14 feet'. (The Cloaca Maxima is the main drain of ancient Rome, perhaps Etruscan-built.)

Virtually everything above ground was destroyed in the Gothic War of AD 408. After the Lombards, who did not engage in sea trade, another harbour was built, now known as Porto Clementino. Its remains are also within the holiday development. In the 1360s and 70s two popes used it on their journeys from Avignon to Rome and back; it was notably improved by Clement XII in 1738, hence the name. It was destroyed in 1944 by the retreating German army.

Still further south are the salt-pans called Saline which were opened in 1803 and for a while met all Rome's needs. After unification in 1870 there was so much competition from Sicily and Sardinia that prisoners were put to work here. Big, seemly buildings – barracks for workers and prisoners – remain. The salt-pans themselves, now enclosed as a nature reserve, keep much of the romantic desolation which marked the whole of this coast until after the Second World War.

Tessennano

Tessennano was formerly Tuscinnana. It grows straight out of the rock it stands on, and its olives, from very old trees, are famous.

Tolfa

TOLFA and MONTEFIASCONE have the most sensational positions of all the towns between the Tiber and the sea.

Today's TOLFA used to be Tolfa Vecchia; Tolfa Nuova was destroyed in 1472. It is on a mountain top (though the altitudes are scarcely Alpine) and its ruined castle is even higher, on a trachitic pinnacle from which you can see to Kingdom Come.

The medieval town was destroyed by French troops in 1799. Rebuilt, it has tall elegant houses in good repair, from which well-dressed old ladies emerge when the church bell rings. The history is of minerals: iron from Etruscan times, alum in the Renaissance, when Paul II (1464–71) bought the whole territory. Annibal Caro (see CAPRAROLA) was sometimes at the nearby mine of Pian Cerasa, working as the Farnese commercial agent and translating the *Aeneid*.

The 17th-century Palazzo Communale has a nice collection – Etruscan, Roman, and Romanesque. The Romanesque mostly comes from the vanished church of Sant'Arcangelo (see TOLFA HILLS). Capitals are wild and ingenious: a twin-tailed mermaid emphatically showing all, with flippers; rabbits butting one another round the corner of a capital; rams sharing one head between two bodies at one corner and vice versa at another. A formal garden behind where old men sit at the breezy end.

Of the churches Sant'Egidio is the grandest, its giant apse straight over the crag. Miners' rows from various dates, with single-roof ridges over many houses. Nothing as grand as the Fabricone in ALLUMIERE; but a far nicer town: a good place for a *pied-en-ciel*.

Tolfa Hills

The Monti Tolfitani or Monti della Tolfa were once a round little archipelago in the sea. Today, they are among the handsomest and least spoiled parts of Italy. Their look is quite different from the more recently and purely volcanic hills to which they are now attached; though small, they are real mountains. A detraction from the pristine is the network of powerlines coming from CIVITAVECCHIA: but they are part of the understandable hurry of people who reached seemly development only forty years ago, and stride gallantly.

Two metalled roads, from MANZIANA to CIVITAVECCHIA and from TOLFA to SANTA SEVERA, are convenient to drive on. Here you can walk or ride all day and meet no one but a shepherd with his carpet-like flocks of sheep, and the white *Maremmana* cattle in the valleys. You may come on the ruins of a Roman villa or a 9th- or 12th-century church, or twelve different orchids. In spring some hillsides are so thick with jonquils you feel faint from the scent.

In the Bronze Age, they were thick with settlements; in the Dark Ages with monasteries; and then with Lombardic and Frankish castles. The monastery of Santa Maria al Mignone, on the river, was large and rich, destroyed by Saracens in 892, and still needs finding. There was an abbey at Sant'Arcangelo and another at Sant'Angelo, unless they were the same, and ruins remain of a church at Piantangeli, unless they were all three the same. There were hermitages – one of the Trinity where St Augustine might have stayed to ponder – and castles at LUNI, vanished, and at SASSO and ROTA, which remain as noble houses.

The quite chunky ruins of the fortified town of Tolfa Nuova can be found at a place hard to describe, more or less between ALLUMIERE and SANTA SEVERA: signposts to La Tolfaccia. It is not known when or why it was new: only when it was destroyed: 1472.

Torre Alfina

One of King 'Desiderius' signal towers. Afterwards the property of one of four Monaldeschi brothers, brought here by Desiderius' son-in-law, the Emperor Charlemagne. BOLSENA's castle bears their name: a battling lot.

Not fine weather, not the lofty site, not even the notice on the road that announces that this is the Marchesato of TORRE ALFINA can cheer the visitor up: the medieval castle has been overlaid with a wilful and gigantic dark brown Victorian version of BRACCIANO and all looks awry. *Maremmana* cows, yes cows, can be seen yoked in pairs to carts.

Torre di Sant'Agostino

Not far north of the power station of Valdilaga by CIVITAVECCHIA was another sea-tower, TORRE SANT'AGOSTINO. There is now an inelegant modern church of St Augustine of Hippo, on which a Latin inscription tells of the Saint's wonderful chance encounter: he had come to this very beach to think, and was

> totally absorbed in meditating on the imperscrutable mystery of the Holy Trinity

when he had a

> prodigious meeting with and message from a very beautiful boy, really holy, who was intent on scooping up all the waters of the sea in the hollow of his childish hand.

After which the Saint withdrew

> into a little trench which he himself had dug at the very edge of the shore, and understood that the matter on which he had begun ... was really immense and impossible for the human mind to comprehend and explain.

As he wrote in his *Confessions*, the nature of the Trinity is

> a mystery that none can explain; and which of us would wish to assert that he can?

Torrimpietra

The name seems not to have the obvious derivation Tower of Stone, but to come from that of the valley, Preyta, or Impreda: *praedo* in Latin is a pirate.

Many places in Northern Lazio have long been occupied but here, in the 1950s, in the depths of a wine-cellar in the tufo the remains of a hunters' settlement were found: bones of mammoth and rhinoceros and stone 'tools' with which the meat could have been cut off them, preserved between gravel and volcanic ash. Potassium argon dating gave the 435th century BC. Re-dating suggests one only a little less amazingly distant.

Little remains of what happened between then and the early 18th century AD: some Etruscan pots, hillsides of untouched woodland, a modest medieval settlement. This the family of Pope Benedict XIII Falconieri bought and turned into a fine place, with a villa and raised garden for the Pope's summer holidays; the other buildings were carefully regrouped and the church was rebuilt octagonal in 1712. It contains three pictures of St Anthony Abbot with his pig, and one sculpture in which the pig has a leather snout and trotters.

The house contains notable frescos by Pierleone Ghezzi and François Simonet, mostly showing open-air scenes of cardinals and ladies picnicking. The most entertaining is an *Expulsion*. Not, to be sure, of Adam and Eve, but of the Falconieri family's own farm manager, one Pagliaccetto, whom they sacked. But a dog, standing outside the (frescoed) frame of the picture, looks faithfully up at him, and so said all of them: the expulsion was thwarted because all the animals, yea verily even the insects – presumably including the valuable bees – followed the young Pied Manager and would not be dissuaded. It was also said of him that he had ninety-nine familiars, *spiriti folletti*, at his command, which made him omnipotent until he bet a certain swineherd that he could plough a longer straight furrow, and the swineherd turned out to have a hundred familiars at his command. A field or two away stands the medieval tower where he lived, still called the Torre di Pagliaccetto.

Ghezzi left a curious *trompe l'oeil* in one of the bedrooms: a standard print of the Madonna, inscribed *Rifugium Peccatorum* (The Sinners' Refuge) and signed and dated 1705, appears rather clumsily stuck up, but the red sealing wax is just paint, and so is the pilaster. Ghezzi almost certainly did not work here before 1712, so this seems to be some kind of darkish joke. The false date distances it from the Pope.

In 1925 Luigi Albertini, then owner and editor of the *Corriere della*

Sera, and a forceful democrat, was deprived of his newspaper by Mussolini; so he bought TORRIMPIETRA and turned it into a model farm of great size and in time fabulous reputation in the still benighted agriculture of Lazio. Even in the 1950s it still produced the only fresh milk you would wish to buy in Rome. Others have now caught up, but the wine is still ahead of local competition.

In 1944 the retreating Nazis hit on the idea of punishing sabotage by shooting the first thirty people they could lay hands on. The Carabiniere Salvatore d'Acquisto, who started life as a footman at TORRIMPIETRA, was among one such group of thirty. When they had dug the mass grave he stepped forward and said he had placed the bomb. It was not true, but it worked, and he alone was shot and now has streets named after him.

TORRIMPIETRA is now the property of the Carandini family. Count Nicolò Carandini, who married Albertini's daughter, was the first Ambassador of the new democratic Italy to London after the Second World War.

Torrita Tiberina

TORRITA TIBERINA is tiny, with a very picturesque crenellated palazzo and a super-crenellated tower.

In the cemetery is buried Aldo Moro, a serious and uncorrupt prime minister who did good by concealing his intentions in such grey language that nobody could tell what he was up to. He was murdered in 1978 and his body was found after many weeks in the boot of a car. The idiotic crime caused much public heart-searching, and terrorism has certainly not advanced in Italy since then.

Down below, the Tiber runs by yellow cliffs and through the green lagoons and reed beds of the nature reserve of NAZZANO-Tevere-Farfa.

Tragliata

Two or three old houses on a vertical *sperone*; a big one below; a church; and a medieval tower. Therefore it is a village.

Treia, the Valley and the Parco Suburbano

The River TREIA ran through the Ager Faliscus and Faliscan settlements dotted its inhospitable catchment area. The Romans conquered and removed most of them. In the Dark Ages, it bolstered the Eastern Empire's defensive boundary against the northern 'barbarians', and in the Middle Ages, the Papacy's against the new Emperors from the north and the Saracens from the west; and even against the Viterbesi.

By the 10th century every rocky spur had been 'encastled': provided with a tiny walled village, a tower, and a church; caves were used for living in. CALCATA, FALERIA, and MAZZANO survive as villages; odd towers or piles of stones in the voracious *macchia* indicate other habitations.

A Parco Suburbano is nothing suburban: it is an area of outstanding interest and natural beauty, which anyone in their right civic mind will treat carefully and enjoy. Communes may start these parks, with financial help from the Region: here it was the Communes of MAZZANO and CALCATA. Nice girls in green jodhpurs patrol informatively and there is a tidy and modest place to eat.

This *parco* covers a stretch of the TREIA where the water is pellucid and nothing is restored or municipalised. Below Montegelato is a small piece of heaven: a couple of ruined medieval towers, a mill, little bridges and decayed leats; springs, pools, waterfalls. Everything man-made is of the native rock – cut and built with, or just carved. In the mill the wheel lies horizontally; it was fed diagonally from above and a shaft drove the grindstone in the room overhead. The people from the *domusculta* of Capracorum (see VEIO) perhaps withdrew here in the 10th century.

Willows; bird-song; moist air. Schubert: *die Steine*.

Trevignano

Until 1960 a walled village on the north shore of the LAKE OF BRACCIANO; now the nucleus of a holiday town. Originally Faliscan and/or Etruscan; then perhaps the site of Roman Sabatia. The hills are the Colli Sabatini, and to the north is Monte Rocca Romana, their highest point, a pure conical form visible for miles around. (Thick scrub to the top, so no views.) The Lake in Latin was Lacus Sabatinus, the fishermen's boats are Sabatine, and there is a Sabatine human type too: short, round, brown, jolly. (Sabines from the land of the hard rock are taller, fairer, more reserved.) When the municipal museum opens, its display will include Sabatia's best find: a great bronze fan as used by Etruscan chiefs on formal occasions – just as Popes and African chiefs still do.

The ruins of the Castle – tall till the First World War – still dominate the scene: it was Giovanni Borgia's 1496 replacement of an older castle he had destroyed in the course of setting up a tiny Borgia empire round the Lake.

The best fresco in any parish church we record is here, in the Assunta just below the Castle. The church was struck by lightning on 18 April 1988, but the damage should soon be made good. The work is a *Death, Assumption and Coronation of the Virgin*, painted in 1517, donor and artist unknown, though the painter certainly belonged to Raphael's studio. Pellegrino da Modena has been suggested, but photographs of his other work are not persuasive, and there is no documentary evidence.

The story comes from Jacopo da Voragine's *Golden Legend*, an early 14th-century collection of lives of the saints and martyrs which provided ideal libretti for painters for the next three hundred years. In the *Death* scene, wicked Jews are trying to steal the body of the recently dead Mother of God in order to prevent the Apostles from claiming she had resurrected like her Son. One has had his hands cut off by a Just Man, and they are sticking to her bier. (Jacopo has it that the Jews in question were converted soon afterward and their wounds healed, so we may imagine those hands joined on again.) As she ascends, the Virgin flings her girdle to Doubting Thomas in a last attempt to convince him of the truth of things: the gesture is so real, so felt, that it suggests a rescue rope for him to climb up.

Behind is a most interesting classical round temple with an open, columned portico, five lines of columns deep (counting the last one, which is pilasters), a sort of open Pantheon with the portico apparently running right into it. Apparently, because the lighting from the left suggests that the round should be behind the whole portico. But it clearly isn't. Here and there in the background are little scenes: fishermen on a lake, travellers with donkeys, people sitting on the ground and eating – all holy stories which happened at a lake in truth very like the LAKE OF BRACCIANO. Also the Castle of TREVIGNANO as it was.

The Madonna being crowned is a woman of some age and the putti above who are pushing the clouds apart are successors of those in Piero della Francesca's *Madonna del Parto*, who were pulling the curtains across her, years before, as she was going into labour. Two prophets look up, waiting to record the events in their marble sketchbooks.

These events are not forgotten in TREVIGNANO. The Festa dell'Assunta, 15 August, is observed most heartily. In procession the statue of the Madonna is taken down to the Lake and on board a boat. (From 1945 till the other day this was the barge from VIGNA DI VALLE across the Lake with the crane on it for lifting engines out of flying boats.) To the sound of amplified and worn hymns, guarded by the priesthood and a mainly otiose choir, preceded by all the fishermen in their boats with lamps lit, and threading her way through tracks of floating nightlights in jamjars, she comes to the other side of town and is disembarked. As she withdraws to the (part Roman) church of St Catherine for the night, attention turns to the firework display which goes on for the next hour.

Formerly this consisted of a competition between two rival and well-provided teams and after the show the village fathers retired to the fine, sober, renaissance town hall, on the façade of which maxi-sparklers were still raining gold fire, to award the prize. When we had been to the *festa* for about ten years, one of us was invited to be a judge. The discussion did not start sober, and there was much singing. We cannot remember if a prize was awarded. Nowadays only one team performs, but the removal of competition has not lowered the standard.

In the Central Italian August it is not only the town authorities who gear everything to the Feast of the Assumption of the Virgin. Nature generously lends colour to the dogma. And what colour. For several days before the 15th the clouds rehearse in ever blacker and whiter precipices, with more and more serried ranks of ruddier or more golden linings, and an ever more brilliantly marked small blue hole for the Assunta herself to go through. Then on the appointed day, up she goes: the lightning leaps out in the eleven different versions known to the Etruscans, the sky is transfigured with flashes from below, the thunder rolls and roars for three days, the light changes from red to pale gold, the temperature falls by fifteen degrees, the sand is no longer too hot for your feet, and the land is cleansed.

In 1988, for the first time in our experience, she was late. The rehearsals went on week after week without any *felix exitus*, and week after week the temperature went over a hundred each day and sank minimally at night. Mankind, creature of habit and faith, celebrated on 15 August just as if something had happened. Is nature signalling a withdrawal of support?

Trevinano

The most northerly place in Lazio, the 'finger' between Tuscany and Umbria. It is a good journey up the valley with a barn on every hilltop and low scrub thinning to bare pasture. From miles below you see the cliffs and castle walls merging: on top, it is cool. The cliffs turn out to be a friable mix of sand and rounded sea stones, a one-time shore lifted long since by vulcanism.

The castle, of many centuries, belongs to the Buoncompagni family. It is strongly battered and rises among ilexes behind; on the cliff-side, a tiny, balustraded hanging garden. In 1910 they were washing sheets in a lower room and the fire under the copper set fire to the oldest part. The substantial, one-room-thick, 16th-century range is lived in.

The wayside chapel of the Madonna della Quercia is richly baroque.

Tuscania

From a distance the towers of TUSCANIA's two great churches and its ruined castle are an impressive cluster, rising on a modest central eminence in the wide Etruscan Plain. The walled town, on the adjacent eminence, has been rebuilt after the earthquake of 1971: it is affable, rather empty: not all those whose houses collapsed have come back. There is much worth seeing, but the two basilicas, San Pietro and Santa Maria Maggiore, are more than that: they are very powerful as buildings and they confound the Christian-educated eye.

Their hill, the Colle San Pietro, has been occupied for nearly three thousand years. The churches both date from the 8th century, before Charlemagne gave the place to the Patrimony of St Peter. They were rebuilt to an unknown extent in the 11th century, when their hill was ringed with towers; and in the 12th; and in the 13th, when the rest of TUSCANIA was first built up and walled, and most of Colle San Pietro's towers were used to build new towers. The churches were then left to themselves on their hill, as they still are.

The rooted apse of San Pietro you saw as you came up, raised high on a rather haphazard plinth, is a one-time acropolis, incorporating Roman and Etruscan remains. You round the later medieval Bishop's Palace with its great hall visible through fine windows above, you pass the pure Carolingian baldaquin standing there in case a passing mighty emperor should wish a while's enthronement in the shade, and the one and a half giant towers, not to mention the Etruscan sarcophagi, and face San Pietro. A sturdy affair, you think, the usual shape for a Lombardic or Carolingian basilica; darkish ginger tufo; white surround for the central door; rose window set in a broad white marble frontispiece above a band of nice little blind arches. Which frontispiece, however, as you approach, you see is intricately, indeed wondrously decorated all over with creatures of great authority, but little to do with the Christian religion.

Above all, who can that enormous bearded three-faced character be, a *trifrons*, who appears twice on the right-hand side of the rose? Why in his lower version is he holding a large snake to himself, which is nuzzling or licking his beard? 'The control of serpents was an art cultivated in Etruria', George Dennis tells us: all right, but this is a church, a millennium and a half later. Anyway, what do his flaming coronets mean, and why has he horns in the top version? What about all that vegetation issuing from four of his open mouths, twining up and down, and framing mermaids, basilisks, and other inscrutables from some dire menagerie on the way? The evangelists' beasts and angel are there, haloed, in the corners of the rose, but the evangelists themselves are not. On the left there are six worthies, two haloed, in round frames set in another enlacement pattern, but with the 'green man' faces spouting vegetation in between; is the animal figure presiding over this clan Christ the Lamb? If so, why no halo? Big winged dragons are hurtling down each side of the rose after prey, but towards you; tufo bulls emerge at the edge of everything; a pair of winged lions stand looking outward just below them, and some other lions are coming out of the masonry; the dentils all have faces. Bottom left is a dancer, perhaps Etruscan, naked but for a pleated cloth over one shoulder, and in the posture of an accomplished windsurfer. We examine *trifrons* more generally, but still inconclusively, in Appendix II.

The arch over the central door is more reassuringly decorated with instances of the crafts: a cooper, a huntsman shooting his arrow at a deer carved in the next stone. Familiar images.

The nave inside is homely and luminous, the aisles dark behind the rather low arcades rising, yes, out of benches: some kind of Christian *majlis*? The capitals, substantial and various, and the Cosmatesque floor, all gloriously faded circles and squares, between them suggest that in this undemanding space many are the tents that have been pitched, many the tribes given shelter. The small-roofed altar and the pergamon up steps and amid low walls in the mistily distant central apse manage to imply there is weather in here too: the effect of the light from the transepts.

The crypt, said Dennis, 'looks more like a mosque, or the subterranean bath-rooms of the Alhambra'; it does indeed have a watery light, twenty-eight ancient marble columns, and elegant Arab influences.

To Dennis, the church of Santa Maria Maggiore lower down the hill was 'still more outrageously grotesque' than San Pietro. To us not, although it has some more than fanciful images – a gryphon holding out a human head on the façade, an evangelist's angel with scythes for wings – but none as traumatic as *trifrons*. Built on the site of a substantial Roman temple, it was the cathedral until the 9th century. Vandals have taken the heads from the statues of St Peter and St Paul by the door: one has been recovered. Note the asymmetry of the lunette over the central door: the powerful Mother and Child half right, the Lamb in a *tondo* right, the 'Sacrifice of Isaac' (in two parts) and the 'Flight into Egypt', all tiny on the left. The few remains of the cathedral at CASTRO suggest it may have looked rather like this: similar colonnettes have been recovered.

The interior is more harmonious and more compact than San Pietro's. It had a local monopoly of immersion baptism and the font is still here. So is a grand high pulpit. In both churches, there are frescos galore, more or less legible: in Santa Maria is a line of twenty-two busts of saints, above the left-hand apse, of about 1500, unusual in its isocephaly. A ragged but tough old bell-tower stands immediately in front.

The Town

TUSCANIA was an important Etruscan centre in TARQUINIA's hinterland, Tirrenia to the Greeks and Tuscana to the Romans. It shared its port with VULCI near MONTALTO DI CASTRO. Conduits, wells, cisterns bear witness to the usual Etruscan skills. The road that became the Clodia came here, crossing the then navigable River Marta; and when the Romans took over in the 3rd century BC, they paved it; a bit can be seen between the great churches and the town.

The Lombards came in 574, doing battle with both Byzantium and Rome for its possession. In 739 one *Rodbertus magister comacinus* was working on St Peter's and had a house and vineyard here and in 774, when Charlemagne conveyed TUSCANIA to the Patrimony of St Peter, the building of the great churches was already well advanced.

At the boundary of Church and Empire, the area was endlessly fought over. Then as the Clodia became less important than the Cassia, TUSCANIA breathed and throve again. In the 13th century it became a free commune, and the great churches were rebuilt.

Pope Boniface VIII Caetani (1294–1303), as punishment for a rebellion, changed its name to Toscanella, under which it went until 1911. (It was also called Salumbrona.) Cardinal Vitelleschi (see

TARQUINIA) recovered it and its fifteen field-castles from the Vico family in 1440 and demolished castles and fortifications. Plague in 1494. Sacked by Charles VIII of France in 1495, though saved from total destruction by a miraculous thunderstorm and rebuilt, smaller, with the basilicas outside. The still scarred and broken hillside and the basilicas' solitude are a monument to this 15th-century vandalism.

There was no grand Renaissance here and much of what over the years had been arduously put together was shaken down in the massive earthquake of February 1971. It has been arduously rebuilt.

The Palazzo Communale is a good 17th-century building. Two mannerist worthies dance on the roof beside a small sail belfry and inside a series of little round frescos recalls local settlements, many no longer known. Most of the churches have been in place since the 10th, 11th, or 12th century: little San Marco has an old barley-sugar portal in its plain square façade and is otherwise rebuilt; San Francesco, where there were splendid pictures, and its convent are a ruin, not rebuilt after the earthquake; Santa Croce, above Piazza Basile, has long held the city archive. The odd-looking part-church, with a pointed arch above, a grated space beneath and a nice lion between, is what is left of San Leonardo on to which a tower fell in 1954. And so on.

There are three sizeable churches: the 18th-century Cathedral in the middle of the old town, which is usually locked, we have not yet managed to get into – its best pictures are in VITERBO. Its broad, calm, façade is 16th-century – provided by Cardinal Gambara (see BAGNAIA).

Santa Maria del Riposo was rebuilt in 1495, after the sack, in memory of a TARQUINIA benefactress, Aurelia dei Mezzopani – 'of the Halfloaves'. A lot of what remained was kept – see some of the windows – and the huge buttresses explain why so much did remain. The interior is taller and more formal and Florentine than the simple façade suggests. 'Green men' appear on some of the capitals and on the pinkish peperino doorway. The handsome wooden altarpiece includes paintings attributed to Perino del Vaga.* The little *Madonna* in the middle is Pastura's. Three paintings by Scalabrino da Pistoia, of which the best is the *Deposition*, a fine mathematical picture in rich mannerist colours, conveying both the weight of the dead body and its symbolism: look at Christ's left hand both hanging and pointing down to the heads of the two Maries.

* Vasari tells how Perino, who was an orphan, was brought to Toscanella by Vaga, an untalented Florentine, to paint on his behalf; but Perino wanted to go to Rome, which he did, so the work here was not completed.

The adjacent convent cloisters now house an excellent small museum. In 1967 and 1970, four generations of the Curunas family were discovered, in three separate unopened tombs of the 3rd to 1st centuries BC, and they are now installed, reclining on their thirty-three sarcophagi, amid a display of their funerary bits and pieces.

Santa Maria della Rosa is an omnium-gatherum: a long flat nenfro façade, with a squat moth-eaten tower attached at one end, a couple of stringcourses inexpertly holding it together, and some oddly placed round windows – one a proper twelve-petalled rose, from which the name may come. There have been several churches here and inside it is far from clear who built which in spite of what. The great transept arches appear to bury a quarter of their length on fully worked capitals inside a pre-existing town wall. After the sack of 1495, this was the cathedral for a while.

Recent restorers have lowered the floor to expose older and holier stones, making the whole *presbitero* into a kind of sanctified picnic site: the Table is on one capital, the pulpit on another, the Crucifix on an upturned third. Overhead are two panels' worth of painted ceiling. What is left of the fresco of the *Madonna Liberatrice*, who saved the town with a miraculous downpour in 1495, presides. There are two fine altarpieces.

Tuscania's Etruscans

The Etruscan necropoles, scattered in the surrounding hills and cliffs, were mostly cleared of their portable contents in the 19th century. Dennis describes the garden of the brothers Campanari, great dispersers of Etruscan artefacts:

> You seem transported to some scene of Arabian romance, where the people are all turned to stone, or lie spell-bound, awaiting the touch of a magician's wand. . . . All round the garden. . . . each seems to be on the point of warming into existence.

The Campanari family had a neat arrangement with the Vatican, whereby *they* excavated (all expenses met), then divided the loot into two equal parts, and the Vatican chose which part to remove to the Gregorian Museum. This left the brothers with plenty to sell on their own account, to the British Museum among other places: the Curunas were lucky to escape.

Some other stone Etruscans, men and women, extracted from their tombs but not expatriated, blindly stare at each other from their sarcophagus lids across Piazza Basile. These were late Etruscans:

their 8th- and 7th-century predecessors had used cremation, with terracotta urns for the ashes.

On the road south, out of the town, near where the Curunas were found, is the Tomba della Regina, which contains a veritable, if small, labyrinth. Further still is the small, tall, box-like, Madonna dell'Olivo: a dignified disused chapel. Beyond that again, along the dust-road to nowhere, the ruined tower of the one-time Abbey of San Giusto shows in a dip. Walling and a doorway with zigzag, and a small vaulted and arcaded crypt with re-used Roman columns: the Abbey, as old as the great churches, was abandoned in 1464. Pigsty since.

Modern Tuscania

Some way along the TARQUINIA road, an estate of post-earthquake housing can be seen to the left; its church began as a district heating plant that didn't work, and was converted with a few deft concrete touches and some bright stained glass; the small cooling tower makes a fine belfry.

For those who cannot get to Tuscania, there is a substitute: the parish church at Wilton, near Salisbury, was inspired by San Pietro and Santa Maria Maggiore, and built in 1841–5, by Wyatt & Brandon for Lord Herbert of Lea.

Vadimone, Lake

The small and now virtually vanished LAKE VADIMONE was famous in classical times for its floating islands. These were probably built up of matted vegetation, but were dense and swift-moving enough to carry off a cow, which would low piteously as the bank receded. The Etruscans believed the milky, sulphurous waters endowed weapons dipped in them with invulnerability: wrongly. Here, in 309 BC and 283 BC, they were defeated by the Romans.

The first victory was secured when the Roman Consul Fabius disobeyed the Senate to pass through the god-infested and forbidden Ciminian Forest to turn the Etruscans' flank. After the second, conclusive, battle the historian Eutropius tells that 'the waters of the Tiber, dyed red near Vadimone, and overflowing with bodies, themselves carried to Rome the news of the victory'.

Vaiano

Not important, despite two churches, but the road from BAGNOREGIO is intensely picturesque. From the hill above VAIANO, a fine view of 'Milan Cathedral', part of the erosion-scape of CIVITA.

Valentano

The hill on the shoulder of which VALENTANO perches is a gigantic heap of cinders, some purplish-red, some greenish-grey. From two large quarries *lapillo* is taken which, treated, makes the red surface for hard tennis courts. The strata displays are grandiose, the layers of volcanic fallout marked by rows of bright green bushes. One quarry acts as home to the country buses, whose rich dark blue shows sumptuously against the red.

After the destruction of CASTRO in 1646, VALENTANO became the capital of the Duchy. The Porta Magenta of 1779 receives you formally, and on Sundays people are notably dressy.

The town's two, but not twin, towers are seen from all around. The Castle was 'improved' in the 15th century by the first Pier Luigi Farnese for his wife. It has a great south-facing arrangement of eleven brick arches, placed over five built of the mauve local stone; from on top of a 20-metre-high battered basement it dominates everything.

Up in the high windy piazza is also the classical church of the Collegiata: the bells are from CASTRO's destroyed cathedral, and the interior is wide and handsome like the streets.

Vallerano

VALLERANO has two churches, each of which *vaut le voyage*.

Compared to its dissimilar twin VIGNANELLO, it has greatly benefited from not getting a straight main street: because traffic can't enter the medieval town, it doesn't try to.

The little church of San Vittore is in this oldest part (as well as a large neo-classical church). 1497. The impression is of a dark, fully furnished, green womb, glinting with silver and glowing with gold, not a square inch unadorned. Single nave and apse, three cubes, the last including the apse. The wooden ceiling, with octagonal coffering and painted with ribbons, roses, and foliage, is unrestored. Rabbit netting catches bits that fall off.

The nave walls are frescoed all over with rich, pale green, acanthus-patterned *trompe l'oeil* hangings, divided by gold-on-dark-blue stripes, and gold-fringed and -tasseled. All four side altars have good pictures, and the frescoed frieze round the small windows above resembles one from the 1570s in the castle at VIGNANELLO. The apse is frescoed, evangelists in the half-dome and apostles in the half-drum, and the panels are stucco-framed in graceful pastry-cooks' patterns, like the local *crostata*. The Evangelist John is watching his pen as it forms the amazing words of Revealed Truth. The *stucchi* have a family ressemblance to the decorations on the façade of the Madonna del Ruscello (see below), which would make them later than the frescos. There are two hanging lamps of some splendour, and a little organ at the west end. This is a rare example of a small renaissance church fully decorated and quite unaltered.

Just below the town, on the south, is the Sanctuary of the Madonna del Ruscello, Our Lady of the Stream. Here is one of the finest 17th-century churches of Lazio outside Rome. It is led down to by a short, wide space, contemporary, with eleven two-storey shops and stables on either side, built to make the most of the pilgrimage trade, and perhaps as contrasting humility. (They are now hardly holding up against time and neglect.)

Perfection, while commonplace in nature, seldom strikes a church façade as it has struck this one. It faces north and is of pale pinkish peperino overall, the friezes darker, and pale brick between the great Corinthian pilasters. The design is tall and majestic, striking from a distance and harmonious from close to; not one of the many figures or motifs, emphatic or slight, familiar or strange, is less than admirable. Two large, human faces, on top of the attic volutes at frieze level, the east one sleeping, the west one yearning, both beautiful, are an unfamiliar motif: to us they have proved unforgettable. Above the door, the Madonna and Child; above the window, the Dove; at the top of all, the Father leans out to us, his hand raised to his triangular halo in a gesture of holy courtesy. Of the Roman church façades, this one most resembles those of Guidetto Guidetti at Santa Caterina dei Funari (1560–4), and of Sallustio Peruzzi at Santa Maria in Traspontina (1556); the latter has high 'heads', but within the capitals.

The church dates from 1605–9; the Farnese lily is ubiquitous in the decoration and there are a few cardinals' hats; the richness of the carving recalls that on the 'Cardinal's Palazzina' next to Santa Teresa at CAPRAROLA, which was due to Cardinal Odoardo Farnese.

The inside is a single nave with side chapels, nicely stuccoed throughout, golden in the evening light, and with good pictures: Pomarancio, Lanfranco and, over the High Altar, the little miracle picture, whose Virgin wept blood. But the real glory is the immense organ, contemporary with the church. Its case is a dark ruddy gold colour and it is alive with *musicanti* angels and cherubs, syncopated pediments and pipe-windows. Played in 1982, it revealed in the big stops a husky roaring tone completely different from the early 18th-century organs we now cultivate and copy so beautifully: indescribably stirring. (Actually they were half-stops: each applying only to one half of the manual.) It sounded best with sustained polyphony, to which it gave an insistent and quite demotic character. It was out of tune and unvoiced, and some of the notes were missing, but like the outside of the church it was unforgettable. The organcase was apparently designed by Chéneriau of Paris, but built about 1610 by Roman craftsmen. We do not know who built the pipework, much of which was still there in 1982, or the action, all of which was. The *cantoria* opposite is attributed to Alessandro Vibani and G. B. Chiuccia, 1644.

Vasanello

The name is either from Bassanello, Little Low Place, or from the clay *vasellame,* pottery made here. Without its walls – demolished in the 19th century – it feels unshelled. The people still have about them an ancient feel of poverty and bad health: feet on stools, limping, obesity, the priest taken ill, drains being put in for the first time. Seeking news of the priest, we wandered through an open door and found ourselves in a kitchen unchanged since the 18th century.

The restored 11th-century parish church of the Assunta has a very ancient portico across the front and the remains of a pagan temple beneath, all mixed up with the remains of the former town wall and a tower. Inside, dark; a 16th-century tabernacle in the form of a *tempietto*; the font a huge egg in two halves, with a door in it: the Villanovan burial form.

Vasanello's best thing is the sumptuous, separate, 13th-century tower of the 10th-century church of the Salvatore: 28 metres high in white travertine. Up-ended ruts show how many of the blocks are paving stones from the Roman Via Amerina just below; a row of Roman heads is a block taken from a tomb. Around, wire-netting; garbage; children playing football in the dust: the scene is more like a decayed grandeur of Asia than of Europe. The church is very much of its date, with three naves and three apses, but rustic: Ionic capitals like Swiss rolls. A 7th-century *cippo*, now the main altar, is carved with a complicated rabbit or deer motif, the beast turning into a tree with birds in it. An altar to the unusual, but here not unexpected, Madonna delle Febbri – Our Lady of the Fevers.

The Castle is handsome and basic of the Renaissance: four plain walls and four round towers. This is where Giulia Farnese brought the body of her murdered sister Girolama to bury (see FALERIA).

There have been important Etruscan finds, recently a 1st-century kiln which shows the instruments and techniques of pottery-making have not much changed, so maybe VASANELLO with a V is right.

Veiano

From the south, VEIANO high above presents its ruinous medieval aspect most picturesquely: lichen-yellow tufo, tufo-yellow lichen, elder, ivy, a few fig-trees, all very dense. The newer town backs up along the main road.

In the 16th century the economy of places like this changed: the valley bottoms, the local historian writes, could be cleared for *potatl* and *tomatl*, newly introduced from Central America and easily Latinised, thus initiating the familiar tomato strand in Italian food. Moreover local wars were no longer smart and building was, even in tiny Viano, as it was then called. The church was restored in 1518. The castle, destroyed by Giovanni Borgia battling the Orsini whose allies the Santacroce of Viano were, was rebuilt in the modern manner. Giorgio Santacroce III (who founded ORIOLO in 1570) built a bridge, and fishponds, and a funerary chapel for his family. (A mixed lot: one Santacroce was Apostolic Nuncio to Germany; two brothers were guilty of matricide and fratricide.)

The Chapel, a sombre and perfect miniature, in effect has no exterior. (The entrance from the street is later.) The style and proportions are those that the great Sangallo practice had found to be most purely classical and therefore most generally and successfully appropriate. (Or vice versa: this is what classicism is about.) But here the proportions are narrowed, shifted from the major key to the minor: the same effect as in the funerary chapel at BOMARZO and, on a much larger scale, Hawksmoor's mausoleum at Castle Howard.

Antonio da Sangallo was already dead in 1554, when the Chapel was first mooted, but Fabrizio Navoni, historian of VEIANO, plausibly suggests a member of the Sangallo team, Bartolomeo Baronino, as the architect. (Presumably the 'Baronino' Vasari refers to as having 'executed' a court and fountain at the Villa Giulia in Rome.) He should be remembered for this little building.

Immediately to its south, the cliff and the houses are falling away.

An attempt, moreover, was recently made to excavate the Santacroce coffins and the floor was opened, in the wrong place, and left unrepaired. Rescue is urgent.

Veio

Heu Vei veteres! et vos tum regna fuistis,
et vestro posita est aurea sella foro:
nunc intra muros pastoris bucina lenti
*cantat, et in vestris ossibus arva metunt.**

O ancientest Veii, you too were a kingdom:
And here in your forum a golden throne stood;
In your walls the horn calls of the slow moving shepherd,
And over your bones the ripe corn is cut.

The 2,000-hectare plateau-site of the Etruscan city of Veii had been settled since the start of the Iron Age and three layers of habitations were removed to put up some of the fortifications the Romans later beat down.

Initially there had been several small settlements round the edge of the plateau, each with its cemetery on the cliff opposite. Then the Veientes developed the idea of supporting their ever-growing centre with farms out in the hills.

Cereal production rose sharply from the 9th century BC on – had they then begun on their remarkable water-management programmes? – and imported Greek objects appeared in the 8th. Forty kilometres of *cuniculi* for water management have been found in the course of studies in the area by the British School at Rome, which is the densest collection yet known. The longest goes 8 kilometres. Their roads too they excavated through the tufo, to secure convenient gradients for their wheeled traffic: several are still in use. Wealth bred talent: in the 6th century Veii produced the grand artist of the bronze Capitoline Wolf and of the great striding, smiling, terracotta Apollo now in the Villa Giulia Museum. In the 4th century BC it had about the same population as Athens.

Though its acropolis was no more defensible than others, Rome stood in more amenable country, controlled more roads, and was itself a port. Veii lost control of the mouths of the Tiber, of their salt supply, of their trade with Greece; and in 396 BC was defeated by Rome. This was despite walls 6 kilometres round, built in the

* Propertius' *Elegies*, IV, X, 27–30; 1st century BC.

manner later used all over Europe by the Romans, with towers and buttresses inside and an earthen rampart 30 metres wide.

Nearly four hundred years later, Livy recorded how the conquerors dug themselves a *cuniculus* to enter the central fortress, the men divided into six parties working in shifts day and night. He also records a story that the Roman soldiers in the tunnel overheard the priest declare, just as the king was sacrificing a victim, that whoever cut up the entrails would be the victor, and rushed them to their general Camillus. Livy observes that 'in dealing with events so remote it is necessary to accept as true all those events that have the appearance of truth'.

The Romans bypassed VEIO with their Via Cassia and ever after made a point of commenting on the dreadful quality of its wine. And this first conquest was the birth of the Roman Empire, the process which in time brought Athens and York, Cairo and Casablanca under one rule of law: a state of affairs that ever after haunted Europe's and the Mediterranean's consciousness. This blank hill is where all that began.

Under the Romans, farming continued in the fertile and convenient Ager Veientanus. When the Empire collapsed, and the Papacy emerged, it was near VEIO that one of the best understood conversions of Roman farming units into a *domusculta* was made, around 780. (See Introduction.) This was Capracorum, where Pope Adrian I, a wealthy Roman, inherited several farms, adding a church, a cloister, and the relics of a martyr, St Cornelia.

Of ancientest Veii there remains little on the surface: just the careful roads, a few ruins and tombs, and near the place called Portonaccio the foundations of a temple, supposedly to Apollo, well displayed, where one can surmise about the development of religion. In front of the classical temple with its pronaos of two columns *in antis* and its nave with two walled-off aisles, we can see the remains of the older, triangular, altar from which lead runnels to wash away the sacrificial blood. It had not been destroyed when the Etruscans built their fine new rational building and set their smiling Apollo and his colleagues on its roof. Although according to Livy VEIO's Juno was promised a fine new temple and carried off to Rome, the Romans generally tended not to disturb, but rather to embrace and rehouse local divinities, as Juno Curite at CIVITA CASTELLANA, Feronia at LUCUS FERONIAE, and indeed Baal when they built their titanic monument to rationality at Baalbek in the Lebanon.

The visitor's main pleasure has to be to wander through the plain pasture and arable tableland where the city stood. Below in the ravines are various natural joys: the waterfall at the Fosso della Mola – unless it is too dirty – and the idyllic valley of the Valchetta and its tributaries. (This last you reach by a road to the *campo sportivo* just below the rock of ISOLA FARNESE.)

On the next tableland to the east is one of the CERVETERI-like tombs, probably 7th-century BC, known as the Tomba Campana, after the Cavaliere who opened it. You can't reach it now, but Dennis's description of its wall-paintings is informative:

> Was there ever such a harlequin scene as this? Here is a horse with legs of most undesirable length and tenuity . . . His colour is not to be told in a word – as Lord Tolumnius' chestnut colt, or Mr Vibenna's bay gelding. His neck and his fore-hand are red, with yellow spots – his head black – mane and tail yellow – hind-quarters and near-leg black – near fore-leg corresponding with his body, but off-legs yellow, spotted with red. His groom is deep-red livery – that is he is naked, and such is the colour of his skin. A boy of similar complexion bestrides the horse. . . . while on the croup crouches a tailless cat, parti-coloured like the steed, with one paw resting familiarly on the boy's shoulder.

Everywhere are dug caves of one sort or another, and the amazing invisible *cuniculi*, which when cleared bramble over again within the year. Things here get ever harder to find and identify: the famous 70-metre-long tunnel, the Ponte Sodo – Solid Bridge – cut to take a river through the rock to prevent flooding, is no longer signposted, and is more or less impossible to visit because of barbed wire and padlocked gates. Rome's pointed neglect of Etruria is still alive and well.

Still, come on a fine spring day, not expecting to bowl up and be bowled over: rather to walk a few kilometres and meditate.

Vetralla

Is this the only town where the mayor has every year to marry two oaks? The Doge of Venice had to marry the sea on his city's behalf, but here it is the vegetable world that the people, in the form of their no doubt sometimes portly and at other times dishy elected representative, and in the presence of the local Passionist Fathers, espouse. In 1206 Innocent III gave wide woods in Monte Fogliano – 'Leafy Hill' – to the town; rival Viterbese claims developed; a later pope repeated the gift; and ever since VETRALLA has taken good care to keep things in order by solemnising the marriage on 8 May. The trees wear ribbons.

It is a dignified town, with solemn palazzi of the 16th and 17th centuries. Its castle, with Zuccari frescos, was mostly destroyed in the Allied bombardment of 1944. The almost gigantic Cathedral, a smooth, severe, pre-neo-classical work of 1711 and onwards, somewhat squashed in its piazza, magnificently commands the plain. Inside it, the quite normal dome and vault-swoops take on a heroic aspect because of their combined scale and simplicity; organ and choir galleries are of positively papal grandeur.

The town was destroyed in 1185 (by the Viterbesi), and rebuilt, and the lower church, now dedicated to San Francesco, was built at that time, using materials from an earlier one. Its three apses have been disentangled from accretive sheds, and now look a bit scrubbed beside the square bell-tower. Inside, it is a small but august basilica with five arches per colonnade, and columns some of whose capitals may have come from the old church. The crypt is older: someone at work reinventing the column. Cosmatesque floors, restored.

The high Gothic monument inside was put up in about 1406 by Giovanni di Vico, who then ruled the town, to his 33-year-old natural son, Briobris. (Who was 'courageous, sociable and fluent' as well as 'prudent, sage, and profound in thought'.) The sculptor was Paolo da Gualdo and originally the tomb was free-standing in the left-hand nave, a canopy over it supported by four columns. It was of a kind with the Anguillara twins' monument, also by Paolo, in the Franciscan church of San Lorenzo in CAPRANICA – though probably less outrageously decorated. It was broken up during a remodelling of 1612 and the sarcophagus now stands alone in the *presbitero*. The first fresco in the right-hand nave is of St Ursula and her eleven thousand virgins: she and they were martyred by drowning, perhaps in the Rhine. (And probably the great size of her maiden retinue is due to a copier's confusion between 'with eleven thousand' and 'with eleven soldiers': *millibus* and *militibus*.) In this picture you can see the little shoe-sized boats struggling out from under her robe, with everybody sinking or scrambling ashore. Most of the rest of the church is covered with frescos of the life of St Francis now attributed to the Assisi painter Francesco Villamena, 1612 and later.

In 1493 the people of VETRALLA rose up against certain deputies of the Papal Governor who had been claiming *droit de seigneur* over young brides, and attacked them during vespers in San Francesco. Bloodshed and death; bombards fired at the people from the castle. When it was all over, the Pope, Alexander VI Borgia, issued a bull in which, 'with clemency and magnanimity', he absolved the aggrieved husband and his friends of murder and sacrilege.

Vicarello

The Roman Vicus Aurelii. Now a foursquare 17th-century monastery building standing high above the LAKE OF BRACCIANO, rather like an Austrian *Stift*; it used to belong to the German College in Rome. The road sweeps up from the lake, punctuated with huge umbrella pines; behind, Monte Rocca Romana; below, an apron of orchard and pasture down to the water. Modern farm buildings make an open, pleasant square. A tiny church on a mound beside for natural religion. Anonymous international money has bought it all.

A kilometre or so north are the Terme di Vicarello, the ancient Aquae Apollinares: a hot spring. A tall 19th-century hotel building still stands against the hillside, out of sight and earshot of the road; closed for years. It would make a splendid hotel again if restored as was.

That stone wall you see wading through the lakeside olive grove is the Acqua Paola (see LAKE OF BRACCIANO), for once above ground; on the other side of the road, those apparent piles of stone are some of its *spie*.

Vico, Lake of

When Rhea the Great Goddess felt that her reign was nearing its end and that the age of the male was due, she knew she must provide for the succession. Her husband Time was in the custom of eating their male children to prevent them succeeding him. After consulting her parents, Earth and Sky, about how to keep her latest son uneaten as the future demanded, Rhea gave Time a stone wrapped in a cloth to eat, and fled with the baby Jove to Crete. There she found two nymphs living peaceably together, Amalthea and Melissa, and with the last breath of woman's authority over the world she bade them bring him up. In secrecy and serenity they fed him on milk and honey and when he began to be no longer a child they took him to see the world he was to inherit. When they came to the CIMINIAN HILLS they found wonderful flowers there: narcissus, periwinkle, anemones, primroses, and asphodel, as well as fine mushrooms. They decided not to go back to Crete.

Hercules joined them. The people came and greeted him and he smiled and felt at his ease. One of the shepherds asked him to show off his strength, which was famous throughout the world, and he said: 'I will stick my club in the ground and one of you will pull it out'. The shepherds tried one by one, and none could do the feat. So then they all pulled together, and still it would not come. Hercules smiled again; he pulled it out, and clear fresh water trickled into the hole, and flowed, and flowed again, and the blue waters rose, and the land around began to shake and heave and all the people ran between fear and joy up into the hills which rose about them until they stood panting on the ridge and saw below them a round, calm, shining lake surrounded by instant woods. (The fate of the young Jove is not recorded in this version, but subsequent events show that Amalthea and Melissa cannot have forgotten him in the scramble. He did kill his father and became King of the Gods.)

The hole that Hercules made is now the LAKE OF VICO, smallest and highest of the three main volcanic lakes in Northern Lazio. (It is 18 kilometres round.) It lies deeper in its crater-bed than the LAKES OF BOLSENA or BRACCIANO. The highest point above it, a small wooded, conical mountain, had the happy name in Latin of Mons Veneris and today is still Monte Venere – Mount of Venus; until the digging of the outlet (see below) it was an almost circular island.*

Only on the west of the Lake is the Ciminian Forest as thick and steep as when it so frightened the Romans. The north shore, called the Valle di Vico, is a shred of paradise: a polychrome wetland of volcanic sand. Some parts are dry, but there are sluggish streams where all is bright green, which at the water's edge wander through a belt of reeds; landward, sheep graze among marram grass, tended by an elderly shepherdess with a great black umbrella. A hawfinch. Clouded yellows. Giant, blue, iridescent bees. Horses ankle-deep in the water turn enquiringly.

Low on the eastern shore ran a branch of the Roman Via Cimina, proving that the level of the Lake had already then been artificially lowered. Above stood the castle of the dread 'Prefects of Vico', from which they terrorised Northern Lazio between the 12th and 15th centuries: its site is a bulging hump above the little old chapel of Santa Lucia with the fountain beside it, the only constructions by the Lake from before 1950. The fountain, ornamented with Farnese insignia cardinalesque and ducal, has a strangely ancient basin, worn by the pulling of inexplicable ropes across its rim.

Here you start the hunt for the outlet, the *emissario*, of the lake. Clockwise along the road from Santa Lucia, you go down a dust

*Venus and all her works have been incorporated into Italian Christianity since the beginning; there is a very pretty place on the west coast of the Basilicata called Santa Venere. There must be a San Priapo somewhere in the south, but we have not yet happened on it.

track 300 metres towards the Lake, then you turn left and walk along a little stream that appears to be going the wrong way, i.e., into the hill. The last few metres it runs between masonry walls, and then disappears into a masonry arch about a metre high. From the sound it must be entering a largish channel. Nothing outside now looks Etruscan: rather of the known 16th-century Farnese restoration. (See RONCIGLIONE.)

The south shore, airless from the closeness of the slope, is built over: already too much so. The richer eastern end is another bit of the *vita olgiata* – the 'life-is-too-precious-to-enjoy' culture (see OLGIATA).

The Lake and its mountains are now a nature reserve, managed by the adjacent communes.

Vigna di Valle

In the 1930s British Imperial Airways operated flying-boat services from Southampton to South Africa, India, and Australia, touching down at St Nazaire, Marseilles, VIGNA DI VALLE, Brindisi, Athens, Alexandria, Cairo, Luxor ... Special Pullman train to Southampton and then daily flights in 'Empire' flying boats carrying twenty-two passengers, with the LAKE OF BRACCIANO for the Rome stopover. In those days, aircraft flew flags which had to be 'struck' by the Flight Clerk before take-off. Antediluvian flying boats still practise take-off and splashdown here.

The Museum of the Italian Air Force is in the old hangar complex and makes a good visit. The first exhibit is a full-size construction of the central part of Leonardo da Vinci's flying machine, which was to fly by beating its four wings, each 'forty arms long', and be powered by one man. From it one gets a good idea of how far Leonardo was from success.

There is also the hot air balloon launched in Paris for Napoleon's coronation in 1804, which touched down on the Lake 22 hours later; a steam helicopter of 1877; one of the Italian 'futurist' hydroplanes of 1907; the engine of the very first Wright Brothers' plane; the first plane bought for the Italian Air Force in 1909, set up by Wilbur Wright himself; a Curtiss Amphibian of 1911; and a series of aircraft, from the first Italian-made warplane – a fighter built by Macchi under licence from a French designer in 1915, down to Second World War, and subsequent NATO planes. And photographs of Nobile's ill-fated expedition by dirigible in the Arctic, accompanied by some misplaced penguins.

Vigna Grande

Quid dicam, iacto qui semine comminus arva/insequitur cumulosque ruit male pinguis harenae/deinde satis fluvium inducit rivosque sequentis/et, cum exustus ager morientibus aestuat herbis,/ecce supercilio clivosi tramitis undam/elicit? illa cadens raucum per levia murmur/saxa ciet scatebrisque arentia temperat arva.

Virgil, *Georgics,* Book I, lines 104–10.

Virgil is praising the farmer

> ... who after sowing works the soil closely/breaking the rich clods up with lean sand,/then draws water enough along parallel channels;/and when the field is burnt up and the stalks are dying,/ behold! from the top of the slope summons a wave/down slippery rocks, to refresh the dry earth/with the growling murmur of bubbles.

This and much else of Georgics husbandry we saw when we spent ten summers here in the 1960s and 70s: pulses or lupins – *tristisque lupini* – grown in 'alternate' seasons, 'firing the shorn stubble with crackling flames' – *levem stipulam crepitantibus urere flammis* – for the nutritious ash. (*Crepitantibus* is nice for the chattering sound of the little flames rattling forward.)

The growling bubbles across dry fields flushed out the mole-crickets – *Gryllotalpa gryllotalpa*: strange thumb-long, earth-coloured creatures, with truly mole-like forelegs, miniature muddy-rubber-gloved, seeming blind, and ferociously busy to return to decent dark underground dryness. By night we saw rain-glistening farm boys clad in the 20th-century loincloth of swimming trunks, lit by blue lightning flashes, as they led the cattle up to shelter from the Lake. On moonlit nights the wild boar brought their striped babies down from the woods to rattle pine-nuts out of cones, snuffling and heaving under our bedroom window in the tower. The palominos, on hot afternoons, trotted into the Lake in line ahead and splashed and pranced and whinnied and trotted out again and rolled in the dust. On the other side of the Lake, ANGUILLARA's pearly little pile approached and receded as the air cleared or hazed.

The place as you see it now includes what is left of the 'ample transformations' carried out by Giacomo del Duca for Paolo Giordano Orsini in the 1580s. From the date one can infer that this, like the contemporary work at the castle of BRACCIANO, was intended for the loving life with Vittoria Corombona which was prevented by the appalling carnage. (See BRACCIANO.) As *ideatore*, Giacomo laid out a little garden by the main building and an 'ample enclosure' to the east, both of which can still be seen. He also worked on a bridge over the stream, its central pylon said to be like those of the Santa Trinità bridge in Florence. Among his employees was a *fontaniere*, and there are still two fountains. Just as he was not paid by the Duke, so did he not pay his workmen. And had to go off to work for the Cardinal at CAPRAROLA.

The main, twin-towered building is mysterious. Substantial remains of a Roman villa and its road and outhouses, of the time of Trajan or Hadrian, lie to the north. A medieval castrum had been destroyed in the 14th century. The fresco in the Vatican Map Room, also of 1580, shows a square building without towers. This could have been a merely emblematic representation of a building which already had its two crenellated towers, or they could have been added later, perhaps by Giacomo: they certainly have a look of ornamental fortification.

The whole was restored by Prince Baldassar III Odescalchi in the 1890s, as a fine heraldic plaque over the door tells. With his Polish mother's money (again see BRACCIANO), he made it a noble stable for the horses of heroes, for Pegasus and Fledge, for Bellerophon and Barset Dobbin III. The soaring stalls and mangers would have served for battle elephants, and when the great doors were open – the courtyard door was made for us – the winds of time blew through.

He made a model farm to show still newly emancipated ex-papal Lazio what a modern farm could be. His descendants today remember him as the Roman Prince who said that if socialism was helping the poor and uneducated to work rationally and become prosperous, then he was a socialist. He imported horses from Arabia, grooms from Ireland, and white donkeys from the Middle East. (White donkeys are almost a symbol of the Papacy.) He planted rare pines and *Magnolia grandiflora* and many varieties of mimosa; he planted peach and pear and apricot where only the fig had been known; he planted mulberry trees and imported silk-worm farmers from Lombardy; cows and grass-seed he got from the Alps; and his *butteri* he kitted out with breeches and feathered hats to be the ideal workforce of late 19th-century ranching and the admiration of the neighbourhood.

In the woods behind, he opened up walks and rides with little bridges and neat arrangements for the Georgics-type irrigation. He opened up a vast *cantina* complex in and on the hillside behind, where underground he installed forty oval barrels, each of 4 metres in diameter, made of oak from Carinthia. And about it all he wrote a booklet (now scarce). In 1902, under the name of 'Castel Bracciano', the white wine from VIGNA GRANDE's vineyards won second prize at the Earls Court exhibition in London. The Roman statues from SAN LIBERATO, and others too, perhaps from Giacomo's improvements, he set up in a great circular grotto round the door of this *cantina,* where most were destroyed and the rest mutilated by a demented US soldier with a machine-gun at the end of the Second World War.

The fine 16th-century *casale* opposite the Castelletto was divided into apartments in the 1970s.

Vignanello

Dennis found VIGNANELLO

> a mean and dirty town with a villainous 'osteria', yet of such importance that a vehicle, miscalled 'diligence', runs thither from Rome twice a week. Its wine has more renoun than merit.

It is still a town to try the temper: thick to the bumpers with traffic, and to the nose with fumes, caught between the high buildings of a grand 16th-century street that seems to carry on for ever. Or at least to VALLERANO: from the CIMINO the two towns show as a single continuous crown above cliffs. *Cantine* line the roads up to both towns. There is a gigantic wine festival in mid-August. The wine is now good.

The Castello Ruspoli is in the grand medieval manner, like SORIANO though not so large. It has four great angled corner towers rising battered out of a deepish moat; and portcullises and drawbridges, one now into the piazza, the other into the vast 'secret' garden which was laid out by Ottavia Orsini, the daughter of Vicino Orsini of BOMARZO. Between the two *portes cochères,* the *androne* is a fine vaulted space, a courtyard until covered over in the 1570s, reputedly by Vignola. The roofed attic floor is set behind the all-round crenellation which now acts as a kind of parapet.

In 1531, Pope Clement VII Medici made Beatrice Farnese its feudatory, whose daughter Ortensia married Count Sforza Marescotti, a 'free-lance' for the Venetians and 'protected' by Pope Paul III; their grandson Marc Antonio married the afore-mentioned Ottavia (and was murdered in 1608), and their descendants, the Ruspoli, still own it. A family tree in a passage holds that the original Marius Escotus (Marescotti) was descended from one of

Charlemagne's generals, who was of the Scottish royal house of Douglas, and Count of Gallivaglia: Galloway, perhaps.

The interior is like a Roman palazzo: sombre great ceilings and ancestral portraits, pleasant frescoed friezes; nothing lighthearted to suggest burdens put aside, no open loggia. The garden is the biggest and grandest of the formal, geometrical, parterres in Northern Lazio. Ottavia's initials and those of her two sons appear in the design, of about 1612. The garden is now clipped box framed in clipped bay, with orange trees in great earthenware tubs and ilexes and cypresses. It spreads forward the whole width of the *castello*. Fountains play no great part. The eastern terrace overlooks the wild leafy falls first of an orchard and then of a great park stretching towards the misty Tiber.

To the south the cliff drops plumb into a yet more secret secret garden: thin, and sun-baked, its box clipped to more wayward patterns. Inserted under one corner of the raised garden is a small church.

Along one side of the piazza runs an elegant balconied building of 1723, where Ruspoli aunts used to live. (Good weathercocks.) The Collegiata was consecrated in 1725. A massive sunburst above the altar with gigantic angels, putti, and clouds frames a hard to see little Madonna and Child by Annibale Carracci.

Clarice Marescotti was one of the eight children of Marc Antonio and Ottavia Orsina. Though avid for wordly success and elegance, after a family row she became a nun. She continued worldly and elegant until, on her sickbed, the chaplain refused her the Sacrament. This fired the spark of her vocation and she instantly changed her life. When she died in 1640 her body had to be hidden because the people believed her to be a saint and tried to take relics. In 1807 the Pope judged they had been right; in a little chapel in the Castello some of the relics of Santa Giacinta, St Hyacinth, are kept, including her scourge and a belt with nails on the inside.

Vitorchiano

The Spinarius – 'that boy, plucking the thorne out of his foote (so much admired by Artists) of brasse, very antique', in Evelyn's description – was a VITORCHIANO shepherd called Martius, who ran through the CIMINIAN Hills, thorn in foot, to warn Rome of the great Etruscan army massing to attack. The statue is a monument.

In 1199 VITORCHIANO, seeking protection against VITERBO, turned to Rome, which was already fighting the Viterbesi over their removal of the bronze Gates of St Peter's in 1167. So the Viterbesi, unable to reach the Romans, attacked VITORCHIANO. So the latter carried off VITERBO's municipal bell, known as the Patarina after the Patarine heretics VITERBO was accused of harbouring. In 1237 a formal arrangement was reached, the *Fidelato*, by which VITORCHIANO, although 100 kilometres away, became an integral part of the Commune of Rome, and provided thirteen macebearers or lictors, called 'the Faithful', to police the Campidoglio. They still have a ceremonial existence, and at the Rome Olympics of 1960 VITORCHIANO men sounded the clarions. The medieval town seal proclaimed in Latin: 'I am the Castle of Vitorchiano and a Limb of Rome', and the castle still greets you with the words *Summa Fidelitas* – 'Total Fidelity'.

The walls and gates, especially the Porta Romana, are in a fine state of preservation and give a vivid sense of medieval reality. Whatever the politics, the street pattern and the way of building are Viterbese, with *profferli* and other useful structures sticking out. The town is prosperous, lived and worked in, and less scraped than VITERBO's San Pellegrino. Walk to the end and look down into the gorge: everywhere great blocks lying about, as at BOMARZO before Vicino Orsini got to work on his *boschetto*.

Outside the walls to the south is the church of the Madonna di San Nicola. You get the key from the adjacent convent of enclosed Clarissae, via a turntable, for the avoidance of eye contact.

The church is entirely covered with frescos by Viterbese painters of several centuries. No single item is 'great art', but the general standard is so high, and there is so much of it, that it seems the whole of life and history was being called to God's attention. Included are the Nativity, the Entry into Jerusalem, and the Passion story. Zuccaresque decorated pilasters. In the apse, angels blowing the trump for the Last Judgement, one holding the scales of justice; hell, heaven, and purgatory. Then the Birth of the Virgin and the Visitation, punctuated by giant herms, and St Barbara holding an up-to-date fortified tower (dated 1548).

A procession from a domed lakeside church, St Augustine at TORRE SANT'AGOSTINO; Duke William of Aquitaine and the Count of Picteviensis, in armour. Note in the Baptism of Christ a Jordan-full of ducks and some donkeys, one kicking his feet in the air, and a very small bridge and tiny boats with masts.

VITORCHIANO has a rich municipal archive, from the 13th century. A study of 14th-century wills shows something went to the Bishop, something to the priests, something to the church or chapels, something to the poor: mostly very small things, individual garments, a piece of lard or dried meat. Also that in 1613 a man was sentenced for life to the galleys for violently kissing a girl of good repute.

Vulci

When Dennis was there in the 1840s, Vulci, or Velx, or Velch was a 'vast treeless moor, without a sign of life' except for the occasional herdsman's *capanna* of rushes. 'The sun gilds but brightens it not'. When D. H. Lawrence was being bounced about in the ruts of the dirt track from Montalto, the hold of malaria was still tight and he saw only '. . . a few forlorn rat-like signs of peasant farming'.

As well as the malaria, there was the texture of the soil: a white, travertine-like cover of volcanic origin, deposited since the Etruscans, had long prevented the traditional ploughs from turning it properly; and the quality of the water, which hangs greyish stalactites on anything it drips or flows along, including irrigation channels, made things worse. The 'travertine' is today piled round the edges of the ruddy fields; the stalactites hang from the dark-stoned Ponte dell'Abbadia.

The Etruscan site starts about a kilometre south of this solitary bridge and castle. The city and its cemeteries covered some 150 square kilometres, in the midst of a wide plain straddling the River Fiora, which provided it with a ring of defensive cliffs. It had five gates, and three bridges connecting with the Etruscan road system; and along the coast it had three ports – Cosa, Orbetello, and Talamone – all now in Tuscany. The Romans conquered it in 280 BC.

Even what little of the city was still there in the 18th century has gone, and only the podium of one large Etruscan temple – 36.50 metres by 24.50 – is visible. Otherwise, remains are ambiguous or Roman, and as Mrs Gray put it, '. . . scarcely a substruction remains amid the barren waste, to tell of the noble fortunes [here] extinguished'.

The scale and density of the necropoles and of the wealth hidden in them indicate it was a huge and rich city, peopled with artisans of extraordinary skill and traders of taste and energy. From VULCI came a flood of 'Greek' – 'Corinthian', 'Ionic', and 'Attic' – ceramics, of 'Egyptian' objects; also of native artefacts: bronzes of all kinds, exported throughout Italy, Central Europe, and Greece; stone, marble, clay, ceramic, gold. Its hinterland, which made it the largest state of southern Etruria, was full of towns today mostly unidentifiable.

Defeated and bereft of its ports and towns, VULCI of course declined. It seems to have had an early bishopric, but that was moved to MONTALTO DI CASTRO in the face of Saracen invasions, and the last settlement had disappeared by the 9th century. An echo of the name – Pian di Voce – remained attached to the site and only Annius of VITERBO had ever come close to colocating place and name. Etruscan VULCI remained blanked out until 1828, when a ploughshare went through the roof of a tomb on the estate of Luciano Bonaparte (see CANINO and MUSIGNANO).

An effort comparable to the mining of Nauru was inaugurated: the rapid excavation of some 30,000 tombs purely to secure objects for sale, combined, George Dennis saw, with 'the ruthless destruction of every article which bore no pecuniary value ...'. However elegant or curious or informative it might be, if it was not marketable, or might bring the price down, it was dismissed as *robba di sciocchezza'* – valueless – by Princess Bonaparte's overseer. '... Everyone who had land in the neighbourhood tilled it for this novel harvest, and all with abundant success ...' As D. H. Lawrence commented, '... that the Etruscans should have left fortunes to the Bonapartes seems an irony: but so it was'.

The Bonaparte excavation business continued for twelve years, furnishing Monaco, St Petersburg, Berlin, Paris, London, and the Vatican with their grand collections.

When the Torlonia family bought out the Bonaparte heirs, they appointed rather more knowledgeable (French) excavators who in 1857 worked on the huge mound, the Cucumella – 18 metres high, 700 metres of tunnel within it. They also discovered the so-called François tomb of the 4th century, with wonderfully vivid wall paintings: strange winged creatures; Achilles' sacrificing of the Trojan prisoners to the shade of Patroclus; two VULCI brothers, Ceclio and Aulovibenna fighting, the former being liberated by Macstarna (see Introduction); a splendid *trompe-l'oeil* key pattern. Dispersion continued: the wall paintings are in Rome.

Tomb-robbing continues unabated. Hydroelectric works caused damage after the first war; drainage and land reform after the second. A small but particularly nice museum has been set up in the Castle of the Abbadia.

This was a monastic advance-castle, built by Cistercians in the 12th or 13th century as a defence against marauders from the sea. In the early 16th century it had become a customs house. Cardinal

Alessandro Farnese built it up again, with its moated, squat-towered *enceinte* and single tall tower, and provided a little palazzo-like extension. Later it was a farm building, and then a pigsty. Restoration has uncovered quantities of ceramic bits, medieval filling the floors, renaissance just accumulated. Today it is all as pretty as you could wish. In the ten or so years since the moat's spring has been re-activated, the water has built itself a little bridge-like spout of travertine to pour down from.

The Abbadia is where it is because of the ancient bridge over the Fiora, the Ponte dell'Abbadia. This is a most gymnastic construction, an exhilarating back-bend of stone into and over the river's vigorous, all-the-year-round, greenery: for much of it, the only greenery in sight. It is tufo and travertine, probably from the 1st century BC and therefore 'Etrusco/Roman'; at one time it included an aqueduct, and there is a *fichu* of stalactite drifting down from it. Indeed the bed of the Fiora below is all petrified lace and froth.

There is a nature reserve, developed where the reservoir of a tiny piece of hydroelectrics, damming some of the Fiora's waters, has created a marsh: two kinds of heron, egrets, godwits, various wild duck, and otters use it.

Viterbo

History

In November 1644, John Evelyn passed through on his way to Rome:

> From Monte Fiascone we travell a plain and pleasant Champion [champain – plain] to Viterbo, which presents it selfe with much state a farr off, in reguard of her many lofty pinacles and Towres; neither dos it deceive the expectation; for it is so exceedingly beautified with publique fountaines, especially that at the very entrance of the Port (being all of brasse, & adornd with many rare figurs) as salutes the Passenger with a most agreable object, & refreshing waters...

Two hundred years later, Mrs Gray found 'Viterbo...seldom visited, and little known to English travellers' despite 'the numerous works of art and science it possesses'.

The observation still applies: VITERBO is least known to the foreign visitor of all the historic cities of Italy. It was the second city of the Papal State after Rome, it was for many years the place where popes took refuge when the Romans drove them out, and for several decades it was the seat of the Papacy itself. It was where kings and emperors jostled to secure the election of the pope of their choice. At other times, it was the place where invading armies massed to threaten Rome, and where papal armies stood to defend it. All this made it, between about 1100 and 1300, one of the great cities of Europe, and today it is among those that retain most extensively their medieval aspect. Add to this that its immediate countryside of lakes, mountains, and great woods is more beautiful than that of any other Italian city, and the world's ignorance of it seems paradoxical.

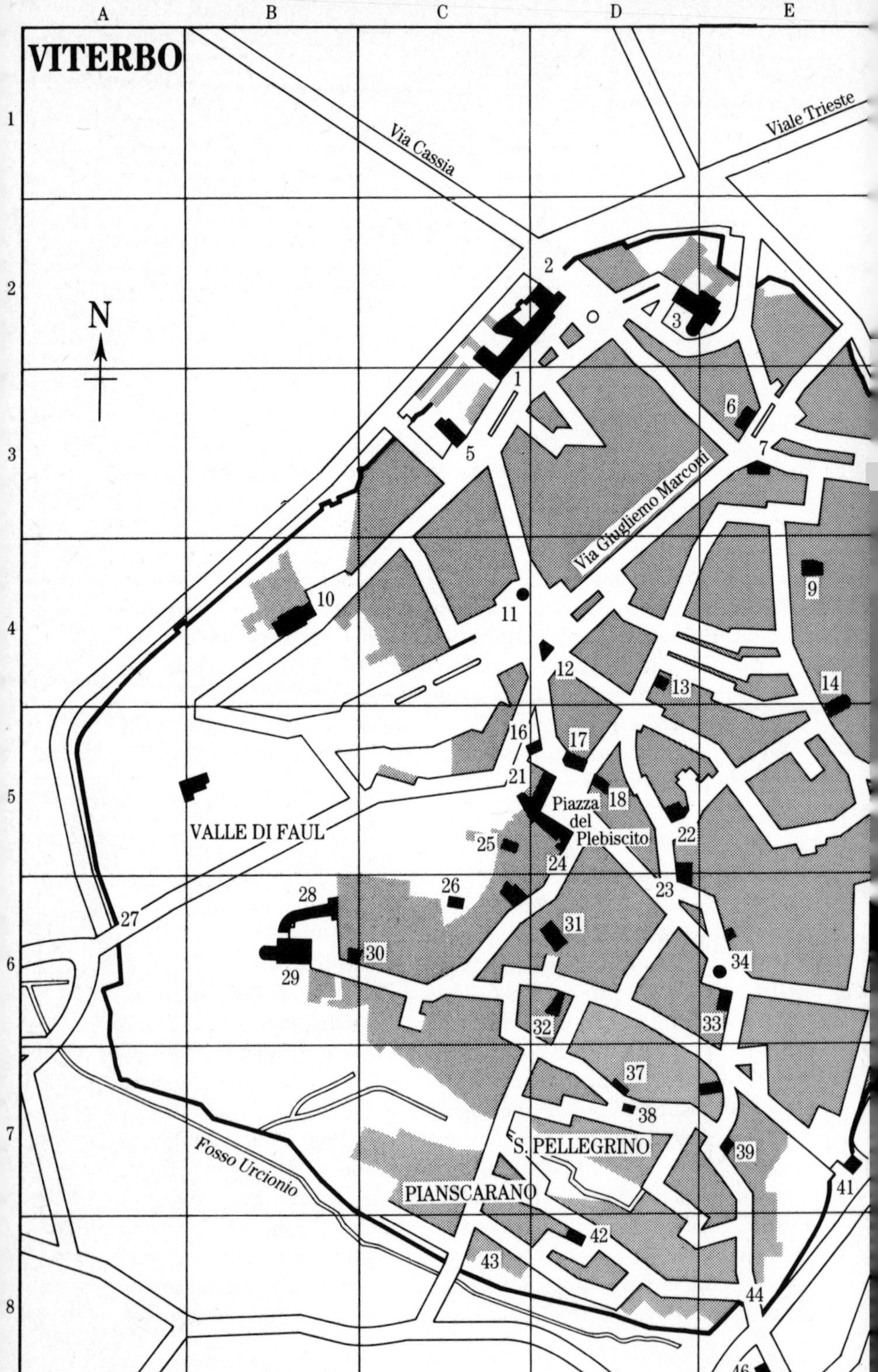

VITERBO
A
B
C
D
E
1
2
3
4
5
6
7
8
N
Via Cassia
Viale Trieste
Via Giugliemo Marconi
Piazza del Plebiscito
VALLE DI FAUL
S. PELLEGRINO
PIANSCARANO
Fosso Urcionio
1
2
3
5
6
7
9
10
11
12
13
14
16
17
18
21
22
23
24
25
26
27
28
29
30
31
32
33
34
37
38
39
41
42
43
44
46

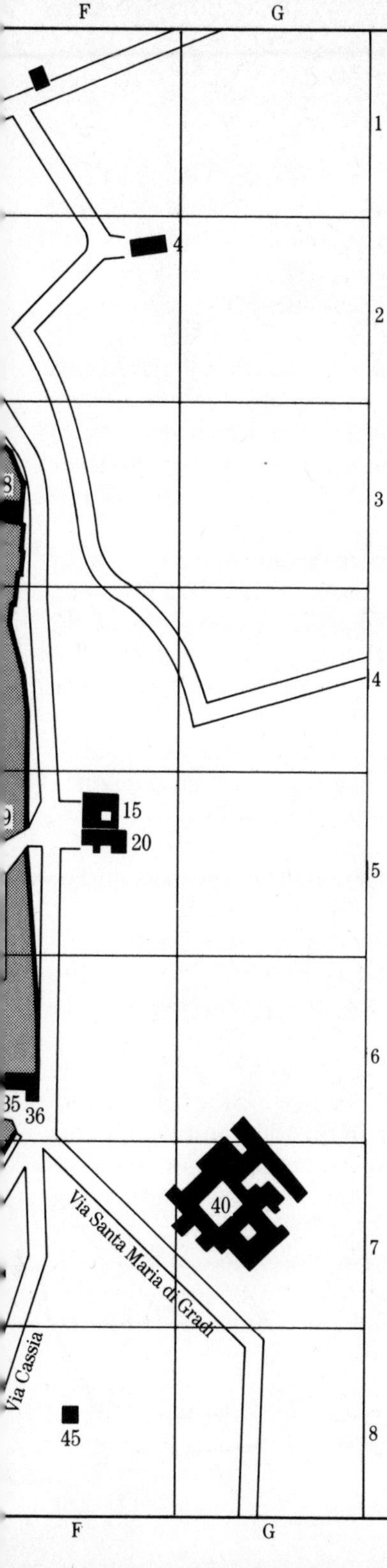

Key

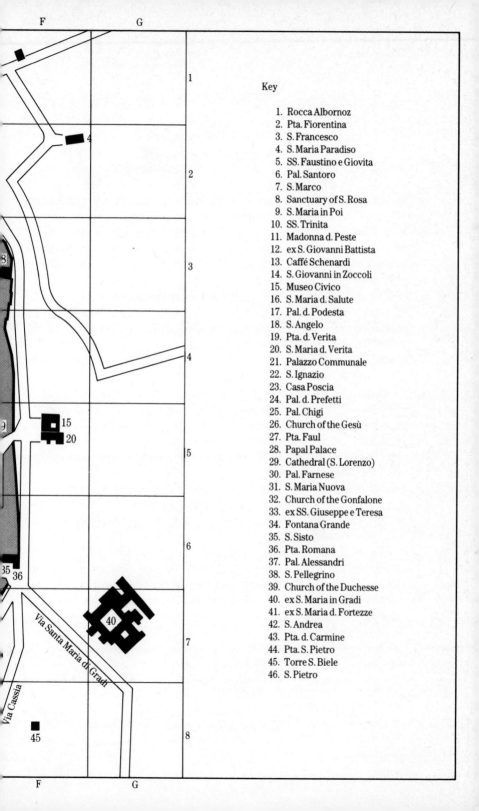

1. Rocca Albornoz
2. Pta. Fiorentina
3. S. Francesco
4. S. Maria Paradiso
5. SS. Faustino e Giovita
6. Pal. Santoro
7. S. Marco
8. Sanctuary of S. Rosa
9. S. Maria in Poi
10. SS. Trinita
11. Madonna d. Peste
12. ex S. Giovanni Battista
13. Caffé Schenardi
14. S. Giovanni in Zoccoli
15. Museo Civico
16. S. Maria d. Salute
17. Pal. d. Podesta
18. S. Angelo
19. Pta. d. Verita
20. S. Maria d. Verita
21. Palazzo Communale
22. S. Ignazio
23. Casa Poscia
24. Pal. d. Prefetti
25. Pal. Chigi
26. Church of the Gesù
27. Pta. Faul
28. Papal Palace
29. Cathedral (S. Lorenzo)
30. Pal. Farnese
31. S. Maria Nuova
32. Church of the Gonfalone
33. ex SS. Giuseppe e Teresa
34. Fontana Grande
35. S. Sisto
36. Pta. Romana
37. Pal. Alessandri
38. S. Pellegrino
39. Church of the Duchesse
40. ex S. Maria in Gradi
41. ex S. Maria d. Fortezze
42. S. Andrea
43. Pta. d. Carmine
44. Pta. S. Pietro
45. Torre S. Biele
46. S. Pietro

The Tales

The name VITERBO is traditionally held to come from the Latin Vetus Urbs – Old City: like Orvieto – Urbs Vetus. Unfortunately no nearby city is available for it to be older than. A sober explanation derives it from Vicus Elbii, the staging post of Elbius, a Roman 'road station', some way off. A more adventurous one, popular in the 15th century, develops it from Vetus Verbum, Old Word, and links the name with the Greek equivalent, Palaeologos, and thus the Byzantine Emperor Michael Palaeologus, who won the throne of the Eastern Empire with Genoese help in 1261. Might not a man from Vetus Verbum have started the dynasty by marrying the daughter of some earlier emperor, thus injecting his name into the imperial register? The tale cannot be squared with history.

The foundation of the city, as narrated in this and other versions by the 15th-century writer Annius of Viterbo, otherwise Friar Giovanni Nanni, is most persuasively illustrated in the great room of the Palazzo Communale. His seven books about Viterbo, which he called *Umbellicus Universi* – the navel of the universe – have long been dismissed as fiction, both text and documentation.

When he wrote, VITERBO's independence was being swallowed by the irresistible machinery of the Papal State: perhaps, he thought, a new emphasis on Hercules might save it.* According to Annius, Hercules had been especially active in the Viterbese. He stuck his club into the ground in several places and pulled it out again, thus creating public utilities of one sort or another: the Bullicame (see below) was one; the LAKE OF VICO another. At VITERBO itself, a most carefully chosen site, he built a castle and gave it his lion for emblem, which is why the fountains and coats of arms of Viterbo sport so many lions.

These and many other fine ideas were so well accepted that when the Sala Regia of the Palazzo Communale was decorated with celebratory frescos by Baldassare Croce in the 16th century, not only does Hercules appear, but the Viterbo civic notables hobnob with Michael Paleologus. Yet another pleasant idea was that VITERBO was the first city founded after the Flood by Noah who, though of course Jewish, looked at the world before the Flood and after, and so easily merged with the originally Etruscan two-faced god Janus, another 'looker-both-ways'. Or it might have been Osiris. The Countess

* A foundling left on the steps of the Palazzo dei Priori in 1472 was even christened Giovanni Ercole Novello, and the woman who took him in was given a substantial sum to bring him up.

Matilda's Donation of Upper Lazio to the Church stands almost alone as a piece of more or less genuine history.

The Annius stories are also illustrated by Pinturicchio in the Borgia Apartments in the Vatican assisted by the Viterbese artist, Pastura. Indeed, to them the world indirectly owes the Raphael *Stanze*: Julius II so loathed his predecessor that he moved out of the Borgia Apartments and had Raphael fresco the *Stanze* on another floor.

As for the mysterious word, or name, or acronym, Faul, which is the name of the westernmost town gate and the valley that leads to it: in the courtyard of the Palazzo Communale an inscription in Latin asserts that 'the former towns of Fanum, Arbanum, Vetulonia, and Longula give this city their first letters: F. A. U. L.', all of which made VITERBO into the 'tetrapolis' – the fourfold town. Higher on the wall, the municipal arms are supported by two Herculean lions and another explanation: *Fanum Auguste Volturne Lucumonum* – 'the August Volturnia of the Lucumons' (see BOLSENA). An origin which seems to us plausible is that Faul is simply the German word: Porta Faul, Dirty Gate. The gate where the little Urcionio flows out is dirty today, and it must have been dirty in the 13th century, when the city was often enough under German rule. (See ÇASTEL D'ASSO.)

The Facts

There are Etruscan tombs in the cliffs, here as everywhere, and some unmistakable Etruscan masonry under the bridge leading to the Cathedral Piazza; it may have been the Etruscan town of Surrena. The Romans sent no great road through it, and VITERBO only begins to have a real history from AD 773 when the Lombard King of Italy Desiderius (the French Didier) fortified it as a base from which to take Rome. Before he could do that, news came that his father-in-law Charlemagne had crossed the Alps: for Desiderius, this meant vassallage or war, and he chose war. He hurried north and was defeated with little bloodshed at Pavia, thus opening Charlemagne's road to coronation as Emperor in Rome in 800. Charlemagne had 'donated' VITERBO to Pope Adrian I in 778, just as Liutprandt had 'donated' SUTRI to Pope Gregory II in 728.

For the next few hundred years VITERBO had three roles in the world. First, it was a pawn between the two great forces, 'Guelf' and 'Ghibelline', which surged round and over its humble head with incompatible claims: the ideal and unrealised force of spiritual sovereignty embodied in the popes of Rome, and the actual force of emerging feudalism and aristocracy, embodied in the emperors, who wished to be recognised as both 'Holy' and 'Roman'.

The second role was that of an Italian provincial city like others; but blest or cursed with a ready-made balance of power to exploit, which allowed it from time to time to consolidate a healthy power of its own, achieving strong fortifications and subjecting the towns and castles of the Etrurian Plain and the CIMINIAN hills to its rule.

The third was a role internal to the Papacy: it was a bolt-hole. In Rome itself the bishops continued to face the tiny and usually sordid suburban feudal barons who were as well aware as any pope of the power of historic names, and sat on the Capitol Hill as Senators of Rome. When they were able to get enough of the plebs on their side, or to appoint powerful enough foreigners 'senators for life', they drove the popes out, and it was VITERBO the popes came to. They found faction here too, and no less bloody than in Rome.

In 1065, playing off various forces, the Viterbesi achieved a victory of proportions which to them seemed sufficient against all future dangers: they captured a small portable altar* from the inhabitants of the ISOLA MARTANA which they believed made them invincible. Certainly by 1095 they owed allegiance neither to Pope nor Emperor, and VITERBO's time as a free commune coincides with the building of its walls and some of its most impressive churches.

The destruction of FERENTO in 1172 opened the way to a major expansion: at the turn of the 13th century, VITERBO's power extended to the LAKES OF BOLSENA and VICO and to the Tiber; it could raise an army of 18,000 men; it had fifty castles under its control; and it was effectively stronger than faction-torn Rome.

In 1145-6 Pope Eugenius III came to VITERBO when the Romans made Rome too hot for him; and resisted a siege. The 'English' Pope Adrian IV, Nicholas Breakspear (though born English he was brought up in Provence), took refuge here from the invading German Emperor Frederick I Hohenstaufen, 'Barbarossa'; who shortly prevailed and installed an anti-pope, Pascal III. The great Innocent III (1198–1216) held a Council here to discuss heresy: VITERBO itself was even excommunicated for giving refuge to Patarine heretics, the name given in Italy to the Manichees who were

*This altar was the second of the Six Nobilities of Viterbo, according to the chronicler Nicola della Tuscia: the first was that it was a free city, answerable to no earthly power; the third was the Beautiful Galiana (see below); the fourth was a woman called Anno whose hair was half red and half green; the fifth was a horse which was so fine and spirited it was the most famous in all Italy; and the sixth was a scholar called Grisigello who made marvellous jokes in new ways – of which alas we know nothing.

being exterminated in the Languedoc by Innocent III's Albigensian Crusade. In 1228, Gregory IX again took refuge from the Romans.

The 13th Century

The 13th century was VITERBO's great age, and the principal medieval palaces – of the Popes, of the Captains of the People, of the citizen Magistracy, of the great feuding families – all date (or dated) from its middle years. There was a long and uninteresting feud between two rich families of long-distant foreign origin, the Gatti, Guelfs, from Brittany (who started building the Papal Palace in 1255, to get the Popes to stay), and the Tignosi, Ghibellines, from Mainz. Round these the other nobility and the citizenry grouped themselves, some with strongholds in the country and many with fortified town houses. The matter was essentially who should hold office: much like what passed in Siena and Florence at the same time. All parties knew what the Papacy was worth to the town, but the feud was nevertheless carried on, by vendetta and affray, and with such repugnant and bloody folly that the popes were frightened away for good. What remained was a papal power – or a vacuum created by its absence – which Rectors or Governors of the Patrimony of St Peter enforced or not. Of the tall towers of the time, most were cut off or pulled down with successive restorations of order by Papal or Imperial forces.

The Emperor Frederick II Hohenstaufen, known as the Wonder of the World, Stupor Mundi, had put a temporary end to the brawls in 1240: he brought VITERBO into his alliance, gave it the title of Aula Imperialis, placed a German garrison in the castle, and started in 1242 to build a palace near the Porta della Verità for himself and his harem. (He lived as much like a Muslim Sultan as like a Christian Emperor, spoke Greek and Arabic, and spent much of his reign in Sicily.)

One day when his back was turned the townspeople drove his Germans out. He raised troops in Tuscany and laid siege to the town in 1243. The Bishop of Viterbo, Cardinal Raniero Capocci, fortified by the support of little St Rose (see below), decided to defend the city, and proclaimed a crusade against him, no less. The Emperor brought up what seemed a whole township of wooden siege towers and commenced the assault.

The story goes that Capocci had tunnels dug through the tufo, along which the Viterbese crawled and then set fire to the wooden structures of the Imperial camp, and thus this city of 60,000 defeated and drove away the Holy Roman Emperor, King of Jerusalem, heir of Julius and Augustus, and master of Germany and half Italy. His still incomplete palace they pulled down in 1250. The Viterbesi still think about it.

In 1257, Pope Alexander IV was chased out of Rome by pro-Imperial nobles and took refuge in VITERBO. The next Pope, Urban IV (1261–4), who was French, was elected in VITERBO, and the next, Clement IV (1265–8), also French, spent much of his reign here: neither ever went to Rome, where the malaria killed pontiffs from the north quite quickly. While their very grand new palace was being built, the Popes occupied the already very grand Dominican convent of Santa Maria in Gradi just outside the walls, and some were buried there.

Clement IV it was who in 1267, from the steps of the new Papal Palace, pronounced the Bull of Excommunication against Conradin – Corradino, the 15-year-old grandson of Frederick II, who had been manoeuvred down into Italy by the German imperialists in an attempt to keep alive the rickety empire asserted there by his grandfather and his grandfather's grandfather. But when Pope Clement stood up on the steps that we still see, and cried with a voice of thunder: 'Let them be excommunicated', and dashed his torch to the ground, and all the clerics echoed him and dashed their lesser torches, and the people melted away in terror, it was not only the Papacy which rejoiced at the extinction of the German boy. Clement was French, and the French King of Naples – Charles of Anjou, the King of France's brother – defeated Conradin's army the following year, and had him beheaded in Naples. A new entity had emerged and was making itself felt: from now on the rivalry under which VITERBO, and Italy, would suffer was that of French Kings and German Emperors.

French Clement died in 1268, and the Conclave of the Cardinals met in VITERBO to elect his successor. Things went slowly. The civic authorities recalled that in Perugia in 1216, and in Rome in 1241, the city governments had locked up the Cardinals, to speed their deliberations. The Captain of the People of VITERBO, Raniero Gatti, proposed that this should be done now, and was immediately excommunicated. St Bonaventure – sunny, tactful, travelled – proposed it again, and it was done. Their food was rationed. The Cardinal Bishop of Porto suggested taking off the roof, since it must be preventing the Holy Spirit from reaching them. This joke seemed good sense to the people of VITERBO, so they did it, and until early in the last century you could see the holes in the floor where the Cardinals then set their tentpoles. This deplorable business, lasting nearly three years, led to the first codification of procedure for electing popes.

For the murder, during this interminable conclave, of the Earl of Cornwall, cousin of the future Edward I of England, see below, under the church of the Gesù.

Several conclaves later, in 1280, there were two Orsini Cardinals in the conclave, two Orsini candidates for Pope, and an Orsini Mayor in VITERBO, Orsino Orsini, all strongly disliked. The Viterbese ousted the Mayor, to the fury of the Orsini Cardinals, who refused to let the conclave continue. Another Orsini, the Duke of the Romagna, rushed to join Orso Orsini in his fortified castle at VIGNANELLO. An instant parliament called in the Cathedral of VITERBO became so inflamed that certain citizens rushed the conclave and extracted three Orsini – two Cardinals, brothers of the Orsini Pope who had just died (Nicholas III), and his nephew – and locked them up.

Another Frenchman, Simon de Brie, was then elected as Martin IV, and to show he had not connived in the abominable brouhaha he instantly left VITERBO, which he excommunicated, and was crowned in Orvieto. He never returned (though he died from eating a surfeit of BOLSENA eels), despite the city's pleas for forgiveness. With burdensome conditions, fortunately not insisted on, this was finally granted in 1285, by the next, Roman, Pope, Honorius IV.

In spite of the excitements this was a time of prosperity for VITERBO; the mere presence of the Papacy guaranteed that. Rents rose; civilised customs spread; grand buildings sprang up. There was even in effect the beginning of a university: the VITERBO Popes, being all old, had brought physicians with them, and a medical school was established. John XXI, Pope for a year, was the only Portuguese Pope and also the only medically qualified Pope, an eye specialist; he died when the floor of his room fell in and was buried in VITERBO.

The Renaissance

With the final departure of the Papacy, VITERBO lost its place in the world. Its economy stagnated. Then the Black Death killed two-thirds of the people, and a great earthquake, in 1349, killed more. The Papacy was now having to take potluck among the monarchs, and made a poor showing. France now prevailed over the other feudal structures and the seat of the Papacy was moved to Avignon.

Hitherto, VITERBO's contending families had been the Gatti and the Tignosi. In the absence of the Papacy, Giovanni di Vico, of the family of the 'Prefects of Vico' – purported hereditary 'prefects' of

Rome – managed to establish himself in VITERBO and to extend his brutish rule as far as CIVITAVECCHIA, TARQUINIA, TUSCANIA, BOLSENA, Orvieto, and beyond. Because of the continuing dual system of government – part papal (now absent), part municipal (and therefore factional) – VITERBO continued at the mercy of one Vico tyrant after another. (Until the defeat and execution of the last, Giacomo, in 1431, by Cardinal Vitelleschi (see TARQUINIA): this was the end both of the family and of VITERBO's independence from Rome.)

Cardinal Albornoz (of whom it was said that he had led as many armies against the Moorish rulers of Southern Spain as he had Christian congregations in prayer) was in 1353 sent by Pope Clement VI as Cardinal-Legate into Italy, charged to re-establish the Pope's authority. Combining political and military skill he regained control of the papal possessions. Arriving in VITERBO in 1354, he established there the permanent seat of the Pontifical Rector, or Governor, of the Patrimony of St Peter in Tuscia and also of the Patrimony's Treasurer, the tax-collector. He built the Rocca that still bears his name, to be the Rector's combined residence and fortress, for safety set on a hill, away from the town centre by the northern gate, and with space before it for the deployment of troops. (The huge church of San Francesco was conveniently at hand for grand ceremonies). Albornoz died at the Rocca in 1367; ten years later, largely by his efforts, a pope was back in Rome.

When Siena flourished in the 14th century, and Florence in the 15th, each owed much of its success to its *signoria*, its ruling families, enough of whom had enough sense of self-preservation not to allow their rivalries to destroy their city. In VITERBO in the 1450s, with the Renaissance bursting out, the Tignosi faction weakened, and the Vico family spent, it appeared that the last Gatti might emerge as a proper renaissance prince. Princivalle Gatti had much going for him: youth, looks, wits, wealth; the friendship of the Pope whose army he commanded and the Emperor who had been his guest; the approval of the people (he got rid of the salt tax); an interest in architecture; a charming wife called Filaldera, and a baby son Giovanni. Alas, on his return from Rome in April 1454 he was murdered by residual Tignosi assassins on the CIMINO. Chaos followed: Filaldera and the baby were besieged by ambitious cousins, greedy for the loot; a new pope, Callixtus III Borgia, and a new Catalan papal governor intervened, and there was a massacre. Filaldera and the baby were imprisoned, and VITERBO itself was widely punished. Pope Pius II raised the penalties, but Giovanni was later done to death by henchmen of the next Borgia pope and the Gatti palazzo dismantled.

In the summer of 1462, Pope Pius II visited VITERBO. With the return of the Papacy to Rome, and of its effectiveness within the Patrimony, substantial building works were in hand, including a new palace for the Governor and a piazza in front of it, and the reconstruction of the Rocca. Complete papal control was well on the way.

Holy celebration also had a place: let us listen to Pius' good-tempered voice.

> All [the Pope's company] were pleased with the country, the kindness of the people, and the pleasantness of the city, in which there is hardly a house without its spring of unfailing water and a garden. There was moreover abundance of fine food, wines of various kinds not inferior to those of Florence or Siena, white bread with a delicious taste, and veal and beef pastured on thyme and other fragrant herbs. Fish came in plenty from the Tuscan sea on one side and the nearby Lake of Bolsena on the other... [All of which is still true.] The Pope lodged in the Citadel [the Rocca] and had hot water brought to him to be used according to his doctor's orders. Almost every day at dawn he would go out into the country to enjoy the sweet air before it grew hot and to gaze on the green crops and the flax in bloom, then most lovely to behold in its sky blue colour.... The Pope inspected all the meadows and crops, riding on different roads every day...

On 17 June came the Feast of Corpus Christi. The Pope wrote a six-page account.

> The Pope attended by the cardinals and all the clergy before a great throng of the people began the celebration of vespers in the tabernacle he had erected. [This was in the Piazza, in front of the church of Sant'Angelo, and a fountain spouting wine was set up beside it.] The sun was still high and its rays, penetrating the woollen walls which imitated the different colours of the rainbow, gave the tabernacle the appearance of a celestial hall and the dwelling of the King of Kings.

He describes the contributions of the various cardinals, ambassadors and officials.

> . . . the Cardinal of Arras canopied the road from the stone bridge that connects the two parts of the city. . . . with stuff that he had recently had sent him from Florence to make new clothes for his household. It was of English wool, between red and russet. . . . The night before the feast there had been a great storm which had buffeted the ropes to and fro and torn a good part of the fabric, thus depriving some of his servants of their expected clothes . . .

The Cardinal of Porto provided

> a huge dragon . . . as the Pope passed, an armed soldier, playing the part of St Michael, cut off the dragon's head and all the demons fell headlong, baying like hounds.

Further on, the Pope

> was met by two boys singing as sweetly as angels . . . [who] went back behind the curtain and chanted in sweet high voices: 'Lift up your gates, O ye Princes, and King Pius, Lord of the world, shall come in.' Inside, five Kings in magnificent attire with an armed escort pretended to prevent his entrance, but when they heard the angel they replied: 'Who is this King Pius?' and the angels, because of the Sacrament which Pius was carrying in the procession, said: 'The Lord of the world'. At these words the curtain was drawn to reveal the entrance and at the same time trumpets and organs sounded.
>
> There was a model of the tomb of our Lord, where our Life, for our sake, fell asleep in God. About it armed soldiers lay sunk in sleep as if dead . . . When the Pope came to this place, lo! there was suddenly let down along a rope as if flying from heaven a beautiful boy with wings like an angel, the face of a seraph, and a heavenly voice, who saluted the Pope and sang a hymn announcing the immediate resurrection of the Saviour. There was a sudden silence. No one spoke; all listened with delight as if an actual event were taking place and it were a real messenger from heaven. When he had finished fire was applied to powders which had been mixed in a bronze urn and the flash of an explosion awoke the sleeping soldiers and dazed them with terror. Thereupon he who played the Saviour was suddenly revealed to all, a man with sandy hair, of the stature and age of Jesus, holding the banner of the cross and wearing a diadem. He pointed to the conspicuous

scars of his wounds and proclaimed in Italian verses that salvation was won for Christendom. . .

After that the Assumption of the Virgin, when 'the tomb opened and a most lovely girl came forth, borne up on the hands of angels.' And finally 'all the ranks of heavenly spirits burst into song and played on their instruments. They rejoiced and made merry and all heaven laughed.'

Then the Pope and all his Cardinals went to the great hall of the Papal Palace and had a very good dinner.

The people of VITERBO had hoped that that 'Resurrection' might be prophetic of the revival of their city. In fact, a pestilence struck before the celebrations were over.

The Renaissance did not quite pass VITERBO by, even though it had little chance to flourish. Benozzo Gozzoli had been called in to fresco the Clarissae's church with the life story of St Rose, in the 1450s; the Mazzatosta family (one of whom was Treasurer to Pope Eugenius IV, and his substantial creditor) had in 1471 commissioned the young local genius, Lorenzo (who died shortly after), to decorate a chapel in the church of Santa Maria della Verità; another fine local painter, Antonio Massari, known as Pastura, had been co-opted by Pinturicchio to assist first at the Cathedral of Orvieto, and then in the Borgia Apartments in the Vatican, and on his return his work was in demand throughout the Tuscia. (His best is now to be seen in the Cathedral at TARQUINIA). In 1502, the local academy, the Accademia degli Ardenti – 'of the Ardent Ones' – was founded. The Piazza del Commune was full of 'improvements' and several buildings in the new style went up – including the two churches by the Ponte Tremolo. Also the 1514 cloister at the Santissima Trinità and Sebastiano del Piombo's great *Pietà*, commissioned for the church of San Francesco.

After the Sack of Rome in 1527 it was to VITERBO and then to Orvieto that Pope Clement VII Medici escaped. Cardinal Wolsey, his ever-ambitious eye on the Papacy, kept 'ambassadors' around the Pope (urging on him the cause of Henry VIII's divorce, and the Pope's own resignation), who reported on his miserable conditions. Famine in Orvieto drove Clement back to VITERBO and in October 1528, he returned to Rome. He remained Pope until his death in 1533, when Alessandro Farnese, by descent and birth and career a son of the Tuscia, was elected, and became Paul III.

He had long been Administrator of the Patrimony of St Peter and he appointed his grandson, another Alessandro Farnese, Cardinal-

Legate for life (see CAPRAROLA). Between them, they were responsible for urban, and other, improvements; monies from the Camera Apostolica were diverted to the Commune; a University with schools of law, medicine, letters, and philosophy was allowed. (It didn't last: the older universities of Siena, Perugia, and Rome were too close.) In 1539, he appointed the Englishman, Cardinal Pole, Administrator of the Patrimony, who is said to have been much liked for his kindness and fairness.

Reginald Pole

Reginald Pole was born in 1500, a relative of Henry VIII. At 21 he went to the University of Padua and corresponded with Erasmus and Pope Clement VII. When Henry VIII's divorce – Henry wished Pole to develop the theological defence – forced him to choose between conscience and King, he chose the former. He took orders, was made a Cardinal by Paul III in 1536, and appointed Papal Legate to England with the job of rallying Catholic opinion to influence the King. But by then, Henry had taken to judicial murder and Pole's mother and brother were executed. Appointed to VITERBO, Pole continued to work at healing the breach in the Church. He was one of the three Papal Legates who opened the Council in 1542.

Henry VIII died in 1547, and Paul III in 1549. Pole could well have been elected, but did not leap at it, and Julius III del Monte succeeded. After Edward VI's death in November 1554 and Mary Tudor's accession and marriage to Philip of Spain, Pole, Papal Legate again, sailed up the Thames, silver cross at the prow, to conduct High Mass in St Paul's Cathedral and to absolve the Lords and Commons 'from their long schism and disobedience'. He went on to become Archbishop of Canterbury and Chancellor of the Universities of both Oxford and Cambridge.

In 1555 Cardinal Carafa (see GALLESE), violently anti-Spanish, became Pope as Paul IV. Warring with Spain (and therefore with Mary's England), he cancelled Pole's Legation, accused him of heresy, and imprisoned his friends in Italy. All hope of healing the divisions in the Church had now evaporated: only Counter-Reformation remained.

Pole's writings show how close his own theological views had been to those of the Reformers, and what at one time it had been reasonable to hope. It was summed up by his VITERBO friend Vittoria Colonna, who wrote: *La barca di Pietro e carica di fango e bisogna rasanarla dal lezzo antico* – 'St Peter's boat is loaded with mud and we must clean it of its ancient stink': Paul III himself had invited Erasmus to 'help him bring St Peter's boat back into port' and invited him to take part in the Council of Trent.

Vittoria Colonna was admired by her fellow sonneteer Michelangelo and painted by Sebastiano del Piombo. Widowed young, she was persuaded against taking the veil but spent time in various convents, including that of the Suore di Santa Caterina in VITERBO. She shared many of Pole's hopes and she corresponded with the Catholic reformist theologian Valdes about a return to a more Christ-like religion, and a Church without nepotism, corruption, or claims to absolute dominion. When she died, leaving money to the Suore di Santa Caterina, Paul IV interpreted it as proof of their complicity in her near-heretical views, and closed their Convent down.

Modern History

When Montaigne passed through VITERBO in 1580, he noted that there were no noble families there. The city lived through the 17th and 18th centuries without much distinction. In the 19th it acquired the usual municipal facilities: a smart café (the Caffé Schenardi – see below), a theatre, a public garden . . .

The Papal State was the last of the Italian princedoms to become part of the unified monarchy. There was, it is clear, a degree of resentment and even contempt in the way it was treated after 1870 – comparable to the treatment of papal Rome (see Appendix II). Ecclesiastical property could then be secularised, and in VITERBO much was: the fates of the Dominican Convent of Santa Maria in Gradi and of the Discalced Carmelite Convent and its neighbouring church of San Giuseppe are told below. The Convent of S. Maria del Paradiso was a barracks, returned to religious use after the Second World War. Parts of the convent building of S. Francesco became the offices of the Military District, but were later returned to the church. The church of S. Maria della Verità became the Civic Museum. The Convent of Santa Caterina became a school. The Convent of S. Maria della Pace was demolished in Fascist times; that of S. Domenico was replaced by the seat of the Fascist youth organisation; that of S. Agostino bombed by the Allies and not restored.

VITERBO suffered greatly in the summer of 1944 from Allied air bombardment. In 1943 Dr Solly Zuckerman, who later served government after government in London as chief scientific adviser (and still today, as Lord Zuckerman, keeps up a salutary barrage against the higher idiocies), was asked to study the effect of air bombing on the railways during the recent campaign in North Africa. He did so, and recommended that aerial bombing should be concentrated on railway marshalling yards which also had repair shops, and which held a lot of rolling stock. By then the US was the senior power in the war, and this advice was soon translated into all railway yards, and the 'interdiction' of power stations, bridges, and just about everything else as well. Operation Strangle, as it was called, covered the whole breadth of Italy and ran from mid-March to mid-May: 21,000 sorties were flown and 22,500 tons of bombs dropped. VITERBO was in a sector assigned to the US 42nd and 57th Medium Bombardment Wings.

The aim was to cause the Germans to withdraw from Rome by cutting their communications. Rome was taken on 4 June, and the bombing was resumed the next day; from then until 20 June the average daily bomb tonnage was 179 tons, and it was in these raids that VITERBO suffered its greatest damage.

In the 13th century VITERBO had 60,000 inhabitants. After the fall to 20,000 in the 19th, it is now 60,000 again.

The City

VITERBO's first nucleus was where the Cathedral and the Papal Palace stand on their high rock – sometimes called the Arx Herculea. A tiny campanile remains visible of an 8th-century church of S. Maria della Cella; the first known castle was of the 10th century.

The city's own governmental centre then moved first to the area around the church of Santa Maria Nuova and what is today the Piazza del Gesù; and then in the 13th century to the present Piazza del Plebiscito. In the 14th century, the Rocca Albornoz was put up at the far northern end for the Papal Governor, distant from, but balancing, the Cathedral and the Bishop's quarters (also fortified) which remained at the south-west.

The course of events in the 15th and 16th centuries, when papal authority was finally established, is illustrated in the history of the public buildings in the Piazza del Plebiscito. During their ascendancy in the 16th century, the Farnese provided the medieval city and its environs with a few straight streets and roads.

Building Forms

All is built almost uniformly of dark grey tufo and equally dark grey peperino. Forms are lower than in Florence or Rome: Viterbo is home to the squat and powerful, like other places vulnerable to earthquakes (though not to the extent of Latin America's 'earthquake baroque' cities). It is also a farming centre, and the people are fairly squat too.

The Walls

Except for a short stretch at the north, the walls are still complete. In the 11th century, they enclosed just the space between the two little rivers Urcionio and Mola (or Paradosso). Then between about 1190 and 1270 they were extended to take in adjacent settlements – the suburban quarters of S. Pellegrino, S. Pietro del Olmo, and Pianoscarano, which had grown up in the fields and orchards outside. Santa Maria in Gradi was to have been included and the curious Tower of San Biele was part of that never-completed scheme.

Today they are some 5 kilometres round, and by our count have at least thirty-one towers and twelve high gates of more or less medieval or renaissance aspect. Of the aggressive domestic towers, only a handful remain: in the 13th century there were two hundred, and pictures show the town looking like a bucketful of them.

The Streams

The city took its eventual shape from the swift little Urcionio which rises in the Monte Palanzana above – Palanzana's springs also feed the city's smaller streams. Formerly it was known as Urcione or Arcione, perhaps from the arches and bridges which spanned the first part of its course. The lower part ran through open horticulture till it ducked under the wall at Porta Faul. By the mid-19th century the first half had been built right over with the new Via Cavour, but the Valle di Faul remained unbuilt on, countryside within city walls. Photographs show it all orchards, gardens, and vines, the odd tiny meadow, a mill or two, and one single big bridge, the Ponte Tremoli, so called because it trembled under the carts. The old Campo Santo, the cemetery, was down there too. Eventually, together with the city's effluents, and the waters from all the mineral baths, and several other little rivers, the Urcionio joins the Marta, the overflow river from the LAKE OF BOLSENA, and reaches the sea just north of TARQUINIA.

The Destructions

The story of the disappearance of that unique valley under carparks, coachparks, and office blocks is one of the stupidest of twentieth-century vandalisms. The Fascist government started it with its bombastic 'urban improvements', and did the most and worst. Even though some of the damage done by the Allied bombing of 1944 has been restored, post-war commercial and financial blindness has carried on the spoiling work with oblivious glee.

The Built City

Within the walls, you are seldom out of sight of a medieval building which would be in black type in the guides to most European cities. In several quarters – Piazza San Lorenzo, San Pellegrino, Piano Scarano – they are solid as far as the eye can reach. Fine post-medieval buildings there are in plenty, but dotted along streets that mostly keep their medieval aspect.

It makes sense to drive in VITERBO only if you live there – and if so your car will be very small. Visitors should leave their cars outside; or, alas, in the great pancake of the central carpark.

Churches

There are still a great many churches and we do not attempt to account for them all.

Our descriptions follow in alphabetical order: those absolutely not to miss are San Sisto (first and foremost), Santa Maria della Verità (for Lorenzo's frescos), the Cathedral (both for itself and for Guidotti's chapel), Santa Maria Nuova, and the church of the Gonfalone (for the 18th-century paintings).

The Cathedral of San Lorenzo

This is the largest of VITERBO's collection of Lombardo-Romanesque churches, and its splendid 14th-century tower, black and white striped peperino and travertine, flags the city's earliest centre. The large, rather boring, façade, with Cardinal Gambara's name all over it (see BAGNAIA), is of course 16th-century, but the building itself is a 12th-century basilica. Post-war restoration has left the stationary grace of its nave arcades clean, lean, and unencumbered.

The columns stand twelve a side and their capitals are ingenious, forceful, and dramatic. The Cosmatesque nave floor is one of the finest and the grey and white of the side-aisle floors, edged in red, frame it admirably. Surviving war and restoration are the tomb of Pope John XXI, on the entrance wall; a fine aediculed font (mostly 1470, partly by Francesco of Ancona), with dolphins sharing heads; and some good pictures – Gerolamo da Cremona's *Redeemer and Saints* (1452); a nice G. F. Romanelli (1610-62); and some by Marco Benefial (1684-1764).

There is one unique glory: the Chapel of Santa Lucia, opening off the left-hand aisle, is frescoed overall by that extraordinary painter, Paolo Guidotti (see BASSANO ROMANO). It is kept definitively locked, and although you may gaze in through the windowed door, you cannot receive the full force of Guidotti's effects. (Water is coming in, moreover.) Here as at BASSANO everything is brilliant and tenacious *trompe l'oeil,* with columns galore. Under yellowish scallop shells 'salt-white' persons in malachite-green niches challenge the normal: this time saints are standing, or peering around columns, or obsessively pouring water. There doesn't seem to be any dangerous message here, but without entering the Chapel it is hard to tell.

Duchesse, Church of the (Chiesa delle Duchesse)

This peculiar name, the 'Church of the Duchesses', is applied to the church of the Visitation because in 1557 Donna Girolama Orsini Farnese, widow of Pier Luigi, first Duke of Castro, founded a convent here for Cistercian nuns, and joined them. So as she was a duchess, the nuns ever after were known as duchesses too. The order is fully enclosed. Here is VITERBO's only baroque belfry, now painted a bright yellow and seen from everywhere.

Gesù, Church of the

This is a small, plain 11th-century box, rebuilt after the bombing, with its frescos all cleaned up, and little old ruinous lions climbing up the shoulders of the façade. It was originally dedicated to St Sylvester, and later given to the Jesuits.

During the conclave of 1271 (see above) a most infamous vengeance murder took place in this church. On the morning of Friday, 13 March, Henry Earl of Cornwall, first cousin of the future King Edward I of England, was at mass here; he was returning from an expedition against Islam in Tunis. (The Kings of France and Naples were at mass in San Francesco.) Ten years earlier, Prince Edward had commanded his father Henry III's forces at the Battle of Evesham, where Simon de Montfort, King Henry's rival for the throne of England, had been killed and beheaded. Henry of Cornwall had not been at the battle, but Simon's sons Guy and Simon now burst in and butchered him as he clung to the altar. Dante put Guy de Montfort to boil for ever in the Bullicame of VITERBO: good evidence that it was hotter then than now.

Gonfalone, Church of the

The name means: Church of the Banner. It was built for a Company of St John the Baptist whose activities included marrying off spinsters and ransoming prisoners from the Turk.

Its interior is VITERBO's best baroque treat – quiet baroque. It was built between 1665 and 1726, has a fine dark street façade, curved, and a simple interior layout: two large spaces, roughly equal in length and breadth. Since one is the chancel, it is up a few steps; between them two giant columns hold up an architrave to form a grand and solemn screen.

The church's glory is its frescos, all by Viterbese painters, all of 1756. The eye leaps to the *quadratura* ceiling; a soaring cortile, all grey and pink *trompe l'oeil* columns and balustrades. It is a worthy member of the genre initiated two hundred years before by Baldassare Peruzzi in the Villa Chigi (later Farnesina) and best 'churched' by Padre Pozzo in the 1690s at Sant'Ignazio, both in Rome. The painter of this one, with its quiet crowds of holy but haloless persons on clouds, its angelic harpers and lutenists, and its glorious dove descending, is Vincenzo Strigelli.

The *trompe l'oeil* goes on: above the organ and the entrance door, the tympanum is a half-domed scene, which we understand is below the cortile in the vault, a sort of dungeon, where St John is being beheaded. The painter here was Domenico Corvi. Opposite, at the other end of the nave, *St John before Herod*, who is surrounded by some of his family, all in 18th-century wigs. The painter is Anton Angelo Falaschi.

The *Baptism of Christ*, a framed picture of the previous century, now hangs from a beam in the chancel, so as to reveal a second picture on the other side. Christ's gesture, *non sum dignus*, is unusual and touching; the colours are firm and subtle. On the reverse is a *Madonna with Saints*: with her blue cloak she is conveying a swirl of grace to a pair of kneeling clerics: she is happy to be needed. The painter of both these was Giovanni Francesco Romanelli, a splendid colourist who remembered Poussin. He later went to France at the bidding of Louis XV.

More: over the second altar on the left in the nave the Virgin

Mary at the *Annunciation* is almost audibly sighing with pleasure. In the chancel, 'God the Father', *grisaille* in clouds. Many Maries. Just as in the work of VITERBO's early renaissance artists, the everyday human emotions continue to find a place in the grand scenes of this not at all negligible school of painters.

Mercanti, Church of the

The Merchants' Church is gone, except for its nice 1371 door, behind which you now find the Indian Dermatological Centre of Bombay.

Sant' Andrea

Sant'Andrea is the centrepiece of Pianoscarano, the ancient low-built suburb between San Pellegrino and the walls, beyond the Ponte Paradosso, where there was a church from the 8th century. Sant'Andrea is a nice squat romanesque barn, almost entirely rebuilt after the bombing, with an open naos, behind geraniums, in deep shadow. Steps rise the full width of the church to the *presbiterio*. Three Lombard apses and two little side doors down to the crypt, which contains a surprise: two little lateral Cistercian vaults, pointed; thus Gothic below Romanesque.

Sant' Angelo in Spata

So called after a family, this stands in the Piazza del Plebiscito, where it forms an unobtrusive but important part of the grand scene.

Like others, the church is built on a sharpish upwards slope. The interior was remade in 1746 and over the high altar is a spirited if rather overfed San Rocco by Pastura. In 1387, the Sant'Angelo in question miraculously delivered VITERBO from one of the abominable di Vicos. The event is celebrated by a joint civil/church festivity every May: all the citizens, two-by-two, are expected to engage in *tripudio* – 'jumping for joy'.

Outside, perched on high curly brackets, and with inscriptions and obelisks above, a fine Roman sarcophagus (removed in 1989) served as tomb for La Bella Galiana. A Roman baron who was laying siege to VITERBO in 1138 promised to raise the siege if she would but show herself to him briefly on the wall. As dutiful to her city as she was beautiful in person, she came and stood on one of the towers, the Torre del Branca, and there he shot her. Alternatively, she repulsed his advances and he threw her off the tower. There are some difficulties – like the tower not being built at the time, and the boar-hunt on the sarcophagus being out of keeping – but VITERBO has a liking for gallant girls.

Sant' Antonio, Hermitage of

Five kilometres outside the town, in the woods up Monte Palanzana, a Capuchin monastery of the 1530s has been brought back into different use. Some twenty years ago rich, scholarly, religious Tomasa Alfieri bought it and she has restored it with love, money, and good taste to be as near as possible what it was. Separate spaces for choir, sacristy, and church. The last is restored to its original forms and furnished in pale grey peperino: newly carved '9th-century' forms. The effect is cool and successful.

The users are a community, some priests, some lay people, called Familia Christiana, who are moved by a laicised version of the Capuchin spirit. A cardinal comes here to draft encyclicals.

Santi Faustino e Giovita

Until the 17th century, San Faustino appeared alone in the dedication: perhaps 'Giovita' should be Gionitas, who had been a prisoner for the faith with Faustinus in Milan, where together they baptised Secundus with water from a rain cloud; all three were then fed the consecrated Host by a dove from heaven.

The church is close up to the walls, of the 13th century, when a convent was attached. Its orchard was the subject of a long dispute with the neighbouring Augustinian Canons, finally settled in 1504 when the priest agreed to plant mulberry trees and share the crop with the Canons. In 1510 Augustinian nuns took over the convent and modishly named the church they built 'Santa Maria in Volturno', in the belief it was on the site of a temple to the Etruscan goddess Voltumna.

The church was altered in 1759 and later, and has some good pictures: *St John on Patmos*, confident and accomplished, is by the younger Romanelli, Urbano. The high altar picture of Faustinus and Giovita (if it be he), having the sacrament brought to them in prison by an angel, is by Vincenzo Strigelli – splendid toplighting, still fully Caravaggesque; the *Slaughter of the Innocents* to the right also his.

San Francesco

A great chilly church, built by the Franciscans in the years after 1236, high up by the Florence Gate; remodelled by a rich family, the Botonti, in 1603; regothicised in 1899; gutted in an air raid in January

1944; and rebuilt in its 13th-century form. The main door is made up of the barley sugar columns of a 1372 predecessor, dismantled but not destroyed in 1465. Inside we face a huge, single, foggy nave, the floor sloping up as usual, the wall frescos gone to illegibility. At the end of the Latin cross, the chancel is square, with a gothic window, now made to ride on a visually absurd – we did not hear it – organ, spread right across the east wall.

The main attractions are the (restored) tombs of Popes Clement IV, who died in 1268, and Adrian V, Pope for six weeks in 1276. Until the State took over the convent and church of S. Maria in Gradi in 1870 to make a prison, St Clement's tomb was there. It had been miraculous in its time, generating much wealth, and therefore much stolen; even by the Cathedral canons. It was made by 'Petrus', the son of Odericus, who both also worked at Westminster Abbey, where they signed the base of the shrine of St Edward the Confessor and the Cosmatesque floor it stands on. Adrian's tomb is held to be by Arnolfo di Cambio, the architect of the nave of Florence Cathedral. Both tombs are very splendid and all three designers later worked together at San Paolo fuori le Mura in Rome.

A slab recalls Vicedomino Vicedomini: he had been present when Pope Adrian V died in 1276, was elected to succeed him, and died instantly. He would have taken the name Gregory XI, which a French pope actually took during the Avignon business. Nevertheless, a splendid painting of 1795, by Vincenzo Milione, which belonged to the Ardenti – now where? – shows him having the pontifical crown snatched from his head by a skeleton.

When the Rocca was the seat of the Cardinal-Legate or the Papal Governor in the 15th and 16th centuries, this was their grand space and Sebastiano del Piombo painted the great Michelangelesque *Pietà* for this church. Turner did a drawing of it still *in situ*.

San Giovanni Battista

A tall rather quakerly church of 1511 (with an older, striped tower like the Cathedral's) which stood at one end of the bridge over the Urcionio, opposite the other renaissance church, Santa Maria della Peste.

When in the 1930s the Urcionio was finally covered up, and its valley and bridge destroyed in order to make room for the Fascist road, San Giovanni was shortened by a bay and the tower was moved and rebuilt. It is now an exhibition hall which you can hire; before that it was a garage.

San Giovanni in Zoccoli

This has a 12th-century façade buttressed across the street by two surprising great arches: a *zoccolo* is a plinth.

San Giuseppe and Santa Teresa

A former 17th-century Carmelite church, in the Piazza della Fontana Grande, its once-potent façade half ruinous. When in 1870 the State took over Church property in VITERBO, it became the Law Courts, and just as it is impossible for visitors to pierce the web of ecclesiastical disapproval and see the great hall of the Papal Palace, so it is impossible for them to gain access to the interior of this ex-church, be they never so armed with testimonials, *laissez-passers*, to whom it may concerns, Egregio Dottores and Caro Pepes. So we cannot describe it.

Sant'Ignazio

A Jesuit church of 1672, domed and cruciform. Although the light does not fall in dramatic beams straight to the altar as in the original Gesù in Rome, it is very grand, no expense spared, the marble all real. It is now used by the Centre of Solidarity of St Crispin of VITERBO, which helps young drug addicts in a cheerful and down-to-earth way, paying good attention to their families.

San Marco

A Cistercian convent church; consecrated in 1198 by Pope Innocent III in the presence of fifteen cardinals. It is like the big and glorious churches, but small, with a little crooked apse. If the fifteen cardinals had fifteen suites, they must have stayed outside.

Santa Maria delle Fortezze

Begun in 1514 to house a Madonna who had long stood against the outside of the city wall, who was revered by wayfarers, and known as Saint Mary of the Forts. Those large and restful forms which stand puzzlingly amputated to the left of the Rome Gate just fell into decay and have been partially demolished: not destroyed in 1944. What remains is the crossing and the apse, still outside the wall. The design of the façade was pure enough to be attributed to Bramante, who died only a year before it was begun. A more likely name is Battista di Giuliano da Cortona.

Santa Maria in Gradi

This was a most grand Dominican convent, built in the first half of the 13th century just outside the Porta Romana. When VITERBO was the seat of the Papacy, this was where the Popes mostly lived while their new Palace was abuilding. The State took it over for a prison in 1870; and in the air raids of May–June 1944 the church was largely destroyed.

The original church was remodelled in 1738 by Niccolò Salvi, architect of the Trevi Fountain in Rome. A drive round the outside of the prison shows the vastness of the ruin: 80 metres by 32. The crossing and part of the tower remain and so does the portico of 1460 and the steps down from it. The main gate of the prison is still Salvi's and what remains within is part of a designed scene little less grand than Monte Cassino at the other end of Lazio. Allow in your mind the wide steps in front of the façade – the Gradi – to run down to the road, with suitable buildings on either side, which was how Salvi laid it out. Originally, when the steps reached the road a great gate turned them straight round and into the city at the Porta Romana. New walls in the 13th century were intended to include Santa Maria: the Tower of San Biele (St Michael), the gate-tower standing alone to the south (and gaping pointlessly above a choppy sea of jerry-built flats of the 1950s and 60s) was part of that grand design.

The 1466 portico at the top of the surviving steps is not only grand, but early for what it is. It may also indicate the sort of thing that was intended at S. Maria della QUERCIA, where an absence is quite strongly felt; the same builder was at work at both places. (And perhaps at CORCHIANO.) Here the outside two arches are narrower than the three in the middle, and the rather portly, even fat, Corinthian columns on their high pedestals make the whole decidedly majestic. The ruin behind is the 18th-century shell, shading forward into the neo-classical.

The sacristy has survived, now surely the biggest prison officers' canteen in Europe: the dado fully 4 metres high. So have two of the three cloisters: the older and more famous (1266–8) may be visited, but not photographed because it is in the secure area of the prison. It has a southern, almost Arabic, look, like the one at Amalfi, though rather bigger: twinned marble columns, lotus capitals, variegated rounded windows above, a lion, a rose, some vaguely Star of David forms. For its wellhead, the bigger, Bramantesque, cloister has the skeleton of an octagonal *tempietto*, terminating at the architrave, of 1480.

The structure plan for VITERBO earmarks land for a new prison near Ferento.

Santa Maria Nuova

Perhaps built as a thank offering to the Virgin for the world not ending in the year 1000, this is the next grandest after the Cathedral. Like the Cathedral's, its long arcades are severe, its capitals brilliant, if respectfully a little less fantastic. The impressive triptych, painted on wood, of Christ blessing two saints, is put in the standard books as 13th-century, perhaps because it was found inside a stone sarcophagus by cowherds in 1283. Its Ravennate appearance might suggest a date some centuries earlier.

The picture of St Jerome, apparently at Stonehenge, is by Pastura. There is good modern work too: the bronze altar rail embodies a *Last Supper*, by Carlo Canestrari, a work of fine moral gravity. See too his stone *Pietà*, in a side-chapel: the Virgin Mary more or less cradling the grown man in her lap. The debt to Michelangelo is obvious, and thus daring, and the dead right arm is his; but the dead head hanging down is all the modern sculptor's.

Externally the apse is decorated with flowers, leaves, faces animal and human: one a Graeco-Roman antefix, showing Jove, perhaps, or an Etruscan deity. St Thomas Aquinas preached from the outside pulpit in 1266.

Santa Maria del Paradiso

St Mary of Paradise is now modern. The cloister is authentic, if odd; 13th-century, built on a slope. Also *polisportivo*, with little cars parked in it and small boys racing bicycles.

Santa Maria della Peste, or Santa Elisabetta

This pretty little octagonal building was put up in 1494, in thanksgiving for the end of a plague, on the site of a little church of St Elizabeth, at one end of the Ponte Tremoli. (BAGNAIA has a similarly placed little octagonal church.) The style is Florentine. The floor tiles are worth peering in at: yellow, blue, and white, full of fancy and variety, and similar to those in the Mazzatosta Chapel in S. Maria della Verita. It is now the memorial to VITERBO's war-dead.

Santa Maria della Salute

This is an early central plan church, which should be better known. It used to face the main street, which came up from the Ponte Tremoli over the Urcionio, to the then new city centre. Fascism reduced that street to an alley and the building now has its back to Fascism's triumphal way. Quite right.

The pink and white patterning in the façade masonry gives it a most genial aspect. It was built in 1320 at the order of a lawyer called Fardo di Ugolino, beside the hostel he had already built for redeemed prostitutes, and it still belongs to the College of Advocates of VITERBO. Inside, the space is high and graceful, square on plan, with a semicircular apse in each wall. One of the apses has two tiny squares attached to suggest a chancel. Above, the ceiling is vaulted up to a small lantern, all very proportionate. It carries the seed of renaissance and baroque achievements in a most engaging way.

The outside doorcase, of the same date, may be from the workshop of Lorenzo Maitani of Siena, who did the finest of the bas-reliefs on the façade of Orvieto Cathedral. The combination of realistic birds and vines with highly formal patterning puts it with the best work of the century.

Santa Maria della Verità

A great airy church, an immensely broad single hall, just outside the walls to the east. It was a 12th-century Premonstratensian foundation, enlarged, and finally rebuilt after the 1944 air raids. In 1912 the church itself became the Civic Museum of VITERBO, but since the rebuilding in 1960 the museum has been moved into the convent next door (see Museo Civico) and the church returned to worship and concerts.

Along the right-hand wall the Mazzatosta Chapel opens out, which contains almost all there is of the work of Lorenzo da Viterbo, perhaps Northern Lazio's only painter of real genius. He worked in this church in 1469 and he painted a *pala*, an altarpiece, for CERVETERI, and that is all.* The CERVETERI *pala*† is dated 1472; it seems likely he died before finishing it, aged about 28.

The frescos were badly damaged in 1944, but have been carefully restored, the *Marriage of the Virgin* from 16,000 pieces it is said. This

* The nice series of illustrations of the life of Sant'Egidio in the Diocesan Museum in ORTE has been attributed to him, but to our minds not plausibly; and so has an equally nice Princess and Dragon at CORCHIANO.

† Currently in Rome.

is on the left wall; above it is a *Presentation of Mary at the Temple*; and above that, the four sections of the vault show Evangelists, with Fathers and Doctors of the Church on either side, and Prophets above them. On another wall is a (part hidden) Assumption of the Virgin. The whole makes a single multipartite composition of great beauty, scrolling the attention upwards in consecutive swoops.

The *Marriage of the Virgin* shows a relaxed, eye-level, linear crowd scene: note that the heads are all at the same level while the feet are not. It is taking place in *un clima di lieta profanità* – 'an atmosphere of happy worldliness' – in Claudio Strinati's words. Many of the heads are evidently portraits of contemporaries and their wonderful variety is what the artist is celebrating. (By tradition, the man facing us in this picture with his hands together is the artist, and the elderly man talking to him is the patron, Nardo Mazzatosta.) Where the *Marriage* is a grand linear design, the *Presentation* immediately above it is all accelerated perspective: the nearest figures are the same size as in the *Marriage*, the furthest, standing at the Temple gate, are tiny; the vigorously patterned pavement is the main vehicle of acceleration; and the buildings and steps all lead up to the distant, ideal, circular Temple. Here too note the relative placing of the heads and feet of the people, near and far. The conclusion to all this is above us, in the vault: the various and highly individual Evangelists, Saints, and Doctors, on their gently inclined clouds, and Prophets above at the golden bar of Heaven. Thirty-five years later, Raphael very precisely combined the two lower scenes – the linear *Marriage* and the vertical *Presentation* – into his own *Sposalizio*. Did he know Lorenzo's versions from his journeys down the Cassia?

Nothing is known of Lorenzo, except that he was born in the parish of San Faustino. His style has been described as deriving from Benozzo Gozzoli, but only because Benozzo had worked in VITERBO (see Santa Rosa, below); or from Piero della Francesca, but only because the 'ideal buildings' in the *Presentation* are thought to resemble those in the *Ideal City* in Urbino, which has not been shown to be Piero's anyway.* In the picture behind the altar the landscape, with its bushes and trees, is very like that still to be seen between NEPI and the Cassia – quite oddly English, as Dennis and we and others have all observed.

* In fact, Strinati points out, his 'urbanism' more resembles that of a little ideal *Veduta* in the Berlin Pinakotek.

For several reasons (see Appendix II), it seems to us that Lorenzo could perhaps be the mysterious illustrator of the *Hypnerotomachia Poliphili*.

The floor of this chapel keeps remains of a majolica pavement, similar to that in Santa Maria della Peste, other bits of which are, regrettably, said to be in the Victoria and Albert Museum in London.

The church contains in its right transept a new organ with mechanical action. But however much the rebirth of church music in Italy is to be applauded, the visual price of these intrusive organs (see also San Francesco) is too high. This one completely obscures a beautiful and richly sculpted 14th-century arcade and archway. It is not too difficult to build unobtrusive organs, and locate them unobtrusively, until organ-builders' visual taste once more catches up with their musical.

San Pietro

This stands just outside the gate of that name, a cold, decent rebuild of a 13th-century church. It is notable only for the very large, apparently 18th-century picture in the apse, showing the Crucifixion of St Peter, with attendant figures, among them four women with faces like stage masks of animals. Pale colours; the drapery with many echoing lines as though blown about by as many separate winds. The foreshortening of St Peter's body makes a special, obscure, point: impressive, but odd.

Sanctuary of Santa Rosa

This huge classical church is bitterly forbidding and funereal. It replaces a convent church of the Clarissae of 1450, which itself replaced their earlier oratory. It was the 1450 church which contained Benozzo Gozzoli's grand narrative of Rose's short life, done in 1453. This was destroyed in redecoration, or perhaps in a fire: the Bishop had copies done in 1632, the painter, Francesco Sabatini, swearing on the Bible to copy them most faithfully. The copies are now in the Museo Civico and the loss is pathetic; some of Benozzo's drawings are in the British Museum.

The present church was built in the 1840s; the dome completed in 1908. Inside, the Saint's less than charming mortal remains are kept in a 17th-century casket. The modern confessionals are modelled on telephone boxes. (Is this witty or not?) Six years after her death St Rose's body was transported from Santa Maria in Poi to the Clares' oratory, the coffin carried by four Cardinals, and the Pope, Alexander IV (1254–61), walked in the front rank of the procession. Had she not been a notable Guelf?

San Sisto

The church of San Sisto, just inside the Porta Romana, is the most impressive building in VITERBO and it is one of the most impressive churches in Italy. The nave is probably 9th-century, on the site of a Roman temple. After being knocked down in the air raids of 1944, it was rebuilt, using the old columns. The chancel, or presbytery as it is called in Italian, which did not suffer, seems to be 11th- or 12th-century. Its three apses, one wide and two narrow, are built into the city wall: you see them from the great rat-race ring-road. The crypt beneath is a largely modern invention. The present façade replaces one which had three tall, narrow blind arches on either side and in the middle a tall broad one with a small crown of blind arches above. The original small Lombard tower is still there: one of its little columns is in human form – a rare 9th-century caryatid. The tall, military-looking tower at the east end with its three bells is a later addition, combining, as indeed does the east wall of the church, the needs of defence and of the faith. In the 15th century not only was St Sixtus' foot kept here, but also St Thomas of Canterbury's sword.

During the 15th century, time of papal visits and renovation, there was a quite large palazzo attached to the church, where the Papal Governor's guests sometimes stayed: Eleanor of Aragon was there in 1473, with her suite. It had a long smart garden along the walls and a white marble fountain.

Having the chancel raised above the nave is common in all Christendom; it derives from the earliest Christian basilicas, which were adapted Roman lawcourts, in which the trial was conducted on a raised platform at one end while litigants, lawyers, and listeners waiting for the next case milled about in the lower and larger part. In VITERBO and around, a variation developed that the nave floor itself should slope upwards to the chancel, usually gently, but sometimes posing the worshipper a stiffish climb.

At San Sisto the peculiarity, the authority, the solemnity, is that the chancel is not up the usual three or four steps but up fifteen in two flights, and steep at that. From the entrance the eye follows the familiar pattern, an aisled basilica with seven smallish columns a side, noting the last to the east is interestingly twisted, and the frothy and whimsical capitals under the tall slab walls which appear to continue through the chancel arch. You are already drawn forward by the steps, and the high walls on either side appear to be closing in. Only as you move up the nave do these further walls reveal themselves as huge, single, acanthus-crowned columns, supporting an arch higher than the chancel arch, and far beyond it. The invitation is to go on, up, and in. The first flight of steps allows you a place to pause, straight under the chancel arch and between like but not identical columned ambos. Just beyond, the steps rise again, and you with them, to be suddenly seized by the quite unexpected height, weight, and grandeur which is opening out around you. In Romanesque architecture, divine order can be thunderously manifest; and here it is that. At each side, the two great single columns are seen to be supporting yet other round arches, narrower, outward, and of still greater height, immense in the upper shadows, and making the first a giant baldaquin. The crossing, if one can call it that, is so huge it could be from another planet: one of C. S. Lewis's, where proportion itself makes godhead.

All this has been happening within a cube, projected upwards, and upwards again, on the far side of the chancel arch. As for us earthlings, we are still not quite at our highest level: there are another two steps up to where the sacrament is kept, against the rounded ashlar of the central apse, which is part of the city wall.

In his *Confessions* (part 12 of book XI), St Augustine tells us: 'My answer to those who ask "What was God doing before he made heaven and earth?" is not "He was preparing Hell for people who pry into mysteries". This frivolous retort has been made before now, so we are told, in order to evade the point of the question. But it is one thing to make fun of the questioner and another to find the answer.' We incline to think he was designing San Sisto.

The Santissima Trinità

The great domed and towered sanctuary church balances the Papal Palace and the Cathedral on the far side of the Valle di Faul, and its still functioning Augustinian convent reaches northwards up to the city walls. In some of the convent buildings are the offices of the new University of the Tuscia, picking up where Reginald Pole's efforts came to naught in the 1540s.

A first church was consecrated in 1258 by Pope Alexander IV, and in about 1315 the then Bishop found two itinerant painters from

Arezzo to paint an image of the Virgin for it. The later grandeurs are all due to the events of 28 May 1320 – Whit Monday. A hurricane was striking the city with awful terror, there were *tenebre horribili et figure de demoni* – 'horrible darknesses and figures of demons' – all over the sky, and the world was about to founder, when the figure of Our Lady appeared miraculously from the little church, and by her grace saved it. *Santa Maria Liberatrice* is now in a big chapel of 1680 in the yet bigger but well-proportioned church of 1745 (architect: the Roman G-B. Gazale). She is surrounded with a wall-full of decorative *ex-votos*, including epaulettes and necklaces; and as madonnas go, she is a honey – not a bit like Superman – and giving her nice baby a little carrot. There are other not negligible paintings, by Strigelli, Bonifazi, and Domenico Corvi.

The convent also has VITERBO's grandest cloister (of 1513): thirty-six monolithic columns carry a smooth, straight entablature, with an arcaded loggia along the church side, above. Everything is calm and tall, and the acoustics are perfect for the play of the low-lying, almost submerged, fountain, to which the cloister pavement gently rises.

Other Buildings

Piazzas and Palazzi

The Piazza del Plebiscito, formerly del Commune, is where VITERBO's centre was established at papal insistence in the 13th century: the intention, no doubt, to get the obstreperous citizen magistracy away from the Papal Palace. It is also where other papal insistences of the 15th and 16th centuries are commemorated; and the administrative centre.

Three large buildings frame the Piazza: the Palazzo Communale – arcaded; the Palazzo della Prefettura; and the Palazzo del Podestà, with the tower attached. There is a bridge between two of them, and it seems likely that all the streets into it were at one time bridged in this way, making it a truly enclosed space as Alberti had recommended.

The two principal buildings of VITERBO's self-government were put up, facing each other, in 1264: the Palazzo dei Priori and the Palazzo del Capitano del Popolo. But the most interesting today is the third, the Palazzo Communale, which was started for papal, not communal, purposes, two hundred years later. It was ordered as a new Palazzo for the Governor of the Patrimony by Pius II, perhaps with the advice of Bernardo Rossellino, to stand in the open space between the 1264 palazzi, to make the most of the fine view across the Valle Faul, and to be proportionately similar to the Palazzo dei Priori, arcaded at ground level, and attached by a bridge to the Palazzo del Podestà. The space in front of the long-existing church of Sant'Angelo was to be enlarged by taking in a cemetery, to become the city's main Piazza, where executions would take place, and lyings-in-state, and summonings of the people.

If you enter the Piazza down the Via Cavour (one of the Farnese streets), on the left is where the Palazzo dei Priori stood: the seat of VITERBO's own and ancient self-government between 1264 and 1510. (The Magistrature consisted of the Priors, or Consuls, and the *Gonfalionieri*, elected by the eighty, sometimes forty, members of the Communal Council.) The 1264 building was replaced in 1779 by the present one, the ex-Palazzo Apostolico, seat of the papal government. (The architect was Francesco Navona – see SAN LORENZO NUOVO.) It is now the Prefettura, the office of the Prefect, an official of the Ministry of the Interior.

In the 15th century, the Priori had energetically 'improved' their palazzo, giving it a loggia facing the view, and in 1466 a grand external staircase, arriving at a 'triumphal doorway' into the *piano nobile*; also new battlements. Then in 1470 they replaced a 13th-century fountain in the Piazza with a 'Hercules' fountain – the two so-called 'honorary' columns and Herculean lions were already there.

Tension between city and Papal State was already high and the Priori, influenced by Annius' patriotic fantasies and aware how fast their independence was disappearing, symbolically renamed their grand hall the Aula Herculea; and in 1487 they commissioned a Roman painter, Giovanni Piacera, to decorate it with the Deeds of Hercules. To ram the point home, they added a story of how five hundred 'well-found men' of VITERBO had had to go to SORIANO to help a conclave bring forth a pope. In 1494, they had arches built to support the floor of the hall where they exhibited the city's collection of Etruscan (and therefore at least non-, if not anti-, papal) sarcophagi.

The Palazzo del Podestà is opposite, with the communal clock-tower attached. When first built, it was the Palazzo del Capitano del Popolo – the Captain of the People – who was indeed elected by the people. When the Podestà, another word for a medieval civic headman, took over is obscure (as is the early manner of his appointment). The present Torre del Commune, 44 metres high, went up in 1487, after the previous one fell on to the Palazzo and badly damaged it and the municipal brothel behind. Today's quite amiable building is still substantially that of 1264, but repaired after the 1487 damage, and encased in more restoration work of 1816.

In April 1510, Pope Julius II's Governor suddenly ordered the Priori out of their 1264 palazzo, for him to move into, to receive the Pope, who was about to visit: they could make do with the one ordered by Pius II, which was still after nearly fifty years unfinished, though Julius' name had already been carved on its internal doorcases and the first of the great rooms frescoed with the papally approved miracles of the Madonna della QUERCIA. The Priori moved in, and the later decorations and arrangements in what had overnight become the Palazzo Communale redound to the credit of VITERBO rather than of the Church.

The building may at first have been just a *piano nobile* on top of an arcade, rather in the manner of the two-arched 13th-century house-front up by the Cathedral, and with battlements above. The curious disjunction between the arcade and the windows is accounted for by the fact that the first 'job' was the central part, five columns below, four windows above; which was then completed with eight of each; and eventually, to provide a correct view down the Via Nuova, a ninth arch was added. The entrance under the arcade shows a still pointed door-frame, whereas even the ground-floor doorcases are fully classical.

Indoors, up the grand stairs, is the Capella dei Priori, or Capella Palatina: frescos, picture, ceiling, and a magnificent late mannerist reredos, all of about 1610. For the moment Sebastiano del Piombo's *Pietà* (see Museo Civico) is displayed here, not very well, because of the thick glass a demented humanity has now made necessary in front of famous works of art.

In the Sala Regia, the Royal Hall, are the six Baldassare Croce frescos of the origin and history of VITERBO, replacements for the Hercules pictures lost in the 1510 exchange of buildings: Noah-Janus founds Viterbo; Etruscan Viterbo is formed by enclosing the four castles F. A. U. L.; Roman Tuscia is given to the Church by Countess Matilda of Tuscany; Celestine III consecrates the first Bishop of Viterbo in 1192; Bernard de Coucy, Rector of the Patrimony of St Peter, presents VITERBO with the Banner of the Church; Paul II invests two Viterbese noblemen with the Order of the Knight of the Lily. On the wall opposite the windows, the middle figure is the Emperor Michael Palaeologus.

The Council meets next door in the Sala degli Eroi, late 16th-century chiaroscuro heroes above, a variegated forest of 18th-century wooden stalls and decorative figures below. The other rooms' frescos and paintings are of more interest for topographic history than as art.

The anti-papal spirit did not die out. In the cortile, a big white marble tablet declares: *SPQV – Senatus Populusque Viterbensis* – 'Strong in its own rights, on the 20th of September 1860 VITERBO shook off the secular papal yoke and on the 11th of October was compelled by Napoleon III, who was devoted to the Vatican, to submit once more to that abhorred dominion. Virile and solemn, it protested.'

'*Arx Herculea*'

The Cathedral, the Papal Palace and the old Hospital gather round the Piazza San Lorenzo. Behind the buildings loggias and one-time *giardini pensili* still string out above the Valle.

The infamous conclave of 1268–71 took place in the great hall of the Palazzo Papale, then newly finished, and the excommunication of Conradin from the steps. It had been built on the initiative of Raniero Gatti, the Captain of the People, to be a dwelling worthy of the popes. The great hall, still called the Sala della Conclava, terminates at its west end where an open arcade stands dramatically above a great low bridge; there was to have been another hall standing entirely on this bridge, which was never built because the popes left. The 19th century restored it all, and well. The 20th century, though rightly still finding the great scene worth using for postcards and wedding photographs, has otherwise treated it poorly. The view down under the arch of the bridge is no longer the little orchards and churches of the Valle di Faul, but a modern bank of ostentatious design, all the more deplorable because it is the regional bank of VITERBO.

The view into the hall from outside is now through a plate glass door kept locked, and beyond that through a second sheet of plate glass – perhaps bullet-proof? What can just be glimpsed is that this once splendid stone space has been whitewashed and is full of packed ranks of plastic chairs. The whole building, hall, collection of paintings from various deconsecrated churches, loggia with fountain, is now the Bishop's Palace and the public is not admitted. Period.

In the interests of our readers, we decided to press the matter. Lest a woman be cause of alarm, the male among us presented himself at the office of the Curia, and there at last found a youngish man, from whose dress you could not tell if he was a priest or not, and explained the case. It was precisely because of such touristic interest as ours that the Bishop had decided to deny all access: tourists write their names on the walls. But, we said, if tourists are to rise above such things, should they not be provided with reliable books, based on research? This was our innocent design. Yes indeed; but if we were researchers we should be in a library, not here. Well, we had actually been in quite a few libraries, and now wished to refresh the memory of our last visit to the great hall, when we and all others were freely admitted: was this quite out of the question? Completely and unconditionally. And moreover, since we had done the research, we clearly had no need whatever to go inside the building, and should proceed forthwith to write our book without bothering the ecclesiastical authorities of Viterbo any further. QED. Catch 22. For a parallel, lay, experience, see S. Giuseppe and S. Teresa, below.

Leaving the Piazza, look at the 13th-century house on the right, with its large, but minimum, two-arch arcade, which the Palazzo del Commune's is kin to.

Townscape

Some Etruscan stones can be seen by the bridge up to the Cathedral. Here too is the Palazzo Farnese, early 15th-century, somewhat amputated and much restored, but still good-looking. It is now occupied by the offices of the ancient Hospital; neighbouring buildings to the north of less or more antiquity are occupied by wards, on whose far side the miniature campanile of S. Maria in Celle can be seen.*

Across the rest of the town, there is a fine scatter of domestic palazzi amid the dense medieval fabric, and a number of remaining domestic towers. The 15th-century Palazzo Chigi/Caetani, towered and sombre, is behind the Gesù. The Palazzo Santoro, of 1466, on the way to the Rocca (and with the theatre now nearby), houses the library of the Accademia degli Ardenti (see above).†

The town's distinction is that 'dense medieval fabric': houses, wells, fountains, gardens enclosed behind high walls. The domestic buildings are embellished by the pleasant invention of the *profferlo*. This is an outside staircase, as many storeys high as permitted by the necessary relation between the *profferlo* form and the overall scale. A quarter of a circle of double-depth building stones goes up the front

* A colossal new hospital building for the entire region of Upper Lazio has been half built on the way up to SAN MARTINO IN CIMINO. Work stopped about 1975 and the abandoned mastodontic skeletons are still nuzzled by Lilliputian cranes.

† Ardenti is actually a rather sedate name: elsewhere there were academies of the Inflamed, the Mad.

of your house, and on the protruding halves rides a straight staircase, diagonally, to your high-level front door; underneath is your stable/storeroom/*magazzino*, or perhaps a lane, or even the main street. The effect of these careful, gawky things is one of lopsided grace. The Casa Poscia, near to the Fontana Grande, has a fine one; and some houses in the Via dell'Orologio Vecchio. At the time, they were everywhere in VITERBO itself and in towns where the Viterbese influence was strong.

The San Pellegrino quarter is a perfectly preserved piece of this kind of townscape, and the little piazza itself is generally held to be the best of the date in Italy. The humbler bits of the quarter continue well lived in, but parts look devilish scraped. The Palazzo degli Alessandri has heavy low arches and a voluminous balcony. It also has a characteristically heavy history of assault, treachery, and butchery in its low vaults and twisting corridors; the Alessandri were of the Gatti faction. There are also picture shops and boutiques and restaurants, which keep the area in use, and a remarkable specialist greengrocer in the Via Cardinale La Fontaine.

Life above, and the half-arched-over life under, the *profferli* is still fully imaginable: this is the Italy Shakespeare's Italians inhabited. A hint: walk slowly. People of taste in 1215 built high and on a very small plot, so things worth looking at happen up there, as well as down here, and they happen every metre.

The Caffé Schenardi

In 1818 a Neapolitan incomer, Raffaele Schenardi, bought the 15th-century Albergo Reale in what is now Corso Italia and opened his famous café. During the Roman Republic of 1849 it posted up despatches each day recording the progress of that stormy and idealistic interlude. A Police Report of 1851 complains: 'And where the malice of Raffaele Schenardi ceases, that of the women takes over, since Schenardi does indeed have two very fine daughters who know well how to attract admirers, and they are definitely of the republican party'. The present interior is the work of Virginio Vespignani (see BOLSENA), 1855, though presumably echoing one built soon after 1818. The two aisles were to have been four; even with the two that were built, the numerous and graceful columns and mirrors produce a sybaritic effect which is outstanding even in the light-hearted history of restaurant design. The acoustics, though, are appalling: one can never make oneself heard without shouting; hence, no doubt, the confidence with which the police reports were filed. Hence too, we are inclined to think, the relative lack of success of the republican and socialist Left in the Papal State between 1820 and 1870. How can you have a revolution without a café to whisper in?

It is recorded that at 9.30 a.m. on 27 May 1938, the Duce sat at the third table on the right and consumed a *cappuccino*.

The Fountains

The sound of running water, which can now be heard only at dead of night, has been famous in Viterbo down the centuries, and the fountains have long been praised for their beauty. They reached a high level of technology and design about 1200. The standard type – and there are plenty of examples – is of stone, on a plinth of steps (which permits adjustment to any slope). The water comes out of brass pipes arranged in rings or squares at one or more levels, falling into round or fancy basins, sometimes cascading from one to another, and adorned with beasts, especially lions, which sometimes have the jets in their mouths. From the casting of the brass they are called Fontane Fuse: Cast Fountains.

The biggest and most famous is the Fontana Grande, in the homonymous Piazza. It was started in 1206 and consists of a Greek-cross basin at the top of five great steps, with a squat central column supporting a smaller basin, with a smaller column, also squat, supporting a decorative and foliated obelisk; water issues from horizontally spouting pipes. Its water comes along a Roman conduit from near Santa Maria in Gradi, and it used to travel a further 9 kilometres to a Roman villa along the Cassia. Other fountains, the one in the piazza outside SS. Faustino and Giovita, for example, have their own indigenous springs. The dashing fountain in the Piazza in Piano Scarano has Hercules' lions spouting water a fine distance into a particularly broad basin. (When the Languedocian Pope Urban V passed through VITERBO in 1367 on his way, as he hoped, from Avignon to Rome, some of his people washed a little dog in this fountain, and there was a riot. The Pope threatened to pull down all the towers; but was dissuaded.) There are more bourgeois 19th-century lions doing their job on the 16th-century fountain in the Piazza delle Erbe.

Museums

Neither the Museo Civico (paintings and Etruscan material) nor the archaeological museum in the Rocca Albornoz are (1989) in full working order: both have collections very well worth visiting, so the traveller should enquire.

Museo Civico

The Civic Museum of VITERBO is housed in the former convent and cloister of Santa Maria della Verita. It began when Annius persuaded Pope Alexander VI that some sarcophagi his court had found while out hunting should be displayed in the Palazzo dei Priori where, of course, they would be valued for their Etrusco/Herculean connotations. The collection was extended by the Academy of the Ardent.

The Museum's most famous possession, one of the great pictures of the Italian Renaissance, is the *Pietà* painted by Sebastiano del Piombo (temporarily visible in the Palazzo del Commune).

The picture comes from the period when Michelangelo was not painting: he was deeply offended, Vasari writes, that 'many artists thought more of Raphael's grace than they did of Michelagnolo's profundity'. But Sebastiano Luciani (later appointed to an office dealing with the leaden seals affixed to papal documents, and thus known as Sebastiano del Piombo) was not among them. Sebastiano was a wonderfully talented Venetian painter and lutenist, a pupil of Giorgione, who had been brought to Rome in about 1512 by the Sienese millionaire Agostino Chigi to take part in decorating his sumptuous new villa. 'Michelagnolo therefore turned to him, being attracted by his colouring and grace, and took him under his protection, thinking that if he gave his assistance to Sebastian in design he might succeed in confounding his rivals under cover of a third person. While matters were in this state . . . someone from Viterbo, in high favour with the Pope, employed Sebastiano to decorate a chapel for him in S. Francesco at Viterbo, with a dead Christ lamented by His Mother. This was diligently completed by Sebastiano, who introduced a much admired shaded landscape, but the invention and cartoon were Michelagnolo's.'

In this painting two powerful and familiar images converge. As Vasari's story makes clear, it is in effect one of the series of *Pietà*s that Michelangelo again and again composed over his long life; but it also embodies the image, familiar from any number of Madonna and Child pictures, of Mary contemplating her miraculous Son, pondering His doom 'in her heart', while He sleeps on the ground, a baby laid on a cloth. In the VITERBO picture, Mary has before her on a cloth on the ground the dead body which in the St Peter's *Pietà* she held on her lap. She is now no longer a young woman and behind her she has a landscape of awful and recent desolation. In her fearsome faith, looking no longer at the Son, but to the Father, she is as brilliantly lit as the vacated, but powerfully undead, body before her. The colours are metaphysical. The lighting, like Caravaggio's later, is instructive of the Almighty's presence high above and beyond the picture.

The collection contains many other good things, some from the closed churches; it gives a proper impression of the particular qualities of VITERBO's art and artists. The best works are only too often on loan or being restored. But look, we say, at least for the following: the Romanelli *Annunciation*; the *Transportation of St Mary of Egypt* by Marco Benefial; an enormous *Death of the Virgin* by the Pisan painter Aurelio Lomi; two fine Pasturas, a large *Nativity* and a formal *Madonna and Child*; a Della Robbia lunette (serious angels in a real hurry to worship while a sleepy Madonna looks patiently out); the young Salvator Rosa's *Incredulity of St Thomas*. Also an affable marble sphinx from Santa Maria in Gradi, signed and dated 'Pasquale Romano, 1286'.

The lower part of the cloister contains the large Etruscan pieces, some from the 1497 collection in the old Palazzo dei Priori. Several sarcophagus lids are from Musarna, a newly found Etruscan site along the road to TUSCANIA. The figures, lying half on their sides with one arm across the body, are sketchy, and the heads strangely turned. One quite ugly woman is lying on her front, chin towards you and forehead away: a gesture prefiguring Michelangelo and Epstein.

One *nenfro* sarcophagus shows Charon, ferryman of the dead, who must surely have a place in the ancestry of our own Mr Punch. Punch certainly derives from the Roman and Neapolitan Pulcinella, but the more that is discovered about Italian folklore and the *commedia dell'arte*, the more its origins recede, certainly to the Romans, and therefore probably to the Etruscans. This Charon-Punch has an enormous nose, an enormous chin turning up to meet it, an eye rather below it, and a quiff coming down towards it. He holds a reversed bow and a long hammer, the latter the Etruscans' symbol for time's ineluctable passage: they hammered in nails to mark it. There is a Persephone – Prspna – at the other end of the sarcophagus, pretty, in a nice frock: no sausage-armed Judy she.

Indoors are the usual fine pots; and the hooks and eyes which are just like ours; and a 6th-century BC jug with the strainer part of the spout. Another jug, a metal one, with a neat gadget to prevent the handle resting against its body and getting too hot. (Gosh, just what I always hoped you'd make me: thanks!...) Note the tiny glass bowl instinct with mysteriously beautiful colours: the experts from Murano say they come from its lying a couple of thousand years in ferruginous water.

The Rocca Albornoz

The Rocca Albornoz is interesting both for itself – it was VITERBO's fortress from the 14th century – and as the new home of a National Archaeological Museum.

Cardinal Albornoz' original fortress of 1354 was many times destroyed and rebuilt before Bramante in 1507 provided the *cortile* with its arcade and inner loggia for Julius II. Paul III had it improved in 1534, with the airy, outward-looking loggia and the great staircase. Cardinal Pole lived in it. After that, decline: leased out; orphanage; occupied by the French; used as a barracks by the new Italian State; bombed, and recently restored.

It used to have several more towers than we see today, and a moat, and a bridged gate, and beetling battlements. The tower beside it is part of the Porta Fiorentina.

The Archaeological Museum

It is now being turned into a fully equipped modern museum. Already the remarkable material from the Swedish excavations at ACQUAROSSA and SAN GIULIANO is on display, which gives an admirable impression of how objects familiar from so many glass cases were actually used.

There is a complete reconstruction of two 'public buildings', from ACQUAROSSA, which together faced a little rectangular piazza. They had stone foundations; their 'Tuscan' columns of oak, with peperino bases and capitals, supported tiled roofs, over an open loggia. Friezes show Hercules stories, with horses and chariots (like the CASTRO *biga*) and various beasts; people dining at two tables: three to each, reclining on a triclinium, a boy pouring wine; and musicians; beneath each table a peaceable long-tailed dog.

The private houses had terracotta decorations too and roof-tiles painted on the inside.

Another exhibition shows just what the Etruscans grew, and ate, and how they cooked it (see Food).

The Macchina di Santa Rosa

The best and strangest day of the year in VITERBO is that of the Machine of St Rose. She lived from 1233 to 1251 and first attracted attention when she was 3 by bringing her recently dead aunt back to life. From then on she divided her energies between prayer, caring for the sick and the poor, mortifying her own person, and unifying the townspeople by her cogent and forceful demand for a firm resistance to the siege of the Emperor Frederick II; this last when she was 10. She sought entry to the order of Poor Clares and was denied that, but allowed to become a Franciscan tertiary.

In 1512, a time of some turmoil when the city fathers were celebrating Hercules and Augustinian nuns naming their church for an Etruscan goddess, an annual procession in her honour was instituted to commemorate the 1257 translation of her body from S. Maria in Poi to the church of the Clarissae. It takes place every year in the evening of 3 September.

At least since 1664 a tall column or reliquary has been carried. The Procession of the Macchina di Santa Rosa – the word is virtually untranslatable: 'machine' seems best – is the most spectacular of all the giant Things which are carried on annual religious processions throughout Italy, though here there is not a priest in sight: the Church has celebrated the day before.

Over the centuries it has got bigger and bigger. In 1801 it went out of control; twenty-two people were trampled to death and the Pope decreed that never again should a machine be more than 10 metres high. In 1967 it swayed dangerously and the course was not completed. A new machine is made every five years. The design is put to competition, and everything is paid for by the Commune.

The *festa* of 1988 was like this. At sunset the Mayor gives a party in the loggia at the back of the Palazzo Communale. Then he and his friends and relations and the Councillors and Deputies and Senators of all parties (and on this occasion a couple of foreign writers lucky enough to be reckoned friendly), elbow their way through the populace from one side of the Piazza to the other, all very politely, and pulling each other through the sticky bits; and line up. Then to a galvanisingly quick march from the town band we set off extremely fast up the hill, between a walk and a run, several lines abreast, each of a dozen people with arms linked. We arrive, flushed, outside the church of San Sisto and do some waiting in the public eye.

Inside San Sisto the Facchini di Santa Rosa, the Porters of St

Rose, are receiving, if you please, Extreme Unction: the sacrament otherwise taken on one's deathbed or before battle. For weeks before they have been training in another church, carrying huge loads while cardiologists take readings. A communist Senator explains that two-thirds of them are communists, and strong: 'Of course; they are sons of the people'. The porters pour out of the church and get introduced to everyone and vice versa, and more mingling is done. There are a hundred and twenty of them.

The Macchina is standing in a giant sentry box built each year for the occasion, just inside the city gate. It is by now no less than 34 metres high, whatever the Pope may have said in 1801. Some of the past *macchine* have been pleasing to look at, varying from the churchy to the wedding cakey. The present one is indeed breathtaking for size and luminosity, but not for the beauty of its design. It is a kitsch, semi-abstract, semi-Tiffany tower, half like a huge slippery woman and half like a huge leek up which smaller women are climbing, with the saintlet puny on top. No matter; the thing is perfectly amazing whatever the design.

But, *Non est factum nisi dictum*, as the Senator says: 'A thing is not done unless a speech is made about it.' So we, and the poor porters, have a ten-minute harangue from the designer of the machine: 'a sculptor not well-known to us: I believe he may be well-known in America'. This was perhaps not the person they wanted to be harangued by because when they came to put this *macchina* down at the end of its first year's journey it leaned alarmingly to one side and the issue was in doubt for some minutes before the emergency levers and ropes could save the day. So it had had to be rebuilt with the centre of gravity lower.

The porters, in their whites with red sashes, and white bonnets, and curious red cushions which they keep in place on their backs by means of strings held between their teeth, are now called by ranks of ten (by size), until eighty of them are underneath the platform: small at the back, tall at the front, for going downhill. (Arrangement reversed for uphill.) Another forty form up outside with ropes to help on the uphill bits, and emergency levers to get the machine upright again if it heels, and stands for putting it down on at the resting places.

The designer it is, too, who gives the word go. The porters underneath take the strain slowly, slowly, and then in a single swift move – hup! – she goes a foot up in the air, and totters for a long moment. The band strikes up again, and again we set off, prancing back down the hill in dozens abreast, and you see why arms are linked: to save anyone who might stumble as the great thing came down behind them. Some even prance backwards, and most of the others peer back over their shoulders at the giant, luminous, white, dreamlike thing rising high above the four-storey houses behind us, breaking all the laws by staying upright and being carried only by men: the Walking Steeple it is called. We almost run to get round a corner to stop and watch it come.

This is the best moment. All of the town's lights are out. Darkness. But the Machine's own light precedes it: a dream luminescence. And then the Saint herself appears over the roofs like some hobbling marsh-light over the unlit mere of the city. And then immediately the radiant height of the whole monument arrives and the house-fronts glow and the people cry out in wonder. It is as near a dream as the waking world can offer: such a huge bright thing cannot happen, and such a thing is happening.

It stops in several piazzas on the way; doing a full turn on its own centre in the Piazza del Plebiscito before the squadron of men under it stand up straight and disperse for a few minutes to kiss their wives and comfort their frightened children. Is it going to fall and kill people? Will so many men faint or fall that they have to give up, like in 1957? Will daddy faint or fall? If one man does, or two or three, they are dragged along by their arms till the next stop, because you can only stop on flat places. If more do – *bo!* They change ends, smaller in front now. The last lap uphill to the cold and deathly sanctuary, is taken at a run, after which everyone shouts 'Santa Rosa! Santa Rosa!' and corks pop.

It is still to do with little St Rose, but by now it is also to do with strength and antiquity and knowing that, even if one knows nothing else, one's family is not going to be the first to give up. Underpinning that high and golden image is an élite ritual: the training, the extreme unction, the extraordinary hardship, and extraordinary merit. Maybe the Macchina itself is phallic: though it commemorates a young girl everything about it says man, man, man. It is about strength, and strength unto death, and the deathlessness of strength, and that is what makes its height and its radiance a centipede dream above the rooftops.

Glossary

Agro	From Latin *ager*: a field. An agricultural area
Ancona	Altarpiece
Androne	Large entrance hall
Antefisso	Terracotta ornament, attached to the end of a line of roof-tiles, etc.
Baldacchino	Canopy over an altar. The word comes from Baldacco, Baghdad, whence the fine cloth used was imported
Bifora	Two-apertured window: trifora = 3 apertures
Borgo	Quarter of a town
Burrone	Deep ravine
Campanile	Bell-tower
Cantoria	Choir gallery
Casa	House
Casale	Big peasant house in open country, often for several families
Cippo	Funerary pillar
Collegiata	A church with a college of priests rather than a single parish priest
Colombario	Etruscan, then Roman, then Christian pigeon-hole-type burial place
Cortile	Courtyard
Cupola	Dome
Duecento	Thirteenth century, and so on. 1250 was in the *duecento*
Duomo	Cathedral
'Earthquake baroque'	A particularly robust, almost squat, version of baroque architecture found in the earthquake-prone parts of Central America
Ex voto	Gifts to the local deity, later to the Virgin Mary or to a saint, in thanks for prayers granted
Festa	Feast or festival, originally on a saint's day. Now any party
Guardiano	Caretaker, keyholder
Hypogeum	An underground chamber or vault
Intonaco	Stucco, as wall finish, used first by Etruscans
Lanzechenecco	Italianisation of the German word *Landsknecht*,

Lanzechenecco (*cont.*)	land-knight. The *Lanzechenecchi* came down into Italy as mercenaries, especially under Charles V
Macchia	French *maquis*, the native mediterranean scrubland, often dense with oak and evergreen shrubs
Mastio or Maschio	Large round tower dominating a castle; also male, as in the response *figli maschi* to a sneeze
Paese	Village; country
Palazzo	Large town or village house, including palace
Pergamon	Lantern of a dome, or something the same shape but smaller, and free-standing, about an altar for instance
Piano nobile	'Noble floor': in effect the first floor, where the great rooms are
Predella	Run of small pictures below a large picture in an altarpiece; the word means 'plank'
Presbitero	Chancel or sanctuary
Putto	Decorative cherub
Rio	Small river
Rocca	Castle, fort, citadel
Romano	Roman (French *romain*)
Romanico	Romanesque (French *roman*)
Sacro Monte	Pilgrimage track up a hill to a sanctuary, with chapels on the way. Samuel Butler described many of them in his book, *Alps and Sanctuaries*
Sagra	Fair at which a particular foodstuff is eaten: e. g. potatoes, mushrooms, beans
Sail belfry	From *campanile a vela*: a small arch on the roof of a church in which a bell is hung
Selva	Wilderness, as in SELVA DI LAMONE
Sperone	Spur of rock, usually of tufo at the junction of two streams
Stemma	Coat of arms or crest
Stucco, stucchi	Interior plasterwork
Talus	Sloping wall of a castle or fortification
Tempietto	Small temple, usually reminiscent of Bramante's influential little circular temple at San Pietro in Montorio, in Rome
Torre	Tower
Tridentine	Pertaining to the Council of Trent, which sat throughout the middle of the 16th century and enacted the Counter-Reformation
Vico	Lane, alley: also, from latin *vicus*, a small staging post. (Also name of Lake.)
Villa	Country house, ancient Roman and Renaissance
Villetta	Villa

Books

Of the innumerable books and pamphlets we have read and consulted, space allows us to list only a few. Our shamefaced regrets to those whose deeply valued work we have plundered without acknowledgement.

As well as studies by outside scholars, there are also many produced by local groups – outstanding among which is Armine, of ISCHIA DI CASTRO.

Throughout, we have depended on:

The various editions of the volumes, *Roma e Dintorni* and *Lazio (non compresa Roma e Dintorni)*, in the series of Guide Books published by the Touring Club Italiano.

George Dennis, *The Cities and Cemeteries of Etruria*, 2 vols., 1848 (edition used, London, 1907). The original drawings and water colours of his illustrator and travelling companion S. J. Ainsley are in the British Museum; some of them have been reproduced in a sumptuous book published by 'L'Elefante', Rome.

Elizabeth Hamilton Gray's *Tour to the Sepulchres of Etruria,* London, 1840, is a remarkably intelligent account for the general reader, which Dennis wrongly sought to disparage; she did not provide his classical references or fight scholarly battles in her footnotes but her book came out eight years before his.

The quarterly *Tuscia*, which the Ente Provinciale per il Turismo of Viterbo has been publishing since the early 1970s, contains much useful and surprising information, including recipes collected by Italo Arieti.

And Giorgio Vasari's *The Lives of the Painters, Sculptors and Architects* beside us (Florence, 1550; edition used, translation by A. B. Hinds, 4 vols., London, 1963).

In the text, we have quoted from the following:

Beckford, Peter, *Familiar Letters from Italy to a Friend in England*, Salisbury, 1805. Peter Beckford was a grandson to a Governor of Jamaica, nephew of Lord Mayor Beckford, and first cousin of William (Fonthill) Beckford; his travels took place in 1787.

Benedetti, Sandro, *Giacomo Del Duca e l'Architettura del Cinquecento*, Officina Edizioni, Rome, 1972–3.

Evelyn, John, *The Diary*, ed. E. S. de Beer, Oxford, 1955, Vol II. John Evelyn was born in 1620, and was 24 when he first travelled in Italy.

Faldi, Italo, *Il Palazzo Farnese di Caprarola*, SEAT, Turin, 1981. Preface, Mario Praz; photographs, Giacomo Casale.

'Paolo Guidotti e gli Affreschi della "Sala del Cavaliere" nel Palazzo di Bassano di Sutri', *Bollettino d'Arte*, No. III–IV (July–December), 1957, Ministero della Pubblica Istruzione, Rome, p. 278.

Franco, Giuseppe, *Orizzonti Etruschi*, Milan, 1987.

Gradoli, 'I Quaderni di Gradoli', *Bollettino del Centro di Studi e Ricerche sul Territorio Farnesiano.*

Madonna, Maria Luisa, 'Momenti della Politica Edilizia e Urbanistica dello Stato Pontificio nell '400: L'Exemplum della Piazza del Comune a Viterbo', in *Il Quattrocento a Viterbo*, De Luca Editore, Rome, 1983.

Montaigne, Michel de, *Voyages en Italie*, Vols. 1 and 2, 1580–1, Oeuvres Complètes, Paris, 1928. Montaigne suffered from the Stone, and visited not only the great places but also the various Baths. While in Italy, he wrote his diary in Italian.

Munari, Mario, 'Monte Romano: Il Borgo Calino', in *Tuscia*, No. 5.

Portoghesi, Paolo, *Rome of the Renaissance*, tr. Pearl Sanders, Phaidon, London, 1972.

Potter, T. W., *The Changing Landscape of South Etruria*, London, 1979. This book provides an admirable general account of the wide-ranging 'South Etruria Survey' carried out by the British School at Rome over recent years.

Siligato, Rosella, 'Due cicli di affreschi nel Castello di Bracciano', in *Bracciano e gli Orsini: Tramonto di un Progetto Feodale* in the series *Il '400 e nel Lazio*, De Luca, 1981.

Strinati, Claudio, 'Lorenzo da Viterbo', in *Il '400 a Viterbo*, Rome, 1983.

Toubert, P., *Les Structures du Latium Mediéval, Le Latium Meridional et la Sabine*, Bibliothèque des Ecoles Françaises d'Athènes et de Rome, Rome, 1973.

'*Tuscia Minore*', Commune di Bassano Romano, Capranica, Oriolo and Veiano.

Zeppegno, Luciano, *Guida al Lazio che Scompare* [*Guide to Disappearing Lazio*], Milan, 1971.

General Matrix

For an explanation of this Matrix, see Foreword, p. ix.
★ = of outstanding interest
● = of interest
○ = nice

1 Pre-Etruscan, Etruscan, Roman
2 High Middle Ages
3 Late Middle Ages
4 Early Renaissance
5 16th–17th centuries
6 18th–20th centuries

Categories = Cat.
A Churches, convents, abbeys, etc.
B Castles, walls, towers
C Villas, palazzi, gardens
D Townscape and urban planning
E Pictures, sculptures, etc.
F Museums
G Ruins
H Land-, lake-, sea-scape, waters, vulcanism, nature reserves
I *Festas*, processions
J Map reference

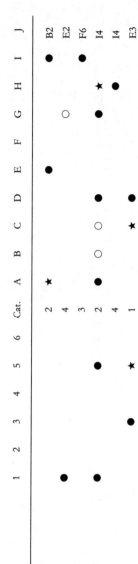

	1	2	3	4	5	6	Cat.	A	B	C	D	E	F	G	H	I	J
Acquapendente							2	★				●				●	B2
Acquarossa	●						4							○			E2
Allumiere							3									●	F6
Anguillara	●				●		2	●	○	○	●			●	★		I4
Baccano							4								●		I4
Bagnaia			●		★		1			★	●						E3
Bagnoregio					●	●	2	●			●				●		D2

Barbarano							3	●			●				●		F5
Bassano in Teverina							3					●		●			F1
Bassano Romano					★		1	●		★		★					G4
Bisenzio	○						4								●		C3
Blera	●						3					○					F5
Bolsena	●	●		★	●	●	1	★	○	●		★		●	★	★	C2
Bolsena War Cemetery						○	3								●		C2
Bolsena, Lake of	○						1								★		C3
Bomarzo	○		●		★		1	●		★		★					E2
Bracciano				★	●		1	○	★			●			★		H5
Bracciano, Lake of	●						1							●	★		H5
Calcata	○	○	●				2				★						H3
Caldara							3								●		H5
Campagnano					●	●	3	●			●						I3
Canale Monterano					○		4	○									G5
Canepina		○			●		3	●					●				F3
Canino				○		●	2	●	○			●					C5
Capena				○			4					○			○		J3
Capodimonte					●		2	○	●						★		C3
Capranica		○	●		●	●	2	●			●	●				○	G4
Caprarola					★		1	★		★	●	★					G3
Carbognano					○	○	4	○	○								G3
Castel Cellesi					●		3				●						D1
Castel d'Asso	●						3							●	●		E4

	1	2	3	4	5	6	Cat.	A	B	C	D	E	F	G	H	I	J
Castel Sant'Elia	○	★					2	★	○					○	●		H3
Castelgiuliano					●		3			●	○				○		H6
Castelnuovo di Porto			○		●		3			●							J3
Castiglione in Teverina				○	●		3	○				○					D1
Castro	○				○		3				○			●			B5
Celleno				○			2		●		●			●	●		D2
Cellere					★		2	★									C4
Cencelle		●					2							★	●		F6
Centeno					○		4										A2
Ceri		○		○			3	●	○			●		○			I6
Cerveteri	★	○					1	○	○		★		●	★			H6
Cesano	○				○		4								○		I4
Chia			○				3		○					●			F2
Cibona					●		3	●									F6
Cimino															★	●	F3
Civita Castellana	●	●	★	●	●	●	2	★	●		●	●	●	●			H2
Civita di Bagnoregio	○	●		●	○		2				●			●	★		D1
Civitavecchia	●				●	○	3	○	●				○				F7
Civitella Cesi					○		3				○				●		F5
Civitella d'Agliano							4		○								D1
Civitella S. Paolo			○				4		○								I2
Commenda, la		○			○		4	○		○					●		D3
Corchiano	●			●	★		2	★				●		●	○		G2

Crocefisso, il						●	3	●									G2
Fabrica			●		○		3	○	●			●					G3
Faleria			○		○		3		●								H2
Falerii Novi	★	●			○		2		●					●	●		G2
Farnese					●		2	●	○		●	●					B4
Farnesiana, la						○	3	○						○	●		F6
Ferento	●						2							●			E2
Fiano Romano			●			○	4	○	○								J2
Ficoncella							4								●		F7
Filacciano					●		3		●		●						I1
Formello			○		●		3	○	○	●				●			I4
Galeria		●			○		4							●			I5
Gallese	○	○			●	●	3	●	●	●					○		G2
Gradoli					●		3	●		●						●	B3
Graffignano				○			4		○								E1
Grotta Porcina	○						4							○			F5
Grotte di Castro	○				●	○	3	●				○					B2
Grotte di Santo Stefano		●					4	○									E2
Ischia di Castro	○	○			○	●	3	●	○		○		●		○		B4
Isola Bisentina	○			●	★		2	★		●					★		C3
Isola Farnese		○					4		○								J4
Isola Martana		○					3							○	●		C3
Ladispoli						○	4										I7
Lamone, Selva di	○						3								○		B4

	1	2	3	4	5	6	Cat.	A	B	C	D	E	F	G	H	I	J
Latera			○		○		3	○	○						○		B3
Lubriano					○	○	3	○		○		○			○		D1
Lucus Feroniae	●						3						○	○			J2
Luni sul Mignone	○						4										F5
Magliano Romano					○		4		○								I3
Malano, Selva di	○						4										E2
Malborghetto	○				○		4										J4
Manziana					○	○	3	○	○		●						H5
Marta			○		●		2	●	○		●				●	★	C3
Martignano							3								●		I4
Mazzano		●					3		○		○			○	○		H3
Mezzano	○						3								●		B3
Montalto di Castro		○					4		○								C6
Monte Romano					●	●	3				●						E5
Montebello					○		4								●		D5
Montecalvello		○			●		3		●		○						E1
Montefiascone	○	●	●		★	○	1	★	●	●	★	●			★		D3
Monterano	○		○		○	●	2	○	○					★			G5
Monterosi					●	●	3	●		●					●		H3
Montevirginio					●		3	○			○						G5
Morlupo				●	○		4		○		○						I3
Mugnano	○		○		○		3		○	●		○					F1
Musignano							4			○							C5

Nazzano	○	●	○	○	○		3	●	●			●					I2
Nepi	○	●	●	●	●	●	2	●	●	●	●	●			○		H3
Norchia	★	○					1							●	●		E3
Olgiata							4				○						I4
Onano			○		○		3		●								B3
Oriolo					●	○	3	○		●	○	●					G5
Orte	○	○	●	●	○		2	●			●	●	●			●	G1
Palidoro					○		4										I6
Palo	○			●	●		2		★						●		I7
Pescia Romana						○	4								○		B7
Pianiano			●				3				●						C5
Piansano	○						4	○				○			○		C4
Pisciarelli						●	3	○				●					H5
Poggio Conte			●				3	○						●			B5
Ponzano		●	○				3	●	○			○					I2
Proceno			○		○		4	○	○	○							A2
Quercia, Santa Maria della				●	○		2	★			●	●	○				E3
Riano			○				4	○	○								J3
Rignano	○	○				○	4		○		○						I2
Rocca Respampani					●		2		●						●		E5
Ronciglione	○	○	●	●	●		2	★	○		●	●			●	●	G3
Rota	○		○		●		2	●		●	○	●			★		G6
Sacrofano	○		○				3	○	○		●						I3
Sant' Eusebio	○	●					3	●									G3

	1	2	3	4	5	6	Cat.	A	B	C	D	E	F	G	H	I	J
San Giovenale	●						3							○			F5
San Giuliano	●						3							○			F4
San Liberato	○	●					4	○									H5
San Lorenzo Nuovo						●	3	○			●						B2
Santa Marinella	○				●		4		●						○		G7
San Martino al Cimino			●		●		2	●			★	●					F3
San Michele in Teverina						○	4			○							D1
Sant' Oreste					○			○	○						○		I2
Santa Severa	●		●		★		2		★						●		G7
Sasso					●		4			●					●		H6
Sermugnano							3		●								D1
Sipicciano		○			○	○	3		○		○						E1
Soracte	○	●					1	●							★		I2
Sorbo, Madonna del				○	○		3	●							○	●	I4
Soriano			●		★		2	○	●	●	●	★					F2
Stigliano					○		4								○		G6
Stracciacappa			○				4		○						○		I4
Sutri	★	●	○	○	●		2	●	●			●		●			G4
Tarquinia	★	●	★	●	★	○	1	★	●			★	★	●		●	E6
Tarquinia, Coast of	○				○	○	4								○		E6
Tessennano							4								○		C4
Tolfa		○	○		●	●	3	○	●	○	○	●	●	●	●		F6
Tolfa Hills	○	○			○		1								★		F6

Torre Alfina						○	4		○								B1
Torre di Sant'Agostino							4	○									E7
Torrimpietra	○					●	3	●		●					●		J6
Torrita Tiberina			●				3		●						●		I1
Tragliata							4								●		I5
Treia, Parco del		○					3							●	●		H3
Trevignano	○				●		2	●	●		●	★	●	●	●	●	H4
Trevinano			○		○		4		○	○					●		A1
Tuscania	●	★	●	●	○	○	1	★	●			★	●	●		●	D4
Vadimone, Lake							4										F1
Vaiano							4								●		D1
Valentano				○	○		3	○	●		○				●		C4
Vallerano				●	★		2	★	○		○	○					F2
Vasanello	○	○	○					○	○								G2
Veiano					●		3	●	○	○							G5
Veio	●						2							●	●		J4
Vetralla		●	○				3	●	○	○		○					F4
Vicarello	●				●		3			○					●		H4
Vico, Lake of	●						1								★		F3
Vigna di Valle						●	3						●				H5
Vigna Grande	○				○		4			○					●		H5
Vignanello			●		●	○	3	○	●	●	○	○				●	F2
Vitorchiano			●	●			3	●	●		●	●					E2
Vulci	●		●		●		2	●	●				●	○	●		C6
Viterbo	★	★	★	★	●	●	1	★	★	★	★	★	★	●	●	★	E3

Viterbo Matrix

	Pre-Etruscan	Etruscan	Roman	High Middle Ages	Late Middle Ages	Early Renaissance	16th–17th Centuries	18th–20th Centuries	Category	Architecture	Art	Objects	Townscape	Other interest	Map Reference
Cathedral of San Lorenzo				★		●	★			★	★	●	●		B6
Church of Gesù				○									●	○	C6
Church of the Gonfalone							●	●			★				D6
Church of Sant'Andrea				○						○			●		D8
Church of Sant'Angelo				○				○					●		D5
Church of Santi Faustino e Giovita					○			○			●			○	C3
Church of San Francesco					○						●				D2
Church of San Giovanni B.				○			○			○			●		D4
Church of San Giovanni in Z.				○		○				●	○		●		E4
Church of San Marco				○						○					E3
Church of Santa Maria delle Fortezze							○			○			●		E7
Church of Santa Maria in Gradi					○	●		●		●			●	★	G7

Church of Santa Maria Nuova				★	●			●		★	○		●		D6
Church of Santa Maria della Peste						●				●		○	●		C4
Church of Santa Maria della Salute					★					★			●		C5
Church of Santa Maria della Verita					○	★			★	○	★				F5
Church of San Sisto				★					★	★					F6
Church della Santissima Trinita							●	●		★	●	●	●	○	B4
Casa Poscia					●					○				○	D6
Fontana Grande				●									●		E6
Museo Civico	○	★	●	●	●	●	★	●	★	○	★	★			F5
Palazzo degli Alessandri					●					●			●		D7
Palazzo Caetani-Chigi						●				●			●		C5
Palazzo Farnese						●				●			●		B6
Palazzo Communale						●	●			●	○		★	★	D5
Palazzo Papale					●					★	○		★		B6
Palazzo del Podesta					○	○		○		○			★		D5
Palazzo della Prefettura								○		○			★		D5
Quartiere San Pelegrino					●								★	★	D7
Rocca Albornoz (inc: Archaeological Museum)		★			●	●	●	○		●		●	★	★	C7
Walls and Gates				●	●	●	●		★	●			★		

Index